AUG 1 2

# FUEL ON THE FIRE

## Oil and Politics in Occupied Iraq

Greg Muttitt

20 YEARS
THE NEW PRESS

Requests for permission to reproduce selections from this book should be mailed to:
Permissions Department, The New Press, 38 Greene Street, New York, NY 10013.

First published in Great Britain by The Bodley Head, London, 2011
Published in the United States by The New Press, New York, 2012
Distributed by Perseus Distribution

LIBRARY OF CONGRESS CATALOGING-IN-PUBLICATION DATA

Muttitt, Greg.
    Fuel on the fire : oil and politics in occupied Iraq / Greg Muttitt.
        p. cm.
    "First published in Great Britain by The Bodley Head, London, 2011"—T.p. verso.
    Includes bibliographical references and index.
    ISBN 978-1-59558-805-0 (hc)
    1. Iraq War, 2003—Influence.   2. Petroleum industry and trade—Iraq.
3. Iraq—Politics and government—2003–   I. Title.
    DS79.76.M89 2012
    956.7044'3—dc23

                                                        2012009267

Now in its twentieth year, The New Press publishes books that promote and enrich
public discussion and understanding of the issues vital to our democracy and to a
more equitable world. These books are made possible by the enthusiasm of our readers;
the support of a committed group of donors, large and small; the collaboration of our
many partners in the independent media and the not-for-profit sector; booksellers,
who often hand-sell New Press books; librarians; and above all by our authors.

www.thenewpress.com

Composition by Westchester Book Composition
This book was set in Fairfield

Printed in the United States of America

2  4  6  8  10  9  7  5  3  1

To the memory of Guy Hughes (1973–2006)

# Contents

*Cast of Characters*      xi
*List of Abbreviations*      xv
*Arabic and Kurdish Words in the Text*      xix
*List of Iraqi Political Parties*      xxi
*Introduction*      xxvii

**PART ONE: OIL AND WAR (1998–2003)**
1. An Immense Strategic Advantage      3
2. The Human at the Center      11
3. Burning Ambition      23
4. Wiping the Slate      40
5. Emergent Iraq      48
6. The Coalition Authority      58

**PART TWO: DEMOCRACY AND VIOLENCE (2003–2006)**
7. Invasion of the Chalabis      73
8. The Advisers      85
9. Anti-Iraqi Forces      95
10. The Hands of Iraqis      105
11. Now It Becomes Legal      119
12. Iraq Divided      131

**PART THREE: THE OIL LAW STRUGGLE (2006–2007)**
13. A Law to End All Laws      145
14. The Pragmatist      158
15. The Laurel Lodge Plan      166
16. The Surge      177
17. A Line in the Sand      185

18. The Ticking Clock                                      195
19. Imposing the Law                                       208

PART FOUR: OIL COMPANIES ON THE FRONT LINE
(2007–2011)
20. The New Iraq                                           227
21. Overwatch                                              242
22. Talking Business                                       255
23. Under the Hammer                                       272
24. A Dirty Business                                       282
25. Winter and Spring                                      295
26. Another Regime Changed                                 311

    Conclusion                                             319
    Acknowledgments                                        331
    Notes                                                  335
    Index                                                  385

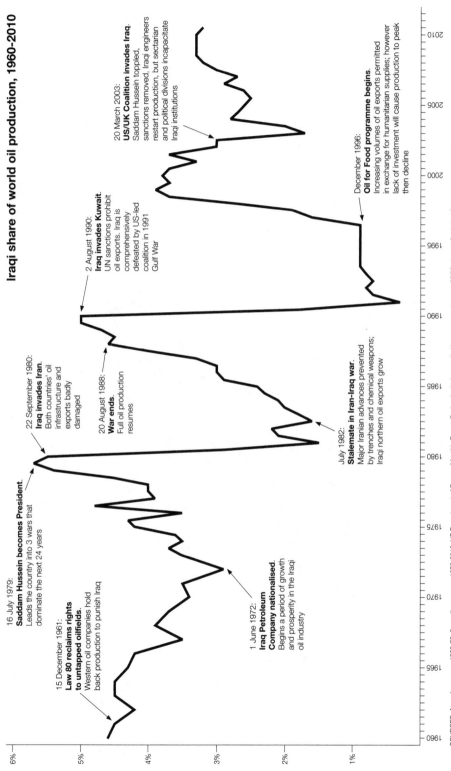

# Iraqi share of world oil production, 1960-2010

16 July 1979:
**Saddam Hussein becomes President.**
Leads the country into 3 wars that
dominate the next 24 years

22 September 1980:
**Iraq invades Iran.**
Both countries' oil
infrastructure and
exports badly
damaged

20 August 1988:
**War ends.**
Full oil production
resumes

2 August 1990:
**Iraq invades Kuwait.**
UN sanctions prohibit
oil exports. Iraq is
comprehensively
defeated by US-led
coalition in 1991
Gulf War

20 March 2003:
**US/UK Coalition invades Iraq.**
Saddam Hussein toppled,
sanctions removed, Iraqi engineers
restart production, but sectarian
and political divisions incapacitate
Iraqi institutions

15 December 1961:
**Law 80 reclaims rights
to untapped oilfields.**
Western oil companies hold
back production to punish Iraq

1 June 1972:
**Iraq Petroleum
Company nationalised.**
Begins a period of growth
and prosperity in the Iraqi
oil industry

July 1982:
**Stalemate in Iran-Iraq war.**
Major Iranian advances prevented
by trenches and chemical weapons;
Iraqi northern oil exports grow

December 1996:
**Oil for Food programme begins.**
Increasing volumes of oil exports permitted
in exchange for humanitarian supplies; however
lack of investment will cause production to peak
then decline

SOURCES: Annual averages, 1960-72; 6-month averages, 1973-2010. US Department of Energy, *Monthly Energy Review* (series), compiled by economagic.com; OPEC, *Annual Statistical Review 1979*, pp.xx,24

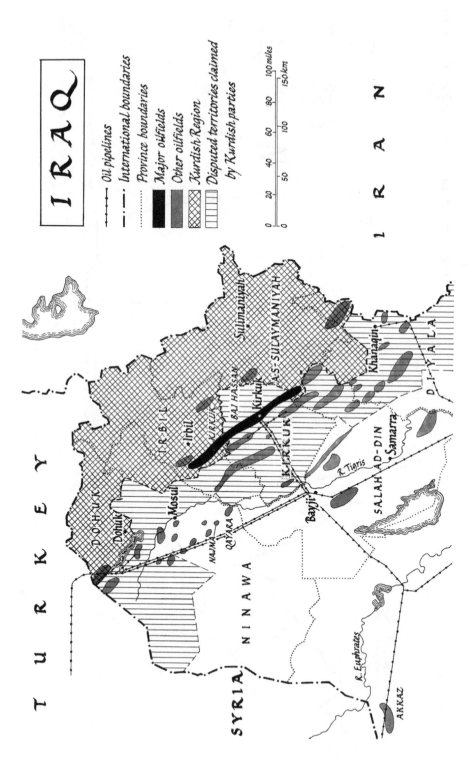

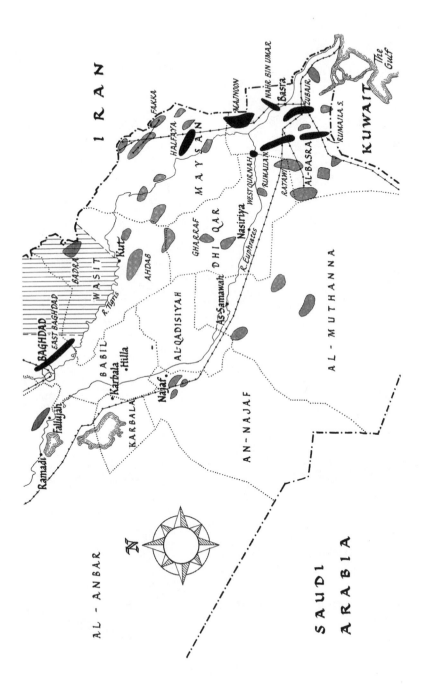

# Cast of Characters

## MAIN CHARACTERS

**Paul Bremer** The viceroy: administrator, Coalition Provisional Authority (CPA) 2003–4

**Ryan Crocker** The careful diplomat: head of Office of Iraqi Affairs in U.S. State Department responsible for Future of Iraq Project 2002–3, head of governance in CPA 2003, ambassador to Iraq 2007–9

**Thamir al-Ghadhban** The compromiser: "chief executive" of Iraq Oil Ministry 2003, minister of oil 2004–5, co-author of oil law 2006, prime minister's adviser on oil 2005–

**Ashti Hawrami** The efficient antagonist: CEO of Exploration Consultants Ltd. 2000–6, which was appointed in 2005 to study the Kirkuk field; minister of natural resources in the Kurdistan Regional Government (KRG) 2006–

**Ron Jonkers** The investment lawyer: USAID-funded legal adviser on drafting of oil law 2006–7

**Hassan Juma'a** The activist: leader of oil workers' trade union in Basra (Iraq Federation of Oil Unions) 2003–

**Zalmay Khalilzad** The hawkish strategist: author of draft Defense Planning Guidance 1992, member of Project for a New American Century, U.S. ambassador to Iraq 2005–7, U.S. ambassador to the United Nations, 2007–9

**Faleh al-Khayat** The affable technocrat: most senior DG (technical) in the Oil Ministry in 2003, manager of operations room March–April 2003

**Meghan O'Sullivan** The political officer: member of Governance Team in CPA 2003–4, President Bush's senior adviser on Iraq 2004–7

**Barham Salih** America's man: Iraq deputy prime minister 2004–5 and 2006–9, planning minister 2005–6, KRG prime minister 2009–

**Tariq Shafiq** The pragmatist: Iraqi oil expert, founding director of Iraq National Oil Company and negotiator with Iraq Petroleum Company foreign consortium in 1960s, oil law co-author 2006

**Hussain al-Shahristani** The lonely politician: Iraqi minister of oil 2006–10, deputy prime minister 2011–

**Dan Witt** The missionary of investment: president of International Tax and Investment Center, a U.S.-based "education foundation" 1990–

## OTHER CHARACTERS

**Adil Abdul-Mahdi** Iraqi finance minister 2004–5, vice president 2005–11

**Ibrahim Bahr al-Uloum** Member of State Department's Future of Iraq Project 2002–3, member of Iraq Reconstruction and Development Council (IRDC) 2003, minister of oil 2003–4 and 2005

**Dhia'a al-Bakkaa** Senior official in (Iraqi) State Oil Marketing Organization (SOMO) until 2003, chief of staff to oil minister 2003–4, DG of SOMO 2004–5

**Sam Bodman** U.S. secretary of energy 2005–9

**Phil Carroll** Senior oil adviser to CPA 2003, former CEO of Shell USA and Fluor

**Issam al-Chalabi** Iraqi oil expert, former oil minister 1987–90

**Robert Ebel** Energy and national security analyst at Center for Strategic and International Studies, adviser to Future of Iraq Project 2002–3

**Michael Eisenscher** National coordinator, U.S. Labor Against the War 2003

**Peter Galbraith** Adviser to Kurdish parties on constitution 2004–5, investor in Tawke oilfield as partner of Norwegian company DNO 2004–8

**Ewa Jasiewicz** Independent activist and journalist in Iraq 2003–4, U.K. representative of Basra oil workers' trade union 2004–5

**Falah al-Khawaja** Telecom engineer, DG of the manpower department of Iraq Oil Ministry 2004–6, DG of State Company for Oil Projects, 2006–8

**Robert Kimmitt** Deputy U.S. Treasury secretary 2005–9, responsible for International Compact with Iraq

**Jabbar al-Luaibi** DG of (Iraqi) South Oil Company 2003–8

**Michael Makovsky** Member of Energy Infrastructure Planning Group 2002–3, U.S. Defense Department official 2002–6

**Abdullah Jabbar al-Maliki** Founding member of oil workers' trade union in South Oil Company 2003

**Mika Minio** Oil/human rights campaigner at Platform 2005–

**Shatha al-Musawi** Member of Iraqi parliament 2005–10

**Saleh al-Mutlaq** Leader of National Dialogue Front, member of Iraqi parliament 2005–

**Rob Sherwin** Middle East oil adviser, U.K. Foreign and Commonwealth Office 2005–7; previously Middle East business development manager, Shell

**Muhammad-Ali Zainy** Energy economist at the Centre for Global Energy Studies, member of Future of Iraq Project 2002–3, member of IRDC 2003

# List of Abbreviations

**AFL-CIO** American Federation of Labor and Congress of Industrial Organizations

**AMS** Association of Muslim Scholars—a post-2003 Sunni organization

**BTC** Baku-Tbilisi-Ceyhan—BP-run oil pipeline through Azerbaijan, Georgia, and Turkey

**CEO** chief executive officer

**CNPC** China National Petroleum Corporation

**CPA** Coalition Provisional Authority—the occupation administration May 2003–June 2004

**CSIS** Center for Strategic and International Studies—a think tank based in Washington, D.C.

**DG** director general

**EIPG** Energy Infrastructure Planning Group—an interagency prewar planning group based in the Pentagon, 2002–3

**FDI** foreign direct investment

**GDP** gross domestic product

**GFIW** General Federation of Iraqi Workers—a trade union federation formed out of the remnants of the Saddam-era unions together with the federation aligned with the Iraq Communist Party

**ICEM** International Federation of Chemical, Energy, Mine and General Workers' Unions

**IDC** Iraq Drilling Company

**IFOU** Iraq Federation of Oil Unions—a grouping comprising unions in the oil sector in the four southernmost provinces of Iraq, led by Hassan Juma'a

**IMF** International Monetary Fund

**INOC** Iraq National Oil Company (state-owned)

**IOC** international oil company

**IPC** Iraq Petroleum Company—the consortium of British, French, and American companies that ran the Iraqi oil industry from the 1920s to the 1970s

**IRDC** Iraqi Reconstruction and Development Council—a group of exiled Iraqi professionals who returned to Iraq in April 2003 to assist the CPA

**ISCI** Islamic Supreme Council of Iraq—pro-U.S. and pro-Iran Shi'a political party led by the Hakim family (formerly SCIRI)

**ITIC** International Tax and Investment Center—an American group led by Dan Witt, promoting business-friendly tax and investment policies

**KBR** Kellogg, Brown & Root—an oil industry contractor and subsidiary of Halliburton

**KRG** Kurdistan Regional Government

**MI6** British Secret Intelligence Service ("MI" stands for "military intelligence")

**MOU** memorandum of understanding—a preliminary, outline contract

**MP** member of parliament

**NATO** North Atlantic Treaty Organization

**NGO** nongovernmental organization—civil society organization

**OECD** Organisation for Economic Co-operation and Development—a grouping of thirty-two industrialized countries

**OEWG** Oil and Energy Working Group of the U.S. State Department's Future of Iraq Project

**OPEC** Organization of the Petroleum Exporting Countries

**PMSC** private military and security company

**PNAC** Project for a New American Century

**PSA** production sharing agreement—a form of long-term contract to run an oilfield, favored by multinational oil companies

**SCIRI** Supreme Council for the Islamic Revolution in Iraq (later ISCI)

**SCOP** State Company for Oil Projects—Iraqi state-owned engineering/contracting company

**SOC** South Oil Company—a state-owned Iraqi oil company

**SOFA** Status of Forces Agreement—legal agreement between the United States and Iraq permitting and regulating the continued presence of U.S. forces in the country

**SOMO** Oil Marketing Company (previously State Oil Marketing Organization, though still known as SOMO)—state-owned Iraqi company responsible for oil marketing, export, and sales

**TAL** Transitional Administrative Law—interim constitution for Iraq, March 2004

**UAE** United Arab Emirates

**UIA** United Iraq Alliance—coalition of Shi'a political parties in the 2005 elections

**UN** United Nations

**UNAMI** United Nations Assistance Mission to Iraq

**UNICEF** United Nations Children's Fund

**USAID** U.S. Agency for International Development

**USLAW** U.S. Labor Against the War

**WMD** weapons of mass destruction

# Arabic and Kurdish Words in the Text

**Arba'in** the religious celebration at the end of forty days' mourning after the anniversary of the death of Imam Husayn (literally "forty")

**ayatollah** senior rank of Shi'a religious scholar

**fatwa** Muslim religious ruling, roughly equivalent to a legal opinion

**hajj** pilgrimage to Mecca

**haram** forbidden under Islam

**Hawza** the scholarly religious establishment of Najaf (in general, a Shi'a seminary)

**imam** either someone who leads prayers in a mosque or one of the twelve descendants of the Prophet Muhammad, beginning with Imam Ali, recognized by Shi'a as the leaders of the faith (literally "leader")

**intifada** the 1991 revolt against Saddam Hussein immediately after the First Gulf War (literally "uprising")

**jaysh** army

**Peshmerga** the official militias of Kurdish political parties, partially unified under the KRG

**Sahwa** the tribal movement that turned against al-Qaeda after 2005 (literally "awakening")

**shari'a** Islamic law

**sheikh** either head of a tribe or a religious leader (literally "elder")

**shisha** water pipe, hookah

**Tatweer** a USAID-funded project for building capacity in Iraqi ministries (literally "development")

**ulema** Muslim scholars (technically a plural, but used to refer to them collectively)

**umma** the community of all Muslims

**wasta** influence through personal connections with powerful people, the ability to get favors such as job appointments or to jump queues for administrative processing

# List of Iraqi Political Parties

## SHI'A PARTIES

**Supreme Council for the Islamic Revolution in Iraq (SCIRI)** Founded in Iran in 1982; fought on Iran's side in Iran-Iraq War (1980–88); close to Iranian military leadership. Moved to Iraq in 2003. Shi'a Islamist, sectarian; political base among middle-class merchants of the Shi'a holy cities. Led by Muhammad Baqr al-Hakim 1982–2003 (killed in terrorist attack), his brother Abdul-Aziz al-Hakim 2003–9 (died of cancer), Abdul-Aziz' son Ammar al-Hakim 2009–. Associated militia: Badr Brigades/Badr Organisation. Renamed Islamic Supreme Council of Iraq (ISCI) in 2007.

**Da'wa (Islamic call) Party** Founded in 1959 by Muhammad Baqir al-Sadr and others. Became an underground resistance movement in 1970s/80s; many of the leaders fled into exile. Returned to Iraqi mainstream in 2003; two major branches comprising those who had been in exile and those who had stayed in Iraq. Shi'a Islamist, somewhat Iraqi nationalist, but at times more sectarian according to political climate. Led by Ibrahim al-Ja'afari 2003–6, Nouri al-Maliki 2006–.

**Sadr Current** Founded in 2005 as the political wing of the Sadr movement, a populist religious and social movement established during the 1990s and led by Muhammad Muhammad Sadiq al-Sadr until his assassination in 1999. Conservative, Shi'a Islamist, Iraqi nationalist (but at times more sectarian), anti-occupation; political base among poorest slum dwellers and rural tribes. Movement led by Sadiq's son Muqtada al-Sadr from 2003. Associated militia: Jaysh al-Mahdi (disbanded 2008).

**Al-Fadhila (virtue) Party** A Basra-based party, offshoot of Sadr movement, led by Ayatollah Muhammad al-Yacoubi. Conservative, somewhat nationalist.

## Coalitions

### (I) ELECTIONS OF 2005

**United Iraq Alliance** Comprising SCIRI, Da'wa, Sadr Current, Fadhila, "independents" (not aligned with a party) led by Husain al-Shahristani and some smaller parties. Won 140 out of 275 seats in the January 2005 election of transitional government; 130 out of 275 in the December 2005 election of permanent government (SCIRI/Badr 36, Da'wa 25, Sadr 29, Fadhila 15, independents 25).

### (II) ELECTION OF 2010

**State of Law** Primarily Da'wa, plus some much smaller groups. Flirted with some Sunni, secular, and tribal parties and groupings in run-up to the election, but by election was utterly dominated by Da'wa. Won 89 out of 325 seats.

**Iraq National Alliance** Primarily Sadr Current and ISCI, plus al-Fadhila, followers of Ibrahim al-Ja'afari (now left Da'wa), and some smaller parties. Won 70 seats (Sadr 39, ISCI/Badr 18, Fadhila 6, Ja'afari 2, others 5).

These two coalitions merged after the election.

## SUNNI PARTIES

**Iraqi Islamic Party** Founded in 1960 as part of the Muslim Brotherhood movement, banned in Iraq from 1961 to 2003; operated from Britain during 1970s. "Moderate" Sunni Islamist. Led by Mohsen Abdel Hamid 2003–4, Tariq al-Hashemi 2005–9, Ayad al-Samarra'i 2009–.

**Association of Muslim Scholars** Founded in 2003, shortly after the fall of Saddam Hussein. Intellectual, mosque-based, Iraqi nationalist, anti-occupation. Boycotted political process. Influential in 2004–7 but declined following attacks by U.S. forces and Iraqi government; largely forced into exile after 2007. Led by Harith al-Dhari.

## Coalitions

**Tawafuq (accordance)** Comprising Iraqi Islamic Party and two smaller parties. Won 44 seats in December 2005 but only 6 in 2010.

# KURDISH PARTIES

**Kurdistan Democratic Party (KDP)** Founded in 1946 as part of the Kurdish nationalist guerrilla movement led by Mulla Mustafa Barzani. Following his death in 1979, leadership passed to his son Masoud Barzani. Conservative, strong tribal character, based in Erbil.

**Patriotic Union of Kurdistan (PUK)** Broke from KDP in 1975. Fought civil war with KDP, 1994–8. Kurdish nationalist, more urban in character, moderately socialist. Led by Jalal Talabani.

The KDP and PUK each governed part of Kurdistan separately from 1992 to 2003, but after 2003 the institutions gradually merged into the Kurdistan Regional Government (KRG), with most unification occurring in 2005–6; some elements remained separate, notably the Peshmerga commands.

**Goran (change)** Broke from PUK in 2009, in response to corruption, patronage, and the two parties' duopoly on power. Became the official opposition in the KRG, and also stood independently in national elections. Led by Nashirwan Mustafa. Won 8 seats in 2010 election.

## Coalitions

**Kurdistan Alliance** Comprising KDP and PUK plus some small parties. Won 75 seats in the January 2005 election; 53 in December 2005, 43 in 2010.

# SECULAR PARTIES

**Iraqi National Accord** Founded in 1991 as secular opposition to Saddam. Worked closely with the CIA; favored by many U.S. officials as an alternative to Ahmad Chalabi. Moved to Iraq in 2003. Secular, capitalist, pro-U.S. Led by Ayad Allawi.

**National Dialogue Front** Founded in 2005. Secular, Iraqi nationalist, anti-occupation. Led by Saleh al-Mutlaq. Won 11 seats in December 2005 election.

## Coalitions

(I) ELECTIONS OF 2005

**Iraqi List** Iraqi National Accord was the major organized political party in the List, but it also attracted various secular/nationalist politicians, many not pro-U.S. Won 40 seats in January 2005, 25 in December 2005.

(II) ELECTION OF 2010

**Al-Iraqiyya** Comprising Iraqi National Accord, Iraqi National Dialogue Front, al-Hadba, followers of Tariq Hashemi (now left Iraqi Islamic Party), and other parties. Won 91 seats (INA 28, NDF 16, Hashemi 7, others 40). Eight MPs split from Iraqiyya in March 2011 to form a new parliamentary bloc known as White Iraqiyya (later the White Party).

# PRIMARILY HISTORICAL PARTIES

**Ba'ath (Renaissance) Party** Founded in Syria in the 1940s then imported to Iraq in the 1950s. Part of the coalition government in 1963, then in power from 1968 to 2003. Pan-Arabist, nominally socialist, totalitarian. Led by Saddam Hussein, 1979–2003. Banned in 2003, but continues an underground existence, mostly overseas.

**Iraq Communist Party** Founded in 1934; was the main organizer of mass protests against the monarchy in the 1940s/50s; minority member of post-revolution coalition government 1958–63; decimated in 1963 through Ba'ath Party assassinations of leaders. Socialist, Iraqi nationalist, secular. Intermittently underground 1963–2003. Returned to mainstream in 2003 but with minimal influence, no longer socialist and now pro-occupation. Allied with Ayad Allawi and intermittently with Kurdish parties, especially PUK. Led by Moussa Hamid.

**Iraqi National Congress** Founded in 1992 as an umbrella group for Iraqi opposition, but collapsed in 1994 and morphed into the political party of Ahmad Chalabi. From 1998 it became the prime recipient of U.S. funds for Iraqi opposition, and provided much faulty intelligence on weapons of mass destruction. Pro-U.S., close to neoconservative movement. In 2005 it reacted to declining political influence by allying with Shi'a parties and stood as part of the United Iraq Alliance in the January 2005 election. Split from UIA in the December 2005 election and won no seats. Rejoined Iraq National Alliance in 2010 and gained 1 seat.

# Introduction

The departure of the last U.S. troops from Iraq at the end of 2011 left a broken country and a host of unanswered questions. Bizarrely, the recent memoirs of George Bush and Dick Cheney still explain the war in terms of the weapons of mass destruction we all know did not exist.[1] Was there ever really a threat to national security? And why did the occupation drag on for nearly nine years, at the expense of thousands of lives, while most Americans, Britons, and Iraqis desperately wanted it to end?

Mainstream media accounts have located the Iraq problem in a string of mistakes: government misread the intelligence; neoconservatives launched a war without preparation and found themselves out of their depth; the invasion force was too small; but things finally started to go right when they changed course with the "surge" in troop numbers under General David H. Petraeus in 2007. This version of the story is more plausible but still leaves questions. Why did the situation in Iraq continue to worsen after the decline of neocon influence in 2003/4? If the 2007 surge turned the war around, how come its accompanying political program failed on almost every count? And why did U.S. forces reluctantly have to leave four years later?

Many Americans have their suspicions about the strategic factors behind the war—but too much of its conduct remains hidden to be able to see how or whether those factors played out. One of the biggest gaps in the account is oil, which lies at the heart of Iraqi and Mideast politics yet has been barely mentioned. At the end of the occupation, it seems a good time to examine what actually happened.

The withdrawal from Iraq came at the end of a year of international up-heaval. Many commentators in the West were surprised by the Arab revolutions that appeared to spring from nowhere. The United States, Britain, and France began by backing Egypt's and Tunisia's dictators before scrambling to express support for democracy as the regimes toppled. Before long, the three countries were involved in another war. Perhaps too we can make some sense of the uprisings, and of the West's responses, by taking a closer look at the war that shaped the previous decade.

I first contemplated the future of Iraq's oil on a Saturday afternoon in February 2003, when I joined more than a million others on a noisy shuffle through London. It was not only Britain's largest-ever political demonstration but also one of its most diverse. Anarchists, Trotskyists, peaceniks, young Muslims, shire Tories, and liberals marched together. NO WAR, MORE PEAS, insisted the banner of one gardening enthusiast. LIBRARIANS SAY SSSSHHH-HHH! DON'T BOMB IRAQ, whispered another. NO BLOOD FOR OIL was one of the more popular slogans. It seemed like an obvious point to make: Iraq had around 10 percent of the world's oil reserves, and its neighbors an additional 50 percent. The United States was the world's largest consumer of oil, ac-counting for around a quarter of total demand.

By chance, I began the march outside the Shell Centre, one of the oil com-pany's two global headquarters. I wondered what conversations about Iraq had taken place inside. Over the following weeks I started reading specialist oil industry magazines to try to find out what the oil companies thought. They told a story quite different from what we read in newspapers and saw on our TV screens. *International Petroleum Finance* observed during the invasion, for instance, "The war in Iraq may have divided the world's politi-cians, but it has united its oil executives—every one of them is wondering how and when the country's 112 billion barrels of known oil reserves, not to mention its huge exploration potential, might be opened up to foreign par-ticipation."[2]

It was not difficult to read those journals and to speak and write about what I read, but it seems no one outside the oil business thought to do so, and I found that a number of people were interested in what I had to say. At the time I was working for a small yet resourceful campaigning charity called Platform, which monitors the activities of oil companies, and over the following years I observed events unfold in the Iraqi oil industry. When I first visited Iraq in 2005, I discovered that it was easier for me to find out in London what was happening to Iraq's oil than it was for Iraqis in Baghdad or Basra. When publicized at all, announcements on new Iraqi oil policies were made in other countries to audiences of diplomats and businessmen rather than to Iraqis. I hoped that by studying Iraqi oil policy I might help inform public debate inside Iraq—after all, oil provides about 95 percent of the Iraqi government's revenues and drives the country's economy and politics. Later, as other groups got involved, Platform became part of an international campaign against American and British interference in Iraqi oil decisions. I worked in the United States with Oil Change International, a group that tackles political obstacles to ending oil addiction. Later still, after I began writing this book, I worked as a freelance journalist, again with a focus on Iraqi oil and politics.

This work took me to events where World Bank and U.S. government officials lobbied Iraqi decision makers, and to meetings at which Iraqi Oil Ministry teams discussed future policy with Western companies. I met some of the executives who hoped to benefit from Iraq's oil and the government officials and advisers they worked with. Generously assisted by my lawyers Phil Michaels and Kel McClanahan, I used freedom of information legislation to obtain hundreds of unreleased British and American government documents that described those governments' plans and activities to reshape Iraq's oil industry. But I also talked to ordinary Iraqis and a few of the country's politicians about what they wanted to happen to their oil. I attended Iraq's first anti-privatization conference in Basra and the meeting in Amman at which Iraq's trade unions decided they would fight the oil law the United States was pushing in Baghdad. I made many Iraqi friends and came to know some of Iraq's foremost oil experts.

When I set out on the venture I expected to focus only on oil, not to get involved in broader political issues. But I found that almost every time I met Iraqis there was something they urgently wanted to tell me and hoped I would convey back home: that Iraqis are not by nature sectarian and that they see themselves first and foremost as Iraqis. This was completely at odds with what I routinely heard about Iraq, and the first few times I heard it I paid little attention. But I discovered that so common are intermarriages between Shi'a and Sunni that most Iraqis I met had a parent, spouse, or sibling-in-law of the other sect. While politicians organized on identity lines and sectarian militias bloodily seized the streets, most Iraqis saw their rhetoric as quite alien.

So on both oil and Iraqi culture, my experiences gave me a very different perspective from what I read in the papers. I've never had much time for conspiracy theories, but human beings have a great capacity to hold (genuine) beliefs about the world that advance or reinforce their own material interests, and it is only from a distance that one can perceive the self-serving nature of those beliefs. Indeed, the architects of the war have not found it hard to see oil behind the actions of Saddam Hussein,[3] al-Qaeda,[4] Iraq's communities,[5] the governments of Russia and France,[6] and even (with historical distance) the British occupation of Iraq eighty-five years earlier.[7] They have seldom seen it behind their own.[8]

It would be wrong to say that the war and occupation were shaped *only* by oil; the reality is messier. But it would be at least as naive to accept the opposite view: that the war had "literally nothing to do with oil," as U.S. defense secretary Donald Rumsfeld insisted in November 2002.[9] Unless we look at the interests involved, and the means by which they were pursued, it is impossible to make sense of the war and occupation, or learn its lessons. Oil is among the most important of these interests. This book therefore tells the story of how the struggles for control of Iraq's oil shaped events during the occupation of that country from 2003 to 2011.

The strategic context in 2003 was of growing concern in the world's major economies for the future of energy supplies. One of George W. Bush's first acts as U.S. president in January 2001 was to appoint a task force, led by Vice President Dick Cheney, to consider policies to address the United States' energy shortfall. The task force recommended that "energy security" be made a priority of U.S. foreign policy, especially in the Persian Gulf region.[10] In September 2004 an unpublished British strategy document suggested, "A modernised, transparent and investment-friendly energy sector in Iraq will be a strong exemplar to other Middle East oil and gas producing countries."[11] In other words, Iraq was only the start; the goal was to reshape the whole region's oil industry.

Concerns about energy supplies grew over the subsequent years. Energy security was the major theme of the 2006 meeting of the G8 group of nations in Saint Petersburg. In 2008 members of NATO agreed that the military alliance should play a role in securing energy supplies, including protecting critical infrastructure and "projecting stability."[12] Six months later Secretary General Jaap de Hoop Scheffer said that NATO's role in energy security should go beyond defending oil tankers and pipelines to helping coordinate the actions of energy-importing countries. Without such coordination, he said, "the energy buyers will not get the best commercial deals, nor maximize their negotiating leverage."[13] In February 2010 U.S. secretary of state Hillary Clinton suggested that energy disruptions be considered "Article 5 actions," under which an attack on one NATO member is an attack on all.[14]

Did the Iraq War usher in a new era of using force to secure energy supplies? Perhaps, but not in the manner of the conquistador loading up his ship with stolen New World gold. A single shipload of any commodity is worth relatively little to a world power, or even to a corporation. A far more valuable prize can be carried in a briefcase or on a laptop computer: contracts, laws, and policies that ensure the flow of resources over decades. And while it would be wrong to simply equate U.S. and U.K. energy interests with those of their corporations, they do overlap. After all, if those corporations were to gain contracts entitling them to extract more oil, that would help provide the secure, increased supplies their governments seek. As the competition for resources becomes more intense, this book is a warning of the fate that may befall other parts of the world if we do not learn from the Iraq experience.

Our story divides into four parts. We begin in Part One by observing the buildup to the war in planning meetings in London and Washington. We see Iraq devastated first by "shock and awe" and then by looting. Under the direct rule of Paul Bremer's Coalition Provisional Authority, the course of the occupation is set, although independent Iraqi civil society groups emerge (or reemerge) with very different visions for the future of the country. We meet the Americans, Britons, and Iraqis who will be at the heart of the coming struggle.

In Part Two we see the first steps toward a new oil policy under Bremer, while the occupation forces attempt to assert control over an increasingly rebellious country. Then, under the interim and transitional governments of Ayad Allawi and Ibrahim al-Ja'afari, a constitution is written and oil plans are firmed up, including the forms of contracts to be offered to companies. We watch in horror as Iraq spirals into violence, with sectarian militias roaming the streets.

In Part Three, which begins with the formation of a permanent government led by Nouri al-Maliki in spring 2006, we go behind the scenes of the most direct confrontation over the future of Iraq's oil. The United States and Britain press the Iraqi authorities to pass a new law to allow foreign investment in the country's oil industry against a popular campaign opposing the law.

In the fourth and final part of the book, spanning the period between 2007 and 2011, the oil companies gradually take over from the U.S. government in leading the West's struggle for Iraq. U.S. influence is already declining by the time Barack Obama becomes president. Meanwhile, new trends emerge—some hopeful and some not—that will shape today's Iraq, and these factors coalesce in U.S. leaders' failure to extend the legal mandate to keep troops in Iraq beyond 2011. And in our last chapter, we consider what Iraq can teach us about events in Libya.

So how do the United States and Britain square all the attention they have given to Iraq's oil with their denials that oil motivates them? Nick Butler, former policy director of BP and founder of the British-American Project, captured a common Western attitude to Iraqi oil in a 2007 *Financial Times* article. He wrote that "perhaps the most useful parting gift that the Coalition could leave . . . is a practical model for renewal of the oil sector."[15] According to this way of thinking, there was no political debate to be had: decisions about the future of Iraq's oil were technical issues, best settled according to the advice of (Western) oil industry experts. But when a country is at war and occupied by foreign troops, where does advice end and coercion begin?

Most Iraqis say they want oil production to stay in Iraqi hands. This attitude was dismissed by occupation officials and Western commentators as old-fashioned, ideological, or even Ba'athist.* Yet when one looks at the Iraqi oil industry, one finds a proud engineering culture. It achieved great successes immediately after nationalization in 1972—as the graph on page ix shows—and maintained Iraq's facilities and operations through the hardships of three wars and thirteen years of sanctions. In place of financial capital, they relied on human endeavor; in place of modern technology, im-

---

*The latter accusation is based on a misperception that the Ba'ath Party was opposed to foreign companies investing in Iraq's oil. While that was the case in the 1960s and 1970s, the Ba'ath had pursued privatization and an open market economy since the late 1980s, and tried to pass management of the largest oilfields to multinational companies during the 1990s.

provised workarounds. For many of the Iraqi oil technocrats I interviewed, all that was required was the purchase of some of the recent technology on which Iraq has missed out. As they see it, privatization has its roots in ideological rather than practical concerns—the direct opposite of the Western advisers' view.

The United States and Britain justified their ongoing intervention by pointing to the political incapacity and sectarian conflict that have plagued Iraq since 2003. Western commentators have tended to attribute these problems to some failing in the Iraqi character, to the immaturity of the country's democracy, or to a hangover from the Ba'athist regime. In truth, the failings of the Iraqi political establishment and the terrible bloodshed were products of a set of actions and decisions by American, British, Iraqi, and other players. I learned that, contrary to the claims of many Western journalists, Iraq's political *culture*—leaving aside its politicians—is in many respects more sophisticated than that of Britain or the United States. There is a keenness to discuss important issues, an interest in the collective good, and a willingness to engage in trying to achieve it. Through this culture comes the most surprising part of our story: a civil society established in workplaces, mosques, and streets that has often succeeded in protecting the rights and broader interests of Iraqis. Despite the United States' unmatchable military, political, and economic power, Iraqi civil society prevented the occupiers from achieving much of what they so badly wanted.

I make no claim to have predicted the events of early 2011. But because I had witnessed the determination and success of Iraqis organizing together, the Arab uprisings were easier to place, and less of a surprise. On the other hand, these pages tell of how the U.S.-led coalition installed and propped up another generation of self-interested autocrats who have no legitimacy in the eyes of their people—and of the damaging effects of Western demands for economic reform, which are now also battering the hopes of liberated Egyptians and Tunisians, and in a different way Libyans.

So this book is the story not just of a war but of the struggle of humanity against power, the clash between strategic interests and principles of justice, the modern-day echoes of an imperial past, and the failure to learn the lessons of history.

A journalist friend once told me that if you fall in love with Iraq, you are destined to have your heart broken every day. At the time I agreed, but in retrospect I think she was only partly right. Having many Iraqi friends and a deepening connection with the country meant I couldn't simply move on to another news story as "Iraq fatigue" set in. But by being emotionally connected rather than just a consumer of news, I was exposed not only to despair but also to hope. And in the darkest moments of 2006 and 2007, as the institutions of Iraqi society collapsed and it looked as though sectarian slaughter would continue for a generation, it was always spending time with Iraqis that lifted me. In this respect I feel privileged.

The final message of this book is therefore one of hope: that the Iraqi people have the ability to make a better future—if they are given the chance.

# PART ONE

# Oil and War
# 1998–2003

# 1

# An Immense Strategic Advantage

On the potential for oil and gas in Iraq, the short answer is that it is huge . . .
Shell and BP could not afford not to have a stake in it for the sake of their long-
term future.

              —Edward Chaplin, U.K. Foreign Office, October 2002[1]

Fourteen months before he became U.S. vice president, Halliburton chief executive Dick Cheney gave a speech to the Institute of Petroleum at London's Savoy Hotel in which he identified a serious challenge facing the oil industry. "For over a hundred years we as an industry have had to deal with the pesky problem that once you find oil and pump it out of the ground, you've got to turn around and find more—or go out of business," he said.[2] "Exxon-Mobil will have to secure over a billion and a half barrels of new oil reserves every year just to replace existing production." And this was growing increasingly difficult.*

The problem was where the oil was located: more than 60 percent lay in five countries of the Middle East, from which the multinational companies had been forced out in the nationalizations of the 1970s. After that they had

---

\* This was only indirectly a problem for Cheney's own company. Halliburton does not run oilfields or hold reserves, as do ExxonMobil, Shell, and BP; instead it provides services for them, such as drilling, construction, and geological surveys. Contrary to the views of some antiwar activists, Halliburton did not stand to be the biggest beneficiary of the Iraq War; its Restore Iraqi Oil contract with the U.S. government was for such technical services only in the first year or two of the war, whereas oil companies such as ExxonMobil seek contracts lasting twenty or more years.

to focus on smaller, technically difficult and more expensive oil provinces, especially Alaska and the North Sea, where they were helped by generous tax and regulatory arrangements from the U.S. and U.K. governments. In the 1990s, as these provinces reached maturity and began to decline, the frontier shifted to the newly independent (and newly capitalist) former Soviet states and to ever deeper water offshore, with its attendant cost and risk. But with potential access now to only 33 percent of the world's remaining reserves, the Western oil companies were playing a losing game, trying to develop ever smaller and more expensive patches of oil.[3]

Things were getting worse for the companies. Financial analysts at Merrill Lynch pointed out that the per-barrel cost of finding and developing an oilfield doubled between 1997 and 2002.[4] In 2003 energy consultant Wood Mackenzie found that the top ten oil companies spent $8 billion on exploration but found only $4 billion worth of assets.[5] And in each of the following three years, the major oil companies in aggregate found less oil than they extracted.[6]

"So where is the oil going to come from?" asked Cheney at the Savoy. "While many regions of the world offer great oil opportunities, the Middle East—with two thirds of the world's oil and the lowest cost—is still where the prize ultimately lies . . . companies are anxious for greater access there."

## The Ultimate Prize

"Iraq is *the* big oil prospect," began the minutes of the meeting at the British Foreign Office on November 6, 2002. "BP are desperate to get in there."[7] The tone was unusually expressive for the notes of a government meeting: civil servants taking minutes normally manage to find blandness in even the most far-reaching discussions.

Iraq, BP's Richard Paniguian said, was "vitally important—more important than anything we've seen for a long time." Paniguian, who speaks Arabic and had studied Middle East politics, was no stranger to high strategy: most of his recent time had been spent troubleshooting the construction of the world's longest pipeline, Baku-Tbilisi-Ceyhan (BTC), in Azerbaijan, Georgia, and Turkey. He would later go on to work for the government, promoting British arms exports. According to the minutes, Paniguian "spelt out why Iraq is special for the oil companies. It has not only the second largest proven oil reserves in the world but unique 'yet-to-find' potential." Furthermore, the minutes continued, "oil production costs—in the range of $0.5–1.0 per barrel—are the lowest in the world."

As war approached, the oil question was naturally a sensitive one. In March 2003 a BP spokesman told the BBC that the company had had no specific talks on Iraq with the government; the subject had only been discussed "en passant."[8] That was untrue.

In fact, that was Paniguian's second meeting with the government about Iraq in the space of a week. On October 31 he and his colleague Tony Renton, along with representatives of Shell and BG Group, had visited minister of trade Baroness Symons.[9] At that meeting the BP men had commented that Iraq "would provide an immense strategic advantage to any company which emerged in a commanding position." All three companies insisted that there should be a "level playing field"—that is, that they should have as many opportunities in liberated Iraq as their American competitors. The companies said they were "very concerned" about rumors that the United States might be making deals with the Russian and French governments, offering oil contracts to their companies in return for support for the war. The U.S. companies would be looked after too, raising the Brits' fears that they'd be left out. Symons replied that "it would be difficult to justify British companies losing out in Iraq in that way if the U.K. had itself been a conspicuous supporter of the U.S. government throughout the crisis" and promised to raise the point with her U.S. counterparts.

The BP spokesman also told the BBC that the company had never initiated any discussions and had only responded to requests from the government for its views of what might happen. That also was untrue. After the three companies met Baroness Symons, Paniguian and Renton requested a follow-up meeting with her without the other companies present.[10] That meeting took place on December 4, 2002.

Shell too was in denial mode. The company's spokesman made a similar claim to the BBC reporter, saying only that "the subject has only come up in normal conversations that we have." But Shell had also had more than one meeting about Iraq. As well as the three companies' meeting with Symons, Tony Wildig, a senior vice president of the company, met Edward Chaplin, the Foreign Office's Middle East director, on October 2. Chaplin reassured Wildig that the "commercial element" was already part of the British government's planning for Iraq. "At any rate, we were determined to get a fair slice of the action for U.K. companies in a post Saddam Iraq."[11]

It took me a five-year struggle under the Freedom of Information Act to obtain the minutes of these meetings. Both BP and Shell declined to comment on the apparent discrepancies between the minutes and their spokesmen's comments. As for the government's account, "the oil conspiracy theory is honestly one of the most absurd when you analyze it," said Tony Blair in a television interview in February 2003.[12]

As war approached, oil companies around the world were keen to ensure they did not miss out on the bonanza. The *Observer* reported in early November 2002 that three U.S. multinational companies had met the Iraq National Congress (INC), the political party of Ahmad Chalabi, who as a favorite of the Pentagon was widely tipped as the next leader of Iraq. INC spokesman Zaab Sethna said, "The oil people are naturally nervous. We've had discussions with them, but they're not in the habit of going around talking about them."[13] The following month Chalabi himself confirmed he had met the companies.[14] According to BP and Shell, Chevron had met with Iraq war hawk and former CIA director James Woolsey, now a member of the Defense Policy Board.[15]

Vagit Alekperov, chief executive of the Russian company Lukoil, spoke to U.S. energy secretary Spencer Abraham at the U.S.-Russia Energy Summit in Houston in October 2002, to try to preserve his company's 1997 contract with Saddam after regime change.[16] According to Nikolai Tokarev, head of Lukoil's partner Zarubezhneft, the U.S. government suggested that companies should finance the Iraqi opposition if they wanted future deals. Tokarev said he had refused, but other, unnamed Russian companies had participated in the "dirty game."[17]

## Echoes of History

It was not the first time BP and Shell had hoped to extract oil from Iraq— nor the first war that would give them the opportunity to do so.

Ninety years earlier, the world's then superpower, Britain, occupied Iraq following the First World War of 1914–18. In many ways the events of the post-2003 occupation have followed that earlier experience. Officially, the British occupation of the new state of Iraq lasted only until 1921, when Britain anointed as king an outsider, Faisal of the Hejaz (now part of Saudi Arabia); the referendum to confirm him was approved by 96 percent. Britain then nominally handed over sovereignty but kept its forces in Iraq under a mandate of the League of Nations, the precursor of the United Nations, which gave it responsibility for security, advising the Iraqi government, and helping represent it internationally. The mandate came to an end in 1932, but British bases remained for another twenty-six years under a bilateral agreement with the Iraqi government. British advisers were kept in most ministries, and few Iraqis saw their country as independent. Britain had not gone but remained in the background—over the horizon, you could say—ready to reengage if its interests were threatened.* In the years leading up to the First World War, Britain had worried about a rising threat from the kaiser's Germany, which, in a direct challenge to the British Empire, aimed to build a superior navy so as to dominate the seaways to its own growing colonies. British intelligence reports warned that the Germans were experimenting with oil-fueled ships, which studies showed could achieve far greater speed, range, and maneuverability than their coal-fired predecessors. Winston Churchill, then first lord of the Admiralty, became convinced that converting the Royal Navy's battleship fleet was essential to keep up in the arms race. The trouble was that whereas Britain had ample supplies of coal within its own shores, oil would have to come from abroad. Churchill's solution was for the Admiralty itself to enter the oil business, to become "the owners, or at any rate, the controllers at the source," of a large volume of foreign oil.[18] And to that end, he proposed that the government buy a 51 percent stake in the Anglo-Persian Oil Company, the precursor of BP. His proposal was approved by Parliament on June 14, 1914, just fourteen days before Archduke Franz Ferdinand was assassinated in Sarajevo.

Anglo-Persian was keen to expand into Mesopotamia (now Iraq), the southern corner of the Turkish Ottoman Empire, which was expected to share neighboring Persia's oil-rich geology. The company's new masters in the British government had the same idea, and in 1915 they ordered an invasion, beginning from the south near Basra. In March 1917 the British marched into Baghdad, and their commander, General Stanley Maude,

---

* That happened during World War II, when an avowedly anti-British government declared alliance with Germany. At that, Britain reoccupied Iraq and put its own allies back in power.

proclaimed, "Our armies do not come into your cities and lands as conquerors or enemies, but as liberators."[19]

The following year, as World War I was drawing to a close, British officials met in Whitehall to review their aims. Sir Maurice Hankey, secretary to the War Cabinet, had spent the previous day examining an Admiralty map that showed oil seepages—an indication of reserves below the ground—near Mosul. Hankey wrote in an urgent memo, "The only big potential supply that we can get under British control is the Persian and Mesopotamian supply. . . . Control over these oil supplies becomes a first-class British war aim."[20] But if that was the aim, the British weren't far enough north. A desperate race up the Tigris ensued, but the troops were still just short of Mosul when the Mesopotamia campaign formally ended on October 30, 1918, with the Armistice of Mudros. Three days later, in breach of the armistice, the British army seized Mosul unopposed.

The British government publicly denied any oil motivation. In December 1920 Winston Churchill—who at the Admiralty had driven the policy of controlling foreign oil—gave a speech to the House of Commons that may have provided inspiration for Tony Blair. Churchill declared the idea that Britain had incurred the expense and risk of a military campaign "in order to secure some advantage in regard to some oilfields . . . too absurd for acceptance."[21]

In 1925 King Faisal's government signed a concession contract with a consortium of Shell, Anglo-Persian, and Compagnie Française des Pétroles (later Total). Three years later, after a long campaign by the United States, a combination of American companies—primarily the Standard Oil precursors of Exxon and Mobil—was added to the consortium, now named the Iraq Petroleum Company (IPC). The contract gave IPC exclusive rights to extract oil over a seventy-five-year period in exchange for a small royalty paid to the government. With two further contracts granted in the 1930s, these rights covered the entire country.[22]

In October 1927, the Baba Gurgur No. 1 well struck oil, and the oilmen struggled for nine days to control the 140-foot gusher. Three days later, high commissioner for Iraq Sir Henry Dobbs sent a memo back to London warning, "The discoveries of immense quantities of oil . . . make it now impossible to abandon control of Iraq without damaging important British and foreign interests."[23]

In the event, IPC's contracts did not last seventy-five years. After a decades-long struggle, as we shall see in the next chapter, they were finally terminated between 1972 and 1975.

## A Fictional Geography

During the 1990s, the isolated Saddam Hussein negotiated oil deals with French, Russian, and Chinese companies—all in an attempt to divide the UN Security Council. In contrast, by 2003 American companies had been out of Iraq for twenty-eight years, as had BP. Officially Shell had too, but it had been trying to get an oil deal in a country, absent from most maps, called East Jordan.[24] Shell's East Jordan team, led by the Austrian Wolfgang Ströbl, had held talks with the Saddam government from 1994 to 2001 about developing Ratawi, a midsized oilfield in the desert fifty miles west of Basra. It was doing nothing illegal in talking to the regime, company men are quick to insist; Shell was simply discussing future business, not actively trading with sanctions-bound Iraq. But among Shell staff the idea of doing business with Iraq was "sensitive"—hence the geographical rebrand.

Shell also concluded an agreement in 2000 with the Australian oil and mining company BHP and its partner Tigris Petroleum to work together in developing the Halfaya field, twenty miles from the Iranian border, should sanctions be lifted. In early 1996 BHP had arranged a "humanitarian" donation of a $5 million shipment of Australian wheat to Iraq. According to an internal BHP memo, "the purpose of the transaction is to establish favour with the Government of Iraq," anticipating that payment could later be exchanged "for a down payment for entry into the [Halfaya field] concession." The company paid for the shipment out of its exploration budget.[25] BHP went even further than Shell to keep its dealings with Iraq secret, preparing a contingency press release to be used if someone found out. But in order to avoid having in its possession a document that itself could implicate the company if leaked, BHP fictionalized history as well as geography in the draft release. In surreal tones, the press release announced:

> X announced today that it had caused a shipment of Austrian eggs to be made to the people of Italy. Mr Y of X said that his company wished to establish goodwill with the people of Italy and would hope to transact business there after Italy has met the conditions imposed upon them by

the League of Nations and when the League of Nations has lifted its
sanctions. . . . The League of Nations sanctions are aimed at forcing
the Government of Italy to comply with nuclear and germ warfare inspection regimes. . . . Italy is a major oil producer; we wish to participate in their industry.[26]

# 2

# The Human at the Center

In our concept, as Muslims, it is the human element which comes first; this is top of the list, followed by means of production, and capital in the last place. The value system held by advocates of privatisation is the opposite of our value system. We emphasize the human element because we believe humanity carries the most value.

—Abu Rabab, Basra refinery fireman[1]

Like any other, Basra's refinery is a labyrinth of pipes connecting oddly shaped buildings: one like a tornado slide, another like a space-village watchtower, a third like an upside-down funnel. Scores of parallel six-inch tubes run down the thoroughfares, until each dives off to the side to carry out its mysterious function. Looming high above is the giant flare tower, spewing forty-foot flames whose heat can be felt on the ground below. And everywhere hangs the dull smell of sulfurous gases.

What is different about the Basra refinery is the aged look of its equipment. Nothing sparkles: this is old chemistry rather than futuristic high-tech. The control room looks like a 1970s movie set, with beige-colored walls covered in switches, knobs, dials, gauges, and golf ball–sized red warning lights. The buildings are tired, their former straight lines now relaxing into old age. And the pipes are shaded with rust—not just in worn corners but over their whole length.

As I walked around the plant in 2005, I felt nervous. I knew that in refineries in Britain and America the failure of old pipes and valves under high pressure was the most common cause of accidents. As I thought about this, I flinched involuntarily. I asked the Basra refinery manager, Mr. Wahid, if there were a lot of safety problems. Accidents were very rare, he replied. Seeing my surprise, he explained, "Every Iraqi loves his work. For the operator, the refinery is part of him. He constantly checks the equipment."

I contrasted what he said with Western practice. In many refineries the workforce has been cut back so much that checking rarely takes place, and faulty parts often are not repaired or replaced. Two months before my trip to Basra, an explosion at BP's Texas City, Texas, refinery had killed fifteen workers when a distillation tower was overfilled with flammable liquids, which were then incorrectly discharged. The underlying causes of the tragedy were not yet known, but an investigation by the U.S. Chemical Safety Board (CSB) later found a lack of leadership competence and insufficient implementation of safety systems. The CSB pointed out that a 25 percent cut in fixed costs between 1998 and 2000 had "adversely affected maintenance expenditures." Training staff had been cut from thirty in 1997 to eight in 2004, and the remaining trainers were given extra duties, leaving less time for training. The number of control board operators was also downsized and workloads increased.[2]

At Basra the most recent fire had been when a large storage tank exploded in 2003. That wasn't the result of failures by the oil company; an F-16 jet had bombed it. During the invasion there were a total of twenty-one fires. Abu Rabab, a fireman at the refinery, told me proudly that he had not dealt with any emergencies in the two years since. Basra had been on the front line of three wars since Abu Rabab started work at the refinery in 1976, each conflict causing huge fires. One of the worst was in 1980, when Iranian aircraft hit four storage tanks of aviation fuel at the refinery. The flames shot hundreds of feet into the sky. Equipped with just two old trucks, a Tatra and a Dennis, Abu Rabab and his team took fifteen days to tame the inferno. "All this was destroyed," manager Wahid said, gesturing to a section of the refinery. "And Iraqi workers rebuilt all of it."

The challenge after the 1991 Gulf War was even greater than during and after the war with Iran, as not only were facilities and infrastructure devastated by the air campaign, but international sanctions prohibited imports of equipment and raw materials and starved the economy of funds. Still, the Iraqis did an impressive job by cobbling together what they could find.

Despite heavy damage, the Basra refinery had its first unit back in operation within nine months.

## A Rebellious Engineer

Iraqis' pride in their oil industry has its roots in how hard they had to struggle to gain ownership over it. Tariq Shafiq was one of the pioneers. With a generous, grandfatherly face and a gentle manner, Shafiq speaks with the weight of forty years' experience and with professional straightforwardness. It is hard not to be moved by the calm reasonableness of his arguments, which he often prefaces with "A rational approach would be . . ." I asked him about the origins of Iraqi oil expertise.

Shafiq completed his degree in petroleum engineering at the University of California at Berkeley in 1953. His father had died during his studies, and it fell to him, as the eldest son, to support the family of eight. He needed a job quickly.[3] He was one of Iraq's few trained oil specialists, so the offer came soon: he would be the government representative at the Iraq Petroleum Company in Kirkuk. Within days he was back in the government oil director's office, having discovered that "the representative is a big shot with a car" whose job was just to take readings on the export gauges. "Is that all?" he asked. "I am a petroleum engineer; that is too silly for words." He turned down the job and was left unemployed.

But not long after, an alumnus of his university became director of refineries in the government and hired Shafiq to work on the Daura refinery in southern Baghdad, which was being built by Kellogg, a precursor of the company that in 2003 would play a central role in Iraq's reconstruction. Shafiq got on well at Daura for four months, but certain things troubled him. Iraqi employees were not allowed in the canteen. Toilets were accessed with keys given only to Western expatriates. Every morning he had to get up before 4 a.m. for his two-hour walk to the bus stop, while the Westerners were picked up by company cars. One day Shafiq invited his Iraqi colleagues to his house to discuss their treatment. "Do we accept this?" he demanded. They all signed a petition calling for equal treatment, and Shafiq took it to a socialist former schoolmate, who published it. The next day the American company manager called in all the engineers and asked who wrote the petition. Shafiq was fired on the spot.

He let things cool down for a week before going back to the ministry. The director agreed to give him another chance and sent him to work at IPC in Kirkuk. On one occasion Shafiq came close to repeating his Daura experience, when a British geologist ordered him to sort the trays used for collecting core samples while he went to talk to a driller. "Not again," Shafiq said to himself. "I've just come out of a battle! Now do I accept instructions from this man? Is it because I am an Iraqi and he is British?"

When the geologist came back and asked why he hadn't done as he was told, Shafiq lost his temper. After a moment of hesitation the geologist backed down. "OK, OK, I'll do it."

"No," said Shafiq, "we'll do it together." He laughed as he told me the story. "That saved me being fired, and very quickly."

After that Shafiq progressed rapidly as his talents were recognized, and he was soon promoted and sent to the London headquarters for a year. Less than ten years after joining IPC, he became head of petroleum engineering in the company. But he could see the situation would not last. The indignities forced on Iraqi engineers, which had provoked the young Shafiq's acts of rebellion, were being replicated with the government and the population as a whole. "The IPC was living a totally separate life from the rest of the country—they were completely isolated from society. They were superior; they were blue-eyed; they had the money. . . . They became an economic, technical, and social enclave. Everybody was looking at that enclave with either envy or hatred."

## A Long Liberation

Throughout the mid-twentieth century, governments of oil-producing countries were in a state of perpetual negotiation with the petroleum companies, whose one-sided contracts had been signed at a time when the Western powers had the upper hand. Although they made some progress, it was never enough. Frank Hendryx, legal adviser to some of the producing governments, wrote in 1960 that the original contracts across the region were "surrounded with an assumed aura of untouchability and permeated with a self-created sanctity."[4]

Governments also talked of the "ghost of Mossadegh," referring to a former prime minister of Iran, Muhammad Mossadegh.[5] Frustrated in his government's efforts to renegotiate the terms of Iran's contract with the now renamed Anglo-Iranian Oil Company (BP), the populist Mossadegh had nationalized the company in 1951. The oil industry responded by closing ranks and boycotted Iranian oil, sending the country rapidly toward bankruptcy. At the time almost the entire world oil market outside the Soviet bloc was controlled by a handful of companies known as the "Seven Sisters": Exxon, Shell, BP, Mobil, Chevron, Texaco, and Gulf. Their market power was such that a 1952 U.S. Senate report described them as "the international petroleum cartel."[6] Two years after the Senate report, the U.S. government joined forces with the British to shore up this cartel. Under the leadership of Kermit Roosevelt, grandson of former president Theodore Roosevelt, the CIA and the British Secret Intelligence Service (MI6) sponsored a coup in Iran. The coup succeeded in deposing Mossadegh and led to the return of Western oil companies, although now in a consortium including American companies, with Anglo-Iranian's holding reduced to 40 percent. The episode remains central to the way people in the Middle East interpret U.S. and British motives to this day.

Nevertheless, across the region the old imperial powers were in slow retreat. On July 14, 1958, the Free Officers' Movement in the Iraqi army overthrew the British-installed monarchy and made Brigadier Abd al-Karim al-Qasim prime minister. It was perhaps the one moment in modern Iraq's history when a government could claim true legitimacy among the population, and July 14 remains Iraq's national day. The front page of the *New York Times* announced the Eisenhower government's policy: in contrast to Mossadegh's fate, "intervention will not be extended to Iraq as long as the revolutionary government in Iraq respects Western oil interests."[7]

Faced with popular demands to throw off that other symbol of foreign domination, Qasim tried for two years to negotiate with IPC. "Iraqis are united on oil as perhaps on no other issue," observed the *Financial Times* in May 1961. "The majority Iraqi view is that the oil agreements now in force were concluded by a regime subordinate to Britain and the validity of these agreements is now in question."[8] The Iraqi press put it more strongly, denouncing the oil companies as a "collection of thieves, monopolists and plunderers of the people."[9] Finally, after three years of failed negotiations, in December 1961 the government issued Law No. 80, a turning point for Western oil companies across the Middle East. Wisely, the law did not nationalize oil production but reclaimed Iraqi rights to the remaining oil in the country, outside the fields already in production. If it had taken everything, the ensuing boycott by oil companies would have left the government with no markets for its oil and hence no income, like Mossadegh's Iran.

The world's demand for oil rose sharply in the early 1960s as postwar austerity gave way to economic boom and as motoring became fashionable. Iraq, however, gained little from the boom. Following Law No. 80, the Seven Sisters punished the country by restraining production there while meeting the demand for growth from other, less problematic countries such as Iran, Saudi Arabia, and Kuwait (the graph on page ix shows the decline of Iraq's share).[10] Although Iraqi oil production continued, meaning the country was not starved, there was a weaker echo of Mossadegh's fate as the stagnant economy eroded Qasim's political capital and left him vulnerable.

In February 1963 the Ba'ath (Renaissance) Party seized power in a coup and showed Qasim's corpse on television to demonstrate his demise. A U.S. hand in the coup was alleged by several observers, including King Hussein of Jordan, who had his own connections with the CIA.[11] In any case, the coup was welcomed by the West. "We think new regime can prove of great significance for Iraq and, by its example, for Arab area," the U.S. embassy in Baghdad reported in a telegram to the State Department the day after the coup. "Embassy believes IPC has potential opportunity of great dimensions to place its relations with Iraq on mutually satisfying basis from which West generally would benefit."[12] The United States was quick to recognize the new Ba'ath government and to offer arms deals.

The Ba'ath Party, founded in Syria in the 1940s, had never achieved mass support in Iraq; instead its Iraqi branch aimed to achieve power through force—assassinations, coups, and intimidation by street thugs. By contrast, the Iraq Communist Party, which had led uprisings throughout the 1940s and 1950s against the monarchy and against foreign control of oil, could mobilize thousands. In the months that followed the coup, the Ba'ath murdered, arrested, and tortured hundreds of senior communists, sending its killing squads house to house using party lists reportedly provided by the CIA.[13] In the event, the Ba'ath Party was in power only for nine months. In November 1963 Colonel Abd al-Salam Arif removed the Ba'ath from government in a palace coup.

In February 1964, Arif's government established the Iraq National Oil Company (INOC) to run the oil industry in the areas Qasim had reclaimed, and appointed Tariq Shafiq one of its founding directors. While Shafiq was as angry at IPC's behavior as anyone else, he thought Law No. 80 had been ill-planned. "It did put us back . . . the IPC froze production. What can you do? What is your next move? The government had no way to retaliate. You do not do that without knowing what to do next."[14] The attitude of Shafiq and many of the technocrats was "You consolidate, take [what you've got], and negotiate further." So in 1964 he was tasked with just that.[15] In June 1965, after 115 meetings, a deal was struck under which IPC would agree to accept Law No. 80—no small feat given Western oil companies' fear of setting a precedent. In return, the land area allocated to IPC would be doubled to include the North Rumaila field, the most attractive untapped prospect. In an important move, IPC agreed to establish a joint venture with the new INOC, which would build Iraqi capacity.[16] To technocrats such as Shafiq, the deal was the best Iraq could get, but it failed to match the political mood of the time. There followed two years of debate, but the 1967 Arab-Israeli War brought a halt to any prospect of agreement.

After the Ba'athists took power for a second time in a 1968 coup, they were desperate to shore up their popularity. They settled on a combination of oil populism and their own brand of bloodthirstiness, and in 1970 Tariq Shafiq was accused of trying to sell out the country to the oil companies and sentenced to death. Fortunately, he was out of the country at the time. He did not return. For all his pragmatism in the negotiations, Shafiq could see IPC would not last. "That enclave was a foreign body in the Iraqi body—it had to be pulled out."[17]

Hazim Sultan, a fellow petroleum engineer who had worked for IPC in Kirkuk since 1966, also favored a gradual approach. But he told me he too could see where things were heading. Assigned to the IPC head office in London in 1969 and 1970, he warned management, "If you continue with your current policy [and] approach, you will be nationalized within three years."[18]

This time the Iraqi government prepared the ground through a technical cooperation deal with the Soviet Union. Meanwhile, the oil market was tightening, strengthening the hand of governments because companies had no spare capacity with which to replace lost production. In mid-May the government gave IPC a two-week ultimatum to meet its demands. When the IPC general manager, a Mr. Gillan, offered Hazim Sultan, now back in

Iraq, the job of pipeline manager for the K3 pumping station, Sultan said he would give his answer on June 2. Why? asked Gillan. "Because on 1 June [the government's deadline] the company will be nationalized."

"Come on, Sultan!" Gillan said. No one took the threat seriously.[19]

On June 1, 1972, the Iraqi government nationalized IPC. The other two contracts, with IPC subsidiaries, were nationalized between 1972 and 1975, so as to build Iraq's position gradually and not precipitate reprisals. Historians Marion Farouk-Sluglett and Peter Sluglett observed, "No action by any Iraqi government since the 1958 Revolution was greeted with such universal enthusiasm, and the Ba'ath was able to live off the moral capital generated by this act for years."[20]

For Sultan, the challenge to Western oil interests spelled future trouble. "Now they will never leave us alone."[21]

## The Golden Age

During the 1970s Iraqi engineers deployed the skills they had learned working for IPC before nationalization to build an industry that was the envy of oil producers around the world. Between 1972 and 1979 INOC increased production from 1.5 million to 3.5 million barrels a day.[22] From 1972 to 1977 Iraqi exploration teams discovered new oil at a rate of 6 billion barrels a year, matching the best years for the whole of the rest of the world put together.[23] They found some of Iraq's largest fields: West Qurna, East Baghdad, Majnoon, and Nahr Bin Umar. Before 1972, production had languished despite the Western companies' superior technology and finance, because the IPC had run Iraq's oil industry according to its members' objectives: in particular, since those same companies (the "international petroleum cartel") then controlled most of the world's oil production, they often restricted their production from Iraq, so as to maintain a high per-barrel price.*

Once freed from foreign companies' control of its oil, Iraq's per capita GDP grew from $1,745 in 1970 to $4,083 in 1980, even as the population increased by nearly 50 percent.[24] For those few years oil was converted into

---

* A few years later, these relative interests were reversed. When most of the major oil-producing countries nationalized oil production, their new state-owned companies came to account for a large share of the world's production. After that, the multinational companies would produce at the maximum rate possible, leaving it to the state-owned companies to restrain production and thereby keep the price higher.

prosperity for much of the population. The Ba'ath regime still felt insecure following the instability of the 1960s and sought to shore up its position by ensuring that the wealth was well distributed.[25] The government invested heavily in infrastructure, agriculture, and industry; established a generous welfare system; and supported the development of a thriving private sector among the middle classes. Baghdad was thoroughly modernized, with new water treatment and sewage systems, housing, roads, and an international airport. During the course of the decade, the other major oil-producing countries of the region followed Iraq in nationalizing their oil.

How had the Iraqis been so successful so soon after nationalizing their oil industry? I began to understand the answer when I met Hazim Sultan in his office in west Amman. I found his fascination with oil contagious as he slipped easily into explaining the characteristics of the Kirkuk reservoir, the properties of the petroleum it contained, and the challenges of extracting it. During the 1990s he had run the Arab Petroleum Training Institute in Baghdad for four years, and he clearly wanted me to share the joy of his specialist knowledge. As he did so, his enthusiasm lifted him.[26] But much of the time he talked with sadness, often looking down, not making eye contact, speaking slowly and deliberately.

Sultan was sixty-two at the time of the 2003 invasion. He headed the committee to bring back oil production once military operations were over, before going on to become head of the Oil Ministry's Reservoirs Directorate for two years. "Had it not been for the invasion, which was totally unwarranted, unfair and totally unjustified . . ." He trailed off and restarted his point. "In any war, nobody is victorious; it's only a question of how much the cost is to each side." His manner carried an inescapable sense of lost opportunities.

As for Iraq's industrial model, he said, "Man is at the center of everything. That requires you to respect him, love him, guide him." And his management style did just that. "You should start from the point that everybody has at least a glimmer of light inside. Let's identify it and get a magnifying glass and see how best we can expand it."

Sultan's comments encapsulated something of the Iraqi oil industry: a focus on people more than technology or finance, a belief in the industry's importance for the common good, and a striving for technical betterment against a background of repeated destruction by war, dictatorship, and outside interference. And through all the destruction Iraqis were forced to improvise, using novel methods or finding any substitute parts that would do the job. Engineer Falah Khawaja explained to me: "We were not engineers but *craftsmen*."[27]

## Islam and Industry

This view of the centrality of the human contribution can be found throughout Iraqi industry. It was most fully articulated in an Islamic theory of economics advanced by Iraq's highest-regarded Shi'a theologian of the twentieth century, Muhammad Baqir al-Sadr. From the age of ten, Sadr studied in the Hawza (seminary) in Najaf, where in the narrow streets around the gold-domed shrine of Imam Ali are found twenty-four theological colleges, some nearly a thousand years old.[28] Concerned about the decline of Iraq's Shi'a leadership, he took on the mission of making Islam relevant to modern life, steering religious jurists into rulings on political and social issues. In the late 1950s, as a young man in his mid-twenties, he co-founded the Da'wa (Islamic Call) Party to give Islam a voice within the political system.[29] And in 1959 and 1961, he wrote his two great works, *Falsafatuna* (Our Philosophy) and *Iqtisaduna* (Our Economics). In them he aimed to set out a vision of society according to Islamic principles.*

Much of *Iqtisaduna* was devoted to a critique of the two dominant economic systems of the time and to defining an alternative. Under capitalism, in Sadr's view, unrestrained enrichment of the successful leads to economic oppression of the weak; unjust distribution of economic wealth inevitably follows.[30] Marxism, on the other hand, focuses excessively on the fight between capitalists and workers, and thus neglects those too weak to work, whom society should support.[31] Class struggle, he argued, draws from a collectivized variant of the (individual) self-interest of capitalism and fails to look at the needs of the whole society.[32] Drawing from Islamic teachings, Sadr aimed to create a different economics with social justice as its central goal.[33]

Sadr's Islamic economics places the human being at its center. When it comes to production, this means the worker; indeed, for Sadr, the only justification for private ownership is physical work, as it is work that improves the situation of society.[34] Islamic economics is best known for its prohibition on charging interest (*riba*) on loans. The reason is that a lender does no work

---

* Although he was prominent within Shi'ism, Islamic economics does not differ between sects. To Sadr and to other economists both Shi'a and Sunni, his work was Islamic rather than Shi'a.

to earn the interest and hence makes no contribution to the advancement of society. Islam does not preclude other forms of finance; the problem in the case of bank interest is that the income is certain. But since the worker is the owner, he should make the decisions.[35] This is the opposite of the Western model, where the providers of capital are the owners and decision makers. A result of the prohibition on earning income without work is that concentration of wealth based on accumulation is not possible. One can only become as rich as one's personal capacity to work allows.

The decisions between 1961 and 1975 to reclaim Iraqi control of its oil industry were made by secular politicians, but it is important to note that in Islam, as articulated by Sadr, Western companies' ownership and control of the Iraqi oil industry are illegitimate. And Iraq's Islamic culture helps explain why the nationalized industry pursued a very different model, and why it was successful.

Yet oil played a contradictory role in 1970s Iraq. On one hand, it provided for major development of the country and contributed to big advances in general prosperity. On the other, the Ba'ath regime used oil revenues to expand the military and fund extensive networks of patronage, and so shored up its political position and intensified its repression of opponents. Having already wiped out most of the Iraq Communist Party, the Ba'ath saw Islamists as its biggest threat. Through the 1970s, it increasingly attacked Da'wa and arrested and killed many of its leaders. Following Saddam Hussein's assumption of the presidency in 1979, more than four thousand Da'wa members were arrested and more than two hundred killed. In April 1980, the regime decreed membership of Da'wa punishable by death and arrested Sadr and his sister Bint al-Huda. After torturing them for three days, the regime executed them both.

In September of that year, Saddam launched a series of air strikes and a major ground invasion against Iran, bringing the development of the Iraqi oil industry to an abrupt end and starting a debilitating war that would drag on for eight years and claim up to a million lives, while neither side ultimately made any political, material, or territorial gains. It was a sign of Iraqi engineers' ability that by the end of the war, Iraqi production had climbed back up to 2.6 million barrels per day. Two years later, in July 1990, Iraq matched the 1979 peak of 3.5 million, the month before Saddam invaded Kuwait in a strategic miscalculation even more catastrophic than the one ten years earlier.[36]

The oil industry's success under extreme adversity has shaped Iraqi attitudes. An oil worker in Basra told me that as a result of rebuilding bombed and shelled oil facilities during and after three wars, their sense of ownership was far deeper than if they had simply hired a company to build or fix them, and they would not willingly relinquish that ownership. When Iraq came to be occupied after 2003, this attitude would put its oil workers fundamentally at odds with the occupiers.

# 3

# Burning Ambition

*Lower prices are a net advantage for the economies of the United States and other oil-importing countries because they help keep inflation low and help their economies grow. However, lower prices increase world-wide petroleum consumption and increase dependence on the Gulf. . . . Iran and Iraq do not accept the new post–Cold War order and their dreams of regional hegemony remain the most significant long-term threat.*

—Zalmay Khalilzad, 1995 strategy paper[1]

No one shied away from saying the 1991 Gulf War was about oil. As then U.S. defense secretary Dick Cheney explained to a Senate hearing, "Iraq controlled 10 percent of the world's reserves prior to the invasion of Kuwait. Once Saddam Hussein took Kuwait, he doubled that to approximately 20 percent. . . . Once he acquired Kuwait and deployed an army as large as the one he possesses, he was clearly in a position to dictate the future of world-wide energy policy, and that gave him a stranglehold on our economy."[2]

With the extent of the oil interests at stake, U.S. strategists all agreed that Saddam's forces had to be kept from attacking Saudi Arabia (which has another 25 percent of reserves) and be driven out of Kuwait. But they disagreed about whether the United States should go further and remove Saddam from power. One of the strongest advocates of pressing on to Baghdad was Zalmay Khalilzad, an analyst in the Pentagon and protégé of Paul Wolfowitz. "You can't stop! We have an opportunity to do a bigger thing," Khalilzad wrote in memos. According to journalist James Mann, Cheney rejected the idea on the grounds that "the Saudis wouldn't like it."[3]

Born in Mazar-e-Sharif in northern Afghanistan, Khalilzad came to the United States in 1975 to study at the University of Chicago under Albert Wohlstetter, a mathematician and critic of nuclear détente who was reputedly the inspiration for Dr. Strangelove in Stanley Kubrick's film. Wohlstetter excited in Khalilzad the ideas of military strategy and introduced him to Wolfowitz, another former student. Over the next two decades, Khalilzad would alternate between working in the government—usually under Wolfowitz—and holding positions in strategic think tanks, notably the RAND Corporation. One former associate commented, "He has a narrow view of the Middle East and South Asia . . . [he thinks of] security to the exclusion of everything else. He tends to look at military solutions as the first, not the last, policy option."[4] Khalilzad's enthusiasm for military strategy and the application of overwhelming power spilled into his family life too: he named his two sons after great emperors, Alexander and Maximilian.

While they had differed on how to end the Gulf War, a few months later Khalilzad forged agreement with Cheney on a radical new course for the wider U.S. posture when he was tasked with drafting the biannual Defense Planning Guidance. In the new post-Soviet environment the primary U.S. aim, Khalilzad suggested, should be to preserve its position as the sole superpower by aiming to "prevent any hostile power from dominating a region whose resources would, under consolidated control, be sufficient to generate global power." A "forward presence"—meaning bases—would be used to project U.S. dominance. Foremost among U.S. interests was "access to vital raw materials, primarily Persian Gulf oil," along with preventing threats from weapons of mass destruction, terrorism, and drug trafficking.[5] Khalilzad reiterated the focus on the Gulf several times.[6]

In early March 1992 the new strategy suffered a setback when a leak to the *New York Times* provoked immediate criticism for squandering the post–Cold War opportunities of both the new multilateral world order and the "peace dividend." Administration officials were quick to distance themselves. An unnamed official close to the White House dismissed what he saw as a "dumb report."[7] But then Defense Secretary Cheney read it. "You've discovered a new rationale for our role in the world," he told Khalilzad.[8] The final version, formally approved by Cheney in May 1992, toned down some of the more explicit references to self-interest, including the vital interest in

Persian Gulf oil, but accepted—in softened language—Khalilzad's core elements of strategic deterrence and forward presence, and even strengthened
his ideas on unilateralism.[9]

Throughout the late 1990s, Khalilzad and Wolfowitz led the growing calls
for a return to Iraq to remove Saddam Hussein. An article they jointly wrote
in the *Weekly Standard* in 1997 left little doubt as to their view: it was headlined "Overthrow Him!"[10] The ideas of Khalilzad's Defense Planning Guidance would form the acknowledged basis of the better-known arguments of
the Project for a New American Century (PNAC), which in 1998 sent an
open letter to President Bill Clinton calling for regime change in Iraq.[11] The
call echoed in regular "black coffee briefings" at the American Enterprise
Institute and became a central rallying cry for the rising neoconservatives.
Many PNAC members and signatories would be appointed to senior government jobs in 2001, and the 2002 National Security Strategy, which laid out
the doctrine of preemption that would be applied in Iraq six months later,
was seen by some neocons as PNAC's "lineal descendant."[12]

## The Affable Technocrat

"Yes, oil was one of the main reasons for the war," said Faleh al-Khayat.[13]
"But it is not just as simple as that, not as simple as 'America wanted to
control the oil in Iraq.' No, it's much more complex." This was how our first
conversation began in Amman in summer 2009. "America, Greg, does not
care much if American companies win the contracts in Iraq," he went on.
"They would *prefer* American companies to win the contracts. But what
matters to them is the pool of oil supplied."

The overriding concern for the United States is not to obtain physical oil
but to boost global supply relative to demand. After all, it consumes 25 percent of the world's oil, and if global supplies are constrained, the largest
consumer suffers the most—economically, strategically, and militarily. The
Defense Energy Support Center (DESC) is the world's single largest pur-
chaser of oil, and in 2003 the U.S. armed forces, via DESC, consumed 143
million barrels of oil, the majority in aircraft.[14] By comparison, this was more
than the oil consumed by Pakistan or Sweden.[15]

Khayat spoke melodiously and warmly, with a voice that could have belonged as easily to an artist as to a petroleum engineer. I immediately liked
him. As he explained to me the details of the Iraqi oil business, Khayat took

his time, making sure I followed every point. His intellectual openness—shared by many of the Iraqi oil experts I have met—could not be more different from the way many Western experts use jargon and privileged knowledge to guard their elite status. British-educated like many of Iraq's leading technocrats, he had started his career in the BP-operated subsidiary of the IPC in 1967; by the time the company was nationalized in 1975, he had become the youngest senior engineer in its history. His generation ran the oil industry after nationalization, using the skills it had acquired in IPC. In 1995, he became director general of planning, one of the Oil Ministry's most powerful positions.

By the early 2000s, Khayat explained, the world's demand for oil was increasing, especially in the rapidly growing economies of Asia, and supply was unable to keep up. Most major producers—Saudi Arabia, Russia, the United States—were already producing as fast as they could. Iraq was the only country that could significantly expand production, since its oil industry was operating well below its potential. Because of wars and sanctions, only about a third of Iraq's seventy-five known oilfields were actually producing oil; the others had yet to be developed. Furthermore, much of the country was still unsurveyed, and geologists expected that the oil yet to be discovered could match or even exceed the country's known reserves.

This underdevelopment of Iraq's oil could be seen by its low share of world production compared with the scale of its resource endowment. At the turn of the century Iraq accounted for less than 4 percent of global oil production, but below the ground it had 11 percent of the world's remaining reserves. Contrast this with the United States, the world's second-largest producer in 2000, which supplied 10 percent of total production but from less than 3 percent of reserves.[16] At those rates of extraction the United States' known oil would be gone in just over ten years, whereas Iraq's would last more than a century. The United States and Iraq were simply the extremes in a broader pattern: OPEC countries produced at an average rate that would exhaust their reserves in seventy-four years, whereas the average for non-OPEC countries was thirteen years. Following these trends, as the rest of the world's oil was depleted, OPEC—and especially the Persian Gulf region—was set to become an even more significant player in the world oil market, with Iraq at the very center of it. More than 60 percent of the world's reserves lie beneath five countries, which form an arch around the Gulf: Iran on one side;

Saudi Arabia, the United Arab Emirates (UAE), and Kuwait on the other; and Iraq the keystone by which the arch stands or falls.

"So the only option for the American administration is to lift sanctions from Iraq and let Iraq export at will and develop its potential," Khayat went on. "But that means keeping Saddam Hussein in power. He will get the billions out of oil; he will rebuild his economy; he will follow his ambition of scientific and military development [and develop weapons of mass destruction]. And suddenly came the other factor into play, the safety of Israel and the new Middle East." At the time there were frequent suicide bombings in Israel, peaking at nearly one per week in 2001 and 2002. "Saddam was banging on the table on television and saying in three days' time, after the man explodes himself, his family will get $25,000 from the Iraqi government. Remember, if five Israelis get killed by a bomb, Israel attacks the whole of Palestine and is ready to start a new war in the Middle East. So how can they accept some leader of a major nation in the area saying that within three days of the man exploding himself, we will give his family $25,000?"

It was a neat explanation. Complex, yes, but more appealing than most other variants of the war-for-oil argument. Khayat's analysis put oil at the center, but without neglecting those other factors in the decision to go to war: the security of Israel and weapons of mass destruction. "The only possibility, they looked around, and they saw that Iraq is possible to be occupied," he concluded. "After it has been weakened by twelve years of sanctions, the destruction of the 1990 war, which devastated its infrastructure, its military industry, its military capability. So it was ripe, it was ready for occupation. And that was the reason for the 2003 war. It's a multidimensional thing."

## The Call for Investment

As the George W. Bush administration came to power in Washington, several think tanks were warning that global oil demand was set to continue growing faster than supplies and push up the oil price. One of the most extensive analyses was the Center for Strategic and International Studies' (CSIS) three-volume *Geopolitics of Energy into the 21st Century*, led by Robert Ebel. The report's central warning was that with energy consumption in the developing world growing rapidly, energy supplies would have to increase by around 50 percent over the next twenty years. But this could be achieved only if Iran, Iraq, and Libya were to produce at full capacity. Unilateral sanctions against Iran and Libya meant U.S. companies would miss out, but the greater strategic worry was that "Iraq, subjected to *multilateral* sanctions, may be constrained from building in a timely way the infrastructure necessary to meet the upward curve in energy demand." Again governments would *prefer* their own companies to get contracts but their more important priority was that "if Western governments are to ensure adequacy of supply early in the twenty-first century, policies must be framed toward encouraging energy producing countries to open their energy sectors to greater foreign investment"[17]—which could come from foreign companies.

An equally influential study in early 2001 led by Amy Myers Jaffe of the James Baker Institute at Houston's Rice University and sponsored by the Council on Foreign Relations warned of a "new era of energy scarcity" in which major investment would be vital to meet growing demand.[18] Jaffe's forty-one-member task force included representatives of BP, Shell, Chevron, Texaco, Eni, and Enron and leading energy and foreign policy members of the George H.W. Bush and Clinton administrations. The report argued that the Persian Gulf region's state-owned oil companies had become reluctant to invest enough to increase production capacity in line with growing global needs. From those states' perspective they had little need to, as they already generated plenty of income to support their countries' needs. In 2001 the International Energy Agency (IEA), the official energy coordinator of the OECD countries, estimated that from a Western perspective the region needed investment in oil production of more than $300 billion by 2010.[19]

The flip side of constrained production was that Iraq was becoming a "swing producer": a country with sufficient surplus capacity to be able to alter the oil price by a policy decision on its rate of production. "Iraq remains a destabilizing influence to . . . the flow of oil to international markets from the Middle East," Jaffe's report warned.[20]

Jaffe's solution to both problems—insufficient production growth and Saddam Hussein's influence over the oil market—was to open Middle East oil industries to foreign investment. "Unless the U.S. government provides leadership in modernizing market and investment structures, there is a clear danger that others will take the reins and develop institutions that run counter to U.S. interests." Furthermore, the report called for a review of sanctions policy: avoiding sanctions wherever possible and focusing them on achieving specific outcomes. "Like it or not, Iraqi reserves represent a major asset that can quickly add capacity to world oil markets and inject a more competitive tenor to oil trade," the report noted. The danger was that lifting sanctions would reempower Saddam Hussein. Therefore, "the United States should conduct an immediate policy review toward Iraq, including military, energy, economic, and political/diplomatic assessments."[21]

There was clearly a meshing of interests between the U.S. government, which needed to expand Iraqi oil production through foreign investment for strategic reasons, and the oil corporations that would provide that investment. "Our wider energy policy objectives for Iraq need to be dovetailed with commercial goals to ensure the best result for the U.K. national interest," the British government observed in its (previously unreleased) September 2004 Energy Strategy for Iraq. "The two sets of goals are mutually enforcing given the need for foreign investment. Iraq's energy sector will provide considerable market opportunities for U.K. firms."[22]

## Iraq and the Bush Presidency

During the 2000 presidential campaign George W. Bush's chief foreign policy concerns were Russia and China, not Iraq.[23] Famously, he said during his second presidential debate with Al Gore, "I don't think our troops ought to be used for what's called nation building."[24] Iraq did appear prominently, however, in his energy policy manifesto. In that document he lamented that under the Clinton administration UN inspections for weapons of mass destruction (WMD) had come to a halt, Bahrain and the UAE had reopened embassies in Baghdad, and Clinton had spent only a "negligible amount" of the $97 million approved by Congress to support the Iraqi resistance under the Iraq Liberation Act of 1998. Quite why these political concerns belonged in an energy policy was then explained: Iraq was becoming "an important 'swing producer,' with an ability to single-handedly impact and manipulate global markets."[25]

Bush promised to make energy security a priority of foreign policy. He would reestablish U.S. "influence and credibility" in the Persian Gulf in order to maintain adequate oil supplies. "Governor Bush understands that ensuring U.S. energy security requires presidential leadership and a comprehensive national energy policy," his team pledged. In his second week in office he established an energy policy task force with leadership from Vice

President Dick Cheney. Meanwhile, the "Iraq problem" of collapsing sanctions and a reempowered Saddam were foremost in the new administration's national security concerns. According to Treasury Secretary Paul O'Neill, Iraq was the main focus of the administration's first National Security Council (NSC) meeting on January 30, 2001. "Imagine what the region would look like without Saddam and with a regime that's aligned with U.S. interests," said Defense Secretary Rumsfeld at the NSC's second meeting two days later. "It would change everything in the region and beyond it. It would demonstrate what U.S. policy is all about."[26] Meanwhile, Jane Mayer reported in the *New Yorker* that NSC staff were ordered to cooperate fully with Cheney's energy task force in a "melding" of "the review of operational policies towards rogue states" such as Iraq with "actions regarding the capture of new and existing oil and gas fields."[27]

Knowledge of the precise workings of the task force is limited due to the secrecy with which they were conducted. On the day it was formed, the vice president's general counsel, David Addington (nicknamed "Cheney's Cheney" for his ability to pull the levers of government and law from behind the scenes), wrote a memo explaining how to avoid demands for documents from Congress under the Federal Advisory Committee Act.[28] When the task force's lead staffer, Andrew Lundquist, suggested releasing the documents—under pressure from the Government Accountability Office—Cheney's reply was "Don't ever suggest that to me again."[29] Cheney believed that "we had the right to consult with whomever we chose—and no obligation to tell the press or Congress or anybody else whom we were talking to."[30]

It would be wrong to assume Iraq was the main topic of the Cheney task force's deliberations. Like the think tank studies, it considered both domestic and international aspects of U.S. energy supply and demand; certainly dismantling environmental regulation of domestic energy development was a key Cheney priority. He was also trying to address the rolling power blackouts across California, which had resulted from Enron's manipulation of the markets. Still, the papers considered by the task force included Robert Ebel's study of the geopolitics of energy, as well as a much-publicized map of Iraqi oilfields and a list of their foreign suitors.[31] On international supplies especially the report reached many of the same conclusions as Ebel and Jaffe. By 2020, it predicted, the Gulf would account for between 54 and 67 percent of world oil production: "By any estimation, Middle East oil producers will remain central to world oil security. The Gulf will be a primary focus of U.S.

international energy policy."[32] The task force proposed encouraging Middle East oil producers to open up to foreign investment, supporting U.S. energy companies in their efforts to enter foreign markets, and reviewing sanctions policy.

Iraq moved more firmly into the administration's target sights following the terrorist attacks of September 11, 2001. Oil remained privately at the heart of the rationale, even as the public reasoning addressed the security threat of Iraq's WMD in the context of international terrorist capabilities. In December 2001 Mark Allen of MI6 wrote a top-secret memo weighing the growing calls for action against Iraq.* In answer to the question "Why Move?" the paper noted, "The removal of Saddam remains a prize because it could give new security to oil supplies."[33]

When U.K. prime minister Tony Blair visited Bush at his Crawford, Texas, ranch in April 2002, the two leaders launched the U.S.-U.K. Energy Dialogue, which again noted the growing importance of Gulf oil supplies. Echoing the warnings of Jaffe and the IEA, their memo on the Energy Dialogue stressed that investment would be needed to more than double the region's production capacity within thirty years.[34] At the same meeting Blair reportedly pledged British support for a war in Iraq.[35]

## The Energy Infrastructure Planning Group

Concrete planning for the Iraqi oil industry began in late summer 2002, when undersecretary of defense Doug Feith hired his former law partner Mike Mobbs to set up an Energy Infrastructure Planning Group (EIPG). By the time President Bush addressed the UN General Assembly in September 2002 to declare the United States would go to war with or without UN backing, Mobbs had assembled an interagency team from the Pentagon, the State Department, the Department of Energy, and the CIA. The EIPG's main role was to plan for the short-term management of the oil sector while Iraq was directly occupied by the United States. And the group proposed two options: a "conservative approach" of restoring existing facilities and leaving major long-term decisions to a future Iraqi government, or an "expansive approach" of awarding contracts to explore and develop new fields.[36]

---

* In 2003–4 Allen famously brokered the rapprochement with Libya's Muammar Qadhafi. Shortly afterward he left MI6 to become special adviser to BP.

"Some would argue that the new Iraqi government should decide," the EIPG noted awkwardly as it weighed the pros and cons in a briefing to Rumsfeld, while the expansive approach had the advantage that it "helps consumers."[37] In the event, the conservative approach was chosen, not least for reasons of contract stability, although that conservatism applied only to the period of direct occupation, and the EIPG's plans would inevitably shape what happened over the longer term.

The group went on to consider how funds from Iraqi oil exports could be spent. The largest items in its budget were contributing up to $60 billion a year to the military campaign and up to $48 billion to the costs of occupying Iraq. But predicting total oil income of just $25 billion a year, it lamented that "demands on petroleum revenue will likely exceed available funds for foreseeable future."[38] It recommended "public diplomacy" statements that were quite at odds with its real proposals—for instance suggesting a public line that "the U.S. will act consistently with applicable legal norms while using proceeds for the benefit of the Iraqi people" even as it considered "whether to use control of Iraqi oil to advance important U.S. foreign policy objectives."[39]

The group is best known for its controversial recommendation to hire the Halliburton subsidiary Kellogg, Brown & Root (KBR) to run the Iraqi oil industry for a year or two after the invasion. Mobbs justified the choice of company—in which he says Cheney's office had no role*—on the grounds that KBR was one of only three U.S. companies capable of doing the work, along with Fluor and Bechtel. With an invasion imminent and planning starting so late, there was no time to carry out a tender process, and KBR already had a logistics contract with the U.S. military that could be extended to include the oil work.[40]

What struck me about the KBR plan was less the allegation that Cheney was engaged in war profiteering than the obvious absentees from the list of potential contractors: Iraqi companies. Hiring an American company, which inevitably would not know the quirks of the Iraqi oil industry—where the infrastructure bottlenecks were and how to work in local conditions—was clearly not the best option to get the job done. In fact, some EIPG members

---

* Mobbs acknowledged that Cheney's chief of staff, I. Lewis "Scooter" Libby, participated in the meeting of the Deputies Committee of the NSC, to which Mobbs had referred the decision for approval. But he points out that the meeting was the first time he had any communication with anyone from Cheney's office about the recommendation.

may not have wanted to repair the oil facilities at all. In an unreleased November 2002 briefing to the Deputies Committee of the NSC (consisting of the seconds-in-command of the relevant government agencies), the EIPG pondered whether Iraqi oil revenues should be spent on repairing Iraq's energy infrastructure. Among the disadvantages of doing so was that it "could discourage private sector involvement." In other words, a functioning and rehabilitated Iraqi oil industry might have little need of foreign companies. Two months later, it seems, that option was rejected when the group prioritized an aim "to minimize disruptions and promote confidence and stability in world markets."[41] This tension—between restoring and preserving Iraqi capacity so as to avoid short-term supply disruptions, and undermining that capacity so as to increase the need for foreign investment in the long term—would shape U.S. policy throughout the early years of the occupation.

Either way, protection of the geological treasure was vital. In one of the more striking semantic contortions of the war, a "senior defense official" gave a briefing in January 2003 to insist that Saddam Hussein's threatened destruction of Iraq's oilfields during the invasion would be "a terrorist act against his own people."[42] Certainly such an act would damage Iraq's economic future, but "terrorism"? Leaving aside the fact that the United States has always avoided a definition of terrorism that can apply to acts by a state (for obvious reasons), the one element of any definition that is generally accepted is that terrorist acts are designed to induce public fear (terror) for political purposes. Fear of damaged oilfields would hardly be foremost in the minds of Iraqis during the invasion; terror was more likely to be seen in the oil markets.

The EIPG prioritized crude oil production over electricity generation or supply of refined fuels to the Iraqi population.[43] Electricity and fuel would be needed by Iraqis, and an occupation power would under international law have a duty to provide for people. But the EIPG's aims were to "avoid unnecessary disruption to supply in the world market" and "to meet the costs of occupation [and] defray costs of administering Iraq."[44]

Another EIPG briefing in January 2003 considered how far a U.S. occupation authority ought to aim to expand Iraqi production. On significantly increasing production, the briefing noted that it "could force questions about Iraq's future relations with OPEC," which it apparently saw as a positive outcome that "may put long-term downward pressure on price" and "may help consumers." On the other hand, it warned of "unwelcome questions about our intentions towards OPEC."[45] It seems this dilemma was not resolved. Outside the EIPG some neoconservatives and libertarians argued that the occupation of Iraq should be used to push Iraq out of OPEC.[46] Neoconservative writer Irwin Stelzer of the Hudson Institute suggested that "competitive [oil] prices would have the same effect as an additional tax cut and would entail none of the long-term negative consequences of the current plunge into long-term federal budget deficits."[47] Put differently, the war could make Americans wealthier by depriving the Iraqi government, rather than the U.S. government, of revenues (not to mention lives). The British government, on the other hand, concluded in late 2002 that a sudden breakup of OPEC would be undesirable because it would cause oil market instability, and instead adopted a policy of using "liberated" Iraq to weaken OPEC from within.[48]

One of the most active members of the EIPG was Michael Makovsky, who had been hired by Undersecretary Feith in summer 2002. Makovsky later told me he saw the two most important roles of the EIPG as the KBR contract and the selection of Iraqis to lead the oil industry.[49] As for the latter, Makovsky had a candidate in mind by the name of Thamir al-Ghadhban, the Oil Ministry's acting director general of planning. Makovsky wouldn't go into how he knew of Ghadhban, but members of the Iraqi diaspora told me U.S. agencies were asking them about possibilities for oil industry leadership, and Ghadhban was one of the options raised in those phone calls.[50] "I just heard that he was apolitical and a good technocrat," Makovsky told me. "Our interest was a functioning Iraq—and the oil was where most of the money came from, so you want that to be robust."

## The Cautious Diplomat

While the EIPG focused on short-term plans during the period of direct occupation (albeit with a set of priorities skewed more to U.S. than to Iraqi needs), some longer-term thinking took place in the State Department, where many officials were more skeptical about the decision to go to war. Diplomats were particularly unhappy both with the prominence of Ahmad Chalabi—whom they saw as unreliable and self-interested—and with the ideological fervor of the neoconservatives who held much sway in the Pentagon: the "fucking crazies," as Secretary of State Colin Powell reportedly called them.[51] State Department officials' skepticism about war was not based on any concern for the welfare of Iraqis, however, nor even on a disagreement about objectives; it was more about strategy. Whereas many in the Pentagon imagined that Iraqis would quickly embrace U.S. values of democracy and capitalism simply by the fact of sudden liberation from dictatorship, their counterparts in State saw this as naive and believed that if a war took place it would entail a much longer and deeper effort to reshape Iraqi society in the aftermath. This became known as the Pottery Barn rule: if you break it, you own it.[52]

One of the skeptics was Ryan Crocker, second-in-command in the Bureau of Near Eastern Affairs and responsible for the Office of Iraqi Affairs. The soft-spoken diplomat had always been fascinated by the greater Middle East. After completing his undergraduate degree in 1970, he hitched from Amsterdam to Calcutta via Kabul. A few years later, when he had to learn Arabic, he chose to live with Bedouin shepherds in Jordan.[53]

While Powell's fears of a military quagmire were shaped by his experience in Vietnam, Crocker's doubts about an assertive foreign policy drew on the U.S. experience in Lebanon. He was working in the embassy in Beirut when it was attacked by a truck bomb on April 18, 1983, killing sixty-three people. The bombing was in retaliation for the presence of U.S.-led multinational forces in Lebanon. The lesson for Crocker, according to the *Washington Post*, was that U.S. involvement in the internal dynamics of this complicated region could have unpredictable consequences.[54]

In late 2002 Crocker was having sleepless nights. "This was not because of what I knew would happen, but because of the totality of what I could not foresee," he said.[55] Powell ordered Crocker to consider the risks of military action. According to Karen DeYoung's biography of Powell, the resulting twelve-page memo (still classified), titled "A Perfect Storm," warned that removing Saddam might unleash long-suppressed ethnic and sectarian tensions: Shi'a and Kurds might try to settle accounts and vie for dominance, while the Sunni Arab minority would not relinquish power willingly. Meanwhile, the United States would have to build a new political structure from scratch and introduce a private economy in place of Saddam Hussein's centralized system.[56] As we shall see in subsequent chapters, this could be seen as a prescription as much as a diagnosis.

## The Future of Iraq Project

To fill in some of the unknowns, Crocker oversaw the State Department's Future of Iraq Project. It was not designed to produce a plan for running the country; rather, it aimed to engage the Iraqi opposition to discuss and think through the issues with a view—like Makovsky and the EIPG—to identifying people with whom the United States could later work ("talent scouting," as an internal briefing on the project put it, for "ideas and people that can play a role in post-Saddam Iraq").[57]

Under this initiative, sixteen working groups of ten to twenty Iraqi exiles and international experts were formed to discuss their visions for the country after Saddam. Mostly the Iraqi members were proposed by the exiled opposition political parties, especially that of Ahmad Chalabi.[58] The Oil and Energy Working Group (OEWG) met four times between December 2002 and April 2003, twice in London and twice in Washington. Its lead adviser from the State Department was Robert Ebel, author of the Center for Strategic and International Studies' January 2001 report. As in most of the working groups, the Iraqi participants in Oil and Energy had varying opinions and abilities. Some spent much of the time expressing their hatred of the Ba'ath regime and their plans for revenge rather than discussing the future of the country. As Ebel put it to me, "There were discussions on who should have positions in the ministry. Sometimes it got very emotional about certain sects that shouldn't be involved."[59] An Iraqi member of the OEWG who asked me not to name him added, "They said we have to eradicate all influence of the Ba'athist people—even to the level of a worker in a refinery."[60] This was an attitude shared by many leading politicians in the exiled opposition.

Fadhil Chalabi (a second cousin of Ahmad Chalabi) was described by Ebel as "the elder person of the group, the one they all looked to."[61] Director of Sheikh Yamani's Centre for Global Energy Studies in London, Fadhil Chalabi is known as one of the strongest Iraqi advocates of oil privatization—an opinion that gets him invited to numerous oil industry conferences. "Iraq has politically always been against the presence of international oil companies," Fadhil Chalabi said to the group. But "Iraq would have to be realistic, and allow at least partial privatization." In particular, he wanted Iraq to offer contracts more generous to foreign companies than those Saddam had signed with Russian and Chinese companies in the 1990s.[62]

Ibrahim Bahr al-Uloum, son of a well-known Shi'a cleric and a follower of Ahmad Chalabi, was one of the members of the group most supportive of what the U.S. participants proposed. Ebel described him as "very reasonable, very sensible."[63] The unnamed OEWG member said he was "completely on their side."[64]

In an interview given at the time, Ebel said many in the group wanted to restrict foreign investment. But "as they realized the tremendous needs for investments, if they wanted to move ahead to expand oil production, that's going to take $35 to $40 billion. They don't have that kind of money. You have to then attract private investment, the foreign oil companies."[65] Ebel suggested a form of long-term development contract known as a production sharing agreement (PSA), which multinational oil companies favored.[66] A paper written by a subcommittee of the OEWG explained why international companies like PSAs. The most important feature from the perspective of private oil companies, the subcommittee said, was that oil companies would be "protected under a PSA from future adverse legislation," a point we shall return to in later chapters.[67] The final report of the working group suggested radical privatization options that went beyond the proposals of the subcommittee. It proposed either to offer *all* fields to foreign companies under PSAs, giving an Iraq National Oil Company (INOC) at most a minority role in the industry, or to privatize INOC itself.[68]

## Blood for Oil?

Although Cheney's task force had identified opening the Persian Gulf oil industries to foreign investment as a "primary focus of U.S. international energy policy," and although the State Department and Pentagon planning exercises considered how to reshape Iraq's oil industry through foreign investment, the administration insisted the war was unrelated to energy interests. The closest advocates of war came to admitting to an oil motive—in the Project for a New American Century's 1998 letter to Clinton, in a speech by Cheney in August 2002, and retrospectively in Federal Reserve chairman Alan Greenspan's book in 2007[69]—was in a reactive sense: Saddam Hussein would seek to dominate the oil production of the region, and intervention by a more moral power was necessary to prevent him. (In a similar vein, George Bush warned in 2005 that al-Qaeda would "seize oil fields" in Iraq were the United States to pull out.)[70] As a rule, politicians find it easy to spot an oil motive in others but almost impossible to see it in themselves. And this was the difference between the two U.S. wars against Iraq: in 1990 Iraq was an aggressor endangering U.S. oil interests, which the United States would defend, whereas it would be quite another thing for the United States to launch an unprovoked war to expand those interests.

Part of the reason the official denials of an oil motive (at least a proactive one) were effective was that they answered a notion in the public mind that the United States and Britain wanted *the oil itself* as some form of imperial plunder. Some critics leapt on the fact that Chevron bought one of the first shipments of "liberated" Iraqi oil. But a few oil deliveries are of little strategic value; what the major powers need is a continuous flow to consumers through purchase, not theft, over many years. These days it doesn't even matter which consumers, as long as the oil keeps flowing.* The captain of an oil tanker from West Africa may not know whether he is headed for Europe or North America as he sets off north, and his destination may change several times midocean as his load is traded and retraded. If Britain doesn't get a delivery from Nigeria, it can get one from Libya in its place.

Popular views on whether the Iraq War was for oil are as polarized as those on whether it was right to go to war. Almost everyone responds to the question with one of two answers: either "Of course it was" or "Of course it wasn't"—the middle ground is barely populated. Because it was a war of aggression (or "war of choice," according to the popular euphemism), there was no single casus belli, as there would have been if it had been a response to an attack on the United States or its allies. Instead, it was necessary to bring together a "coalition of the willing" even *within* the United States, inside which there were differences of interests, objective, and strategy. As Paul Wolfowitz put it, "For reasons that have a lot to do with the U.S. government bureaucracy, we settled on the one issue that everyone could agree on, which was weapons of mass destruction."[71]

The weight of evidence—no WMD, no links with al-Qaeda, no serious subsequent effort to respect or protect human rights in "liberated" Iraq, and the prioritizing of U.S. control above Iraqi democracy—encourages us not to believe what our leaders said. Should we also doubt what they *thought*? Is it possible that they honestly held an irrational belief based on unconvincing intelligence that Iraq was developing WMD? Psychologists use a concept

---

* Apart from some minor limitations according to the grades of crude a refinery can accept.

known as confirmation bias, a cognitive flaw whereby a person subcon-
sciously collects or interprets information in a biased way so as to back up
preexisting beliefs. Could this be the reason that Western policy makers
apparently feel more strongly about human rights abuses in Iraq or Iran than
in the Congo or Saudi Arabia? Or that they were more fearful of WMD in
Iraq than in North Korea (which in 2003 posed a greater threat)? Perhaps
their interests in a country serve to condition and sensitize their reactions
to humanitarian causes there?

Still, if simplistic articulations of the war-for-oil argument were easy for
the U.S. government to dismiss, more complicated versions, with all their
abstractions and qualifications, could readily be portrayed as conspiracy
theory. A long-winded explanation can come apart at any weak link in the
chain of reasoning and risk sounding like it has been contrived to fit the political prejudices of the theorist. Our media culture craves the simple image
that reveals a greater truth. And perhaps it is enough to know that Iraq holds
around 10 percent of the world's oil, and that the Middle East as a whole
holds more than 60 percent. As Robert Ebel put it to me in 2009, "What did
Iraq have that we would like to have? It wasn't the sand."[72]

# 4

# Wiping the Slate

*The intent here is to impose a regime of Shock and Awe through delivery of instant, nearly incomprehensible levels of massive destruction directed at influencing society writ large, meaning its leadership and public, rather than targeting directly against military or strategic objectives.*

—Harlan Ullman and James Wade, *Shock and Awe*[1]

March 19, 2003. The streets of Baghdad were empty. Most of the shops were shut. Hospitals discharged all but the most urgent patients to make space in their wards. A heavy sandstorm blew in from the west, turning the city into a fog of orange. "I feel sorrow. It's like waiting for somebody to come and slaughter you. We have paid dearly for something we haven't done," Jihad Hashem, a fifty-year-old engineer, told Reuters. That night at 4:00 a.m. George W. Bush's deadline would expire, and after that the war would start. "Our fear of danger increases with every passing hour," said Nasman Bahjat, a shopkeeper. "All this powerful buildup of troops in such massive numbers on a country like ours is terrifying. They talk about new weapons, about a nine-ton bomb, about new missiles . . . All this news is frightening."[2]

It began at 5:30 a.m. on March 20. Forty Tomahawk cruise missiles, launched from surface ships and submarines in the Gulf and Red Sea, struck the city, along with four 2,000-pound bunker-buster bombs. It was over within a couple of hours—shorter than Baghdadis had feared. Some even began preparing to reopen their shops the next day. The following night saw a larger but still modest air attack. However, any relief was short-lived. At

8:00 on the third night the full force of U.S. airpower was unleashed in the shape of 504 cruise missiles and 1,700 air sorties.[3] This was nearly twice as many cruise missiles in a single night as the 282 that were fired in the entire forty days of the 1991 Gulf War. The ground shook with each explosion; shock waves pulsed through the city, forcing windows from their frames and showering people with glass in their homes. Bright orange fireballs lit up the sky, revealing thick smoke emanating from buildings across the capital. "There will not be a safe place in Baghdad," warned one Pentagon official.[4]

The attacks became relentless, no longer restricted to nighttime. Through-out the day the steady rumble of B-52s far overhead was punctuated with the shrill whiz of low-flying cruise missiles and the subsequent shuddering blasts. On March 26 the television station was bombed. On March 28 B-2 stealth bombers dropped two 4,600-pound bunker-busters on a communica-tions center in downtown Baghdad, destroying most of the telephone net-work. Now residents could no longer check on the safety of loved ones. Horrific rumors started circulating of the devastation of southern cities by the advancing armies. Iraq Body Count, scanning media and official reports of casualties, counted 6,616 civilian deaths caused by U.S.-led forces be-tween March 20 and April 9.[5] Spokesmen for the U.S. military insisted that strikes were carefully targeted to avoid what was still glibly referred to as "collateral damage."

## An Untidy Freedom

"In the second week and the third week of the war morale started to collapse with the news, of course," Khayat told me. "There was a general air of resig-nation that unless a miracle happens, Iraq is going to be occupied. But what will happen after the occupation? We were numb to think of it." With the war so long anticipated, Iraqis in the Ministry of Oil had spent months stock-piling supplies. The storage facilities of every organization—naturally the army, but also ministries, schools, hospitals—were filled with fuel. The Oil Ministry also kept its own stores, so as to be able to provide people with cooking gas and fuel for heating or transport if the refineries were knocked out during the war.[6] Once the war started, a central operations room was set up to oversee storage and distribution, and to shut down the refineries if necessary. It was led by Faleh al-Khayat, whose war-for-oil theory we saw in the previous chapter. The room was in an annex of the Oil Ministry, its doors protected by sandbags. Top officials remained there, sleeping in the cellar, as bombs fell on Baghdad.

The team stayed—hearing worsening news or often no news at all—until the morning of April 9, the day U.S. Marines pulled down the statue of Saddam Hussein in Firdos Square. Oil Minister Amr Rashid then said good-bye to his remaining staff and wished them luck. Although he was only an ordinary member of the Ba'ath Party, not part of its command structure, he was one of the last ministers to leave his post. In his final days he ordered that salaries be paid to all of the employees of the ministry two weeks ahead of schedule, as it might be some time until they were paid again. Leaving the ministry, Khayat moved his family to the outskirts of Baghdad, where there was less fighting. As he traveled across the city that afternoon the first looters were already busy—pickup trucks and handcarts loaded with furniture, young men carrying computers on their shoulders.

For more than a week the looters swarmed over the city. The most widely reported looting in the Western press was that of the National Museum. Here were housed priceless relics of the ancient civilizations of Mesopotamia. This land between the Tigris and Euphrates, commonly referred to as the cradle of civilization, was the home of the world's first cities. By around 3000 BCE inhabitants numbering in the tens of thousands thronged Eridu, Larsa, Uruk, and Kish in the kingdom of Sumer. The Sumerians were the first to practice year-round organized agriculture and the first to use writing, in the cuneiform script. According to some sources, 150,000 cuneiform tablets— some of the world's oldest writings—were smuggled out of Iraq per year from 2003 onward.[7]

At least as devastating to most Iraqis was the loss of records of the country's Islamic and modern history. A thousand years ago, while Europe was lost in the Dark Ages, newly founded Baghdad was not only the official capital of the Islamic Caliphate under the Abbasid Dynasty (750–1258 CE) but also the cultural and intellectual capital of the world. In Baghdad's Bayt al-Hikma (House of Wisdom), scholars translated the ancient scientific and philosophical works of the Greeks, Romans, Chinese, Indians, and Persians and created a great repository of knowledge. They made considerable advances in medicine, optics, astronomy, and literature. Algebra was discovered, the twin-cylinder water pump invented, the astrolabe perfected, and the foundations laid for modern chemistry.

Established in 1920, the Awqaf (religious endowments) Library held the

oldest public manuscript collection in Baghdad; it was looted and then completely destroyed by fires on April 13 or 14, 2003. Twenty-two trunks of
manuscripts were carted away, while ten trunks were burned, destroying
600 to 700 manuscripts. Some 5,000 of the collection's 7,000 manuscripts
had been removed by staff for safe storage, although their location is still
unknown and the library remains closed.[8] Around 45,000 rare books and
periodicals were destroyed in the fires, including 5,000 in the Ottoman
script, 5,000 medical books, and 5,300 books on Shi'a jurisprudence.[9]

The Iraq National Library and Archive (INLA) was one of the most
important repositories of documents. On April 10, U.S. tanks entered the
INLA complex to destroy a statue of Saddam in front of the building; they
then departed, leaving the complex unprotected. It was looted and burned
on April 10, 12, and 13. About 60 percent of the archive's state records and
documents were lost, dating from the nineteenth century under Ottoman
rule up to the Saddam regime. They included records of property ownership, political history, state administration, and relations with other states,
including treaties, border demarcations, and agreements over oil and water
resources. In short, the archive contained the documents that define the
Iraqi state.[10] As political scientist Charles Tripp put it, "This is really a terrible thing for Iraq. One of the problems has been establishing an identity, a
place in history and in the future. If you lose those documents you are subject to remolding of history which will be extremely dangerous."[11] For many
Iraqis, the "liberation" had parallels with the Mongol sacking of Baghdad in
1258, when the Tigris reportedly ran red and black with the blood of its
citizens and the ink of its destroyed books.

All public buildings—except one, the Ministry of Oil—suffered the same
fate. The Ministries of Agriculture, Irrigation, Education, Industry, Planning, and Trade were looted and burned.[12] Of the country's 4,422 secondary
schools, 1,683 were looted and a further 446 damaged by being either burned,
bombed, or used by the military.[13] And 84 percent of higher education institutions were burned, looted, or destroyed.[14] The vital al-Kindi Hospital in
northeast Baghdad was stripped of everything, including beds, electrical
fittings, and medical equipment, and was forced to turn most of its patients
away.[15] Corpses were piled in the entrance hall before being buried in the
hospital's own grounds.[16] Staff asked U.S. troops for help when two of its
ambulances and medicines were stolen but were told the forces had no orders to intervene.[17] Looters took everything from the 1,200-bed Yarmouk

Hospital, including fundamental equipment such as blood-pressure moni-tors, thermometers, and stethoscopes, and even tore air-conditioning units from the wall.[18] Many smaller hospitals closed down because they could not defend themselves against looting.[19] When hospitals were protected, it was by their own staff or by locals.[20]

At least five UN agencies (the Office of the Humanitarian Coordinator for Iraq, the High Commission for Refugees, the World Food Programme, the children's agency UNICEF, and the World Health Organization) called for urgent action to avert a humanitarian crisis.[21] Yet the following day Donald Rumsfeld was telling jokes: "The images you are seeing on television you are seeing over, and over, and over, and it's the same picture of some person walking out of some building with a vase, and you see it twenty times, and you think, 'My goodness, were there that many vases?'"[22]

Why did U.S. troops stand aside as Baghdad was looted? Why was no order issued to stop the looters? It was not that the military did not know looting would happen; they had been repeatedly warned.[23] "This is not something that surprised us. We knew there would be a period of chaos," Secretary of State Colin Powell said on April 11.[24] Yet it was another five days before the first order was given to ground commanders to stop some of the looters, even at the National Museum—after an intervention by a curator at the British Museum.[25] Before the war started, Pentagon officials had prepared such an order, yet it was never issued. In fact, Ambassador Barbara Bodine, the ini-tial U.S. civilian coordinator for Baghdad, told documentary filmmaker Charles Ferguson that there were instructions from Washington *not* to in-tervene to stop the looting.[26]

Did U.S. leaders actually *want* Iraq to be looted? Perhaps not, but they did not object when it was. In part, their complicity lay in a mythologized notion of small government: that through exertion of military power, "free-dom" could be created, that a society could function or even thrive when government was swept away and resources handed back to the (unorganized) people.[27] This approach would later be formalized under the Coalition Pro-visional Authority, whose director of economic policy, Peter McPherson, approved when Baghdad's bus drivers started driving their own routes and keeping the fares. He saw this not as theft but as "privatization that occurs sort of naturally."[28]

Many American and British officials seemed to assume there was nothing of value in the Iraqi society, culture, or state. John Agresto, appointed to run the higher education system, deliberately read nothing about Iraq before he arrived. "I wanted to come here with as open a mind as I could have," he told the *Washington Post's* Rajiv Chandrasekaran.[29] At best, Iraqi institutions were seen as contaminated by Saddam's dictatorship and would have to be disinfected, if not erased altogether. Some of the arriving Americans were obsessed with turning Iraq into a testing ground for an experiment in extreme neoliberal economics. Lee Schatz, a U.S. senior adviser on agriculture, commented that the destruction of the Ministry of Agriculture building would help in the process of modernization. "Had everything remained in place, there would have been a temptation to continue business as usual," he said.[30]

Intended or not, the destruction of Iraq's infrastructure and institutions would ensure that power remained with the occupiers, on whom the Iraqis would come utterly to depend.

## An Industry Stripped Bare

Only one public building was protected from looting: the Ministry of Oil. Fifty tanks surrounded the complex; razor wire was laid; snipers were stationed on its roof. U.S. Marines stood guard on the steps up to the central octagonal block. In fact, at first only the front door of the ministry was protected. The Future of Iraq Project member who asked me not to name him had watched the fall of Baghdad on satellite television; now he saw the city being torn apart by looting. He spotted looters walking in through the back entrance of the ministry. He also saw them looting the Rafidain Bank and the National Museum. He called the State Department, the people he had worked with on the Future of Iraq project, in a panic. "Please prevent it," he implored. "The museum is being vandalized, being attacked—and you are there. I can see your tanks are there." He sent an e-mail with a sketch of the Oil Ministry and its surrounding area, of where the bank was, and of the museum. An hour later his State Department contacts called back. The back entrance of the Oil Ministry was now secure. But they couldn't do anything about the other buildings.[31]

The rest of the Iraqi oil industry did not get the same privileged treatment. Dhia'a al-Bakkaa, a senior official at the State Oil Marketing Organization (SOMO), the body responsible for oil exports and sales, said SOMO staff saw masked men arrive in force on April 10. SOMO had little worth stealing: no expensive machines, not even many computers. "All we had was documents—we didn't expect it. No one took equipment. Instead they broke it and burned it." The attackers started fires in the shipping, finance, and administration departments. "The whole history of SOMO was burned." Staff rushed to two nearby U.S. tanks to ask the soldiers to protect the building. They replied that they had no orders to do so. The next day, the remaining staff including Bakkaa decided to protect SOMO themselves. Every night, they divided guard duty among themselves, taking two- or three-hour shifts at a time. Some raiders were deterred just by their presence; others were persuaded when the guards fired over their heads.

In the south of Iraq, too, oil facilities were hit by looting. At the time of the war the Iraq Drilling Company had about a dozen rigs, mostly dotted around the stony southern desert. These 150-foot structures penetrate two or three miles into the earth and are what keep the oil flowing. Nasir Mohsin Mohan, manager of a drilling site in the Rumaila field, told me that every meter, gauge, and control panel was taken from the rigs after the invasion. Copper wire was stripped off to be melted and sold. All that were left were steel skeletons, and no doubt the looters would have taken these too if they could. The looting of drill rigs went on for four whole months until July 2003, while a British unit was based nearby. "All the looting happened with Coalition forces present," Mohan explained to me. "They did nothing to prevent it."[32]

## Underground Treasure

The fate of the National Museum and archaeological sites prompted an international outcry, but not the destruction of Iraq's schools, universities, or government offices, nor even the loss of its manuscripts, archives, and public records. The fundamental difference was that the archaeological treasures from beneath Iraq's soil—a record of one of humanity's earliest civilizations—had value to foreigners, whereas the others were of immediate value only to Iraqis. National Museum director Donny George reports that before the war he heard from reliable sources that some British archaeologists and collectors were saying the Iraqis did not understand the value of their archaeological remains and so did not "deserve" them; the artifacts should instead be brought to Britain.[33] And in the United States William Pearlstein, treasurer of the art dealers' lobbying organization the American

Council for Cultural Policy, criticized Iraq's prewar policy on its cultural heritage as "retentionist" and envisioned a post-Saddam government that would liberalize the issuance of foreign-dig permits in Iraq and allow "some objects [to be] certified for export."[34]*

As it turned out, the U.S. military did not care much about culture or history, but it did care rather more about Iraq's other underground treasure. The First Marine Expeditionary Force seized the Rumaila field near Basra within twenty-four hours of its entry into Iraq. Despite claims that the oil was being safeguarded as the Iraqi people's nest egg, it was increasingly seen as belonging instead to the people of the world (or, more accurately, its major oil consumers) and Iraqis had no right to be all "retentionist" about it. As the International Energy Agency's deputy director put it, "The importance of the Middle East and North Africa (MENA) to global oil and gas markets cannot be underestimated. These countries have vast resources, but these resources must be further developed. Investment should not be delayed."[35]

Why, then, protect the Ministry of Oil but not SOMO? Why prioritize preventing Saddam Hussein from sabotaging oil wells while allowing drilling rigs, control rooms, and other infrastructure to be destroyed by looting? The difference is between oil and the infrastructure for extracting it. Had Saddam ignited the wells, he might have damaged the geological structure of the oil reservoirs beneath. And the ministry was the storehouse of all the data on what lay below ground, a treasure far more valuable in the eyes of the invaders than dusty ancient artifacts in museums. On the other hand, the trading records at SOMO, though vital to an independent Iraqi oil industry, were worth little to the United States. And drilling rigs and flow stations could be rebuilt by U.S. contractors—after all, the occupation bureaucrats thought they were doing the Iraqis a favor by replacing their decrepit equipment with state-of-the-art American products. The destruction of the aboveground elements of Iraqi state, society, and culture included the institutions and infrastructure of the country's oil industry. What was protected was the oil that lay beneath the ground.

---

* In making these comments, he was apparently not representing the association, whose president subsequently stated that its work on Iraq did not seek to change Iraq's antiquities laws. See Ashton Hawkins, "Protecting Iraqi Antiquities," letter to the editor, *Science*, May 2, 2003, 737.

# 5

# Emergent Iraq

*Iraq, we were told by our leaders in Washington and others, was trapped in a relationship of submission and victimization; its people were voiceless, deprived of the power to determine their own destiny. Once the dictator was removed, by force if need be, Iraq would be free, a tabula rasa on which to build a new and different state.*

—Anthony Shadid, *Night Draws Near*[1]

Abdullah Jabbar al-Maliki had not written about trade unions for more than sixteen years. Now, just a few days after the regime fell, he had to handwrite his poster because there was no equipment to print it. "Help me rebuild the unions!" he urged his fellow workers on the poster. He pinned it to the wall of South Oil Company's headquarters at Bab al-Zubair in southern Basra, where he worked.[2]

Abdullah, an electrician in the company, comes across as weathered but undeterred by his decades of activist experience—the thankless frustrations of grassroots organizing. But to him activism is as necessary as eating; he rolls up his sleeves and gets on with the job. He first became involved in trade unions in the 1970s, when he learned about the labor movement in the Workers Cultural Institute in Baghdad. In 1976 Abdullah was arrested and imprisoned for seven years, "for union activities and for my left-wing ideas." His son was taken as well, and to this day Abdullah does not know what happened to him.

After his release from jail in 1983, Abdullah was sent to work in Fao, fifty miles from his home in Basra. While there he began training trade unionists. But things had changed: the regime had its people everywhere, and some wrote reports on Abdullah's activities. So he was removed from his job and sent to the Iranian front. In 1987, the year before the war ended, Saddam passed Law No. 150, which redefined all public sector workers as government employees, who were prohibited from joining unions. Unions were now permitted only in the private sector (which did not include oil), and these were official bodies whose purpose was to monitor the workforce to report any dissenters.

Most unionists ceased their activities at that point for fear of being arrested or killed, but Abdullah and about ten others continued meeting in secret. They would talk to managers to help resolve workers' problems, "but in a friendly way, not as a union, because that was not allowed." Most of them joined the Ba'ath Party so that they would not be considered suspicious. In the meantime, they "waited for the regime to change so we could restart the unions." In April 2003 that moment came.

## Sponsoring Civil Society

"Democracies don't work unless the political structure rests on a solid civil society," Coalition Provisional Authority (CPA) administrator Paul Bremer said in his first meeting with CPA staff in May 2003. "They protect the individual from the state's raw power." In this he was right, but as he saw it, Iraqi society effectively no longer existed: the country was a cultural and civic terra nullius.[3] Therefore, civil society would have to be created from scratch by the occupying powers.

In 2003, setting up nongovernmental organizations (NGOs) became big business in Iraq. The U.S. Agency for International Development (USAID) distributed 5,200 grants totaling $337 million during the first three years of occupation, through its contractor Development Alternatives International.[4] Similar, smaller funding programs took place through other USAID programs and through the International Republican Institute and the National Democratic Institute, the international foundations historically tied to the two U.S. political parties.[5] Inevitably, these programs supported groups prepared not to raise concerns about the activities of the occupation forces or the new political structure, and many actually consisted of a single individual, often a businessman with an office who knew how to fill out forms. But with worsening security, it soon became unsafe for such organizations to recruit, build their constituencies, or even carry out projects. Some NGOs were actually manufactured in the United States to gain entry into Iraq. Women for a Free Iraq was established in Washington, D.C., in February 2003 by the Foundation for Defense of Democracies. The latter organization counts among its directors and advisers neoconservatives Jeane Kirkpatrick, William Kristol, and Richard Perle. It brought together fifty Iraqi women, mostly U.S. citizens. And its press launch was hosted by Undersecretary of State Paula Dobriansky.[6]

But in a nation with roots as deep as Iraq's, history and culture are not easily forgotten. So while Saddam Hussein had shattered the institutions of civil society, no amount of brutality could erase the ideas from the minds of the Iraqi population. Following the collapse of his regime, the sheet of Iraqi politics would be far from blank, whatever Paul Bremer thought.

Since the founding of modern Iraq in the 1920s, political thinking and organizing in the country have drawn from five main sets of principles: Iraqi nationalism, socialism, and Islam, together with (among their respective communities) Arab and Kurdish nationalism. The country has been shaped at different times by struggles within and between these ideas and movements, and of them all against foreign interference or internal repression. The nationalization of oil, for instance, was popular because of nationalist attitudes within the population, and successful in part because of an Islamic industrial culture.

In this political environment lay a set of threats for the post-Saddam occupation. First, each of the strands, in different ways, contains a strong emphasis on solidarity and the collective good, in contrast to U.S. ideas of individualistic "freedom." Second, with the possible exception of Kurdish nationalism, each points to an approach to economics, especially oil policy, fundamentally different from that favored by the West. And third, each strand has a deep history and culture of resistance against oppressors. It may be because of this last feature that we never hear about them, except occasionally as caricatures attached to the Ba'ath Party or al-Qaeda. Most of the Western media have shown little interest in reporting Iraqi views or the complex dynamics of its society. Instead the only Iraqis who appear in our newspapers and on our TV screens are politicians—no wonder, then, that many in the United States and Europe have such a dim view of Iraqis.

In the days immediately following Saddam's fall the first new organizations to emerge—long before the grant programs arrived—were in the two venues where Iraqis had continued to come together: the workplace and the mosque. Even Saddam could not destroy Iraq's religious institutions, nor could he abolish workplaces. With an immediate mass base, these new groups were able to continue to organize as security deteriorated over the coming months. And they had little need of sponsorship by the occupation authorities.

## Building a Union

When Abdullah pinned his handwritten poster to the wall of South Oil Company (SOC), he was one of the last two unionists who had met in secret through the 1990s. The second was named Faleh Chayyid. The others had retired or died. Even before the poster, Abdullah and Faleh's first move was to speak to a man who until that point had had no connection with unions, Hassan Juma'a Awad. Hassan had worked in the oil industry for thirty years and was now head of engineering workshops, a midranking position in SOC. His career had started in the IPC's Basra subsidiary the year before it was nationalized in 1975. He was well known in Basra as a leading activist against Saddam Hussein's regime. In 1991 he "took part"—that's all he would tell me—in the intifada, the Shi'a uprising against Saddam in the wake of the Gulf War.[7] He was charged with "opposition to the government" and imprisoned for three months in "very harsh circumstances. Ali Hasan Majid was there, so what do you expect?" Again, he declined to give any specifics. Chemical Ali, as he was better known internationally, had been put in charge of Basra security after the uprising. Hassan's colleagues told me he was jailed on at least two other occasions. Despite his years of struggle against the regime, Hassan did not see the 2003 war as in any way altruistic on the part of the United States and Britain. He later explained, "It would have been easier to topple Saddam Hussein in 1991 after the U.S.-led coalition had driven the Iraqi army out of Kuwait, [when] there was a popular uprising in fourteen cities across the country. It was U.S. policy during this time not to remove the regime, as it did not have an alternative to Saddam Hussein, so it abandoned the Iraqis and the uprising was crushed."[8]

Throughout the 1991 Gulf War, President George H.W. Bush and his officials had encouraged Iraqis to rise up. "The Iraqi military and the Iraqi people should take matters into their own hands to force Saddam Hussein the dictator to step aside," said Bush in a speech on February 15, 1991. The message was widely disseminated among Iraqis via leaflets and radio broadcasts.[9] But when the Iraqi military and people did rise up, U.S. forces stood by—often stationed just outside Iraqi towns—as Saddam's forces moved in and slaughtered the activists. Worse, the surrender agreement had permitted Iraq continued use of helicopters, which played a key role in the clampdown. The regime killed indiscriminately by firing artillery into residential buildings and mowing down anyone found in the streets. Tens of thousands were killed, many of their bodies discovered in mass graves in 2003. If the U.S. government hoped to be seen as a liberator in 2003, it surely hoped Iraqis had forgotten its previous betrayal.

Abdullah and Faleh found Hassan at work, although the invasion was still taking place. "It was easy to go to the company during the invasion," Hassan told me, "because the U.S. and British forces opened the doors to looters to let them do whatever they liked. So when I and my colleagues wanted to go to work, we did not find it difficult to do so, because the forces thought we were looters. . . . We continued to work not because we are more patriotic than others, but because it was easy."[10] Abdullah, Faleh, and Hassan recruited another well-known activist against the regime, Faleh Abood Umara, to form the core of a new union and waited for a response to Abdullah's poster. Some made contact but declined to join because they were afraid that unions would not be permitted. "There was no work; foreign troops were around the city," Abdullah explained. "The view ahead was not clear, so most people were scared."

Abdullah asked the acting director general of SOC, Jabbar al-Luaibi, for permission to reestablish the union. Luaibi refused. A few days later, as more workers agreed to get involved, Abdullah asked again, and was turned down a second time. "So we relied on ourselves to build the union." Within a few days they had an organizing committee of twenty and called a meeting. According to Hassan, two hundred workers attended the first meeting on April 20, just eleven days after the fall of Saddam. Their next move, Abdullah thought, should be to make a more public demonstration, to reach out further. He called for a demonstration on May 1, thinking the date would help emphasize that they saw themselves as part of a global labor movement rather than as a local political group. But with the atmosphere uncertain and foreign troops on the streets, only fifty people showed up.

Once again he would have to do it the hard way. Abdullah established a committee to organize elections for the union leadership. Neither he nor Faleh Chayyid wanted to lead the union; as experienced unionists, they wanted to work behind the scenes to build up the membership. Both were also associated with the Iraqi Communist Party, whereas Hassan and Faleh Abood had no party affiliation. The decision to avoid politicization was a smart one. All of the other unions in Iraq—mostly renascent or emergent rather than new—were aligned with one or more political parties; as a result, their fortunes would ebb and flow with those of their political patrons, and it was far easier to dismiss them when it suited the government or occupation authorities to do so. In contrast, the new union in South Oil Company attracted communists, democrats, Islamists, and others. The only political rule was that party and religious affiliations must be left at the door when doing union work.

Abdullah and Faleh spent May 2003 touring the dispersed SOC work sites across southern Iraq. None of the managers supported them, but they succeeded in establishing a foundation of union committees at each site. Hassan was elected head of the union committee for the Bab al-Zubair site. He quickly contacted the new committees on the other sites and encouraged them to hold elections too. Wisely, they ensured that the elections were witnessed by SOC lawyers and by officials of the Basra judiciary.

The new leaders of the oil union had three aims. First and most pressing was to get the workforce to restart production. This may sound odd from a Western perspective, where unions are understood primarily as organizing tools to pressure management. However, in Iraq's socialist and Islamic culture, workers see it as their duty to work for the benefit of their fellow Iraqis. As a result, a cooperative relationship developed with some managers, who recognized the union's role in helping get the job done. The unionists' second aim was to defend the rights of workers, especially as Iraq was now under foreign control. "The situation was very bad," Hassan told me. For example, "our wages were very low, insufficient to live on. The wages were being paid very late, and occupation forces weren't addressing this issue of the wages. They were not concerned with Iraqi people's problems. Workers in Iraq didn't know what the future held for them."[11]

Third was to protect the industry from foreign control. Hassan had noticed that U.S. and British forces had moved immediately to protect the oil fields. "We fear that the purpose of the occupation was to take control of the oil industry," he said in an interview. "Without organizing ourselves, we would be unable to protect our industry, which we have been looking after for generations. It was our duty as oil workers to protect the oil installations since they are the property of the Iraqi people."[12]

## Religion and Resistance

In contrast to Abdullah's poorly attended street demonstration on May 1, a week earlier the roads to Karbala had filled with up to a million Shi'a pilgrims. They were marking Arba'in, the end of forty days of mourning after the anniversary of the death of Imam Husayn.

Husayn was the son of Ali, a cousin and son-in-law of the Prophet Muhammad who had served as the fourth leader (caliph) of the new Muslim nation following Muhammad's death in 632 CE. Ali and his sons Hasan and Husayn were the first three of the twelve imams revered by the Shi'a. After Ali was murdered by a rival in the mosque at Kufa in the year 661, the caliphate passed—briefly via Hasan—to Mu'awiyah, the founder of the Umayyad Dynasty in Damascus, and then to his son Yazid, a brutal and irreligious tyrant. Hasan was poisoned by his wife, on Yazid's orders. Husayn led a small force from his base in Medina and tried unsuccessfully to foment an uprising against Yazid in the Euphrates valley. Vastly outnumbered by Yazid's army, Husayn and his followers fought valiantly but were cut down and their heads taken as trophies to Damascus. Their bodies were buried at the site of the battle, around which was built the city of Karbala.

For Shi'a the battle symbolized the struggle of the pious against the overwhelming military force of a wealthy but unjust empire, and U.S. troops sensibly stayed away from the 2003 Arba'in procession. Ahmad Chalabi was singled out for particular scorn, even though his U.S.-trained "Free Iraqi Forces" nominally provided security for the event. "Chalabi is a thief!" some shouted. "We want to be free, and we want to choose ourselves."[13] Chalabi epitomized the politicians who had lived abroad in luxury, courting the United States and the United Kingdom, while most Iraqis suffered through the darkest years of Saddam's rule.

Distaste for self-interested, out-of-touch exiles was also in play when an anti-U.S. demonstration called by the Supreme Council for the Islamic Revolution in Iraq (SCIRI) attracted only around three thousand pilgrims in Karbala despite the popularity of its message.[14] SCIRI was an Islamist political party, led by the Hakim family, that had been founded in Tehran in 1982 at a ceremony attended by Ayatollah Ali Khamenei. SCIRI's military wing, the Badr Corps, had fought against Iraq in the Iran-Iraq War under the command of Iran's Islamic Revolutionary Guard.

The elitist SCIRI contrasted in many Iraqis' minds with the movement established in the 1990s by Muhammad Muhammad Sadiq al-Sadr, a cousin and pupil of Muhammad Baqir al-Sadr, theorist of Islamic economics and founder of the Da'wa Party. Like his mentor, Sadiq al-Sadr saw the Shi'a religious establishment as too distant from ordinary people, and he established relief charities to help a population that was starving under sanctions. Whereas the Hakim family's constituency lay in the middle classes of merchants and intellectuals, Sadr reached out to both the urban poor and rural tribes and immersed himself in their concerns. An often-repeated story tells of a Shi'a who was deciding which of the Najaf ayatollahs to follow and asked them all the price of tomatoes. Only Sadr knew the answer.[15] His activist methods and engagement were combined with simple conservative rulings, which had wide popular appeal in a time of strife. His Friday sermons at Kufa attracted up to a quarter million attendees.[16]

Despite the persecution of Shi'a under Saddam, Sadr called for Islamic unity, using the language of Iraqi nationalism; on one occasion he led his followers to pray in Sunni mosques.[17] As his popular support grew, his criticism of the Ba'ath regime became more overt. From 1998 he preached in a white funeral shroud, an acknowledgment that he would not be allowed to live much longer. On February 19, 1999, Sadr and his two eldest sons were gunned down in their car as they returned home from prayers. One son survived, Muqtada.

Muqtada al-Sadr was young in 2003 and had had little religious training. Whereas his father Sadiq and cousin Baqir had established their legitimacy as learned clerics, Muqtada relied heavily on associating himself with their legacy. At Arba'in and other demonstrations and at Friday prayers, followers carried posters showing the three Sadrs, sometimes also with Grand Ayatollah Ali Sistani, the highest Shi'a religious authority in Iraq. On April 11, 2003, Muqtada gave his first sermon in the Kufa mosque, where his father had preached.

Muqtada moved quickly after the invasion to reestablish his father's movement, appointing clerics in mosques around the country, and gained wide popular support, unlike any other post-2003 Iraqi politician outside

Kurdistan. Soon after the invasion the Saddam City slum in east Baghdad was renamed Sadr City, after Muqtada's father, to commemorate his work for its poor residents. Over the following weeks it became Muqtada's principal power base too. Sadrist gunmen provided security; Sadrist clerics preached in Sadr City's mosques.[18] The movement set up its own courts, applying strict shari'a law, punishing those who bought or sold alcohol or listened to Western music, or women who went out with their heads uncovered. It took over the hospitals and furnished services that the collapsed state could not provide.[19]

It was not just Shi'a clerics who were beginning to organize. On April 14, 2003, twenty Sunni intellectuals gathered at a conference center in Adhamiya in north Baghdad, beginning what would become the Association of Muslim Scholars (AMS), which aimed to serve as a Sunni equivalent of the Shi'a establishment in Najaf. The AMS also organized charitable activities, providing aid for the poor and supporting the families of those killed. As it expanded, the AMS set three conditions for membership: applicants should be from the intelligentsia, they must not be committed to the former regime, and they must be prepared to take action.[20]

The AMS established its headquarters in Adhamiya, from which it gradually built a network of clerics and mosques. Later that year it moved into a more famous base, the Umm al-Qura mosque, of which one of its members was the imam. The mosque had been built by Saddam Hussein in a display of triumphalist vulgarity following the 1991 Gulf War and was originally named Umm al-Ma'arik (Mother of Battles); four of its minarets are shaped as Kalashnikov rifles and four as Scud missiles. After Saddam's fall, it was renamed Umm al-Qura (Mother of Cities), a reference to Mecca.

Muhammad Bashar al-Faydi, one of the co-founders of the AMS, told me that he and his colleagues suspected dark motives lay behind the occupation. "The Americans opened wide the army arsenals to everyone to collect weapons without restrictions. We know the Americans are not naive, and they know what this means. What is the consequence of civilians taking heavy and light weaponry?" The AMS was one of the first bodies to call for Islamic unity in Iraq. Its leaders visited Sistani, Sadr, and SCIRI leader Muhammad Baqir al-Hakim, as well as Christian priests. "We signed agreements for keeping [not spilling] Iraqi blood." At the same time, "we carried out education about the occupation," al-Faydi told me. "We noticed many people in our society thought the occupation came to make them happy and the country prosperous and stable. That's why we had to act, and demonstrate that the occupation came to demolish our country."

When U.S. forces arrived, they did not find the expected blank slate. New strands were emerging in the Iraqi social and political fabric, many of them echoes of earlier movements. The Pentagon's war planners, including Defense Secretary Rumsfeld and Undersecretary Feith, had envisaged a short occupation of at most a few months. After that, power would be handed to "Iraqis," by whom they meant their ally Ahmad Chalabi. These plans had been torn up by early May 2003, in favor of an approach the State Department had advocated in which the occupation would exert direct control on shaping the country's future.

# 6

# The Coalition Authority

*Is it not for the benefit of the people of that country that it should be governed so as to enable them to develop this land which has been withered and shrivelled up by oppression? What would happen if we withdrew?*
—David Lloyd George, British prime minister, on Iraq, 1920[1]

Which Iraqis would take over the Oil Ministry after the invasion? As we saw in chapter 3, this was the principal question asked by the prewar planning exercises. Would the ministry be run by those who had lived in the United States and Europe during the Saddam years or by those who had stayed in Iraq? Would it be those—in either group—who favored privatization of the oil industry or those who believed it was best kept in the public sector? Would they have genuine authority or be mere puppets of the Americans? In April 2003 four Iraqis were seen as possible leaders of the Oil Ministry: Faleh al-Khayat, Thamir al-Ghadhban, Muhammad-Ali Zainy, and Ibrahim Bahr al-Uloum.

From the existing establishment and supported by some of the key officials at the time, the obvious candidate was Faleh al-Khayat, the most senior of the twenty-two directors general (DGs) in the Oil Ministry at the time, who expounded his war-for-oil theory in chapter 3 and who ran the operations room during the invasion.[2] Among the four potential leaders, he was the most strongly opposed to privatizing the oil industry. "I am not anti-foreign, by the way," he told me when we met in 2009. After all, he had earned his degree in Britain and begun his career in the BP-operated Basra Petroleum

Company, an IPC subsidiary, in 1967.[3] "Actually I am too cosmopolitan in my ways, as you can see," he said, holding up his Cohiba cigar. "But state companies have characteristics that no foreign contractor can have." For instance, he explained, state enterprises never declare force majeure, invoking a contractual clause that releases a company from its obligations if subject to circumstances beyond its control such as war, terrorist attack, or "act of God." In a state-owned company, "whatever happens, you try to keep on producing. If the planes bomb you, you will hide, and when the planes go, you resume loading, resume production. If fifteen of your workers get kidnapped, you pray for their safety and continue production. Now, a foreign company does not do that. If an airplane hits it, it packs up. It needs guarantees; it will not go back immediately."

Khayat's example illustrated an attitude common among Iraqi oil technocrats. They were concerned with the technical question of how production can be optimized. For them, the argument for keeping oil in the public sector was that the industry would be more effective and efficient. In the Iraqi context you would privatize only for political motivations. Western commentators saw things the other way around.

The second candidate, Thamir al-Ghadhban, was favored by Michael Makovsky of the Pentagon's Energy Infrastructure Planning Group. A balding, jowly technocrat with sunken eyes, fifty-seven-year-old Ghadhban had served under Faleh al-Khayat in the ministry's planning department for seven years. When Khayat was moved to head the technical department in 2001, Ghadhban was promoted to acting DG of planning. In March 2003 he was Khayat's deputy in the operations room. "He is not an ordinary man; he is very talented," said one colleague who asked to be described as a former close friend.[4] "When he was young, he was seen as one of the stars." With a master's degree in petroleum engineering from Imperial College London, he began work at IPC's Basra subsidiary in 1973, two years before it was nationalized. By the late 1980s, he had risen to DG of planning in record time. No doubt his rapid rise was helped by his roots—he came from a well-known Ba'athist family in Karbala—and his own role as a local leader in the party during the 1970s. Conversely, it was falling out with the party that halted his ascent. In 1992 he spoke out against the building of expensive houses for party officials and was jailed for forty-eight days, then demoted. According to the former friend, his promotion to DG had been "too quick, and bypassed others more deserving. We thought that when he fell it was only a correction."

The other two candidates were exiles who arrived in Baghdad in April 2003 hoping to take senior roles in the Oil Ministry. Both had been members of the State Department's Future of Iraq Project, but were among 150 Iraqi professionals who came to Iraq as part of the Iraq Reconstruction and Development Council (IRDC), an initiative set up by deputy defense secretary Paul Wolfowitz in February 2003. The more senior of the two was Muhammad-Ali Zainy, an economist who was moderately skeptical of a foreign role in the Iraqi oil industry. With him came forty-nine-year-old Ibrahim Bahr al-Uloum, whom the Americans had especially liked in the Future of Iraq Project. He had worked in a few petroleum engineering firms but had little high-level experience in oil. One Iraqi official who worked with him said, "He didn't even speak oil language—it was as if he wasn't an oilman. He couldn't argue with any expert about any issue—even in his own specialism of reservoirs."[5]

## The Compromiser

Since leaving the operations room and taking his family to the relative safety of outer Baghdad, Faleh al-Khayat had stayed at home to see what would happen.[6] After a week, a fellow DG from the ministry visited him at home. "Where are you? Why don't you attend the ministry?" he asked.

"What ministry?" Khayat replied. "There isn't a ministry anymore."

But his colleague had talked to the Americans at the Meridien Hotel— which they were using as a contact center to meet Iraqis—and they had asked him to reassemble the Oil Ministry. "Military authorities in a hotel? What's that got to do with the Ministry of Oil?" Khayat asked. "If they want the ministries to function again, they should declare on the radio that all of the ministries' officials—except the minister and deputy ministers—should report for duty. . . . Why should we go individually and look like collaborators?"

In the end they agreed that a group of six or seven DGs would go in together. As they entered the hotel, Thamir al-Ghadhban appeared. He demanded, "What are you doing here? Why did you come to this hotel?" Ghadhban had been the most junior DG two weeks earlier; now he ordered the others to go to a building in Karrada, where the ministry was temporarily operating. When they got there, they found a group of second-rank officials treating Ghadhban as the boss.

Just three days after Baghdad fell, on April 12, Ghadhban had walked several miles to get to the Oil Ministry, where he introduced himself to the U.S. military. It is not clear whether Ghadhban had communicated with the Americans directly before they arrived in Baghdad; what is clear is that of all the DGs, he was the most willing to accept the new political reality of occupation. As he told a former colleague at the time who asked why he took the job when the Americans had all the power, "Well, being there is better than not being there." The friend explained: "He's a compromiser. Whenever there's a dispute between different factions, different parties, he plays a peaceful mediator position between the two parties."[7] Ghadhban opted to stay and do the best he could, rather than leaving it to others who were less capable.

But another friend said his compromising instinct went too far: "If there's a decision, he will make the weakest, that disturbs the least number of people." The reason, he said, was Ghadhban's ambition.[8] A third friend warned, "There's a thin line between ambition and opportunism."[9] Many of those I spoke to had mixed feelings about him. Even while criticizing his political instincts, all respected his technical abilities. In contrast to their comments on other oil ministers, none would put his name to a criticism of Ghadhban. However he got there, Ghadhban was now in charge. His position was confirmed by Coalition officials on May 3, 2003.

Ghadhban apparently found it difficult to accept that others were less willing to quickly adapt to the new reality. When OPEC did not invite any Iraqi representatives to its meeting in June, on the grounds that there was no internationally recognized Iraqi government, Ghadhban took it as a snub. "None of our dear Opec countries has contacted us, not even a telephone call," he complained. "Forget about the ministerial level, even the junior officials, none of them has extended any help—not even from the secretariat or from the friends we used to sit in conference with. . . . Surprisingly, they haven't contacted us, even as friends, to ask us how we are doing."[10]

The different attitudes of Faleh al-Khayat and Thamir al-Ghadhban illustrated the dilemma faced by many Iraqi oil professionals. Here was the industry to which they had devoted their lives and on which the country depended, but an occupying force would be in control. Should they keep working and do their best to protect the industry while making the necessary compromises to keep their positions? Or should they work to rule, or even refuse to work, and allow the occupation to make its own mistakes?

Khayat decided to work to rule, and even then only until he could get his pension. Ultimately, over the following months and years, those who refused on principle to work for the government would either remove themselves or be removed, creating space for others who were prepared to compromise. Almost without making a conscious decision, the United States would have a compliant ministry.

## The Viceroy

Just as in the Oil Ministry, the overall leadership of the country—both Iraqi and American—remained subject to debate during April 2003. The neoconservative Zalmay Khalilzad and Arabist Ryan Crocker (both of whom we met in chapter 3) were sent to Iraq to oversee the selection process through meetings in Nasiriyah and Baghdad, while retired general Jay Garner attempted to address humanitarian and administrative issues. Both Khalilzad and Crocker had worked with Kurdish and exiled opposition parties since early 2002, meeting with members in London and, in Crocker's case, in trips to Kurdistan. In that first month of occupation, however, it became clear that exiles such as Ahmad Chalabi were too unpopular to lead a government unless they were propped up by the U.S. military, while indigenous leaders who could wield authority were likely to do so on the basis of articulating popular opposition to the occupation and its political agenda.[11] U.S. strategy therefore changed in early May 2003, with the appointment of Paul Bremer as administrator of the Coalition Provisional Authority (CPA) and the new absolute ruler of Iraq, replacing Garner and beginning a long U.S. occupation. Before he arrived, Bremer demanded the removal of Khalilzad for fear that the latter would compete with his authority. But since he knew nothing about Iraq, Bremer kept Crocker as his political adviser.

Bremer had the superior air and false generosity of a Victorian colonialist, though perhaps less charm. Of the many books written about Iraq since 2003, Bremer's memoir, *My Year in Iraq*, gives the best insight (albeit unintentionally) into why the occupation failed so badly. It achieves the rare feat of casting the author himself as a character for whom the reader can feel no empathy. His insistence throughout the book on capitalizing the word "Liberation" gives an indication of his fervor. He makes much of the aphorism he displayed on his desk—"Success has a thousand fathers"—but shows no awareness in his book of the rest of the saying, "failure is an orphan," as he casts blame at officials in Washington, at the military, or most often at the Iraqis, who he says were too divided, incompetent, or self-interested to help their own country.[12] Only Bremer knew how to solve Iraq's problems.

As Bremer arrived in Baghdad, the principal security issue was looting—during June 2003 there were only six attacks per day on Coalition forces[13]—so he and the U.S. government were ambitious in their plans. He arrived with two documents in his briefcase intended to cleanse Iraq of Saddam's dictatorship: executive orders designed to dismantle both the Ba'ath Party and its security apparatus. The first, CPA Order No. 1, had been drafted in the Pentagon, but Bremer had asked to delay its publication until his arrival, to emphasize its importance. The order had two elements: first, it would remove all Ba'ath members (regardless of their degree of involvement in the party) from the top three tiers of management in all public institutions; second, it would remove all but rank-and-file party members from public sector jobs at any level. The decision not to target just Ba'athists who had been complicit in crimes and abuses or just the most senior party leaders, as was proposed in early Washington versions of the policy, crippled many ministries and public institutions by removing their leadership and large numbers of technical specialists.[14] The result would be Iraqi dependence on the United States and, as some planners had hoped, an opportunity to refashion the country from scratch, but it would leave Iraqis bereft of many services.

During the U.S. occupations of Japan and parts of Germany after World War II, which CPA officials often imagined as their model, the local civil services were left largely intact to run the countries under U.S. leadership, and purges of the old regimes were mostly restricted to the military and security services. De-Ba'athification in Iraq was much more far-reaching. Iraqis disagree as to how, and how broadly, de-Ba'athification should have been applied. Some believe that it should have focused only on the leaders of the party and reviewed members who were more junior through a calm and gradual process along the lines of South Africa's Truth and Reconciliation Commission. Others feared that unless the purge was wide ranging, there was a danger that the Ba'ath might return. After the decades of all-pervading tyranny—the paranoia, the informants, the violence—that view was understandable, but the undiscriminating approach taken could hardly be seen as just, nor would it help the country to rebuild.

CPA Order No. 2 dismantled all security forces, including the army. This decision has been widely criticized for angering 400,000 trained and armed soldiers, many of whom subsequently joined the resistance, and for depriving Iraq of security in the post-invasion chaos. At least as damaging, however, was the removal of an important symbol of national identity and sovereignty, which since its foundation in the 1920s had been seen as professional rather than political.[15] Again, the order did not differentiate between those involved in repression and abuses or those closest to the dictator, such as the Special Republican Guard, and the majority of soldiers and officers who had no loyalty to the Saddam regime. In fact, Saddam consistently mistrusted the army as the source of a possible coup, and for this reason established elite units led by family members and loyalists.

## The Political Officer

Three days after arriving in Baghdad, Bremer went over CPA Order No. 1 with his governance team, led by Crocker. Bremer noticed that one earnestly enthusiastic team member had marked her copy with different-colored markers and neatly printed margin notes.[16]

Then thirty-three years old, Meghan O'Sullivan, a redhead of Boston-Irish roots, almost hadn't made it to Iraq. On Columbus Day weekend in October 2002, she told her State Department boss Richard Haass during a walk, "You know, if this happens I really want to be a part of it." She had always been interested in the region—in second grade she wrote an essay about Palestine—and with the Gulf War occurring the year she graduated from college, she felt Iraq in 2003 was her generation's war. Eventually, when the CPA's precursor Office of Reconstruction and Humanitarian Affairs was set up in January 2003, Haass got her a place on it. But three weeks later Defense Secretary Rumsfeld ordered her off the team.[17]

O'Sullivan was a classic Washington dove, associated with the more progressive end of mainstream policy but careful never to question the morality of U.S. positions. In February 2001 she had advocated a slackening of the sanctions on Iraq—not because of the suffering of Iraqis but because "the widespread misperception of Western culpability for and indifference to" that suffering was losing the United States allies. Less than a month after Bush became president she wrote, "If a modified Iraqi sanctions regime can give the world another decade in which Saddam Hussein is restrained, if not totally tamed, then it is worth pursuing."[18] That proposal—although blaming Saddam for the problem—could hardly have been more at odds with the hawks in Bush's new government. Ten days after the attacks of September 11, 2001, she even implicitly criticized the Bush policy of targeting state sponsors of terrorism, arguing that the United States should pursue a differentiated and multifaceted approach, rather than lumping countries together—for example, in what would in January 2002 become the "axis of evil."[19] In short, she seemed to have the knack of publicly criticizing hawkish positions that would become official policy a few weeks later.

Those sent to Iraq were carefully vetted for their ideological purity, and O'Sullivan simply did not fit. "I just was angry because I really, really wanted to be a part of it," she told the CPA historian in December 2003. She felt she should have been ideologically acceptable. "Even if you look at my book [*Shrewd Sanctions: Statecraft and State Sponsors of Terrorism*] and my section on Iraq, which was written not long before the war, it's not against the war at all."[20] Eventually her State Department superiors managed to get her back on the team.

Now working closely under Bremer, O'Sullivan showed none of her earlier soft pragmatism. Bremer and Crocker made her the point person on de-Ba'athification: she worked through the details of what it meant and how it would be implemented. And she argued that it should be implemented "vigorously," while some colleagues would have preferred a more moderate approach. For example, whereas some wanted to interpret the top three levels of management as ministers, deputy ministers, and undersecretaries, she specified that it should also include directors general. She also decided that top-level position holders would be presumed to be Ba'athists until proven otherwise, and therefore all should be suspended from work pending investigations. This, she believed, "delivers the strongest message about our seriousness regarding de-Ba'athification."[21] She saw little room for flexibility.

> Somebody would come to me and say, you know, "Mr. Muhammad. He's a really good guy and he had to join the Ba'ath Party because he wanted his son to go to college; and, you know, he's a *firqa*-level person [the banned fourth tier of the party]; but, you know, he's a harmless guy. Do I really have to de-Ba'athify him?" And my answer was always, "Yes." You know, "Yes, you do. There is no scope for flexibility except if you want to apply for an exception, but the grounds on which you make the

exception case is not that he's a really good guy or that he didn't mean it or that he didn't like Saddam, it is that he is critical to carrying out Coalition objectives."[22]

## Protest in Basra

Two months into the occupation workers at Basra refinery had still not been paid their wages.[23] According to the CPA's deputy oil adviser Gary Vogler, the problem originated in Baghdad with Dave Oliver, the CPA official responsible for salaries. Vogler told an interviewer that Oliver was unwilling to recognize the Iraqi pay system, as it "violated" the superior system he was developing. As a result, no one was paid.[24] As CPA head of finance and budgets, Oliver presided over the disappearance of $8.8 billion. Asked in a later interview where that money went, he responded, "I have no idea. I can't tell you whether or not the money went to the right things or didn't. Nor do I actually think it is important." The BBC interviewer was clearly shocked, saying, "Yes, but the fact is billions of dollars have disappeared without trace—" Oliver interrupted him: "Of their money. Billions of dollars of their money disappeared. Yeah, I understand. I'm saying what difference does it make?"[25]

At 7:15 a.m. on June 20, 2003, around a hundred workers arrived at Basra refinery and, rather than going to work, placed a crane across the access road in protest, preventing vehicles from getting in or out. It did not take long for Coalition troops to arrive, and several armored vehicles accompanied the next convoy of tankers. The soldiers threatened to shoot. In response, some workers tore off their shirts. "Shoot!" they shouted, pointing at their chests. Others ducked under the tankers. At first their aim was simply to stop the trucks from driving off, but as the tension escalated, some of them took out their cigarette lighters and threatened to set fire to the tankers. The military offered to negotiate. Throughout his discussions with a British general, the refinery director kept in touch with union leaders by radio. By noon the problem was resolved: salaries would be paid within twenty-four hours. Ibrahim Radhi, the head of the refinery union, explained, "That they faced down the troops was the fundamental card the workers had in negotiations."

The showdown at the refinery demonstrated to previously doubtful workers what a union could achieve. According to Ibrahim, membership mushroomed from one hundred to three thousand that day. "Workers came to the union themselves to fill out forms; we didn't have to actively recruit."

Dave Oliver dismissed the protest. "In the one-product economy Saddam's disastrous economic policies had developed for Iraq, the oil workers were accustomed to being specially pampered, and not reluctant to express their displeasure."[26]

## The Horse's Legs

Two weeks after Thamir al-Ghadhban was confirmed in his position in the Oil Ministry, Bremer published CPA Order No. 1. "We had started to move the horse," said Dhia'a al-Bakkaa, who had fought off the looters at SOMO and was now Ghadhban's chief of staff, "and then somebody said we had to cut its legs off."[27]

Counseled by Ghadhban, the CPA senior oil adviser Phil Carroll applied to Bremer for sixty exemptions to the de-Ba'athification policy. "I have to have these people; otherwise I am wasting my time here," he told Bremer. Bremer granted all of them. According to O'Sullivan, Bremer granted fewer than ninety exemptions in total, so around two-thirds were in the oil sector, which was considered "critical to carrying out coalition objectives."[28] Carroll did not share O'Sullivan's uncompromising approach. "Two of the people I got exemptions for were men who were in Iranian prison camps from the Iran-Iraq War," he recalled. "One was there for sixteen and the other for eighteen years. When they came home, Saddam's present to them was a high rank in the Ba'ath Party. Which they of course accepted. They were not key people, but they both got exemptions, to keep their job. It would have been unjust to fire them."[29]

Compared to other ministries, I was surprised to learn, the Oil Ministry had relatively few party members. Engineer Falah Khawaja, who hated the Ba'ath Party, told me it was a "fallacy that former employees were Ba'athists. This was never the case. In the Ministry of Oil most of the hard workers were not Ba'athists. They were tolerated because they were good technocrats and because they were outside politics. And what more does Saddam or his party want?"[30] Faleh al-Khayat, on the other hand, had been a member— "not up, not down, just a member"—since February 1979. He was in a minority in the ministry, a point he illustrated to me with a story.[31] One evening in 2002 he was working late in the office when the phone rang. The minister of oil, Samir al-Najm, who was a member of the Ba'ath Party national command, asked Khayat to go up to his office.

"What is this? Where are we?" demanded the minister when Khayat arrived.

"What, sir?"

"Out of 154 heads of departments [the rank below director general] in the Ministry of Oil, I found out that only one of them is a member of the Ba'ath Party. Where are we living? In Kinshasa? Where are we? In Nigeria? In Russia? What's this? This is a country ruled by the Ba'ath Party."

"Sir, you should be proud of that," Khayat replied.

"How come?"

"It means the Ministry of Oil is a highly technical department which only takes technical ability into consideration. You should be proud that after all these years of Ba'ath Party rule only one out of 154 are members."

The minister stopped to think about what he had said. Khayat was taking a risk in speaking freely. "OK, you've convinced me," said the minister, and he gave Khayat a cigar—one of Saddam Hussein's cigars—as a present. Saddam used to hand out Cuban cigars in cabinet meetings. Many ministers didn't smoke, so they kept them for their friends. And Samir Najm gave Khayat one to reward him for explaining why the Oil Ministry was not full of Ba'athists.

## An Industry Crumbling

Even as Phil Carroll and Thamir al-Ghadhban sought to protect the Iraqi oil industry from excessive de-Ba'athification, it was being starved of resources and deprived of authority.

Falah Khawaja was part of the group working with Ghadhban to restart work at the Oil Ministry in April 2003.[32] Khawaja's spirits were lifted by finding people at the Daura refinery hard at work, after having fought off looters. His first job had been as a project engineer building the next-door power station. "So there was a new spirit of '89," he told me, recalling the optimism after the end of the war with Iran. "The war is over; the regime is over; let's develop our country."

He was soon disappointed. "Had they given the money to us, we would have developed Iraq. OK, we would not have returned it to perfection, but it wasn't perfect anyway. As we did in 1991, and as we did in 1988." But the Americans did not trust Iraqis to rebuild their own oil industry, preferring instead to rely on the U.S. Army Corps of Engineers and its contractor Kellogg, Brown & Root. For three months the Oil Ministry was not even given a budget: every expenditure, from salaries to equipment, had to be individually authorized by U.S. officials.

In the event, those Iraqis who worked under KBR were so disempowered and unmotivated that they simply did what they were told and nothing more. Much of the new equipment installed was inappropriate and unusable.[33] U.S. managers commissioned endless studies of specific problems and then got KBR to do the work without any overview of the industry or accountability for their results. For instance, at the Rumaila oilfield's Qarmat Ali water treatment plant, which cleans water to be injected into oil reservoirs to maintain pressure as oil is extracted, KBR replaced the pumps only to discover that the pipes that supplied them fractured under the higher pressure.[34]

The Pentagon's Energy Infrastructure Planning Group had set a target of achieving 3.1 million barrels a day of Iraqi oil production, within nine months in a best-case scenario or twenty-one months in the worst case.[35] In the event, that level has not been reached even at the time of this writing, in December 2011. And the damage done to the Oil Ministry's human and institutional capacity in 2003 played a central role in this failure.

Faleh al-Khayat told me he could see where things were heading in the meeting on May 3 at which Thamir al-Ghadhban's leadership and a new list of directors general were both announced. At the end of the presentation by Tim Cross, the British second-in-command at the temporary reconstruction authority, Khayat asked a question. "Sir, you appointed us DGs, but you did not tell us about our competencies and authority. Shouldn't you have added somewhere that our existing competencies continue, or that new competencies will appear in the future?" Khayat recalled Cross's reply: "As for your competencies, your competencies come through us."

Able and experienced Iraqis were reduced to advisers at best, even as KBR proved incapable of doing the job. As Khayat described it, "They made our people layabouts, the executives and the U.S. people around them going to meetings, putting in specifications and schedules on paper that were never executed. On the ground nothing happened. This is not the way to rehabilitate! Get the people to do it. . . . But they came with different ideas, like picking generators off the shelf. It was useless."

It would get worse. Later in 2003 Oil Ministry officials and their U.S. advisers identified $1.2 billion of urgent capital investments needed to keep the industry running. Dave Oliver cut the allocation to $800 million and then eliminated it altogether. Oil officials and advisers hoped the cash would be reallocated in the 2004 budget, but it was reduced to $200 million when Bremer met the oil minister in April of that year. The frustrated CPA senior oil adviser at the time, Mike Stinson, wrote in a memo, "If there is a fight I can enter with the hope of winning this funding, let me know where and when it is."[36]

## A Disappointment

By July 2003 Muhammad-Ali Zainy had sunk into a deep depression. As a member of Paul Wolfowitz's Iraq Reconstruction and Development Council (IRDC), he had come back to Iraq, he thought, to be lead adviser to the Oil Ministry, possibly even interim minister. But he found himself redundant when Phil Carroll filled that role at the CPA. "We arrived in Iraq on 28 April," he told me. "To my surprise, and to everyone's surprise, we found full American teams, and they were in charge of the ministries. Somehow that was very disappointing."

Zainy and other members of the IRDC found themselves not working in their area of expertise (in Zainy's case, oil and economics) but accompanying American officials to meetings to provide cultural advice or even translation. The Americans, he said, were polite and respectful, but there was no substantive role for the Iraqis. At the same time, Zainy was saddened and frustrated by the chaos, mismanagement, and corruption, and by disastrous decisions such as disbanding the army. In August, thoroughly disheartened, he resigned and returned to London. "I don't know why they misled us from the beginning," he said. "We were supposed to be the elites, the cream of society. And if we were treated that way, how are they going to treat people in the street?"[37]

# PART TWO

# Democracy and Violence
# 2003–2006

# 7

# Invasion of the Chalabis

*The people themselves are patently unqualified and are apparently being placed*
*in the Ministry for religious, political or personal reasons. . . . [On the other hand,*
*the] people who nursed the industry all through Saddam's years and who brought*
*it back to life after the liberation, as well as many trained professionals, are all*
*systematically being pushed to the sidelines.*

—Rob McKee, CPA senior oil adviser, 2004[1]

Many Iraqis were glad that the Americans and British had toppled Saddam.
When I first visited Basra in 2005, I was surprised to find far more people in
favor of the war than against. However, almost all were absolutely opposed to
the continued U.S./U.K. occupation once Saddam had been removed. "All
donne, go home," suggested some misspelled graffiti in Baghdad's Firdos
Square.[2] But going home was not on the agenda: Paul Bremer had been sent
to establish a long-term occupation, and the agenda now was to find a
means to govern the country.

The protest at Basra refinery was one of several manifestations of liberation that did not fit in with Bremer's plan. While increasing numbers of
Iraqis (and some U.S. officials) called for early elections, the CPA instead
appointed an advisory body of selected Iraqis.

On July 13, 2003, the Iraqi Governing Council was presented in a press
conference in the Green Zone conference center. "It will represent the diversity of Iraq: whether you are Shiite or Sunni, Arab or Kurd, Baghdadi or
Basrawi, man or woman, you will see yourself represented in this council,"

Bremer said on Iraqi television.[3] There were indeed all those categories among the council's members. To be precise, there were thirteen Shi'a Arabs, five Sunni Arabs, five Kurds, one Turkoman, and one Assyrian Christian. Three were also women, and one a tribal leader. But few of them other than the Kurds could be said to represent those communities, and most had neither a mandate nor significant support.

In fact, lack of representativeness was a positive advantage for the Americans who created the body. For instance, Sondul Chapuk, the Turkoman member, was barely known within her own community but was selected because the CPA "felt that it was time to break the back of" the Iraqi Turkoman Front (ITF), which had historically represented the community. Scott Carpenter of the CPA's governance team explained that ITF was considered too close to antiwar Turkey and not malleable enough for U.S. objectives. Chapuk was also a woman, and the CPA was feeling short on its female quota.[4]

Some secular members of the council were categorized simply on the basis of their personal religious identity. Hamid Moussa of the Iraq Communist Party and Ayad Allawi (much of whose constituency was in fact Sunni) were both chosen as Shi'a representatives, although neither would have identified as such. Meanwhile, it was a strange notion that there could be a single representative of "the tribes" (unselected by them), given their complex alliances and enmities.

Bremer referred to the six-week selection process as "Iraqi math."[5] A more accurate label would be "Bremer math," as most Iraqis simply did not think of themselves in such categorical terms and did not want politics to be run on the basis of communal identity. In September 2003 polls showed that only 29 percent of Iraqis believed it important that a leader should represent "my sect."[6] The process of selection was led by CPA head of governance Ryan Crocker, who, having worked in Lebanon in the 1980s, should have known the consequences of allocating political positions according to sectarian quotas. Instead the formation of the Governing Council allowed Crocker to feel his job was done; after that he returned home.[7] Iraqi politics would now not be about ideas or policies; representing (or claiming to represent) a sect or ethnicity was the only ticket to political participation.

Was the sectarian selection the product of a divide-and-rule strategy? Or some racist notion of Iraqis as consisting of no more than their primordial identities? Or a desperate attempt to impose categories on a country its new rulers did not understand? Probably it was all three. Whether through ignorance or by design, the effect was to build structural weakness into the future government, as politics would be fundamentally based on communal differences. Even if this could be overcome, the removal of policy from politics helped ensure that politicians would not represent Iraqi points of view that might be at odds with those of the United States. In fact, unwanted ideas were deliberately purged. For example, Bremer's condition for accepting an Iraqi Communist Party member on the Governing Council was that "we could find someone who had cast off communism's misbegotten ideas about how to run an economy."[8]

That weakness was exacerbated by the fact that of the nine rotating presidents of the council, six had been in exile and two based in autonomous Kurdistan; only one had lived under Saddam during the 1990s. The exiles thus would have little political strength independent of the United States. Undersecretary of Defense Doug Feith saw the fact of their exile as making them more ideologically suitable: they were "better positioned to understand concepts of democracy than are those who do not have exposure outside Iraq."[9] Bremer echoed the point: "Anybody who'd been in Iraq for the last 30 years had seen a totally socialist government-dominated [economy]."[10]

## Sects and Sectarianism

While criticism of the occupation had largely been in generic terms up to that point, the formation of the Governing Council prompted more explicit Iraqi rejection of the Americans' approach. The following Friday Harith al-Dhari, who would become leader of the Association of Muslim Scholars in late 2003, gave his sermon at the Umm al-Qura mosque in Baghdad. "This council has divided Iraq along communal and ethnic lines for the first time in its history. It is the creation of the occupation forces," preached al-Dhari. "It is formed of parties that . . . do not express the will of all the Iraqis, whether Sunni or Shi'a. . . . The divisions on which this council is based are unacceptable, as they divide Iraq into communal and ethnic groups. It sows the seeds of hostility among the people of this society."[11]

In a sermon at his father's mosque at Kufa the same Friday, Muqtada al-Sadr denounced "the illegitimate council created by the United States and their servants." He called for the establishment of a Jaysh al-Mahdi, an army of the "hidden imam." The Mahdi was the last of the twelve imams of the Shi'a faith who disappeared at Samarra in 878 CE. Shi'a believe that he did not die but was hidden by God and will return to rescue them from oppression. "No, no to the United States. No, no to Israel. No, no to the Governing Council," chanted the worshippers at Kufa.[12]

So was this really the first time Iraq had been divided along communal lines, as its critics claimed? Over the years that I worked on Iraq, this was a subject Iraqis would raise with me more than any other. Iraqis do not think of themselves as Shi'a and Sunnis, I was told time and again; they think of themselves as Iraqis. A typical conversation took place when my fixer Ahmed and I met secular politician Saleh Mutlaq in the Rasheed Hotel on the edge of the Green Zone. Mutlaq spoke in Arabic but always corrected Ahmed when his English interpretation didn't quite capture what he was trying to say. He spoke with a weariness brought by Iraq's recent burdens, but much in his manner harked back to a time when Iraq was happier: his bushy mustache, his shiny tweed sports jacket, his black slip-on shoes, even *Tom and Jerry* on the TV in his hotel room.

Mutlaq: "We didn't practice sectarianism in this way. People didn't even know who were Shiites and who were Sunnis. We didn't ask—it's not good to ask if you are Shiite or Sunni. But after the occupation it became so obvious."

Ahmed: "My sister is a Sunni; she's married to a Shiite guy. When the violence started, and people started to ask, I'd say, 'Let's talk about their kids. Which one are they gonna kill, their mother or their father?'"

Mutlaq: "I am married to a Shiite also. And my wife used to cook on religious occasions, during Saddam's time. But after the occupation happened, sectarianism started, and I told her please stop it now."

Ahmed: "We used to ask people from which tribe they are, and we used to know from their accent from which province they are, but the sect didn't interest us at all—we are all Muslims."[13]

As for the sectarianized politics, Mutlaq wrote an impassioned condemnation titled "Our Problem with America" in the newspaper *Asharq al-Awsat*.

> We, the people of Iraq, never understood the homeland to be merely a farm that can be divided when rivals differ or when they want to differ. For us, Iraq is a sacred historical and religious concept, which

represents our existence, which is a genuine symbol of the existence of our ancestors, and which is dedicated to our coming generations. . . . We did not and will not reduce the concept of the great Iraqi people in a naive manner by dividing them into Shiites, Sunnis, Kurds, Christians, Turkmen, Sabians, and Yazidis. This is because the Iraqi people, as God created them on this land, are a combination of all these components.

I would learn over these years that while Islam is an important part of most Iraqis' identity, religiosity and sectarianism are not the same thing.* A January 2004 survey by the Iraq Centre for Research and Strategic Studies, for instance, asked people which description suited them best: Sunni Muslim, Shi'a Muslim, or "just Muslim." The largest group, 40 percent, chose the last option.[14] Some Iraqis say that until they were adults they were not even aware that there was a difference.

That is not to say that no prejudices exist. Some Sunni Iraqis grumble at the uneducated Shi'a masses with their "crazy rituals." Conversely, some Shi'a readily accuse the Sunnis of having collaborated with the Saddam regime. But the differences are small compared to the perception of them in the United States and Europe. Take this early 2003 comment by Doug Feith: "Democracy . . . would mean Shiite predominance in a country that was 60 percent Shiite Arab. That alone ensured that the region's [Sunni] Arab leaders would be hostile."[15] He was assuming that since the Shi'a were the majority in Iraq, the government would necessarily have a Shi'a character. In contrast, no one supposed that democracy in Russia in the early 1990s would mean a women-led government since Russia's population was 53 percent female. It's not that womanhood was irrelevant to Russian identity or society, but rather that there were simply other, more important factors in shaping its politics. The same could be said about religious sects in Iraq.

Yet occupation planners and administrators seemed to see Iraqis as divided into three quite distinct and largely homogeneous groups: Sunni Arabs, Shi'a Arabs, and Kurds. The Sunnis, according to this picture, had ruled

---

* Sectarianism is the pursuit of the interests of one sect over and above or to the exclusion of those of others. This is contrasted with (Iraqi) nationalism, which puts the interests of the whole nation above those of any of its component communities, and also generally rejects interference by foreigners. Finally, that too is different from ethnic nationalism, such as Kurdish nationalism or Arab nationalism, which prioritizes the interests and identity of that ethnic group.

Iraq for decades and repressed the other two groups. In our information-rich age, such shorthand constructs become the meat and drink of newspapers and websites, and so the notion spread to foreign observers at large. Unfortunately, it obscured more about Iraq than it revealed. While it is true that under Saddam Hussein Sunni Arabs were disproportionately represented in the Iraqi middle classes and in the most senior positions in government, that too was routinely overstated. Reports of Iraq referred to its Sunni government, implying incorrectly that most government officials were Sunnis or that most Sunnis supported the regime. In fact, of the deck of fifty-five playing cards issued in April 2003 with pictures of the United States' most wanted members of the regime, thirty-five were Shi'a.[16] The majority of the early leaders of the Ba'ath Party were Shi'a, including the man who introduced the party to Iraq, Fu'ad al-Rikabi, and the leader of the 1963 coup, Ali Salih al-Sa'di. And outside the places that benefited from Saddam's patronage, notably his hometown of Tikrit and some tribal areas, many Sunnis hated his regime as much as Shi'a did.

The development we saw in chapter 5, where two of the most significant post-2003 social movements in Iraq were religious in nature, one Shi'a and one Sunni, is a reflection less of Iraqi culture or society than of the previous totalitarian system and the resistance to it. Saddam Hussein was always driven far more by securing his own power than by any ideological goal. To that end he would execute or persecute anyone who challenged him, Shi'a or Sunni, Arab or Kurdish. He marginalized and then crushed civil society, with the result that religion became—for Shi'a opponents of the regime—the only space for organizing. This led, for instance, to the Da'wa Party's central role in focusing discontent against the Ba'ath regime during the 1970s. As the regime saw the potential for opposition organizing through Shi'a religious networks, it focused its repression on religious institutions and individuals, essentially forcing them into the role of an underground resistance. When those same networks organized the 1991 intifada, the regime again counterattacked a religiously defined enemy. Shi'ism was the vehicle rather than the reason for the resistance. Shi'a institutions thus became a natural space for organizing once the regime fell.

Mutlaq told me a story. "Once I was asked by both Condoleezza Rice and the foreign minister of Britain, Jack Straw; they asked me in the presence of the other politicians—Jalal Talabani, Tareq al-Hashemi, Adil Abdul-

Mahdi—they said, 'Do you think sectarianism has gone deep into people in the street?' I told them sectarianism is only among us who are sitting in the room—it does not extend to the ordinary people. And Condoleezza Rice was shocked. 'Is that so?' she said. I said, 'Yes, it was only brought to us when you came to Iraq. Before you were here, we never knew sectarianism, only when you came.'"[17] In his article in *Asharq al-Awsat*, he was more scathing: "The U.S. Administration found itself drowning in the Iraq problem because it entered Iraq based on tourist information about the country, with which it was supplied by some Iraqi opposition figures close to it." But it wasn't only ignorance. Why, I asked him, did the sectarian parties become the U.S. allies? "Because they are weak," he replied, "so they will obey what the Americans tell them to do."

Mutlaq's own position—while representing the secularism popular among a significant strand of Iraqi society—was complicated by his association with the Ba'ath Party, which led some of the new crop of politicians to dismiss him. Under Saddam he had been responsible for chicken factories in Tikrit. More significant, during the years of occupation he would speak positively of the Ba'ath, at least in comparison to what had replaced it. I challenged him on this. "Well, this is not a shameful accusation anymore," he replied. "Let them [politicians] say that I'm a Ba'athist, because the performance of the Ba'athists was much better than their performance. But I assure you that I'm not a Ba'athist. I was expelled from the Ba'ath Party in 1977." I asked why. "You will be surprised. I was expelled in that time because I stood against the leadership when they wanted to execute five people in Karbala who were demonstrating against the regime. . . . Then I came to know that they belonged to al-Da'wa Party, the [Shi'a] party of al-Maliki. I defended them and they were Da'wa Party!"

Not only did the West's view of Iraq overstate the role of communal identity, it tended to assume that the social dynamics of sect and ethnicity were the same: that the Shi'a Arabs' position was equivalent to that of the Kurds. In fact, the identity issues, politics, and intercommunal relations are quite different. Most Arab Iraqis consider themselves to be Iraqi first, Muslim or Arab second, and Shi'a or Sunni only a distant third or fourth. For most Kurds, however, their ethnicity is the primary element of their identity. They have their own language and a distinctive culture and mostly live in quite a different environment from their Arab compatriots—mountains rather than desert and river plain. The struggle for Kurdish rights since the formation of the modern Iraqi state, including for autonomy and potential future independence, is correspondingly the driving force of Kurdish political culture. An individual's status is still strongly determined by his previous role in the Peshmerga militias. The brutal repression that met this struggle has strengthened Kurdish identity over the decades. But the Western assumption that Shi'a Arabs in Iraq were as culturally distinct as Kurds and as desirous of dedicated political representation and autonomy led to the dominance of politics by sectarian politicians, and consequently to many of Iraq's greatest problems.

Identity politics can take a range of forms. Some politicians simply use identity as a means to organize—using the social infrastructure of the mosque, for example—but advocate a political agenda that is not focused on the exclusive interests of their sect or ethnicity. Others, more objectionably, practice a kind of zero-sum politics, claiming to represent their sect in competition with other communities, and even attacking members of the others. As Gary Younge put it in his recent book *Who Are We?*, "While identity is a crucial place to start, it is a terrible place to finish."[18]

## Even Worse Than the Looters

Armed attacks on Coalition forces increased from an average of six per day in June 2003 to fifteen per day in August and fifty in September.[19] August saw the first mass-casualty truck bombs—targeting the Jordanian embassy and the UN headquarters in Baghdad—which were apparently carried out by foreign Islamist fighters in the al-Qaeda mold. The first killed at least ten and the second twenty-two, including UN special envoy Sérgio Vieira de Mello. Later that month an even more deadly car bomb in Najaf killed Muhammad Baqir al-Hakim, the head of the Supreme Council for the Islamic Revolution in Iraq (SCIRI), and one hundred others. Suicide attacks and vehicle bombs would punctuate the coming months with increasing frequency. Politicians now represented their sects—or themselves—and violence was set only to worsen.

Following the establishment of the Iraqi Governing Council, the new politics began to grip the Oil Ministry. While Muhammad-Ali Zainy left Iraq in disgust, his IRDC colleague Ibrahim Bahr al-Uloum proved better suited to the direction politics was taking. Not only was Bahr al-Uloum the State Department's favorite from the Future of Iraq Project and a supporter of Ahmad Chalabi, his cleric father, Muhammad, was a leading member of the Governing Council. In September 2003 Bahr al-Uloum was appointed oil minister, replacing Thamir al-Ghadhban. One of the Governing Council's early tasks had been to nominate ministers to run the bureaucracies under the CPA. Unable to agree on the twenty-one appointments, the council increased the number of ministries to twenty-five, so that each member could choose one. Most were family, allies, or members of the same party as their appointers; few were qualified or competent. Faleh al-Khayat called it "the invasion of the Chalabis."

None of the Iraqi technocrats I spoke to was impressed with Bahr al-Uloum's leadership; neither were the American advisers. One Iraqi member of the Future of Iraq Project oil group told me on condition of anonymity, "Every time I talked about the ministry and the national oil company, you would find Bahr al-Uloum saying, 'No, there is nobody who knows anything in Iraq . . . the people in Iraq, they cannot do it, so we have to find a replacement for them.'" The replacements Bahr al-Uloum proposed were the multinational oil companies. But now, with this appointment, my source asked, "How can you be a minister of a ministry you don't believe in?"[20]

One of the early victims of the new order was Mohammed al-Jibouri, the head of the State Oil Marketing Organization (SOMO). A pious and well-liked man from Mosul, he had been appointed to the position in May after he overwhelmingly won in a vote by SOMO's senior staff.* His immediate job had been to rebuild the organization after the almost complete destruction of its offices, records, and equipment by looting in April 2003. By June, he had succeeded in organizing the first export tender of Iraqi crude.

In order to stamp out the corruption and patronage that had grown during the sanctions era—in which certain traders were favored and benefited from price differentials and commissions—Jibouri adopted a policy of selling Iraqi oil only to its end users (refineries) rather than to traders. From that first

---

* The following month, Bremer would outlaw the practice of managers being elected by their staff, despite the obvious advantages of avoiding Ba'athists and ensuring that competent people were appointed.

tender, however, one trader tried to persuade Jibouri to award his company a tender. Jibouri refused, both because the trader's company was not an end user and because it had been involved in questionable dealings during the sanctions/Oil-for-Food period. Over the following weeks, the trader tried repeatedly to change Jibouri's mind "with a carrot and a stick." But Jibouri would not bend. "I am not accustomed to their way of business," he explained. "It is shameful to take bribes."[21]

After several refusals, the trader came to Jibouri's office in late September and said, "I am going to show you what I can do—within a week or two." The next day, articles began appearing in newspapers—primarily those associated with Ahmad Chalabi—accusing Jibouri of corruption. The new oil minister, Bahr al-Uloum, offered Jibouri a transfer from SOMO to the ministry headquarters. He refused. Then one week after the meeting with the trader, Jibouri was called into Bahr al-Uloum's office again. This time he was removed from his post. It is not clear by what means the trader's threat was carried out, but Jibouri has no doubt that that was the reason for his removal.[22] It was an early sign that honesty and competence were not the way to get ahead in the new Iraq.

Meanwhile, over the summer Meghan O'Sullivan had started to feel that the de-Ba'athification policy of CPA Order No. 1 was too blunt an instrument; it needed to be more discriminating, and she proposed transferring the process to Iraqi control. She was right that Iraqis would be better able to judge than Americans which Ba'athists were criminals and which had joined the party because they had to; however, rather than handing de-Ba'athification to a judicial body, the Governing Council proposed a commission led by Ahmad Chalabi. Bremer agreed. Chalabi had left Iraq in 1958 at the age of fourteen and was known for his blanket hatred of the Ba'ath and his ambition for personal political advancement. His deputy in the De-Ba'athification Commission was Nouri al-Maliki, the future prime minister, who had been out of Iraq for twenty-four years since fleeing in 1979, when Saddam became president.* The new commission's first two decisions were to cancel all exceptions to the policy and to expand the ban on Ba'athists in public employment to public activities in civil society and the media. As a body of politicians, its fervor was far greater even than the CPA's, and vast numbers of government officials were removed from their

---

* At the time he went by the name Jawad al-Maliki.

posts, making way for the friends and allies of the newly arrived leaders. O'Sullivan later admitted that handing over de-Ba'athification to the Governing Council had been a mistake.[23]

While many senior Oil Ministry personnel had been protected under Thamir al-Ghadhban, Bahr al-Uloum launched a massive purge. By the end of the year seventeen of the twenty-four prewar directors general had either been removed from or left their jobs, along with hundreds of midranking technicians.[24] In November 2003 Faleh al-Khayat was called in to meet Bahr al-Uloum.[25] "You come highly recommended," said the minister, "but I have to remove Ba'ath Party members from their posts as DGs." He offered to demote Khayat rather than fire him, but Khayat refused. "If I accept demotion, it means I accept I have done something bad," he told the minister. "I don't accept that." So he was given retirement.

In any case, Khayat had had enough. The CPA's insistence on keeping control of the ministry had thoroughly demoralized its staff. "I cannot live in a society where people come at their own time and leave at their own time, obey what they want and neglect what they want," he said to me. "The structure lost its respect and lost its hierarchy. I used to walk in my office and my people used to love me and I loved them. After the occupation, I walked in and I saw nobody there. They all did their own business and meetings. People were working for personal benefit . . . the only cohesive was self-interest."

Another senior oil official, who asked me not to name him, said of Bahr al-Uloum, "His only concern was to remove people from their posts. He never listened." And the impact on the Iraqi oil industry was "even worse than the looters. This was an historical loss that cannot be replaced."[26]

Under "the Chalabis" the purge went far wider than actual members of the Ba'ath Party. Anyone with a grievance would accuse a rival of being a Ba'ath sympathizer. Conversely, the best proof of anti-Ba'ath purity was membership in a former opposition party, preferably one aligned to the minister. Ironically, occupation policies created the very problems they were supposed to solve. Following de-Ba'athification, staff were employed on the basis of party membership to a greater extent than ever under the Ba'ath, and now without even having the relevant technical qualifications.

At the same time, the Oil Ministry was increasingly staffed by friends and loyalists of the minister and directors. Recruitment also took on a sectarian tone. "If you are a Sunni you are left alone, but don't think of your future—no prospects," said Faleh al-Khayat (who is Shi'a). The minister "began to bring in people from Denmark, Norway, and England. I remember one of them was a pizza cook or something like that . . . the ministry went down and down."

# 8

# The Advisers

*The idea that Iraq's energy development needs are best served through FDI [foreign direct investment] will be politically sensitive, both in Iraq—touching on issues of sovereignty—and internationally. We will wish to push the message on FDI to the Iraqis in private, but it will require careful handling to avoid the impression that we are trying to push the Iraqis down one particular path.*
—U.K. Energy Strategy for Iraq, September 2004[1]

On May 19, 2003, two and a half weeks after President Bush declared "mission accomplished" on the deck of the USS *Abraham Lincoln*, Australian foreign minister Alexander Downer attended a secret meeting at the London residence of his country's high commissioner. Across the table sat three executives from BHP, the company that had prepared the press release about exporting eggs from Austria to Italy in 1996, along with Malcolm Rifkind, a former British foreign secretary who was now a consultant to the company.[2]

David Regan, leading the BHP team, explained to the diplomats the value of Halfaya, one of five undeveloped "strategic fields" in the south of Iraq. BHP and Saddam's Ministry of Oil had "substantially agreed" upon the commercial documentation but had never executed the contract because of sanctions. BHP had recently signed a three-month contract with Shell for a feasibility study of the field, a partnership that the company believed would bring political as well as technical and financial advantages because Shell was based in another Coalition country. With the commercial terms already negotiated and a development plan drawn up, the field could be developed quite quickly—a significant advantage to the Iraqis, Regan explained.

Rifkind said it was "critical" that BHP's interest be registered early with the United States. The Americans had warned their Coalition partners "not to behave like the English," said Rifkind—in other words, to let their oil interests be known to U.S. officials rather than trying to make their own arrangements with the Iraqis. While contracts could not be signed until there was an Iraqi government, he said that the United States would ensure that commercial interests were protected, though it might ask that U.S. companies participate in any consortia. Rifkind said he planned to seek a meeting with Vice President Cheney to raise BHP's claim.[3] Downer warned that oil was a sensitive issue but agreed to raise the point both on his next visit to Washington and with Paul Bremer in Baghdad.

Three weeks later, on behalf of unnamed oil company clients, Rifkind wrote to Patricia Hewitt, U.K. secretary of state for trade and industry, to urge that contracts be signed as soon as possible by the Iraqis appointed by the occupation forces. He noted that many were saying that no decisions would be made on awarding oil contracts until there was a sovereign Iraqi government. That, he wrote, "would be a significant recipe for delay, as I understand an Iraqi Provisional Government is unlikely to come into office for at least six months. It would be a pity if all decisions were deferred for that reason."[4]

At the end of May, British civil servants met at the Department for Trade and Industry to discuss the future of Iraq's oil industry.[5] An unreleased policy paper presented at that meeting outlined a set of objectives quite at odds with ministers' public shows of indifference as to what the Iraqis chose to do. The paper called for "an oil sector open and attractive to foreign investment" via long-term contracts known as production sharing agreements, and which thereby "acts as a role model for how other Middle East countries might open their oil sectors to foreign and private participation"—recalling the idea of Iraq as the keystone in the Persian Gulf's arch. Iraq should be "a reliable world oil supplier where production is robust to potential disruptions" and "a member of OPEC but on the dovish side—favouring greater output at more sustainable prices."

The officials were under no illusions as to the Iraqis' views. "It is inevitable," they acknowledged, "that there will be a temptation . . . to use regional role models as opposed to international (Western) ones." This should, they suggested, be avoided as "it is unlikely that such a comparison would lead

INOC [Iraq National Oil Company] down a road of management professionalism and transparency." But, while noting the scale of the Coalition's task in changing the Iraqi oil industry to what it would like to see, the paper noted awkwardly, "almost anything the Coalition does to move the industry towards a Western management model may well give rise to accusations of interventionism."

Still, some civil servants suggested that the Coalition had a moral duty to intervene. Department of Energy officials noted that UN Security Council Resolution 1483, which had endorsed the occupation of Iraq, held the United States and the United Kingdom jointly accountable for any actions they took as occupying powers. "Given this accountability of the U.K. towards the UN and the international community," they wrote in a briefing, "it is most important that we are closely involved in the policy making and decision taking processes affecting Iraq's major revenue source."[6] A more natural interpretation might have been that they would be held accountable for abusing their role as occupiers to pursue their own energy interests.

## The Elder Statesman of Oil

Paul Bremer saw Iraq's nationalized oil industry as a product of "Saddam's vicious brand of socialism."[7] Yet while he set about remaking the Iraqi economy from its foundations—in what the *Economist* called a "capitalist's dream"—he left the oil sector untouched.[8]

To some that was a missed opportunity. Some libertarians and neoconservatives called for urgent wholesale oil privatization, like that applied to Russian companies in the 1990s, and handing out shares in state companies to all Iraqis. On this model the state was to be taken apart and its assets distributed to free Iraqis in a free market.[9] But in Russia privatization had been a disaster, as vouchers granting rights to shares rapidly became concentrated in the hands of a few entrepreneurs who bought them up for cash and became multibillionaire oligarchs, while the state was left virtually unable to function. To Ariel Cohen of the Heritage Foundation and Gerald Driscoll of the Cato Institute, Russia's main problem was in fact that it hadn't gone far enough: pipeline companies had not been privatized, and private ownership was restricted to Russians, not foreigners.[10] Fortunately, others disagreed with the idea of repeating Russia's experiment. "I told everyone that I would have no part in it," CPA senior oil adviser Phil Carroll said. "For 25 million people to lose control of the one thing they have that is of value would be highly irresponsible, and thankfully this did not happen."[11]

Carroll arrived in Baghdad on May 7, 2003. He had been one of a handful of former industry men to advise the Pentagon's Energy Infrastructure Planning Group back in late 2002, at Michael Makovsky's recommendation. To many war critics, including myself, the appointment of a former head of Shell USA appeared intended to clear the way for multinationals to resume control of Iraq's oil.

I met Carroll—a dignified, understated seventy-one-year-old—in his tenth-floor office in central Houston in summer 2009. On a display case, alongside a model of a Pemex gas compressor and books on military history, were pictures of Carroll with Margaret Thatcher and (separately) with the man she had famously branded a terrorist, Nelson Mandela. That strange juxtaposition suggested a man who spent a lot of time with politicians but didn't care much for politics. He had a lot of affection for engineers, however. "I went to the Daura [refinery] control room. It was like a museum. It's amazing that the Iraqis can make the systems work," he told me. "They find a way. They are creative, and it's amazing."

His idea was to employ a corporate model, appointing Thamir al-Ghadhban chief executive with himself as chairman. The day after Carroll arrived in Baghdad, he and Ghadhban agreed upon four objectives. First, get fuel to the Iraqis, who were queuing for three or four days at gas stations. Second, get crude oil production and exports back on line, as this was the primary source of funds for the country. Third, begin introducing modern and transparent systems of accounting, procurement, metering, and the like. Finally, there was the question of "what Thamir would propose to a sovereign minister with regard to further investment in the Iraqi oil sector." This, Carroll said, could be anything from keeping the oil in Iraqi hands in the public sector to handing out concessions to multinational oil companies. "I made it clear that it was not something that I could decide. I could offer advice and opinion, but that is only something a sovereign Iraq could decide."

Carroll's relative caution and his respect for the Iraqis contradicts the view held by some that it was the Pentagon that pushed for privatization of Iraq's oil while State Department planners tried to keep it in the hands of the Iraqi government.[12] The theory sounds at first plausible but makes the mistake of assuming all radical measures were associated with the neocons (and implemented via the Pentagon) and moderation with the "realists" (mainly in State and the CIA). As we have seen in chapter 3, the Pentagon planning unit looked mainly just at oil industry repairs and contingency operations for the first few months after the invasion, and appointed the noninterventionist Phil Carroll and the technically able Thamir al-Ghadhban. Although both favored bringing in foreign companies, each tried to protect Iraqi expertise from the de-Ba'athification cull in summer 2003. The State Department planning exercise, on the other hand, considered extreme models of privatization and championed the politicized Ibrahim Bahr al-Uloum, who oversaw a more sweeping cleanout.

Still, while Carroll opposed wholesale privatization on the Russian model, his advice and opinion was that Iraq would need some involvement by foreign companies. "They [Iraqis] badly need not only investment, but more importantly an infusion of technology. They have been starved of it."

None of Iraq's five-year plans for its oil industry had been achieved since 1980, interrupted as they were by wars. But Ghadhban kept the habit of thinking in five-year plans. The current one, from 2001, would need some dates amended, but foreign investment would fit in order to allowed the planned production increases. "There is room for Arab and foreign investment, in particular in the upstream," Ghadhban said in May. "We are part of the international community. We don't see any problem with encouraging foreign investment, but it has to be on a mutually acceptable basis and in the best interests of the Iraqi people." In the meantime, he pointed out, "I'm not the prime minister of Iraq. I'm not the minister of oil. I'm the chief executive, heading an interim team doing the day-to-day work of the ministry. I'm not a politician. I'm a technician with 30 years' experience in the industry."[13]

## Helpful Advice

Contrary to Malcolm Rifkind's call for speed, oil investment contracts would not be signed just yet. Corporate lawyers warned that major oil companies would not invest billions of dollars under contracts with an occupation authority that could later be ruled illegal. Ideally, deals should wait until there was a constitution and a permanent government. "There has to be proper security, legitimate authority, and a legitimate process . . . by which we will be able to negotiate agreements that would be longstanding for decades," said Phil Watts, chairman of Shell.[14] BP had told the British government even before the war that it "would not wish to be involved on opaque, ambiguous arrangements" that might occur before the formation of a proper government.[15] That did not mean doing nothing. "Shell has not been inactive with regards to developing future business in Iraq and has been involved in building long-term relationships," explained Wolfgang Ströbl, the Austrian who had led Shell's deal making in "East Jordan" in the 1990s.[16] When the time came for contracts to be signed, those relationships would be key.

Carroll put out a call for oil companies to send representatives to Baghdad. Most were too nervous for that, although some sent security advisers to look around and set up front offices. Mostly they began the relationship building outside the country. Carroll's old company, Shell, was ahead of the pack. It sponsored the participation of senior Oil Ministry officials at conferences and "donated" nine tons of scientific journal back issues to Baghdad University (the donation was paid for by the British Council). When the British government established a joint board to coordinate training for Ministry of Oil staff, Shell was the most active member of the board, with several of the meetings taking place in the Shell Centre.

But if formal decisions were to be left to a sovereign government, advocates of a new oil policy would need to conduct what the U.S. military calls "shaping operations" to make sure the future Iraqi government did not make any unfavorable decisions. Throughout 2003 and 2004 the future of Iraq was a hot topic in the corridors of Whitehall and Washington. How could an Iraqi democracy be established? How could the country's economy and infrastructure be rebuilt? Many were excited by the opportunity to design a country from scratch. Government officials and academics—whatever their views on the war—now offered opinions on what would be best for the Iraqis. Think tanks produced reports; the UN held conferences; diplomats theorized over coffee. They shuddered at tales of Saddam's mismanagement of his people's patrimony. He hadn't invested in the oil industry for years: equipment was creaking and the oilfields geologically damaged. Clearly investment was needed, along with access to the latest technologies. It was a frenzy of advice and opinion that would be repeated eight years later when the regime of Muammar Qadhafi fell in Libya. Political questions were overtaken by technical ones: how to attract investment and how to determine terms for an optimum outcome. While the Iraqis would supposedly decide how to manage their oil industry, the U.S. and U.K. governments would advise them on how to do so.

However patronizing the advice may have been to Iraq's capable engineers and technocrats, it would have been hard to ignore when the advisers arrived accompanied by 160,000 soldiers. Furthermore, any advice was far from impartial. I put this criticism to a British civil servant who worked on the Iraqi economy. It was a fair point, he said. "Obviously the U.K. government has a particular point of view. We don't go round advising countries to set up cooperatives and organize big consultations."[17]

## The Missionary of Investment

For the most part the oil companies left the shaping operations to their home governments. But one man was keen to offer advice on their behalf. Dan Witt was head of a "research and education foundation" called the International Tax and Investment Center (ITIC), which aims to "create [a] neutral table to bring guys to share their knowledge with the policy-makers."[18] More specifically, ITIC's mission is to "share knowledge" of business-friendly tax and investment policies in "transition" countries. According to Kent Potter, a Chevron vice president and active participant in ITIC, the organization is "like a private-sector version of the OECD or IMF."[19] Although the majority of ITIC's funds come from its hundred corporate sponsors, about a quarter of which are oil and gas companies, Witt insists that he is not a lobbyist and does not *represent* those corporations. Rather, their financial support is philanthropic, and ITIC's work is educational, not advocacy.

A short, enthusiastic American with round spectacles and neatly combed hair, Witt has been described by one colleague as "a bundle of energy." It is not unusual for him to visit three or even four countries in a week as he moves between his home in Washington, D.C., his second office in London, and projects in capital cities around the world.

As major combat operations were coming to an end in May 2003, Witt realized Iraq was going to be redrawn, essentially on a blank sheet. So, he thought about "what we started in '93, '94 with the Kazakhs . . . Let's take some pages out of that playbook with the Iraqis."[20] The parallel was clear: ITIC had made its name shaping the tax and investment policies of post-Soviet Russia and Kazakhstan during their own period of rapid political change. Witt took his Iraq idea to the ITIC board, and in subsequent strategy planning meetings ITIC's directors and sponsors agreed, suggesting that the ultimate goal should be to regain companies' access to the region's other oil-rich countries, such as Iran and Libya too. Board members chose a military metaphor: the Iraq work should be "considered as a 'beachhead' for possible further expansion in the Middle East." Witt approached six of ITIC's sponsors—Chevron, ExxonMobil, BP, Shell, Total, and Eni—who agreed to fund the Iraq project on top of their normal contributions to ITIC, and then he set about constructing a vision for the country's oil industry with which to educate the Iraqi government.[21]

## Pushing the Ball up the Field

Phil Carroll left Baghdad in early October 2003 after a five-month tour of duty. "I thought I came here to teach the Iraqis," he said in a speech at his farewell party, "but in fact they taught me."[22] Michael Makovsky of the Energy Infrastructure Planning Group suggested Rob McKee as his replacement.[23] Until April McKee had been second-in-command at Conoco-Phillips, where he'd worked for thirty-five years. He was friends with Dick Cheney from the vice president's Halliburton days. After two trips to Washington for briefings, he was on his way to Baghdad, where he was installed in a plywood trailer next to the palace.

McKee took up where Carroll had left off on improving fuel supplies and restoring oil production. He had an extra challenge: securing the pipelines against the growing resistance movement. During October–December 2003 there were twenty-two attacks on oil pipelines, compared to just nine over the previous three months.[24] But while Carroll had been busy getting a grip on day-to-day operations, McKee began to look at the longer term. "I pushed hard to move the ball on the field a bit. I wanted to leave something behind that was not just a day-to-day firefight," he told me, using very Texan metaphors. And this meant Carroll's fourth objective: the future shape of the Iraqi oil industry.

Less than a month after his arrival in Baghdad, McKee commissioned a study on how oil and gas regimes worked in other countries, for Iraqis to learn from. He contacted Makovsky to make the arrangements. Makovsky decided to give the work to Virginia-based BearingPoint, the spun-off consulting arm of accountants KPMG. Under that contract BearingPoint was tasked with designing and implementing a Comprehensive Privatization Program focused on selling key firms and industries to "strategic investors," "especially those in the oil and supporting industries."[25]

BearingPoint completed its report on December 19, five days after a bearded and bedraggled Saddam Hussein was dragged from a hole near

Tikrit. Someone at USAID sent me a copy of the study. It set out to weigh the pros and cons of the oil systems of Venezuela, Azerbaijan, Kuwait, Iran, Malaysia, Saudi Arabia, and Indonesia. The evaluations were far from neutral, however: the report found lots of drawbacks to keeping oil production in the public sector and not many to opening it up to international companies. For instance, it counseled that the public option "would tend to limit future production levels to at-or-just-above prewar levels. Achieving higher levels of output through self-financing, though possible, will require a number of tough and potentially controversial decisions, including . . . possible underinvestment in other areas of the country's economy." Saudi Arabia, Iran, and Kuwait, it argued, had suffered delays, restricted development, and political divisions because of their nationalized oil industries.[26]

The predominantly BP-run Azerbaijan, on the other hand, was the great success story of the report. Despite "less attractive geology and governance"—Azerbaijan ranked sixth most corrupt out of 133 countries, according to Transparency International[27]—it has "been able to partially overcome [its] risk profile and attract billions of dollars of investment by offering a contractual balance of commercial interests within the risk contract, one that is enforceable under U.K. and Azeri law with the option of international arbitration."[28] In Iraq too, the report said, contracts needed to meet companies' wish lists on legal terms, including mechanisms for economic stabilization, international arbitration, investment protection, and freedom to repatriate profits.[29] (We shall see the implications of some of these in chapter 13.) In short, the report did what was asked of it in proposing how to develop a "modern, workable, and sustainable" structure for the oil industry—but with the multinational oil industry's views on what would meet those criteria. Signed off on by Bremer, Oil Minister Bahr al-Uloum, and adviser Thamir al-Ghadhban, it would shape the development of Iraq's oil policy over the following years.

## Oil and Politics

Mike Stinson, who replaced Rob McKee's as senior oil adviser in March 2004, told me that, as he saw it, a major problem in the Iraqi oil industry was its politicization during the Saddam era, so one of his principal aims was to get the industry on a more professional footing. He sketched out on my notepad the new structure he had envisaged, with divisions for exploration, production, and refining, and their management boards. But it was the top of the organization diagram that caught my eye, where there was another layer, an advisory board above the minister. This would, Stinson said, help ensure that the economically vital oil industry was run more on the basis of technical and economic decisions and less politically. Who would be on such a board? "Oh, it could be, let's say, people like Lord John Browne," he replied, and perhaps also some university professors and Iraqi businessmen. Lord Browne was former head of BP.

With that comment I understood the role of advisers in Iraq's oil sector. To an oil professional such as Mike Stinson, an advisory board led by someone like Browne made perfect sense. He was no longer with BP and so would not necessarily have a conflict of interest, and to a fellow oilman Browne was one of the very best. This was the impact of appointing former executives of multinational companies to advise the Iraqis. They weren't going to favor their own companies or do anything unethical or improper. It was just that, according to their worldview, multinationals would naturally be best at the job of developing Iraq's oil.

# 9

# Anti-Iraqi Forces

*With a heavy dose of fear and violence, and a lot of money for projects, I think we*
*can convince these people that we are here to help them.*
                                        —Lieutenant Colonel Nathan Sassaman,
                                        U.S. 4th Infantry Division, December 2003[1]

In late March 2004 members of the First Marine Expeditionary Force in Fallujah came up with a new name for their enemy: "anti-Iraqi forces." Apart from the obvious perversity of the term—it referred to Iraqis fighting foreign invaders—it revealed the existence of notions of Iraq or Iraqis quite independent of what the citizens of that country did, thought, or believed.* In reality, notions of a pro-U.S. Iraq "democratically" governed by identity-based parties with a liberalized economy were explicitly opposed by most Iraqis.[2] And Iraqis also opposed the "pro-Iraqi" forces of the United States and its partners: a CPA poll in May 2004, for instance, found 81 percent of Iraqis wanted Coalition forces to leave, compared to only 7 percent who wanted them to stay.[3]

Yet Paul Bremer and his colleagues remained convinced that only U.S. stewardship could bring democracy and that most Iraqis shared their vision for the future. The problems they were facing, they deduced, must be put down to antidemocratic forces in Iraq committed to returning the country to its old ways.[4] Therefore, their solution was military: to destroy them.

---

* A more subtle and widely accepted linguistic trick was to label fighters against the occupation an "insurgency" (against the government) rather than a "resistance."

## Two Battles

The largest U.S. offensive was in Fallujah, the "city of mosques" forty miles west of Baghdad. The attack on that city is remembered by most Americans and Europeans as a response to a mob attack on March 31, 2004, in which four Blackwater private security guards were killed and their bodies hung from a bridge over the Euphrates. The resulting outrage in the United States did lead President Bush to order a dramatic escalation, but in fact the Fallujah operation had started five days earlier, on March 26, and was under way at the time of the Blackwater killings. In mid-March Bremer had warned U.S. generals that "the situation is *not* going to improve until we clean out Fallujah."[5] The reason Fallujans were so strongly opposed to the occupation dated back to April 2003, when U.S. forces opened fire on a peaceful demonstration at a local school and killed seventeen people. Two days later, at a demonstration protesting the killings, troops again fired into the crowd, killing three.[6]

The few foreign civilians in the city when U.S. Marines attacked it— al-Jazeera's Ahmed Mansour, independent reporters Dahr Jamail and Rahul Mahajan, and human rights activist Jo Wilding—all reported that numerous civilian Fallujans, including women and children, were shot dead by U.S snipers.[7] Wilding reported that each time she went out in an ambulance to collect the dead and wounded, the vehicle—though clearly marked—was repeatedly shot at; at least one ambulance had to be withdrawn from service because it had taken so much damage from U.S. fire.[8]

Iraqis around the country were appalled at the brutality of the attack. On April 8 the Association of Muslim Scholars called on Iraqis to donate food, medicine, and blood for the suffering residents of Fallujah. Many Iraqis who had almost nothing themselves gave what little they had. The first convoy from the Umm al-Qura mosque to the besieged city contained more than ninety vehicles.

Three members of the Iraqi Governing Council threatened to resign, including the staunchly pro-American Adnan al-Pachachi. Bremer subsequently ruled Pachachi out of consideration for future office because of his "overly emotional reaction" to the attacks on Fallujah.[9] The threatened resignations would, however, have made the council—Bremer's sole claim to Iraqiness—likely to collapse, especially as all three were Sunnis and thus key to Bremer's idea of balance. As a result, the Marines were forced to declare a cease-fire on April 10.

At the same time as the attack on Fallujah, U.S. forces tried to take out another troublesome group. On March 28, 2004, troops closed down Muqtada al-Sadr's newspaper *al-Hawza*, which was printing strident criticisms of the occupation.* "Bremer Follows in the Footsteps of Saddam" was one of the paper's headlines. Following the closure, thousands of Sadr supporters marched in protest to the Green Zone, chanting, "Just say the word, Muqtada, and we'll resume the 1920 revolution."[10] This was a reference to the great uprising of Shi'a and Sunni religious leaders, tribes, the urban poor, and the middle classes against the British occupation, subsequently put down by an extensive Royal Air Force bombing campaign.[11] U.S. special forces' arrest of Sadr's deputy Mustafa al-Yacoubi on April 3, on suspicion of involvement in the murder of a pro-occupation Shi'a cleric in April 2003, prompted an uprising across southern Iraq. On April 5 Bremer issued an arrest warrant for Sadr himself, declaring, "He is attempting to establish his authority in the place of the legitimate authority. We will not tolerate this. We will reassert the law and order which the Iraqi people expect."[12]

Sadr's forces concentrated their efforts in the holy city of Najaf. U.S. tanks took the major streets. The Sadrists retreated into the labyrinthine Wadi as-Salaam (Valley of Peace), the world's largest cemetery, and to the shrine of Imam Ali, which U.S. forces did not dare attack. With no means of achieving his principal aims of arresting Sadr or dismantling the Jaysh al-Mahdi, Bremer accepted a negotiated resolution through supporters of Grand Ayatollah Sistani. The eventual deal in late May secured Sadr's withdrawal from the shrine in return for a removal of U.S. troops from Najaf.

The Shi'a Sadrists and the mostly Sunni Fallujans were seen as national heroes for standing up to the Americans.[13] Shi'a families donated food to the besieged Fallujans as enthusiastically as their Sunni co-religionists, and aid convoys carrying rice, grain, flour, and sugar traveled to the city. Shi'a and Sunni alike gave blood for the wounded. Jaysh al-Mahdi fighters arrived to

---

* Shutting down newspapers would be officially endorsed later that year in a new U.S. Army counterinsurgency manual that listed indicators of enemy activity, spotted by political scientist Eric Herring. Among these were rhetoric against the mission force in the local media, circulation of opposition petitions, political themes in religious services, and even "entertainers with a political message." These indicators—which might equally be considered manifestations of the much-vaunted "freedom"—were interspersed in a list among more conventional signs such as terrorist acts and attacks on patrols. See U.S. Army, *Counterinsurgency Operations*, Field Manual-Interim FMI3-07.22, October 2004, Appendix E, cited in Eric Herring and Glen Rangwala, *Iraq in Fragments* (London: Hurst, 2006), 176.

fight alongside the Fallujans. Posters of Muqtada al-Sadr began to appear in Sunni mosques, and some fighters from Fallujah joined the besieged Sadrists in Najaf. In a poll the following month, 64 percent of respondents believed the battles in Fallujah and Najaf had made Iraq more unified, compared to 14 percent who felt they had made it more divided.[14]

Speaking at an April 2004 press conference in the Green Zone, General Rick Sanchez, commander of U.S. forces in Iraq, warned of the Americans' greatest fear: an Iraq united against the occupation, and which the United States was no longer able to manage politically by playing on communal interests. "The danger is, we believe there is a linkage that may be occurring at the very lowest levels between the Sunni and the Shi'a, and we have to work very hard to ensure that it remains at the tactical level."[15] He added, with unintentional irony, "We will not let terrorists inspire and create sectarian violence."

## Abu Ghraib and the Salvador Option

It was not only through crushing, full-frontal confrontations that U.S. forces sought to pacify the country. In April 2004, ten months after dismantling the Iraqi military, Paul Bremer passed Order No. 69, creating the Iraqi National Intelligence Service (INIS), following input from the CIA.[16] INIS was staffed by a mixture of former Ba'athist intelligence officers and members of the exiled parties the United States had covertly trained immediately after the fall of Saddam.[17] Whatever they thought about de-Ba'athification in general, Iraqis were dismayed that Bremer appeared to be bringing back precisely those Ba'athists from the security and intelligence services who had been most involved in Saddam's repression. Bremer was seen to prioritize crushing the anti-U.S. resistance over preventing a return to tyranny.

Later that month Bremer's decision was placed in an even more sinister context when Seymour Hersh published a *New Yorker* article detailing the systematic abuse of Iraqi captives at Abu Ghraib prison, one of Saddam's most notorious torture sites, now run by the Americans.[18] The abuse included chemical burns, beatings, sodomy, and the use of dogs. A CBS *60 Minutes* episode showed the now-infamous photos of Private Lynndie England and colleagues grinning over naked prisoners forced into humiliating sexual positions.

September 2004 saw the formation of the five-thousand-strong Special Police Commandos, a counterinsurgency force staffed by ex-members of elite units of the former regime, such as the Republican Guard. General Adnan Thabit, commander of the new unit, came up with the idea of a grim reality TV show for the al-Iraqiyya network called *Terrorism in the Grip of Justice*. In the daily show, detainees—often showing clear signs of beatings—would confess to their crimes on camera, as well as drunkenness or sexual deviancy.

Counterinsurgency continued to get dirtier. On January 8, 2005, *Newsweek* published an article headlined "The Salvador Option."[19] The title of the piece referred to the Reagan administration's support during the 1980s for the Salvadoran army and right-wing death squads, which fought a leftist insurgency through executions, disappearances, and torture, often of civilians. According to the article, the Pentagon was considering using special forces to train paramilitary units composed of militias associated with Iraqi former exile groups, with the aim of using them to assassinate or capture enemy targets. The chief of the new INIS was quoted as saying, "The Sunni population is paying no price for the support it is giving to the terrorists. From their point of view, it is cost-free. We have to change that equation."

## Two Men in a Hurry

On June 28, 2004, Bremer left Iraq, the handover to interim prime minister Ayad Allawi secretly brought forward by two days. It was hardly a dignified exit. Bremer left the country just minutes after his early departure had been made public. Journalists' mobile phones were confiscated at the press conference; after waving good-bye as he boarded a C-130 cargo plane, he waited for everyone to leave before dashing across the runway to a waiting Chinook helicopter. It was his parting vanity to imagine that Iraqi fighters might want to impede his departure.

Bremer had failed to assert control over Iraq. This would be left to Allawi, whom Bremer chose to succeed him because he thought Allawi the most capable of clamping down on the resistance. "Allawi was tougher than any of his colleagues," wrote Bremer in his memoir. "And a newly sovereign Iraq would need a tough leader."[20] Bremer had also failed to convert Iraq into his hoped-for "Singapore on the Tigris." Although he had put in place a radical free market legal framework, companies were not sufficiently interested in profiting from it, especially in the poor security environment. It was only oil—driver of the economy—that could have generated the cash to feed other sectors (as in the Gulf states), and postwar oil production still had not returned to prewar levels. He later said that economic liberalization "is a process that will take years. The occupation need not last as long as that process if you can turn over to indigenous forces that . . . are committed to continue."[21] Allawi was chosen also to take this process forward. Officially, however, the main duty of Allawi's interim government was to prepare for elections in January 2005. Those would elect both a one-year transitional government and the committee that would draft the constitution, before a second round of elections in December 2005 to form a permanent government.

Bremer was not the only one in a hurry in June 2004. On June 29 a small Norwegian oil company called Det Norske Oljeselskap (DNO) announced that it had signed a contract with the Kurdistan Regional Government (KRG) to explore and develop an area of fifteen hundred square miles around the town of Zakho, close to the Turkish and Syrian borders. DNO managing director Helge Eide felt he "had to do it before the interim government came in."[22] As a result, the contract would be subject to the legal authority of Kurdistan's post-1991 autonomy, rather than the post-2003 legal regime, under which Iraqi governments might be able to challenge it.

The hills near Zakho are dotted with ponds of crude oil seeping naturally from the ground. In one gully near the village of Tawke, a stream of oil runs down the hillside.[23] These were the seeps War Secretary Hankey observed on the Admiralty map in 1918, prompting the call for the push northward as a first-class British war aim (in chapter 1). DNO had been negotiating with Kurdish officials for a contract there since late 2003, after being introduced by former U.S. diplomat Peter Galbraith, son of the celebrated economist John Kenneth Galbraith.[24] The younger Galbraith had known the Kurdish leaders since the 1980s, when he was one of the first to alert the U.S. administration to Saddam Hussein's al-Anfal campaign of genocide against the Kurds. In 2004 Galbraith was both paid as a consultant by DNO and awarded a 5 percent stake in the contract through his Delaware-registered company, Porcupine LLP.[25] His interest would not become public until five years later. Galbraith's role was reminiscent of that famously played by the Armenian businessman Calouste Gulbenkian, who became known as Mr. Five Percent after gaining the same stake when he brokered the Turkish (later renamed Iraqi) Petroleum Company's 1925 concession contract.

The DNO/Galbraith contract and others like it would shape Iraqi oil debates over the coming years. An Oil Ministry official who asked not to be named had a warning of trouble to come when he was called one day by DNO's local director, who said he needed help with some data on the border. "What? You mean the border with Syria or Turkey?" asked the official. The DNO man had meant the boundary between Kurdistan and the rest of Iraq. Realizing his mistake, he tried to cover it up, but he had shown how he was thinking. "The KRG is acting as if it is a separate country," the official concluded.[26]

## Returning for the Kill

The United States was not prepared to let its April 2004 truces with either the Sadrists or the Fallujans stand, as both served to undermine its authority. "How could you have control in Iraq when you have this cancer called Fallujah?" asked General Richard Natonski, who took command of the Marine Expeditionary Force (MEF) in August 2004. "So it had to be eradicated before you could even conceive of having a successful election."[27] The challenge for U.S. commanders following the April battles was how to achieve military victory without again suffering political defeat.

In returning to the fights later in the year, three main things would be done differently. First, the two battles would be fought at different times: the Sadrists in August and Fallujah in November. In this way, Fallujans would worry about a coming attack on them but would not see any immediate advantage in helping the Shi'a fighters. In April, when both groups were attacked simultaneously, cooperation had been their best tactical option. General James Conway, commanding general of the MEF at the time of the April attack on Fallujah, commented, "We never wanted to see a general uprising of both Shi'a and Sunni because we did not have enough forces to handle both of those writ large."[28] Second, an Iraqi face—that of Allawi—would be put on the decision to attack. "Blasting our way into Fallujah" would not solve the United States' problems, Bremer said in late April, "until we had strong Iraqi leadership in place to support these moves."[29] Third, U.S. military leaders recognized that the greatest driver of Iraqi solidarity was knowledge of the suffering of the Fallujans. One of the U.S. conditions for the cease-fire in April had been that Ahmed Mansour and his al-Jazeera crew, who had been transmitting regular live reports on the battle, leave Fallujah.[30] This time U.S. forces would ensure no information got out.

But Najaf was first. On August 5, 2004, the Marines attacked. The fight began in the old city, whose narrow streets the U.S. forces bombarded with artillery and aircraft. The Iraqi face of the operation was emphasized even though the nascent Iraqi security forces made little military contribution. In the first two days the Marines claimed to have killed three hundred "anti-Iraqi" fighters,[31] although Iraqi television showed women's bodies among the corpses in the streets.[32] A few days later the Iraqi authorities ordered journalists to leave the city.[33] The scale of the attack attracted immediate criticism. "I think that killing Iraqi citizens is not a civilized way of building the new Iraq," said Ibrahim al-Ja'afari, interim Iraqi vice president and leader of the Da'wa Party.[34] Half the Najaf provincial council resigned in protest.

There were demonstrations in Fallujah against the Najaf attack, with placards reading HE WHO DEFENDS AL-FALLUJAH AND DOES NOT DEFEND AL-NAJAF IS NOT AN IRAQI. The Association of Muslim Scholars issued a fatwa—a rare event—forbidding collaboration with the Americans in the operation. Worshippers at the Umm al-Qura mosque chanted, "Sunnis and Shi'a are united to kick out the occupation." And on August 18 a delegation of religious and tribal leaders from Fallujah led an aid convoy to Najaf carrying blankets, food, and medical supplies.

Again, the United States failed to decisively crush Sadr. Ultimately a settlement that allowed Sadr to keep not only his freedom but also his militia (both of which had been red lines for the Americans) was brokered by Sistani, who did not want to see Najaf destroyed.

The second attack on Fallujah, code-named Operation Phantom Fury, started six days after the U.S. presidential election, on November 8, 2004. It began by cutting off water and electricity supplies to the city, although 50,000 of its 300,000 residents remained. Men of "military age"—between fifteen and fifty-five—were denied exit from the city on the apparent assumption that no men of that age were civilians. Prime Minister Allawi had closed al-Jazeera's Baghdad bureau in August. A few days before the assault on Fallujah, U.S. forces entered the city and ordered all TV crews to leave.[35] On the other hand, more than ninety reporters were embedded with the attacking forces and were able to show the battle from their perspective.

One of the first moves of the attackers was to capture the hospital. Along with its strategic location, the reason for this was that putting the hospital out of action—in violation of the Fourth Geneva Convention[36]—would eliminate a location at which the media could see and film mass casualties. If the wounded and dead had to remain in their homes or in the street, in other words, they would be out of reach of the cameras. "The Fallujah hospital had long been used as a propaganda organ by insurgent forces. . . . Without this portal, the enemy had a much weaker voice," wrote General Thomas Metz.[37]

This time the city was flattened. U.S. officials estimated that more than half of Fallujah's 39,000 homes were damaged and about 10,000 destroyed.[38] Some 60 mosques, 65 schools, and 8,500 businesses were also damaged.[39] The bombardment so crippled the water distribution system that supplies could no longer be piped to 60 percent of homes. Five months after the attack only half the city had electrical power at all.[40] The United Nations' IRIN news agency reported that there were between 650 and 1,300 civilian deaths.[41] Most controversial internationally was the Americans' use of white phosphorus munitions, which under international law is banned from use in civilian areas because it burns deep under the skin, cannot be extinguished, and poisons the body through the burn.

Leaders of the AMS were arrested days before the attacks on both Najaf and Fallujah, "maybe as a message to us," spokesman Muhammad Bashar al-Faydi speculated to me.[42] And this time U.S. forces thoroughly sealed the city, denying entry to all aid.[43] According to the charity Doctors for Iraq, food aid trucks were prohibited from entering and food shops and markets prevented from opening. With piped water supplies cut off, Doctors for Iraq distributed food and bottled water but reported that U.S. Marines shot at water containers left outside the doors of homes.[44] There was again some action by other Iraqis, but with aid unable to enter and no one allowed to leave the city to say what was happening, nor any media coverage, the response was far more muted.

Meanwhile, Muqtada al-Sadr had realized that direct confrontation was delivering diminishing political returns. The strategy of mass peaceful demonstrations, at which the Sadrists were most effective, had ceased to be viable when the United States began attempting to arrest the movement's leaders. But, clearly, neither could they win by force. Sadr therefore hedged his position, accepting indirect involvement in the official political process by allowing some of his allies to stand in the coming election while never formally endorsing the political process With unfortunate timing, Grand Ayatollah Sistani had issued a fatwa the day before the November attack began on Fallujah, ordering his followers to vote as an "individual duty." Given his unrivaled influence over Iraq's Shi'a, and since U.S. propaganda efforts focused on distinguishing between the "legitimate" elections and "anti-Iraqi" resistance to the occupation, the effect was to leave the Fallujans isolated.

## Creating the Sunni "Insurgency"

The official justification for the November 2004 attack on Fallujah had been to create security for the coming election. In fact, it had precisely the opposite effect on Iraqis' willingness to vote, as most Sunnis decided to boycott.

Meanwhile, since the beginning of the occupation the United States had identified the resistance as "Sunni"—exemplified by labeling its geographical center the "Sunni Triangle." The reasoning was that Sunni Arabs were angry at having been forced from power, and their insurgency was targeted at the Shi'a and Kurds who had usurped the government. Like much of the official narrative, this contained a grain of truth. As we have seen, the government and military elite had been disproportionately, though far from exclusively, Sunni Arab during the Ottoman, British, and republican periods. However, not only were numerous Shi'a involved in resisting the occupation, but the discourse of Iraqi resistance—especially in the first year—was almost entirely nationalist and anti-occupation in character, not sectarian. This was hardly something the liberators of Iraq would want to admit.

Eventually, however, the diagnosis became self-fulfilling. As the United States consistently identified its enemy as Sunni Arab and the government as Shi'a and Kurdish, the entire Sunni community began to feel religiously persecuted. The ferocity of the second assault on Fallujah was final confirmation. The less violent attack on the Sadrists in Najaf—based on the rationale that the occupation could not afford to risk angering the Shi'a majority—undoubtedly served to undermine solidarity between the two communities. The linkage between Shi'a and Sunni, about which General Sanchez had been so worried, was being broken.

# 10

# The Hands of Iraqis

*The authorities are saying that privatization will develop our sector and be useful. But we do not see it as development at all; we view any plan to privatize the oil sector as a big disaster.*

—Hassan Juma'a, February 2005[1]

While battles raged for control of Iraq, the oil companies continued to develop their relationships with Iraqi officials and politicians, to ensure that they were well positioned, ready for when the time came. A headline in December 2004's *Petroleum Economist* magazine characterized the mood as "snuggling-up time."

In August 2004 Shell created the new position of external affairs officer for Iraq, whose principal role would be "to build relationships." It contracted with a headhunting agency to find the right person, described as "a person of Iraqi extraction with strong family connections and an insight into the network of families of significance within Iraq."[2] The position was filled by Luay Jawad al-Khatteeb, a nephew of Muhammad-Ali Zainy.

BP, meanwhile, hired Sir Jeremy Greenstock, who had served as Tony Blair's envoy in the CPA, as a special adviser in June 2004. He had also been British ambassador to the United Nations, responsible for making the case in 2002 for a second UN resolution on attacking Iraq. The U.K. Advisory Committee on Business Appointments (ACBA) barred him from business trips to Iraq or dealings with Iraqi companies for six months, but this was hardly a serious restriction, as most Iraqi oil business was still done outside

the country and oil companies such as BP get their business from governments, not companies.[3] In September, he represented BP at a private meeting in London with prime minister Ayad Allawi,* apparently to lobby for an
interim contract on the Rumaila oilfield.[4] The previous time they'd met, in
March, Greenstock had been representing the country with the second-
largest occupying force. Clearly BP had bought some serious influence.

People in Greenstock's position are usually precluded from taking up
their new employment at all for six months. Greenstock was offered an earlier start date if he focused on non-Iraqi issues at BP for the first six months.
Greenstock admitted that he had already discussed Iraq with BP less than
two months after leaving his CPA post, albeit in a "preliminary and rather
general" way. He argued that he would not give the company any commercial advantage, as "I never got into the oil area in the CPA."[5] Following that
e-mail, the Foreign Office recommended a three-month delay before starting his employment, which the ACBA accepted. However, it seems Greenstock might have misremembered his time in Iraq: in January he had met oil
adviser Terry Adams—a former executive of BP and number two at the CPA
to Rob McKee—"to discuss the state of the oil sector and decision-making."[6]
He also seemed to know, when he gave a presentation to the Asia Oil and
Gas Conference in June 2004, that "the current Oil Ministry recognizes the
need to work with foreign companies and to allow these companies to participate in production through Production Sharing Contracts."[7]

As time went on, the companies' efforts become more substantive. In
June 2004 Chevron signed a memorandum of understanding (MOU) with
the Oil Ministry under which it would provide technical training and advice
on ministry projects and strategy.[8] The latter included advising on the supergiant oilfields West Qurna and Majnoon, which Chevron was interested
in developing. The move was followed by other companies. In October 2004
Shell signed an MOU to develop a Gas Master Plan advising Iraq on a strategy for developing its natural gas resources. It also entered into an agreement to advise on fields in Maysan province, together with BHP. By
mid-2005 around thirty multinational oil companies had signed MOUs.
Luay al-Khatteeb estimated that each company spent around $50 million
between 2003 and 2009 on studies, education, and training. "That's pea-
nuts to the oil companies—it's petty cash," he said to me. "But they get intel-

* Also present were BP CEO John Browne and BP Middle East president Mike Daly.

ligence on the geological, the technical, and the political details of Iraq. They weren't doing Iraq a favor; they got to study a lot of Iraq."[9]

## The First Oil Policy

At the first meeting of his Supreme Council on Oil Policy in August 2004, interim prime minister Ayad Allawi presented a set of guidelines as the basis for Iraq's future oil policy.[10] Iraq has about seventy-five known oilfields, of which only twenty-five have been developed.[11] Allawi proposed that these twenty-five producing fields remain in the hands of a reconstituted Iraq National Oil Company (INOC), while the development of the fifty known but undeveloped fields, as well as exploration for new ones, would be undertaken through private sector investment. That should happen "as soon as possible," and field development should be arranged through twenty-five-year production sharing agreements (PSAs). This broadly fit with what Phil Carroll, Rob McKee, and the other Western advisers had been thinking.

But Allawi's guidelines went on to exclude Iraqi companies from having any role in the new fields at all: "New ventures should specifically not be allowed to partner with any state-owned enterprises, including INOC, in order to ensure state impartiality and avoid the pitfall of state interference in corporate enterprise management." Furthermore, the terms of contracts should be generous and profitable to foreign companies. "Should we spend months and years trying to extract the last penny in negotiating the commercial terms? I would suggest that there is no need to waste time. Time is of the essence." Most radical of all, he suggested that "INOC may be partially privatized through wide distribution of ownership among Iraqis"—precisely the Russian model that Phil Carroll had cautioned against.

Thamir al-Ghadhban, who had led the Oil Ministry alongside Phil Carroll until the invasion of the Chalabis, now returned as oil minister under Allawi. He shared Allawi's preference for PSAs but sought a more balanced approach than his new boss. "Our declared policy is to depend on ourselves and seek outside help too," he said.[12] "The first principle is getting the best that is in the interest of the Iraqi people. This means we must negotiate contracts whose terms and conditions provide the highest possible revenues."[13] To get the best terms he began talking to companies all over the world—in China, Russia, and Arab countries—as well as the Western multinationals, in order to strengthen his bargaining position. There were also political advantages, he believed. "I look at the issue of involving IOCs [international oil companies] in Iraq from a strategic point of view in the context of the regional balance of power," he later explained. "I think they would add strength to the country vis-à-vis our relations with neighboring countries."[14] Meanwhile, he also sought to prioritize the use of Iraqi skills and manpower in any development.

## The Beachhead

Dan Witt's ITIC published its report in autumn 2004. Titled *Petroleum and Iraq's Future: Fiscal Options and Challenges*, some of its proposals were similar to Allawi's, especially a focus on PSAs. It went into some detail on how investors' profits would be protected: contracts should give them full freedom to export oil regardless of OPEC quotas, insulate them from changes to Iraqi law, and allow them to go to international courts to defend their interests if they got into a dispute with the government.[15] As for the economic benefits, the report proposed a structure whereby the state would receive "a minimum (if any) resource rent" until the investor achieved its target rate of profit. Such an approach would effectively guarantee the foreign companies' profits, and any cost overruns (even if the fault of the investor) would be paid by the state.[16]

ITIC admitted that there was no objective *need*—either economic or technical—to open the Iraqi oil sector to foreign investment. Rather, it was a political decision. And playing on the short-term mind-set of politicians, the report calculated how much foreign investment would "save" the Iraqi government during the investment period ($4.2 billion) but did not consider the longer-term cost to Iraq: once the revenues started to flow, a large share of them would go to the foreign companies.[17] It is as if I decided to take out a bank loan based only on how much the additional money would improve my finances in the present and not on what it would cost to repay it later.

The "advice" did not come entirely without some embarrassment. "Who the hell are you to be sharing stuff if you've not been there? It's a bit hypocritical," said Witt as he admitted to me he'd never been to Iraq.[18] His euphemism matched the language of the form of contract that was taking hold in Iraq, the production sharing agreement. The idea of sharing sounds fair enough; in fact, language was one of the principal reasons PSAs looked attractive to the advocates of foreign investment in Iraq's oil.

## Production Sharing Agreements

A consensus was now emerging around PSAs as the mechanism of foreign investment in Iraq's oil. They were advocated by Allawi, Witt, McKee,[19] the State Department's Future of Iraq Project, and its member Ibrahim Bahr al-Uloum when he later became oil minister.[20] Shell called for greater use of PSAs across the Middle East in October 2003.[21] So what is a production sharing agreement?

As we have seen, the value of oil lies less in a single shipment (which is generally worth a few tens of millions of dollars) than in the long-term right to extract from an oilfield, which can provide many tens of billions of dollars of profit. In order to release this profit, a company must invest capital up front in rigs, pipelines, storage tanks, and expensive drilling operations before the first drop of oil is extracted. It will do so only if it has a guarantee that it will receive a sufficient share of the oil later.

The traditional form of contract, the concession, granted companies all the oil they extracted, for which they compensated the host state through taxes and royalties—like the Iraq Petroleum Company's 1925 contract. PSAs were developed as an alternative contract structure by Indonesia in the late 1960s, when nationalism was surging through oil-producing countries. Like concessions, they give foreign companies exclusive rights to extract oil on predefined terms for a long period of time; however, in an ingenious conceptual twist, PSAs invert the flow of payments. Rather than compensating the state for the oil they take, in a PSA companies are labeled "contractors," and the state compensates them for their investment and their operating costs. For example, in a concession a company might take the oil and give 70 percent of profits back to the state in taxes:* in a PSA the company would extract the oil for the state and be given a 30 percent share of profits as its reward for doing so. The economic effect is the same: either way, the state gets 70 percent and the company 30 percent. As for who controls the oil development, the foreign investor—despite being called the "contractor"—still makes the operational decisions, and the state's power to intervene is defined in the contract just as in a concession.

---

*Tax rates vary from less than 30 percent in countries with little or expensive oil, such as Ireland, to above 95 percent in the most prolific countries, such as Libya.

In one of the standard textbooks on oil contracting, industry consultant Daniel Johnston comments, "At first [PSAs] and concessionary systems appear to be quite different. They have major symbolic and philosophical differences, but these serve more of a political function than anything else. The terminology is certainly distinct, but these systems are really not that different from a financial point of view."[22] But in a country such as Iraq, where foreign ownership of oil is unpopular, such a terminological distinction has a clear advantage. Thomas Wälde, an oil law expert at Dundee University, put it more colorfully:[23]

> A convenient marriage between the politically useful symbolism of the production-sharing contract . . . and the material equivalence of this contract model with concession/licence regimes in all significant aspects . . . The government can be seen to be running the show—and the company can run it, behind the camouflage of legal title symbolizing the assertion of national sovereignty.

## Speed

With the consensus now in place around PSAs, Oil Minister Ghadhban suggested that in order to get foreign companies in more quickly, work could take place on model contracts in parallel with the political and constitutional processes, "so that when the time comes, we'll be ready," he said. "We will not put this work aside until the situation allows us to move forward. . . . if, theoretically, we shake hands with an oil company who is ready to take risks and do work based on the contracts available in the interim period, and if it's acceptable to the cabinet and approved by all, I don't see why it should be stopped once governments change."[24]

The trouble with this rush was that Iraq was an occupied country and so would have little bargaining power in negotiating contracts. Their terms would nonetheless be fixed for the contracts' duration—generally between twenty-five and forty years. Oil contracts could thus effectively preserve the economic circumstances of occupation—partial sovereignty, political division, and violence—well beyond the withdrawal of troops. When I interviewed Witt in summer 2006, he admitted that long-term deals are often seen as unfair in retrospect: "It's really easy to sit here today, and I have these discussions with Kazakhs, with Azeris—'Oh, well, maybe we gave too much

away, maybe we didn't get enough government take, maybe the foreign investors aren't paying a fair share.'" But, he argued, "you've got to really look at
the political risk and what other industries are prepared to invest in an unstable, risky environment."[25]

During summer and autumn 2004 Witt had a series of meetings with
U.K. government officials to discuss the most effective strategy for persuading the Iraqis to adopt his organization's views. With few contacts of his own
in Iraq, he was eager for help—and the government was happy to oblige.
When ITIC completed its report in September 2004, it was formally sent to
Finance Minister Adil Abdul-Mahdi by the British ambassador in Baghdad,
Edward Chaplin.[26] This was not just some lobbyist the minister could ignore
if he chose. After all, Abdul-Mahdi had been directly appointed to his job
by the occupation powers.

British MP Alan Simpson asked the government what representations the
ambassador had made on behalf of ITIC or in favor of PSAs. "None" was the
one-word answer from Kim Howells, the Foreign Office minister responsible for the Middle East. I gave Simpson evidence from ITIC that the ambassador had sent the report. Well, "the Embassy did pass a copy of ITIC's
report and an invitation to an ITIC conference to the Ministry of Finance at
ITIC's request," admitted Howells. But "this was done without representation or endorsement by the Ambassador or other Embassy staff of its content
but simply because security conditions were such that ITIC could not themselves pass on the report direct."[27] And even though the United Kingdom did
not endorse the report, "The development of a strong energy sector is vital
for Iraq's future. . . . It is right that the U.K. should do what it can to support
the Iraqi authorities in this area."

The British also helped ITIC organize the formal presentation of its report at a workshop in Beirut in January 2005. Chris Brown, a senior diplomat at the Baghdad embassy whom Witt describes as "an excellent guy,
perhaps one of the most knowledgeable people in terms of what was going
on in the Ministry of Oil and helping to bring them best practice," advised
Witt on which Iraqi officials and ministers to invite to the meeting and
helped deliver invitations to them.[28] It was combined with a workshop organized by the International Monetary Fund and the World Bank. Iraqi minds
were no doubt sharpened by the presence of these two institutions, which
would have the power to shape the terms of the country's repayment of its
debts as well as future access to international funds.

## The Activist

The consensus on PSAs did not extend to Iraqis outside the Green Zone, who hadn't been told what was in store for their oil. I first met the Basra oil workers' leader Hassan Juma'a in February 2005, a few days after Iraqis' purple-dyed fingers were broadcast around the world to proclaim the country's new democracy. The thickset fifty-three-year-old spoke with calm authority and uncompromising conviction about the oil workers' duty as guardians of the nation's oil wealth. He was in London for a week, and we met at Platform, the charity where I then worked, to exchange what we each knew of the plans for Iraq's oil. The union of oil workers had grown rapidly in the two years since it was formed. It now numbered 23,000 members, around half the oil industry workforce in the three southern provinces of Basra, Maysan (Amara), and Dhi Qar (Nasiriya).

Hassan's visit to London had been organized by a young British activist from a Polish family, Ewa Jasiewicz. Energetic and determined, she was one of a handful of antiwar activists and freelance journalists who had traveled to Iraq in 2003 without the comfort of organizational backup, funds, or body-guards. There she found herself working with nascent groups of Iraqis campaigning for their rights. Almost all the independent Westerners stayed in Baghdad. In November 2003, after about five months in Baghdad, Ewa traveled to Basra to investigate the state of civil society there. She was immediately impressed by the oil workers' union and by Hassan. "He struck me as a very dignified, strong, uncompromising, charismatic person," she recalled. Everyone in Basra knew him as a leading activist against the Ba'ath regime: "He was so well respected that we thought he might be some sort of religious leader or part of some political party." She was pleased to find he was neither. (Some of the union's detractors in Islamist parties would later accuse Hassan of being a communist, while others with communist sympathies would accuse him of being Islamist!) The oil workers' union had genuinely emerged from the grassroots, growing from existing relationships in the workplace rather than from some ideology or political organization. Ewa contrasted this with unions led by semiprofessionalized bureaucrats, which "were organizing from the top down. You know, 'This is our union, all we've got to do is get the members in.'"

The oil union had become established through the June 2003 protest at the refinery and a strike at the South Oil Company two months later, which succeeded in reversing a decision to use KBR-hired foreign workers rather than locals. But the unionists needed to know more about how to organize, how to structure their organization, how to train the new generation. They also needed information about what was being decided by the CPA. As Ewa put it, "They didn't know who was attacking them, what was being planned against them; they just knew something was going to happen." So she spent her time disseminating information on Bremer's orders, on privatization, and on International Labour Organization standards and conventions. The other help the union needed was international recognition. When Ewa returned to London in early 2004, Hassan asked her to serve as the union's international representative, along with an Iraqi-British engineer named Munir Chalabi.* She began promoting the union: writing about it, speaking about it, contacting British unions to ask for their support.

I asked her about the response to her solidarity campaign. "It was *rubbished!*" she replied. Some British trade unionists accused her—partly because of union politics—of misrepresenting the oil union, trying to distort its view to suit her politics, or even having Ba'ath sympathies.[29] Few could be more innocent than Ewa of the last charge: on arrival in Iraq she was quicker than many other critics of the war to understand the legacy of dictatorship, and she worked as much to help heal that legacy as she did to hold the occupation to account. Things changed when Hassan visited London himself in 2005 and met British unionists. He spoke of opposing the occupation and of creating a culture of civil resistance. "Finally [the British trade unionists saw] it was not just me making it up," Ewa recalled. "It tallied up with what I'd been saying." If Ewa had not persevered when others were mocking or dismissing her, the oil union would be in a far weaker position today. Hassan's trip to London, and a subsequent one to the United States, created the union's relationship with the international labor movement, a relationship that would be vital in defending the union later on.

## A Rich Country?

When I met Hassan, the oil workers were beginning their engagement in longer-term issues of oil policy, and in May 2005 they organized the country's

* A very distant relative of Ahmad Chalabi.

first post-2003 public conference on privatization, in Basra. I attended, along with Ewa and three other international participants.

It was only after four days there that I noticed, behind the disfigurement of bombed or half-rebuilt buildings and avenues lined with mounds of rubble instead of trees, that Basra is a beautiful city. On one street lay a huge pile of tank tracks and turrets, testament not just to the current situation but to twenty-five years of wars in which the city had been on the front line—against Iran, Kuwait, and now the United States and the United Kingdom. The city once had been known as the "Venice of the East," but we couldn't see any water in the canals, which were packed solid with trash.

Hassan worked seven days a week, starting at seven o'clock in the morning. In the Basra climate, early morning was the only time one could actually concentrate. Hassan disagreed with the new government's decision to reduce the working week from six to five days. "People need to work more, not less," he said, fearing a plot to weaken the Iraqi economy.[30]

The oil union was still officially illegal—Saddam's 1987 law was still in force—but in the workplace itself it was informally recognized. Since the union's successes in organizing the workforce, the managers of most companies (now including Jabbar al-Luaibi of South Oil, who had twice refused Abdullah al-Maliki permission to reestablish the union, as we saw in chapter 5) were willing to deal with it and allow its leaders time for their activities. Hassan himself was permitted to work full-time on union activities while being paid by SOC and was given a seat on the company board. We stayed the night in the guesthouse at the Basra refinery, which, like the conference venue and the vehicles in which we traveled, had been provided by the company to support the union's work.

We visited Hassan's crumbling rented house in Jumhuriya, one of the poorest neighborhoods of Basra. Although meticulously tidy, the house was sparsely furnished. A few walls bore peeling paint; most were bare plaster, some of them with widening cracks. His two oldest sons had married and left home; he lived with his wife, three daughters, and youngest son, cheeky six-year-old Hamoudi. "Iraq is a rich country, but its people are poor," Hassan explained as we sat on the floor of his austere living room.

The privatization conference, attended by around 150 workers and other Basrawis, took place in the South Oil Company's cultural center, a gray 1970s polygon of a building adorned with tourist photos of the marshes around Basra in more peaceful times. Local religious and political leaders sat in the VIP armchairs at the front, with tissues and plastic flowers on knee-high tables in front of them. A banner at the front of the auditorium displayed the conference slogan: TO REVIVE THE PUBLIC SECTOR AND TO BUILD AN IRAQ FREE OF PRIVATIZATION.

Several speakers lamented the lack of debate on privatization in Iraq. Abdul-Jabbar al-Hilfi, a well-known economics professor from Basra University, worried about the apparently ideological motives for privatization; little study had been done of the state of Iraqi industries and their needs. Ultimately, he argued, their future must be the people's decision. The government had a responsibility to make sure people understood the issues, and the parliament should make any decisions only after a full debate.

I gave a presentation about oil and production sharing agreements. Another of our group, Justin Alexander, coordinator of the Jubilee Iraq debt campaign, spoke about how the International Monetary Fund uses debt obligations to impose privatization and other unpopular economic measures on countries. Iraq was already in discussions with the IMF. David Bacon, a labor journalist representing U.S. Labor Against the War (USLAW), spoke of examples from around the world where civil society had effectively blocked privatization and other neoliberal economic policies.

Summing up the discussions, the conference's closing statement concluded, "The public sector economy of Iraq is one of the symbols of the achievement of Iraqis since the revolution of July 14, 1958. It represents the common wealth of all Iraqis who built this sector." Calling on members of parliament to block any moves to privatize public companies, the statement added, "The conference participants believe that the privatization of the oil and industrial sectors, or of any part of them, will do great harm to the Iraqi people and their economy."

U.S. officials still struggled to take Iraqi trade unions seriously. The embassy labor attaché reported of a meeting with unions, "We were surprised to be told that the number-one labor union concern in Iraq today was neither poverty nor unemployment, but rather their allegedly deteriorating legal status under successive governments since 2003." The labor attaché should have known that in 2003 Paul Bremer had reaffirmed Saddam's Law No. 150, banning unions in the public sector, and that in 2005 the Iraqi government passed Decree No. 8750, empowering a committee of ministers to seize all union funds. "On our side, we spoke out for an integrated approach to economic reform based on anti-corruption, privatization, subsidy cuts and attracting investment," the attaché went on. "We suggested that the union leaders risked marginalizing themselves if they tried to deny that economic reform in Iraq is urgently needed."[31]

After I returned from the Basra anti-privatization conference, I worked with the British organization Crisis Action, which was led by my friend Guy Hughes, to expand my conference paper into a longer report explaining the plans for PSAs and what they would mean for the Iraqi economy. *Crude Designs* was published by Platform and Oil Change International in November of that year in association with four other campaigning organizations in Britain and the United States.* I spent the following weeks rushing between newsrooms and TV studios as media organizations reported the findings. The Arabic version of the report was downloaded from our website more than ten thousand times, although we'd done almost nothing to promote it. I met one Iraqi who told me he'd made a hundred photocopies to distribute; another said he'd made his family read it, then passed it to his neighbor, who did the same, until everyone on their street had read it. The popularity of the report was not due to any great skill on my part; rather, it was indicative of an unsatisfied public demand for information both in Iraq, where people wanted to know what lay ahead for their economy, and in the United States and Britain, where people suspected their governments had lied to them about oil. The rapid spread of the report in Iraq also reflected the gulf between Western plans and the desires of most Iraqis.

## Iraqi Unionists Stateside

In June 2005, two weeks after the Basra conference, Hassan Juma'a and oil union general secretary Faleh Abood Umara traveled to the United States along with two leaders each from two other union federations, the General Federation of Iraqi Workers and the Federation of Workers' Councils, on a visit to meet American workers, organized by U.S. Labor Against the War. "Both of them are extremely powerful personalities: they have a real presence," USLAW's national coordinator Michael Eisenscher said of Hassan and Faleh. "At the same time, not a hint of ego. Neither of them were prima donnas, as you sometimes run into with international labor people. They're

* Global Policy Forum, Institute for Policy Studies, New Economics Foundation, and War on Want.

very down to earth, very warm, and I thought they had a very clear and well-worked-out analysis of their situation."[32]

Activism and the labor movement are in Michael's blood. With patient determination and political intelligence, he has spent most of his adult life as an organizer, negotiator, and educator. He gained a reputation for being one of very few unionists to organize in Silicon Valley in the 1980s, a time when trade unions were the last thing the valley's entrepreneurs wanted to see. By the time of the attack on Afghanistan in October 2001, three weeks after the 9/11 terrorist attacks, Michael and other Bay Area trade unionists had already pulled together an ad hoc antiwar committee. During 2002 the committee began to build relationships with people in other cities, and in January 2003 a conference in the Teamsters Hall in Chicago attracted two hundred delegates from labor organizations across the country.

By early 2004 Michael and his fellow organizers knew what they were going to do. Their target was the convention of the AFL-CIO, held every four years. Nicknamed the "AFL-CIA" by some, the federation had never in its history criticized a U.S. foreign policy, let alone a war. USLAW's aim was to change that.

The Iraqi unionists spent five days in Washington meeting members of Congress, union leaders, and antiwar activists. The Iraqis then traveled separately for ten days: Hassan and Faleh to the West Coast and the other union representatives to the East Coast and Midwest. Between them they attended more than seventy events in twenty-six cities. "They just left a huge impression on people here," recalled Michael. "Up until that point, for a lot of people the idea of Iraqi unions or [an] Iraqi working class was an abstraction. . . . It made real for people that there are real human beings who are very much just like them, at the other end of this thing."

It was an exhausting—and at times emotional—schedule. One of the most memorable moments for the Iraqi visitors came during a service at Plymouth Congregational United Church of Christ in Washington, D.C., near the end of the trip. "We have got to come together if we're truly going to stand in unity and solidarity with these workers from Iraq and with the people from Iraq!" preached the Reverend Graylan Hagler. "Bring the troops home now! Stop the war! Come together in unity and let's begin to bring into existence the peace! God bless you." A tearful Hassan Juma'a—not usually one for open displays of emotion—rushed forward to hug the reverend, and was joined quickly by the other five unionists.[33]

Before their departure the Iraqi unionists drafted a joint statement with USLAW opposing the occupation and privatization, calling for the repeal of Saddam's 1987 law banning unions, and asserting their shared belief that a strong, free, democratic labor movement is the bedrock of democracy. "We commit ourselves to strengthening the bonds of solidarity and friendship between working people of our two countries," concluded the statement.[34]

Four months later sixteen resolutions were presented to the AFL-CIO's convention, calling for a rapid end to the occupation of Iraq. Given the federation's conservative history, Michael later recounted, "many people in the labor movement just thought we were nuts: this was not going to happen. But we had a strategy based on bottom-up organizing. And when we got to the convention we had enough influence on the floor of that convention that we were able to steer a resolution to the floor."[35]

After negotiations with USLAW activists, the AFL-CIO's leadership agreed to support the resolution, which passed without opposition thanks to many months of organizing by activists and to the inspiration provided to grassroots American workers by meeting the Iraqi unionists. "Once that happened," Michael said, "it changed the entire posture of USLAW in the labor movement. Our credibility went through the roof." It marked a turning point not just for U.S. public opposition to the war but also for solidarity with Iraqi civil society.

# 11

# Now It Becomes Legal

*Actually, there was no policy after 2003, nothing at all. Only personal adventures and endeavors, no institutional or collective work. The men in the kitchen . . . represented their own personal, party, ethnic, or sectarian interests. . . . Before, with the de-Ba'athification, the problem was political. With the constitution, it becomes legal.*

—Dhia'a al-Bakkaa, former director general,
Iraqi State Oil Marketing Organization[1]

If there had been a good time to resolve the nature of the Iraqi state and economy, it ought to have been during the drafting of the country's constitution. Should oil, which utterly dominated the economy, remain in the public sector or be privatized? Iraq's interim constitution of 1970, which was in force prior to the 2004 Transitional Administrative Law, states that "natural resources and the basic means of production are owned by the People. They are directly invested [in] by the Central Authority in the Iraqi Republic, according to exigencies of the general planning of the national economy."[2] The constitutions of Iraq's neighbors Kuwait and Iran also carefully guard public ownership of their oil.[3]

However, during the drafting of the Iraqi constitution in 2005 the provisions dealing with public ownership were not considered for removal or replacement; they were not discussed at all. Instead, Iraq's new politicians were far more interested in the question of which of them would control the country's oil wealth.

## The Election

The January 2005 election, which determined the composition of the parliament that would oversee the writing of the constitution, could hardly have delivered a worse result: 215 of the 275 seats were won by parties with an explicitly sectarian or ethnic agenda—140 Shi'a and 75 Kurdish. And those parties represented just two of Iraq's three principal communities, most Sunni Arabs having boycotted the election to protest the destruction of Fallujah. Ayad Allawi won 40 seats.

Like the Kurds, the Shi'a members were organized into a single bloc. In late 2004 Grand Ayatollah Sistani had called on the Shi'a Islamist parties to fight the election as a coalition, which became known as the United Iraq Alliance (UIA). At the top of the UIA's electoral list was Abdul-Aziz al-Hakim, who had taken over as head of the Iran-founded Supreme Council for the Islamic Revolution in Iraq (SCIRI) after his brother's death in 2003. SCIRI was both the most organized of the Shi'a parties and also the best able to exploit its connections with the religious hierarchy in Najaf. The other major party in the coalition was Da'wa, the party founded by Muhammad Baqr al-Sadr and now led by Ibrahim al-Ja'afari.

As war approached in 2002 and early 2003, SCIRI had maintained an ambiguous relationship with the United States based on their common hatred of Saddam Hussein and pragmatic desire for power, tempered with a strong mutual distrust. Nonetheless, SCIRI was sufficiently connected in the exile community to win a place on the Iraq Leadership Council, and in turn in the rotating presidency of Paul Bremer's Iraqi Governing Council. Bremer gave political officer Meghan O'Sullivan the job of building a relationship with SCIRI. "I approached it by venturing into Baghdad and talking to people who happened to be near SCIRI signs," she told me. "I would ask them, 'Do you know anyone in this political party and can you bring me to their house to meet them?'"[4]

During the course of Bremer's rule, O'Sullivan's efforts transformed a wary relationship into mutual cooperation. One focus of her charm offensive was Adil Abdul-Mahdi, the party's second-in-command. A trained economist, he was seen as more Westernized and pragmatic than many other Islamists, having lived in France for more than twenty years. And his roots were secular: he had begun his political career as a Ba'athist, then joined the Iraq Communist Party when he fell out with the regime. After a brief flirtation with Maoism, he eventually sided with SCIRI. Bremer would use O'Sullivan as a go-between whenever his relationship with Abdul-Mahdi broke down. In later advocating Abdul-Mahdi for Iraqi prime minister in 2006, O'Sullivan would characterize him as "amiable" and "experienced."[5] Others in the U.S. administration worried about his links with Iran.

## A Managed Democracy

The absence of Sunnis was not the only unrepresentative feature of the new parliament. Apart from Allawi's party, with forty seats, and some smaller groups, there was no voice representing nationalist or secular attitudes. This was despite the fact that just four months before the election a poll had found 52 percent of Iraqis believed religion and politics should not interfere with each other.[6] And apart from a handful of seats held by allies of Muqtada al-Sadr, there was no voice critical of the occupation—even though large majorities of Iraqis favored withdrawal.[7]

One reason for the disconnect between the views of the elected parties and those of the people who elected them was that the rules of the election, which had been set by the interim constitution negotiated between Bremer and the Governing Council, the Transitional Administrative Law (TAL), made the entire country a single constituency. This ensured that the parties with a national profile had a large advantage over local political groupings, and the national political process up to that point had been dominated, by definition, by pro-occupation parties whose members had been appointed to first the Iraq Governing Council and then the interim government of Allawi. Those parties had in turn been chosen for their lack of Iraqi political base, being led by former exiles, so they would neither represent Iraqi points of view nor have the power to challenge the occupation even if they did. Furthermore, the Governing Council had been created on an identity basis so as to remove policy from politics.

It appears that the U.S. intention was to use the eighteen months of appointed government bodies in this way to establish their favored parties in Iraq before elections. Indeed, the CPA had resisted calls for early elections, warning, "Elections could create a legitimate counter authority to the CPA, making its ability to govern more difficult," and would "largely sacrifice Coalition control over the outcome."[8] In a memo in July 2002 Defense Secretary Rumsfeld compared the situation with the late stages of World War II, when Churchill and Roosevelt installed Charles de Gaulle's government-in-exile in liberated France, out of fear that otherwise "the Communist-dominated resistance would have been the only significant political force on the ground in the country. . . . [Instead] De Gaulle, in power from 1944–47, was able to expand his own political movement and effectively neutralize the Communists."[9]

The United States should manage Iraq's path to democracy, Rumsfeld said, by "consistently steer[ing] the process in ways that achieve stated U.S. objectives. The Coalition will not let a thousand flowers bloom." If it had let a thousand flowers bloom, those that bloomed largest or brightest likely would have been those that best represented Iraqi desires and interests. And on a range of questions, including oil and the continuation of the occupation, those would be fundamentally at odds with U.S. objectives. The longer the delay until elections, the better established would be the U.S. allies.[10]

Naturally, the United States had no desire to boost the anti-occupation constituency. Still, most in the U.S. administration—apart from Meghan O'Sullivan—did not welcome the dominance of the Shi'a Islamist parties, especially given their links with the United States' archenemy Iran. With Allawi defeated, the Americans were keen to find a new foil to offset those parties' influence, and this necessitated a change of strategy. Under viceroy Bremer and subsequently Ambassador John Negroponte, the approach had been to try to crush the "Sunni insurgency" in order to allow the political process to go ahead, while emphasizing the Shi'a-Kurdish character of the government. In the post-election situation, hawkish strategist Zalmay Khalilzad was appointed ambassador, tasked with bringing Sunnis back into the process. Faced with a sectarianized politics, the U.S. approach was thus to add a third pole to the divided scene. Since leaving Iraq at Bremer's insistence in 2003, after several months courting the exiled and Kurdish oppositions, Khalilzad had been ambassador to Afghanistan. He was of the region, a Muslim, and an Arabic-speaker, and so was chosen to broker a new political settlement.

## Profiting from Division

Since the fall of Saddam Hussein in April 2003, the Kurdish parties of Masoud Barzani and Jalal Talabani had been the most organized players on the Iraqi political scene, and the new constitution was their chance to formally decentralize more powers to the semiautonomous region they con-trolled. Not only were they the most unified bloc and the most tactically sophisticated in the negotiations, the process itself was stacked in their favor.[11] Through the 2004 Transitional Administrative Law (TAL) they had effectively secured a veto in the constitutional referendum, with a rule that the text could be rejected not only by a nationwide majority but also by a two-thirds majority in any three provinces. They could easily achieve this in Irbil, Dohuk, and Sulaymaniya. With this veto they would block any constitution that did not give them more autonomy than was provided in the TAL.

The most prominent of the Kurdish parties' international advisers was Peter Galbraith, the new Mr. Five Percent. "Adviser" significantly understates his role; in reality he was often a direct participant in negotiations and also wielded clout through his articles in the U.S. media and his ability to work the U.S. system. For example, at a late stage of the negotiations, a British treasury official noticed with alarm that the Iraqi national government had no power to levy taxes. "He was about to charge into a meeting of Iraq's politi-cal leaders," Galbraith wrote in his memoir, "when a quick-thinking Kurdish constitutional adviser grabbed an available Westerner—me—to explain the situation. The omission, I told him, was no mistake and he might want to consult with his ambassador before reopening an issue that could bring down Iraq's delicate compromise."[12]

In particular, he argued, any federal region must have control over its own oil contracts (such as his undeclared deal with DNO and the KRG). In one of the murkier episodes of post-2003 Iraq, he was in fact arguing for a political position that would happen to boost his business interests—which he would later value at over $250 million—while hastening the disintegration of Iraq and laying the ground for greater violence. The title of Galbraith's 2006 book, *The End of Iraq*, was not a lament but a policy proposal—and one that would help make him very rich. It was not until October 2009, through investigative work by the Norwegian financial newspaper *Dagens Næringsliv*, that Gal-braith's role in the DNO deal was publicly confirmed. The paper showed photographs of Galbraith walking his dog in Bergen and then sprinting away, dog in tow, when its reporters tried to challenge him.[13]

In his defense Galbraith has argued, "I undertook business activities that were entirely consistent with my long-held policy views. I believe my work with DNO (and other companies) helped create the Kurdistan oil industry

which helps provide Kurdistan an economic base for the autonomy its people almost unanimously desire."[14] But at the time no one knew about his
involvement in the DNO deal. Writing in the *New York Review of Books* and
the *New York Times*, he portrayed himself as an independent-minded advocate for justice for a wronged people and an unpaid adviser to the KRG.[15]

## In the Kitchen

The driving force of U.S. policy during the drafting of the constitution was
that the process must be completed by August 15, 2005, the deadline set in
the TAL. "That's the timetable," said President Bush during Prime Minister
Ibrahim Ja'afari's visit to the White House in late June. "And we're going to stay
on that timetable. And it's important for the Iraqi people to know we are."[16]

The U.S. administration argued that passage of a constitution and Iraq's
transition to democracy would quell the armed resistance, but the figures
flatly contradicted that belief. In the year following the departure of Paul
Bremer in June 2004, attacks on Coalition forces had risen steadily, from an
average of forty-seven a day to seventy in summer 2005. Improvised explosive
devices (IEDs) had become highly effective and were now accounting for
around half of U.S. troop deaths.[17] The idea that the constitution would serve
as a national compact was even less credible, as the election had excluded
precisely the constituency identified most strongly with the resistance/insur-
gency. Most of those involved in the constitutional negotiations believed
Bush's hurry had more to do with a desperate desire by his administration to
demonstrate progress to an increasingly skeptical U.S. public.

The TAL had envisaged six months to draft the constitution—February
to August 2005—which was already an unrealistic schedule. South Africa,
generally recognized as one of the best examples of post-totalitarian and
post-conflict constitution making, took two years—in more stable circumstances than Iraq. Ukraine took four years. Afghanistan took fifteen months.
But with two months of haggling over ministerial positions and policies, the
Iraqi government was not formed until April 28 and the constitution-drafting
committee a month later. Further bargaining eventually brought in Sunni
members, and the expanded committee held its first meeting on July 8. So it
had five weeks.

Meghan O'Sullivan returned to Iraq in July and suggested to Qasim

Daoud, a member of the drafting committee, that some of the details of the constitutional settlement could be decided after the constitution itself had been written. "This constitution, perhaps, may best be regarded as a framework document that does not seek to resolve every contentious political issue definitively," an embassy cable recorded her as saying.[18] This might have felt like a way of keeping everyone happy while sticking to the timetable, but it was at odds with precisely what constitutions are supposed to achieve—to resolve the major issues and to do so with some permanence.

On July 31 the chair of the constitution-drafting committee, Humam Hamoudi, indicated his desire to expand the time frame. That wish was shared by several senior committee members and also by representatives of Iraq's minorities and civil society groups. But Ambassador Khalilzad called private meetings with the political party leaders and insisted that the deadline must be met.[19] So no formal extension request was made. But on August 8 Hamoudi declared that his drafting committee could not complete the task in time. Now the only way to meet the deadline was to end the deliberative process and leave it to a deal among the leaders of the main political parties. In reality, only four leaders were invited: Abdul-Aziz al-Hakim of SCIRI and Ibrahim Ja'afari of Da'wa, both Shi'a; and Masoud Barzani and Jalal Talabani, both Kurds. Negotiations took place in the private homes of Hakim, Barzani, or Talabani, and sometimes in the U.S. embassy. Iraqis say that the constitution was produced "in the kitchen"—cooked up behind closed doors.

As well as transferring negotiations from the drafting committee to the kitchen, the rushed schedule also increased the U.S. role in brokering agreement between the leaders. Rather than considering the issues from first principles, the TAL became the starting point for discussion and amendment. According to one British official I spoke to, many of the provisions that had been debated and formulated by the committee were stripped out; in their place the negotiators "pasted in the provisions of the TAL."[20] Khalilzad shuttled between the four leaders, suggesting new text and trying to triangulate between their various positions and U.S. objectives. On August 12 the U.S. embassy even circulated its own draft of the constitution, proposing specific changes from the committee's version.[21] Clearly there was no time for public consultation or engagement with civil society.[22] With the official political process ever more divorced from the views of most Iraqis, a meaningful consultation would only have steered the constitution away from the type of text the United States would like to see. Even politicians—apart from the four party leaders—were excluded from drafting; the negotiation was between the United States and its four Iraqi allies.

Three of the Iraqis present were pushing for a similar vision of a divided Iraq. Adil Abdul-Mahdi of SCIRI had grumbled to U.S. diplomats in June that anything the Kurds had, the Shi'a should have too, and that the nine Shi'a-majority provinces in the south should be allowed to form a federal region with the same powers as Kurdistan.[23] Such a structure would give the dominant Shi'a parties, led by SCIRI, exclusive control over the vast oil wealth of southern Iraq. On August 11, four days before the constitution-drafting deadline, the plan went public when Hakim spoke to an orchestrated demonstration in Najaf, calling for such a Shi'a superregion. The effect would be to split Iraq into three ethno-sectarian regions: Kurdistan in the north and northeast, Shi'astan in the south, and Sunnistan in the west. In his comments to U.S. embassy staff, Abdul-Mahdi showed little concern that the Sunni region would be resource-poor and might only comprise two provinces.

The "three-state solution" had other proponents in the United States besides Peter Galbraith. Most prominent was Joseph Biden, then ranking member of the Senate Foreign Relations Committee, who the following year would co-author a New York Times op-ed calling for the establishment of "Kurdish, Sunni and Shiite regions [that] would each be responsible for their own domestic laws, administration and internal security."[24]

The idea reflected neither demographic reality nor the desires of most Iraqis outside Kurdistan. Most areas, especially cities, are mixed, comprising Shi'a, Sunnis, and Kurds. Baghdad and Kirkuk are the best-known examples, but even Basra in the far south traditionally had a sizable Sunni minority—up to 40 percent of the population before 2003, according to some estimates. A July 2005 survey by the International Republican Institute found that 69 percent of Iraqis thought "the new Iraqi constitution should establish a strong, central government," whereas only 22 percent believed "the new Iraqi constitution should give significant powers to regional governments." In southern areas the results followed the national figures, and in the Shi'a-majority Middle Euphrates, which includes the holy cities of Najaf and Karbala, 85 percent favored strong central government, versus just 5 percent for regionalization. Only in Kurdish areas did a majority favor empowering regional governments.[25] Nevertheless, in the first week after the constitution-drafting committee handed over to the kitchen, the leaders added a procedure for forming new regions and radically devolved power from the center to the regions.[26]

## Oil in the Constitution

The role of foreign oil companies in Iraq was not an issue during the constitutional negotiations as by this stage, more than two years into the occupation, genuinely representative voices were largely absent from the corridors of power. In the end the constitution committed Iraq to a foreign role in the oil sector in bland and vague terms: fields would be developed "using the most advanced techniques of market principles and encouraging investment."[27] More significant, though, was what was left out compared to Iraq's previous constitution and those of its neighbors. This was not a principled discussion of the nature of the country, its economy, and its politics, but rather a power struggle between a set of parties and individuals and the sects and ethnic groups they claimed to represent.

While the foreign role in the oil industry did not feature in the negotiations, the relative powers over oil of the center and regions were at their very heart. Would regional or national government manage the industry, including setting policy, awarding contracts to foreign companies, and overseeing operations? And who would receive the revenues from oil production and export? The final text of the constitution largely adopted the Kurdish parties' position, which had first been suggested to them by Galbraith in early 2004: that "current fields" would be managed by the national government in partnership with the regions and their revenues fairly shared, while management of "future fields" would devolve to the regions. As Galbraith pointed out, "Because there were no commercial oilfields within Kurdistan as defined by the March 18, 2003, boundaries, this proposal had the effect of giving Kurdistan full control of its oil," with the exception of the Kirkuk field, were Kirkuk ultimately to join the Kurdistan region.[28] At the same time, they would not lose their 17 percent allocation of national revenues derived from the major current fields elsewhere. In effect, the proposal gave them autonomy over oil in Kurdistan without relinquishing their stake in the rest of the country's oil.

Most experts believed the decentralization of the oil industry would be a disaster. In an open letter published in three Iraqi newspapers, eleven technocrats—each with between twenty-five and forty-eight years' experience in the sector—warned that as new fields were allocated to the regions, "the role of the central government in the production will be thus temporary depending on the life span of current fields. In the long term this means that the federal government's role will be limited to participating in the design of strategy for the sector. This is a marginal role compared to the regions."[29] Furthermore, they pointed out, the regions didn't have the technical skills, which would "weaken Iraq's bargaining position" when negotiating contracts.

Tariq Shafiq, who as a young engineer had rebelled against foreign arrogance (in chapter 1), was dismayed. Combining the favoring of "market principles and encouraging investment" with the decentralization of contracting, "a wholesale [sell-off] of Iraq's future oil riches is expected to go to IOCs' [international oil companies'] sole operations, effectively denationalizing Iraq's oil and gas assets. This would take Iraq back to . . . near total financial dependence on IOCs," he wrote.[30]

## Dismantling the State

Sunni negotiators were invited into the kitchen only on August 25, when they were presented with a finished package with all the main points agreed upon between the four Kurdish and Shi'a leaders. When the U.S. embassy suggested compromises, Adil Abdul-Mahdi "pushed back hard," according to a diplomatic cable. "The Sunni Arabs were impossible to deal with, and changing one part of the draft constitution might look easy but would cause dissatisfaction in the Shia community."[31] The constitution would therefore go forward to a referendum without support from the Sunni politicians.

Khalilzad was desperate to get at least one Sunni party to endorse the draft to prevent it from being seen as representing only two of the three major communities and to reduce the risk that the three-province rule, originally designed to give the Kurds a veto, could derail the constitution through a Sunni rejection in the referendum. He finally succeeded in persuading the Iraq Islamic Party—a Sunni Islamist party that had had a representative on the Governing Council—to support the constitution by adding a clause that the document would be reviewed within the first six months of the new parliament.

In the event, on October 15 people in the Kurdish and Shi'a majority areas voted overwhelmingly in favor of the constitution; the vast majority of Sunnis voted against it. Al-Anbar and Salah ad-Din provinces returned "no" votes of 97 and 82 percent, respectively. But in the more mixed province of

Ninawa (Mosul), 55 percent voted against it (and in Diyala the "no" vote was 49 percent), so only two, rather than three, provinces achieved the two-thirds majority "no" vote necessary to block the constitution. The ethnic and religious split in the vote was a sign of how the sectarianization of politics at the center was feeding through to the electorate. Most newspapers and TV stations were run by political parties, as were local services, so Iraqis' principal sources of information were filtered through the parties.

Addressing the Iraqi people, President Bush said, "Thank you for doing what is right, to set the foundations for peace for future generations to come."[32]

In fact, the failed constitutional process delivered precisely the opposite result. The resulting document offered little to bind the country. It did not define a national identity, nor did it create a functioning state structure. It was supported by two of Iraq's major communities while being rejected by almost all members of the third. Its drafting had not engaged ordinary Iraqis; the different visions for the future of Iraq had simply not been debated. It was explicitly impermanent, with a review process written in, while contentious points—including key issues such as the role and structure of the upper house of the parliament, presidential deputies, and the Supreme Court—were left ambiguous or vague, and deferred to future legislation to resolve.[33] An internal report by the UN team advising on the constitution noted that the list of exclusive powers granted to the national government "does not include all the powers that are necessary for a stable functioning of the State." The constitution did not address powers of taxation and policing. It made no provisions regarding regulation of the environment, animal diseases, and air traffic control, nor management of interstate relations regarding water.[34]

The influential conflict resolution organization International Crisis Group noted in unusually immoderate language:

> The disparate class of former exiles and expatriates that has ruled Iraq since the war and has drafted both the TAL and the current constitution is virtually as out of touch with popular sentiment as it was in April 2003. Some are seen, with a certain justification, as carpet-baggers intent on capitalising on skills learned in exile. Others have proved incapable of bridging the yawning gap between their worldview and that of most Iraqis, who have never had the chance to express themselves freely, develop their political views or travel outside the country.[35]

Peter Galbraith, however, was delighted. "Iraq's constitution has two great virtues: first, it provides a structure for Iraq's Shiites and Sunni Arabs to form their own institutions of self-government that may facilitate economic development. . . . Second, the constitution provides a formula to resolve the contentious issues that could widen Iraq's civil war."[36] Less than six weeks after the constitution was approved, in late November 2005, the DNO project in which Galbraith held a 5 percent stake began drilling its first well.

# 12

# Iraq Divided

*In essence, many politicians now engaged in backroom bargaining are ultimately embroiled in a resource conflict—rather than a conflict of ideas and visions. What has been lost is even a minimal sense of a common national interest.*
—Kamil Mahdi, University of Exeter, summer 2007[1]

By summer 2006 numerous unofficial checkpoints had sprung up across Baghdad, manned by militiamen in police uniforms. The way to survive these checkpoints was to accelerate through them. If you stopped, your tortured, mutilated body would be found on a trash heap the following day.

There were also official checkpoints. At these you had to stop. If you didn't, and if they didn't manage to shoot you as you sped through, they'd call in U.S. air support, which would rip open your vehicle, and you, with a single missile.

On a daily basis, Baghdad residents had to make the choice: two pedals, accelerator and brake, one for life and one for death, and at best a few seconds to decide which to press.

## To Be an Iraqi

Ali, an architect, left Baghdad in late 2006. After receiving a scrawled note threatening to kill him, he knew it was time to go. A few weeks later, in a café in Amman, he told me about his experience registering as a refugee after he entered Jordan.

"What's your religion?" asked a UN official.

"Muslim."

"Are you Shi'a or Sunni?"

"Just Muslim."

"Look, I have to write something on this form. Shall I put Shi'a?" The note of frustration in the official's voice indicated that he regularly had to deal with this answer.

"What about ethnicity? Arab, Kurd, Turkoman . . . ?"

"I am Iraqi," Ali replied.

It's a common story. Most Iraqis are proud of their country's ethnic and religious diversity, which, along with its ancient and Islamic history, is part of its national identity. And when it comes to religious sect, as we have seen, the dividing lines aren't nearly as neat as many in the West seem to imagine.

By 2006, however, identity had become communalized through fear. Especially in Baghdad and central Iraq, Shi'a people had come to live in Shi'a areas, protected by Shi'a militias from Sunni killers. And vice versa. This duality sat uncomfortably on Iraq's uneven terrain of identity. Mixed families—of which there were many—had to keep quiet. Some people carried two identity cards so that they could show either a Shi'a name or a Sunni one, as required. Abu Ghaith, a painter from Baghdad who also escaped to Jordan, was born in Najaf and is a member of the Jumayli clan, which is mostly Sunni. "I was chased by all sides," he told me—for being from Shi'a-dominated Najaf and for having a Sunni background. "Before 2003 I felt a patriot, an Iraqi. You can't pay your bills, but you have a dignity as an Iraqi. But afterwards I lost my identity, even when I was still in Iraq. I felt alienated from the country."[2]

Despite Iraqis' unwillingness to think of themselves in categorical terms, foreigners could not see beyond sect and ethnicity. In summer 2008 I gave a presentation on Iraqi oil developments to a British energy studies group. The chair told me that a few weeks earlier they had heard "the Sunni perspective" in a presentation by former oil minister Issam al-Chalabi. This struck me as odd. I knew Issam al-Chalabi reasonably well but had no idea what his religion was. He had never spoken of it, and in his public presentations and written papers his position was technocratic and nationalist. Would the chair have introduced me as giving "the British perspective" or even, relying on my family background, "the Christian perspective"? Why was it so difficult to imagine that Iraqis might have views that were not sectarian?

A year earlier I had encountered the same problem in another context. Through 2006 and 2007, while working at Platform, I felt that the views of ordinary Iraqis were being excluded from the mainstream debate about oil policy, which instead was being negotiated between the United States, multinational oil companies, and various Iraqi political elites. I was part of an international campaign of antiwar and human rights groups calling for decisions on the country's oil to be made democratically by Iraqis without outside interference. We decided to survey and publicize Iraqi views. Polls were regularly looking at Iraqi opinions on a range of issues—security, the occupation, the performance of the government—but none had asked about oil, the driving force behind the economy.

The poll, conducted in summer 2007, found that by a majority of two to one, Iraqis wanted their oil to be managed by Iraqi state-owned bodies rather than foreign companies. Only 4 percent of Iraqis felt they had been given "totally adequate" information about oil plans, with 76 percent considering the information they had received "inadequate."[3] The shocking feature of the poll was not its results but its methodology. I had asked to see it beforehand, but the polling company sent it only after the poll had been conducted. Along with our questions the poll contained demographic items, some of them quite straightforward—age, marital status, and so on. When it came to ethnicity, however, there was a note to the questioner: "If respondent is reluctant to answer, probe for response, as 'It is important for my supervisor, who is checking my work.'" On religion, the questioner was instructed, "If respondent says Muslim ask: 'Do you consider yourself to be Sunni or Shi'a?'" And then, "If respondent is Muslim and refused to be classified as Sunni or Shi'a, please enter your [the questioner's] estimate of whether he or she is Sunni or Shi'a." The gathered data did not record those who considered themselves simply Muslim. Respondents were pressed to choose Sunni or Shi'a, and if they declined to do so, their category would be chosen for them. Peacefully or violently, Iraqis were being forced into these categories.

## Divide and Rule?

As we have seen, at the time of the war sectarian attitudes were present in Iraq to a limited degree, but after 2003 these dramatically intensified, and ethnic and religious identity became the dominant feature of Iraqi politics. "The first time Iraqis heard of ethnic divisions was when Iraq got invaded," said Hassan Juma'a (who is Shi'a and whose wife is Sunni). "We do not deal according to religion or ethnicity. I am fifty-three years old and never heard of these divisions before." The roots of the problem for Hassan lay elsewhere: "If the U.S. did not whip up divisions, they could not divide and rule."[4]

So to what extent was he right about the divisions being whipped up by the United States? In the early weeks of the occupation identity-based politics was introduced to Iraq through the quota system of the Iraq Governing Council, set up by Paul Bremer and his head of governance, the State Department's Ryan Crocker. Members could participate only on behalf of an ethnic or religious group and not to represent their political ideas or constituencies. This suited the exiles who now took power. With no base in Iraq, appealing to sectarian identity was the only way they could succeed in elections.

In 2010, I asked Meghan O'Sullivan if she accepted the criticism that early CPA decisions enshrined sectarianism in Iraq. "I think it is only partially valid," she replied. "It is true that the division of positions by ethnicity or sectarianism began with the Governing Council." But while she recognized the political problems that caused, she argued that it was a necessary outcome, because the CPA had established "a high priority in seeing that the Shi'a community—more than half the population—participated in the political process. And they would only do so if they were assured that a majority of the seats of the Governing Council went to Shi'a members. So while this did set an unhealthy precedent, the 'Iraqi math' came about not from naïveté, but out of a necessity of bringing the Shi'a on board."[5] The argument seemed to me circular.

Meanwhile, a vacuum was being created into which these ethno-sectarian forces stepped. First the looting, then the far-reaching and zealous de-Ba'athification, and finally the occupation's insistence on control even while it lacked the capacity to assert it—all of these factors emasculated the institutions of state. The army, a principal symbol of Iraq's nationhood, was dismantled. And finally the 2005 constitution, as we saw in the previous chapter, failed to articulate a national identity or establish a functioning apparatus of state. Instead, as its ethnic and sectarian drafters squabbled for their piece of the pie, the constitution formalized a divided politics. There was now no effective state over whose direction politicians could compete, no purpose to bind Iraqis, no national basis for power or decision making. Its people, land, and assets were for the taking—by parties, sectarian leaders, and militias.

This suited the United States—as long as Iraqi leaders were fighting over subnational interests, the overall direction of the country could be shaped from outside. But by 2006 the divisions had spawned violence to the extent that the country became ungovernable by anyone. Whatever strategic benefits there may have been in dividing Iraqis, whatever respite was gained by diverting violence inward and away from coalition forces, whatever legitimacy had been garnered by turning public attention from rejection of an unwanted occupation to wanton intercommunal killing, whatever excuse was made for the continual presence of an impartial foreign policeman—U.S. interests were not served by the levels of uncontrolled slaughter that eventually broke out. The Bush administration faced growing political pressure at home to withdraw from an unmanageable situation. At times U.S. and U.K. forces did try to prevent the fighting. At others their policies and military strategies worsened it. But whenever given the choice between minimizing Iraqi social divisions and maintaining control over the country, the United States consistently chose the latter, as we saw in chapter 9 in the response to cooperation between fighters from (Shi'a) Najaf and (Sunni) Fallujah.

## Three Phases of Killing

Feeding off the new politics of communal self-interest, sectarian violence escalated in three phases. The first phase, lasting from summer 2003 to early 2005, was characterized primarily by jihadist terrorist attacks on Shi'a religious symbols. On August 29, 2003, a massive car bomb killed the head of SCIRI, Muhammad Baqir al-Hakim, along with nearly a hundred others, as he exited the Imam Ali shrine in Najaf. Six months later, on March 2, 2004, at least five suicide bombs exploded in the shrine cities of Karbala and Kadhimiya during the Ashura processions to commemorate the death of Imam Husayn, killing 270 people. Both attacks were blamed on Abu Musab al-Zarqawi's organization, Tawhid wal-Jihad (Monotheism and Holy War), which would in October 2004 become al-Qaeda in Iraq. For the most part, during this phase, these attacks failed to achieve their aim of provoking Shi'a retribution.

Most attacks on Sunnis came instead from American forces. U.S. leaders saw the greatest threat to peace in Iraq as an insurgency—against the new democratic order, as they saw it—rather than a sectarian conflict and so did not shy away from characterizing their enemies as "Sunni." Patrols were explicitly focused in Sunni areas, houses were raided, and bombs dropped. Arrests were made using broad and undiscriminating sweeps. In 2005 more than 75 percent of Iraqi detainees held by the United States were Sunni Arabs, compared to around 20 percent of the population as a whole.[6] A team from the International Committee of the Red Cross reported in February 2004 that it had been told by military intelligence officers that between 70 and 90 percent of detainees were innocent of what they had been accused of and had been arrested by mistake.[7] The result was an overwhelming sense of persecution of the Sunni community by U.S. forces and their Shi'a and Kurdish allies.

At the same time the CIA was training Iraq's new parties (who were mostly organized on sectarian lines) in lethal operations, according to an exposé by Knight Ridder journalists Hannah Allam and Warren Strobel. Immediately after the fall of Saddam, the CIA recruited agents from SCIRI, Da'wa, the two Kurdish parties, Ahmad Chalabi's Iraqi National Congress, and Ayad Allawi's Iraqi National Accord and taught them how to turn raw intelligence into targets that could be used for operations.[8]

From summer 2004 the resistance to the occupation began to broaden its approach from relatively unproductive attacks on well-protected Americans to hitting softer Iraqi targets who could be labeled collaborators: politicians and the nascent police and army. The attacks were mostly labeled by their perpetrators as acts of resistance but by the authorities as sectarian. The new police forces were predominantly Shi'a and to a large extent saw themselves as such, partly because they were selected by Shi'a political leaders, partly because the United States continued to talk of a Shi'a government and a Sunni insurgency.

The second phase of sectarian conflict began with the appointment of the transitional government of Prime Minister Ibrahim al-Ja'afari in April 2005. The United States' key ally SCIRI, as the leader of the Shi'a UIA coalition, was now the country's most powerful party and was determined to gain control of the security apparatus. SCIRI conceded the prime ministership to Da'wa's al-Ja'afari in return for appointing its own Bayan Jabr Solagh as interior minister. Solagh quickly replaced officers of the police and security forces with leaders from the Badr Organization—SCIRI's militia—who were often promoted above their experience and abilities. A month after the new government took office Firas al-Nakib, a Sunni and a senior legal adviser in the Interior Ministry, told McClatchy reporter Tom Lasseter that more than

160 senior members of the ministry had been dismissed and many police commanders replaced by members of Badr or others associated with SCIRI. "They are putting in battalion commanders who are loyal to one idea and not the whole country," Nakib said.[9] Sunni members of the forces were intimidated and many resigned, only to be replaced by additional Shi'a recruits.[10]

Soon after SCIRI took over the Interior Ministry, its Special Police Commandos began targeting Sunni civilians. In one of the first such attacks, on May 5, 2005, they raided a vegetable market outside Baghdad and arrested fifteen Sunni men. The men's blindfolded bodies were found in a mass grave nearby with smashed skulls, marks of burns and beatings, and their right eyeballs removed.[11] By summer 2005 there were increasing numbers of reports of people detained by the police commandos turning up as corpses in Baghdad's morgues a few days later.[12] In July 2005, according to John Pace, chief of the UN Human Rights Office in Iraq, Baghdad's morgue received eleven hundred bodies, up to three-quarters of which bore evidence of torture or summary execution,[13] compared to a monthly average of three hundred in 2002.[14] "It's being done by anyone who wishes to wipe out anybody else for various reasons," said Pace, "but the bulk are attributed to the agents of the Ministry of the Interior," which he described as "acting as a rogue element within the government."

The first official U.S. and U.K. expressions of concern came on November 13, 2005, when 170 detainees were found in a secret Interior Ministry bunker in Baghdad, kept in inhumane conditions. According to Ambassador Khalilzad, more than a hundred of them had been abused.[15] A month later a unit of the new Iraqi army raided a second detention center, finding 625 detainees, at least twelve of whom had been subjected to "severe torture" according to Iraqi officials. The techniques used included extracting fingernails, applying electric shocks to genitals, and beating until bones were broken.[16] The bunkers were run by the notorious Wolf Brigade of the Special Police Commandos. In spite of the Interior Ministry's involvement in sectarian cleansing and tortore under SCIRI, the party remained the United States' top ally in Iraq.

Meanwhile, some Sunni elements of the resistance, which had previously targeted occupation forces and their perceived collaborators, began to converge in 2005 with al-Qaeda. In part it was the Americans who unwittingly strengthened their principal foe. So concerned were they with controlling the country that they treated the nationalist resistance and jihadists as a common enemy, which helped drive the two together and encourage sympathy among Sunnis for attacks against the "Shi'a/Kurdish" government as well as the Americans themselves. As the pro-American Sheikh Tariq al-Abdullah put it to me, "They are using this same word against the resistance—they call them insurgents—and they call al-Qaeda insurgents. But there is a *big* difference."[17] For him, despite his sympathy for and business interests in the West, the tribes of al-Anbar province supported the resistance because the Americans were behaving as occupiers, not as liberators.

The third phase of sectarian violence was the bloodiest. Whereas in the first two phases the principal actors were known, in the third few victims even knew who their assailants were. In Baghdad especially, Iraqis feared attack from any quarter.

At 6:55 a.m. on February 22, 2006, explosives were remotely detonated on the four supporting columns of the golden dome at the al-Askari shrine in Samarra. A fifth charge exploded just beneath the dome, which collapsed. The once-lustrous beacon of the city's skyline, containing 72,000 gold tiles, was reduced to a shattered dull-brick skeleton. Mosaics covering the walls of the shrine were blown apart, littering the area with rubble. The ninth-century shrine, third-holiest site of Shi'a Islam, contains the tombs of the tenth and eleventh imams, Ali al-Hadi and Hassan al-Askari. Next door, in the same complex, is the Blue Mosque, under which is the cellar from which the twelfth ("hidden") imam Muhammad al-Mahdi disappeared. The blast ignited Shi'a fury and tore through the country's social fabric.

Rumors abounded about the perpetrators of the attack. Officially, the bombing was blamed on al-Qaeda, but unlike with many other high-profile attacks, the group did not claim responsibility and denied involvement. Construction minister Jasim Muhammad Ja'afar remarked, "The bombing was technically well conceived and could only have been carried out by specialists."[18] He estimated that it would have taken at least twelve hours to drill the holes into the pillars where the explosives were placed, which would imply complicity from local security forces. The shrine's caretaker reported that just before the eight o'clock curfew the night before, men wearing the uniform of Interior Ministry commandos had entered the building, beaten him, and locked him in a room, from which he could hear drilling all night.[19]

Religious and political leaders called for calm, urging their followers not to take revenge. They were not heeded, and levels of violence, especially in

Baghdad, radically escalated. Immediately afterward Sunni leaders reported that more than twenty Sunni mosques were attacked.[20] In the week after the al-Askari shrine was bombed, up to thirteen hundred died in sectarian tit-for-tat killings.[21] The Jaysh al-Mahdi, despite Sadr's earlier efforts to bridge the sectarian divide, became involved. Over the next eighteen months its black-clad units became the most prolific killers in the worsening sectarian cleansing of Baghdad. There were increasing indications that large parts of the Jaysh al-Mahdi were no longer under the control of Muqtada al-Sadr; however, he declined to condemn attacks on Sunnis, instead responding to accusations of his followers' involvement with counteraccusations of Sunni atrocities.[22] Militias that had been set up to fight the occupation were drawn into the sectarian fighting in self-defense. New militias sprang up to protect communities or to pursue other agendas.

The sectarianization of politics and of the streets merged as militias served political interests. Most major parties had their own forces to settle scores with rivals or seek advantage in ever more complex struggles. The largest were SCIRI's Badr Organization, Sadr's Jaysh al-Mahdi, and the Kurdish Peshmerga. "Control equals money and power," a U.S. military officer told journalists from the *Times* of London.[23] "The more districts your ethnic group controls, the more potential influence you will have in the Council of Representatives and the government of Iraq through legal and non-legal means."

Residents could only speculate who was behind four-wheel-drive vehicles that turned up in communities to carry out targeted killings. Death came from every direction. As with the occupying forces, the acceptance of collateral damage was rationalized as self-preservation trumped compassion and as the attainment of idealistic goals gave way to the pursuit of power and control. Militias no longer operated only defensively but went on the attack to preemptively kill perceived enemies. In some places sectarian cleansing took the form of terrorizing the "enemy" into submission. Whereas "shock and awe" had sought the same end with unmatchable levels of firepower, the death squads employed sheer savagery.

Some used methods inspired by Saddam Hussein: a single bullet, execution-style, to the back of the head, or torture with electric drills. For others, even these were no longer shocking enough, and instead new horrors of symbolism were created. Fruit crates filled with severed heads would appear in the street. One story told of a son kidnapped, his decapitated body returned to the family's doorstep with a metal tap attached to his aorta at the top of his severed neck.

Across Baghdad drifted the stench of death. No one cleared the piles of trash or animal corpses for fear that they contained IEDs; some of these piles also concealed human bodies. Elsewhere, corpses were dumped in ditches or backstreets. At 120 degrees Fahrenheit, they rotted quickly.

The initial spectacular acts of terror gave way to a grim routine of everyday violence. In July 2006 more than 3,400 civilians were killed, straining the ability of the morgues to keep up. In Baghdad alone more than sixty people were killed every day.[24]

## Militias Enter the Oil Business

The militias grew stronger as the violence spiraled and as fearful residents saw them as the only protection available. They targeted members of the other sect within their neighborhoods, out of fear that the other might harbor rival militias and also to consolidate their control over territory. Baghdad's mixed neighborhoods became increasingly homogeneous, and militias used their control of an area to accumulate wealth from seized property, protection money, unofficial taxes, and corruption. The proceeds of these activities made the militias even stronger as they invested in weapons and salaries for new recruits. The identities and aims of the groups with nationalist, sectarian, political, or criminal motives blurred.

Outside Baghdad the most lucrative militia activity was oil and fuel smuggling. A June 2006 report by the Iraqi Oil Ministry's inspector general described some of their methods. A smuggler would fill up a tanker truck with fuel from an Iraqi depot at subsidized prices. Rather than delivering it to a gas station, he would then cross the border into Iran, Syria, or Turkey, where the load could be sold at a much higher price. Returning to Iraq, sometimes with a tankful of water instead, he would bribe officials at the original destination to sign his documents stating that he had delivered the fuel.[25]

Some groups coordinated their smuggling activities with attacks on the oil infrastructure. For instance, blowing up a fuel pipeline forced more to be transported by truck; damaging a refinery or its crude oil supply pipeline required more to be imported. Both tactics fed the smuggling trade. Frequently the tankers were escorted by police cars, the drivers taking a cut, as

they crossed the border. "We use the same methods we used during Saddam. Instead of Ba'athists and generals, it is now Shi'a militias and their
cronies who are doing the business," a smuggler in Basra told Ghaith Abdul-
Ahad of the *Guardian*.[26] It was easy to smuggle refined fuel products, but far
more profitable was smuggling crude oil, either by carrying extra, unme-
tered volume or by showing fake paperwork authorizing a shipment.

Officials were bribed at every stage of the supply chain and then employed for protection of the load. "It depends on the officials manning the
terminal when the tanker arrives. Usually it's a committee of three to four;
they are all of one party. Your contact with that party arranges everything in
advance," said the captain of a smuggling vessel. "If we are arrested by the
Iraqi Navy, it's easy. They are involved in the party, after all."[27]

In August 2006 the U.S. special inspector general for Iraq reconstruction
estimated that oil smuggling and corruption amounted to $4 billion a year,
around 10 percent of Iraq's GDP.[28] And the Iraqi government estimated that
up to half of this went to the militias.[29] Corruption appeared to go to the
heart of the Oil Ministry. On May 2, 2006, days before a new government
took over, a fire in the ministry building destroyed large sections of the finance department, including its records. Ministry officials blamed a power
surge on a tea urn, prompting cartoons in Iraqi newspapers satirizing "terrorist electric cables."[30] But, despite the black humor, things would get a lot
worse as the militias grew ever more powerful.

# PART THREE

# The Oil Law Struggle
# 2006–2007

# 13

# A Law to End All Laws

*The arbitration is in Paris not in Baghdad. And the Paris Chamber of Commerce works according to the letter of the contract. So you will be standing as the great state of Iraq, 31 million people, in front of a BP executive who says to you, "Well, I don't think you are right."*

—Faleh al-Khayat[1]

In order to help Iraqi policy makers "understand what would be needed to have a successfully functioning [oil] industry,"[2] on April 4, 2006, the United Nations arranged a three-day meeting on the shores of the Dead Sea in Jordan. The meeting venue, the Jordan Valley Marriott, is the most luxurious of the five upmarket hotels at the northeast corner of the world's saltiest sea. While most Jordanians head for the public beach a couple of miles south, this patch of shoreline is reserved for wealthy Gulf Arab and Western tourists. At the Marriott they are pampered with five restaurants, well-watered gardens, and the safe exoticism of professional belly dancers and *shisha* waiters.

The UN Assistance Mission to Iraq (UNAMI) had focused on helping the Iraqis write their constitution the previous year. Now, with the messy constitution passed, it turned its attention to the six-month review of the text. The Dead Sea meeting was one of a series of UNAMI-sponsored meetings for Iraqi politicians to talk through the most contentious issues. Until that point I had seen the United Nations as a neutral broker, playing a constructive role, respectful (in contrast to the United States and Britain) of the Iraqi right to lead in decision making. On the constitution, it was para-doxically that approach that had made the UN ineffective: while the United States was ordering the Iraqis around, the noncoercive UN ended up with little impact on the process, despite its best efforts.

But this meeting was different. Of the thirteen speakers on the original agenda, only one was Iraqi. Five of the others came from the World Bank and two from the British government's Department for International Devel-opment (DFID). Mike Francino, representing DFID, had previously led the Iraq team for Adam Smith International, the consultancy arm of the Adam Smith Institute, a pro-privatization think tank. Another speaker was Roland Priddle, a former Canadian energy regulator who was appointed to the Ca-nadian Petroleum Hall of Fame in 2001 because, while working for the government, he "played a central role in breaking old Canadian habits of government intervention in the petroleum industry, and in doing so earned respect throughout the Canadian oil and gas community."[3]

Not everyone in UNAMI approved of this lineup, and at least one staff member pressed for greater participation by Iraqi experts. One of the result-ing invitations was sent to Kamil Mahdi, an Iraqi-British economist at the University of Exeter. Kamil replied in an e-mail to the organizers:

> This is one of the worst talking-down "workshops" I can imagine. It reeks of racism and colonialist arrogance. . . . There is not a single Arab, Iranian, Venezuelan or other expert [on the agenda]. There is no one from OPEC or OAPEC* or even from the hapless UN itself, and no expertise on developing countries.

Kamil's intervention sent the UNAMI team scrambling to reclaim legiti-macy for the event. At the last minute Iraqi experts were added as speakers, including Tariq Shafiq and Issam al-Chalabi, an Amman-based technocrat (unrelated to Ahmad Chalabi) who served as oil minister from 1987 to 1990, one of the very few to have risen through the ranks of the ministry rather than being appointed for his party loyalty.†

Under the hastily reworked agenda, it turned out to be the Iraqis who lec-tured their intended advisers about how the oil should be managed. I arrived

---

*The Organization of Arab Petroleum Exporting Countries.
†Unrelated to Ahmad Chalabi.

for the last day of the conference to find something I'd never seen before: World Bank experts subdued, almost shy, chastened. The day before, the Iraqis at the meeting had even questioned outright whether Iraq needed external capital to develop its oil, or whether it could instead be done with Iraq's own resources. After all, the costs of developing Iraqi oil were so low and the returns so high that a relatively small outlay would quickly be returned, generally within three to five months of production coming onstream.[4]

Issam al-Chalabi was speaking as I arrived. He argued that now was not the time to make decisions about long-term contracts; Iraq should instead rebuild oil production from existing fields, using its own companies, money, and workforce, and make a decision on foreign investment later, after a few years. This point resonated with the Iraqis present. For now, according to al-Chalabi, the priorities should be to depoliticize the Ministry of Oil, reestablish INOC, and "put the right man in place [as minister] and let him get on with it."

Iraq could get loans from banks if it needed to, pointed out Khaled al-Mukhtar, a geology professor at Baghdad University. Most Iraqis, he said, were open to using multinational oil companies through technical service contracts, but not concessions or PSAs.

Tariq Shafiq spoke strongly against signing PSAs in the current circumstances, noting the ease of finding and extracting Iraqi oil. "Couldn't Iraq then hold on unnecessary long-term exploration PSA contracts for a few years or at least until stability prevails and big powers' pressure subsided?" he wrote in a paper.[5] "In the meantime, the industry can concentrate its capital investment and limited human resources on production capacity growth to bring in the necessary revenue."

These were not the conclusions that had been planned for the meeting.

## Evading Parliament

Until the December 2005 elections, no major multinational oil company had been willing to invest in Iraq. Companies wanted to ensure that their investments would last for decades, not be swept away by political changes, and be built on the foundations of contracts that could be enforced by international courts if necessary. In 2006 there was to be a permanent government that would be considered sovereign under international law. It seemed the companies' wait was nearing its end.

There was one other obstacle to signing contracts, however. In 1967 a law,

No. 97, had been passed to try to prevent a repeat of Iraq's unhappy experience with the Iraq Petroleum Company. It specified that for foreign companies to develop Iraqi oilfields, each contract would come into force only
when the parliament passed a specific law to ratify it.[6]* And although the
2005 constitution provided for Iraq's oil to be developed "using the most
advanced techniques of market principles and encouraging investment," it
also stated that this would be governed by legislation. Until that legislation
came into force and repealed the 1967 law, the restriction would still apply.

The requirement for parliamentary scrutiny was not an unreasonable one,
as oil exports provided around 95 percent of government revenue, and any
one oilfield contract could account for a significant percentage of that. Nor
was it unusual: parliamentary approval of major oil contracts is required in
both Venezuela and Russia, two of the three major oil countries that allow
foreign investment. And it is also required in other countries in the Mideast,
such as Syria, Egypt, and Yemen. But from the perspective of advocates of
foreign investment, this presented a challenge. If each contract could be approved, rejected, or amended by the parliament, that could open contracts to
an inconvenient degree of scrutiny, especially given Iraqis' natural suspicion
of foreign oil companies. Far less politically awkward would be for the parliament to pass a law delegating a general power to the executive branch of
government to sign contracts. Using that approach, the parliament would be
dealing with the abstract, rather than with real jobs, real oilfields, and real
revenues.

As Iraq approached the establishment of a permanent government, the
United States and Britain began to get the issue of an oil law onto the
agenda. In November 2005, even before the election, British ambassador
William Patey wrote a cable to London outlining "key issues which the next
government will need to address early on" and recommending lobbying of all
potential candidates for Iraqi prime minister so that when one was selected
he would already be briefed. Among these priorities was restructuring "the
oil industry . . . on a commercial basis, and preparing legislation to create
the right environment for private investment in it."[7]

One of the first formal calls for a new oil law came just eight days after

---

* All contracts signed since then—mostly the more limited service contracts—had been accord-
ingly ratified by parliament, even under Saddam.

Iraq's election, on December 23, 2005, when caretaker finance minister Ali Allawi (a cousin of Ayad Allawi) signed a financing agreement with the International Monetary Fund (IMF). Known as a Standby Arrangement, its purpose was not so much to raise funds (it created a reserve facility) as to demonstrate compliance with international requirements—yet it was signed a week after elections, when Allawi's mandate had expired.[8]

By 2003 Iraq had accumulated crippling debts to foreign lenders, incurred largely to pay for the war with Iran, Saddam's vanity projects, and interest accrued during the sanctions regime. The Paris Club of wealthy creditor countries conditionally agreed in November 2004 to reduce Iraq's debts to its members: by 30 percent immediately, a further 30 percent when Iraq entered into an agreement with the IMF, and a final 20 percent three years after the agreement, subject to a satisfactory report from the IMF. An alternative route would have been to apply the legal doctrine of "odious debt," under which a country becomes immune from paying its prior debts if they were incurred without the consent of the country's people and to their detriment. But the U.S. Treasury rejected this idea, perhaps for fear of setting a precedent.[9] The 2004 interim finance minister, Adil Abdul-Mahdi (of SCIRI), had agreed. "Iraq's need for very substantial debt relief derives from the economic realities," he said in an interview with *Euromoney* magazine. "Principles of public international law such as the odious debt doctrine, whatever their legal vitality, are not the reason why Iraq is seeking this relief."[10] He later added that lenders would be offered economic benefits for reducing Iraq's debts.[11] In other words, the deal came not through recognition of the injustice through which the debts were incurred under dictatorship but with economic strings attached. The details of those strings were set out in the December 2005 IMF agreement.

The most controversial of the IMF's conditions was the requirement to slash public subsidies on fuel—including cooking gas, lamp oil, and the diesel and gasoline crucial for keeping generators running when many Iraqis still got less than four hours of electricity per day. The resulting tripling of fuel prices, suddenly and without alternative social protection programs in place, led to protests on the streets and the resignation in January 2006 of Oil Minister Ibrahim Bahr al-Uloum. Largely unnoticed in the small print of the agreement was another condition: a December 2006 deadline for passing an oil law to "define the fiscal regime for oil and establish the contractual framework for private investment in the sector." It stated that IMF staff would review progress on the drafting in their quarterly review of the Iraqi government's performance.[12]

It was not just about making oilfield contracts legal (and without parliamentary scrutiny); there was also the question of what rights, powers, and obligations investors would have. Much as Western advisers liked to talk of an objective standard, a "modern" or "practical" way of doing things, there was in fact a range of possibilities. To what extent would the corporations be subject to Iraqi laws? How would the environmental impact of their activities or the safety of their workers be regulated? How would any future disagreements with the Iraqi government be resolved?

Multinational oil companies wanted more legal armor to ensure their profits would not be affected by future laws and other government actions. A new oil law—eventually backed up by an international treaty—would determine their rights and powers. So, as one of its first tasks, the new government would have to pass a new oil law "setting that framework that will attract the kind of investment it needs," said Ambassador Khalilzad in March 2006. "The oil companies will be very interested in ensuring how they have the support in terms of the legal rights to returns for their investment, and if there are any disagreements in contractual arrangements, how those are handled in courts and how they are enforced," he said. This would mean "ensuring that there is a robust system in place, that if you have an issue, a legal issue, that you take it to the courts, you have a sense of fairness in that process, and then also once you get a determination that that determination can be enforced appropriately."[13]

## An American Lawyer in Baghdad

After lunch at the UN meeting, I joined a few of the advisers who had retreated to the poolside to lick their wounds. From the terrace we could smell the Dead Sea's salt below. Fink Haysom, the South African head of the UN constitutional support team, was keen to hear about how Algeria had liberalized its oil and gas from Eliodoro Maygoro, a World Bank economist who had worked there. Algeria was becoming a favorite model for Iraq's advisers—an Arab country and OPEC member that had opened its natural resources (primarily gasfields) to multinationals on the back of the country's bloody civil war in the mid-1990s, and where BP now dominated the economy. "What Iraq needs is some twentysomethings who've just got their MBAs; *they* understand investment," Haysom sighed. "These old-school Iraqi nationalists just stop anything moving forward."

Across the table another adviser was keeping quiet; in fact, he'd said nothing all day. Ron Jonkers was listed as representing the "Iraq Ministry of Oil." In a way, he worked for the ministry, but that wasn't who paid his salary. Jonkers, an investment lawyer, worked for BearingPoint, the consultancy that had written the report in December 2003 for Rob McKee on how to develop Iraq's oil sector. BearingPoint and Jonkers had recently been enlisted by USAID to work on drafting the Iraqi oil law. This would appear to be in breach of the American Bar Association's rules, which state (rule 1.8), "A lawyer shall not accept compensation for representing a client from one other than the client unless . . . there is no interference with the lawyer's independence of professional judgment or with the client-lawyer relationship."

I introduced myself to Jonkers. "Yes, I know Platform," he told me. At the time my job was to research Iraqi oil policy and its likely consequences and to try to encourage debate among Iraqi civil society. But it was my previous work at Platform that Jonkers knew about, on BP's Baku-Tbilisi-Ceyhan pipeline. Platform had been part of an international campaign to prevent human rights violations and environmental damage being caused by the export pipeline for Caspian oil through Azerbaijan, Georgia, and Turkey. As assistant general counsel at the Overseas Private Investment Corporation (OPIC), Jonkers had been part of a team of lawyers that drew up a set of agreements to effectively put BP's pipeline above the law. "Without having to amend local laws, we went above or around them by using a treaty," said George Goolsby, head of the legal team, in 2002.[14] The treaty he referred to had been signed by the presidents of Azerbaijan, Georgia, and Turkey in Istanbul in November 1999, watched over by U.S. president Bill Clinton. The pipeline contracts—signed the following year, between the BP-led consortium and the three governments—became annexes of the Istanbul treaty.

The combined effect of the treaty and contracts became clear in November 2002, when BP proposed to build the pipeline through part of Borjomi-Kharagauli National Park, a protected nature reserve, site of a famous health spa, and also the source of Georgia's largest export, Borjomi mineral water. The country's environment minister, Nino Chkhobadze, protested that "BP representatives are requesting the Georgian Government to violate our own environmental legislation."[15] But, Chkhobadze would soon discover, that legislation was irrelevant.

The contract with BP set a firm deadline for the government to approve construction, subject only to BP's submission of the correct documents and not to government acceptance of their contents.[16] It exempted the project from any laws that applied stricter standards than the contract itself. Through the treaty, the contract had been lifted to the status of international law, which trumps any national laws. This is what George Goolsby meant by going above and around the laws. On November 30, 2002, the day of the deadline for approval, Chkhobadze was still insisting on the rerouting to avoid Borjomi. BP refused. The following day President Eduard Shevardnadze called the minister into his office and kept her there until she signed the approval. Chkhobadze was forced first to concede the Borjomi route with environmental conditions and then to water down her conditions. She finally emerged in the early hours of the morning.[17]

I was working on the campaign against the BTC pipeline when Chkhobadze was forced to back down. Despite the cynicism I had accumulated through years of researching the oil industry, I'd still not imagined it would be so easy to override national laws. My friend and colleague Nick Hildyard, though, was ahead of the game. Working for another environment, development, and human rights group called the Corner House, Nick was a master of using the law for campaigning. In fact, Nick was a master of using any opportunity available. When asked what he thought was the best campaigning manual, he once said his inspiration lay in Richmal Crompton's *Just William* series. The books, first published in 1922, describe the adventures of eleven-year-old schoolboy William Brown as he tries to subvert the authority of parents, teachers, or other adults (and usually succeeds). If you work for a campaigning charity, Nick said, you have almost no resources compared to your opponents, and the system is thoroughly stacked against you. So, like William, you have to exploit any tiny opportunity.

Working late into the night, sustained by endless hand-rolled cigarettes and strong coffee, Nick pored over contracts and investment treaties. Sometimes consulting a lawyer to check his interpretation, sometimes translating the dry legal language into real English, Nick saw what he called a new corporate colonialism unfold on the page. The longest section of the BTC pipeline ran through Turkey, which, Nick observed, was "now divided into three countries: the area where Turkish law applies, the Kurdish areas under official or de facto military rule, and a strip running across the entire length of the country, where BP is the effective government."[18] BP spokesman Barry Halton denied that the company was trying to circumvent legislation.

Eighteen months later, as I tracked events in Iraq in the oil industry magazines, I could see that the oil companies and their counterparts in the U.S. and British governments were talking about using the same legal provisions they'd utilized in Azerbaijan, Georgia, and Turkey. That's when I started looking more closely at Nick's work and began my own study of investment law. My research focused on PSAs, the type of contract that oil companies and Western advisers were advocating for Iraq.

## The Legal Frontier

Sitting with the advisers by the pool at the Jordan Valley Marriott in April 2006, I wondered what similar meetings Ron Jonkers and the others had attended five or ten years earlier in equally plush hotels, in Baku, Tbilisi, Moscow, or Almaty. For the oil multinationals, the collapse of the Soviet Union had smashed down a geographical frontier and opened up a treasure house of resources. Just as important, they had advanced across legal frontiers that elsewhere had defined the boundaries of foreign rights over resources under the postcolonial settlements of the mid-twentieth century. With the former Soviet republics rapidly embracing capitalism as they cast off the old ways, oil companies saw a blank sheet on which their lawyers would write new rules and set precedents to be rolled out around the world.

Under one of these rules, investor companies effectively became immune from new laws. Using a measure known as a stabilization clause, contracts froze, or "stabilized," the body of law with which investors had to comply. If a government wanted to pass a new law affecting investors at any point during the length of a contract—which could be up to forty years—it had to either exempt investors from the law or pay the cost of their complying.[19] So, for example, a government could not adjust its environmental regulations when more is learned about environmental pollution, when new international standards or technologies become accepted practice, or as the country develops.

Why should a government surrender its powers to this degree? It might do so if it were weak and desperate for investment, or while its institutions and parliament were too disorganized or divided to properly monitor what was being signed away—precisely the circumstances that existed in the former Soviet states in the early 1990s and in Iraq in 2006. For investors the risk is that once the country recovers, the government and or the populations will reject what they see as an unfair deal. Investment lawyers call this the obsolescing bargain. In order to prevent this from happening, corporations have increasingly sought to enforce their contracts under international rather than national law. Contracts and investment treaties usually specify that any dispute between the government and the investor will be heard in investor-friendly international arbitration tribunals, in Paris, London, Stockholm, or Washington.[20] Whereas domestic courts might try to balance an investor's right to stable terms with the rights of citizens, such as the right of workers to a safe workplace, investment tribunals consider purely commercial issues. Most arbitration rules do not permit appeals except on purely administrative grounds. And in many cases they are held in secret, so the citizens of the country concerned might not even know that a case is being heard.

Following the legal innovations applied in Russia, Kazakhstan, and Azerbaijan, the number of investment treaties around the world exploded from 385 in 1990 to 2,495 in 2005.[21] But the collapsed Soviet Union was not the first new frontier for investment lawyers. The rush of lawyers into the newly independent former Soviet states marked merely the latest advance in the expanding territory of corporate legal powers. Its roots can be traced back, according to arbitration lawyer Anthony Sinclair, to the events following Prime Minister Mossadegh's nationalization of the Anglo-Iranian Oil Company's (BP's) oil production in Iran in 1951.[22] The British government took a case against the nationalization to the International Court of Justice, but the ICJ declined jurisdiction, since there was no explicit treaty protecting the contract—only the agreement made in the contract itself.

After the 1953 CIA-sponsored coup achieved what the courts could not by overthrowing Mossadegh (as we saw in chapter 2), the company tried to apply the lessons it had learned. On January 20, 1954, just five months after the coup, the company's legal counsel Elihu Lauterpacht advised that subsequent contracts "be incorporated or referred to in a treaty between Iran and the United Kingdom in such a way that a breach of the contract or settlement shall be *ipso facto* deemed to be a breach of the treaty."[23] Over the following years, investment treaties empowered the investors themselves to take cases against host governments in international arbitration tribunals without needing to rely on help from their home governments.

## Imported to Iraq

Now I could see why Ron Jonkers would seem a good choice for the Iraqi oil law job. He was one of the many veterans of the campaigns to liberalize the former Soviet economies who were now trying to do the same in Iraq. Others included Dan Witt, whose International Tax and Investment Center started out in Russia and Kazakhstan and who was pushing for PSAs in Iraq; Richard Paniguian of BP, who went from overseeing the BTC pipeline to lobbying the British government for access to Iraqi's oilfields; and Dan Speckhard, President Clinton's envoy to the newly independent states from 1993 to 1997 and now head of U.S. reconstruction efforts in Iraq.

Perhaps they hoped that Iraq was the new frontier, that companies would achieve even greater legal rights than they had in the post-Soviet republics. The lesson they had learned in Russia was that a future stronger government—in that case, that of Vladimir Putin—can make life very difficult for investors, even if the legal position is unambiguous. However, Iraq seemed to offer scope for an even more radical experiment: not only installing powerful legal artillery to protect investment, but deploying it against a flimsy government that would never be politically strong enough to fight back.

In December 2008, two and a half years after the UNAMI conference, I attended a one-day workshop for international companies and Iraqi legislators on the legal aspects of oil investment in Iraq. Our trainer for the day was J. Jay Park. Based in the oil hub of Calgary, the fifty-year-old Park was head of the global oil practice of law firm MacLeod Dixon and Canada director of the Association of International Petroleum Negotiators; he had been named twice by *Who's Who Legal* as the world's leading oil and gas lawyer. The oil law was not enough, Park told the workshop. He wanted Iraq to sign an investment treaty to elevate contracts to the status of international law (as the Istanbul Treaty had done for BP's pipeline) and also to sign the New York Convention on Enforcement of Foreign Arbitral Awards. The latter is one of the most powerful weapons in the investors' legal armory. Under the convention, if the losing party in a ruling by an international arbitration tribunal fails to pay the compensation ordered by the tribunal, the winning party is empowered to seize the loser's assets in any of the 140 countries that have signed the convention.

All these measures to protect investors' profits from political circumstance were especially significant in the context of Iraq. It was only a few years since Iraq had been governed by a dictatorship, and since then the country had been occupied by foreign troops and torn apart by ethno-sectarian interests. Inevitably, the rule of law and the framework for protection of citizens' rights were poorly developed. But if the investment lawyers got their way, either Iraq would be frozen in its post-dictatorship state or, if new laws and regulations were introduced, the government would end up paying the investors' costs of complying with them.

It's worth stopping to illustrate what all this could mean in practice. Let's imagine that in five years' time a new Iraqi government decides finally to repeal Saddam Hussein's Law No. 150 of 1987, which prohibits all public sector employees, including those in the oil industry, from joining a trade union. A foreign oil company would be entitled to complain about the change, pointing to the stabilization clause in its contract.* The government should either exempt the company's operations from the change in law, the company would argue, or compensate the company for its extra costs—for example, higher wage levels resulting from negotiations with workforce representatives.

Now imagine that the government repeals the law regardless, without compensation. Iraq is a sovereign nation, the government might argue, and companies operating there should be subject to its laws. At this point the company and the government would be in dispute, and the company could take the case to an arbitration tribunal. At the tribunal it would be difficult for the Iraqi side to defend its position. Although other narrow legal issues may be raised—such as questions of jurisdiction or the status of the contract—the tribunal will consider only the terms of the contract and not the broader range of national and international law (let alone public interest), except insofar as it relates directly to investment. If the tribunal finds in favor of the oil company, it would decide on an appropriate amount of compensation for the company's burden in having to deal with unions and order the Iraqi government to pay the company. If the government failed to do so and if Iraq had ratified the New York Convention, the company would then be able to seize Iraqi assets in other countries, such as financial investments, property, and companies owned by Iraqis to recoup those extra wage costs.

It was strange to reflect on all this while sitting in the luxurious surroundings of the Marriott with well-educated and well-traveled men who spent

---

* Under a PSA, oil developments could still be treated as being within the public sector, even though managed by a foreign private company.

their time with ministers and chief executives, lawyers, and bankers. The unspoken subtext was that such meetings were needed to civilize the Iraqis. But the tone—however clothed in utilitarian rationality, even philanthropy or humanitarianism—was really about power. The issue at stake was not so much bettering the lot of Iraqis, as the advisers claimed, but determining who would make decisions about their natural resources. What they proposed could in fact be seen as a *decivilization*: a hollowing out of public institutions such that the desires and opinions of Iraqis would be unattainable and the parliament and even the government in crucial respects irrelevant.

# 14

# The Pragmatist

*We professionals are caught in the middle—we get it from both sides. . . . If you
are a professional and try to think in a professional way, you can't win.*

—Tariq Shafiq[1]

Ron Jonkers arrived in Baghdad in March 2006 to begin work on the new oil
law. That gave him a two-month head start on the new Iraqi government.
Both the U.S. government and his employers BearingPoint were careful to
insist that Jonkers was only advising, not drafting the oil law. BearingPoint
spokesman Steve Lunceford said his company was "providing a single expert
that consulted to the government on its oil industry. . . . Note, this does not
equal 'drafting' the proposed hydrocarbon [oil and gas] law."[2] And the government said in response to a Congressional Research Service inquiry in
March 2007 that the "U.S. Government did not provide any drafting input
to the recent hydrocarbon law; the Iraqis have not asked for that kind of
assistance."[3] (The oil law was referred to as the hydrocarbon law in some
circles.)

However, drafting is exactly what Jonkers was hired to do. His project
charter, provided by USAID through its contractor BearingPoint, which I
later obtained under the Freedom of Information Act, listed six main tasks.
Among them was—in discussion with multinational oil companies and the
State Department—the "creation of drafts, reviews, amendments of proposed legislation, regulations, and other legal documents."[4]

## A New Oil Minister

On May 20, 2006, six months after the election, the Iraqi government was finally formed, a government of national unity that included all the sectarian parties. Former prime minister Ja'afari had been removed at U.S. insistence and replaced by his number two in the Da'wa Party, Nouri al-Maliki.[5] Like most of Iraq's most prominent post-2003 politicians, Maliki too had lived in exile: he fled Iraq in 1979 and lived in Tehran and Damascus, and his two most important aides, Tariq Abdullah and Sadiq Rikabi, had both spent the 1990s in London. Maliki had been deputy of Ahmad Chalabi's De-Ba'athification Commission since its inception in 2003, when it oversaw a sweeping and vindictive cleanout. He was also a keen supporter of the constitution, having noted that Sunnis might not like it, but Shi'a and Kurds were nonetheless agreed on the issues. A U.S. embassy cable at the time commented that he was "thought to be harder line on relations with the Sunni Arabs."[6]

Hussain al-Shahristani, a sixty-four-year-old from a religious family in Karbala, became oil minister. He had beaten Thamir al-Ghadhban to the post after months of haggling. Two days later Shahristani set out his top priorities in an interview with Reuters. "The first thing we are going to work on is an investment law to reassure the big oil companies," he said.[7]

A devout academic with aristocratic features, Shahristani had cultivated a reputation as one of the most honest of Iraq's major political figures. In 2003 he had called for scientists worldwide to refuse to work on weapons of mass destruction—following his own example as Iraq's foremost nuclear scientist in the 1970s, when he refused Saddam's order to focus on "strategic applications." For his stand he was imprisoned in Abu Ghraib in December 1979, shortly after Saddam Hussein became president. His jailers tortured him for twenty-two days and nights in prison. "Still," he recounted to an interviewer, "the most painful thing in those torture chambers was to hear the screams of children being tortured to extract confessions from their fathers." During his subsequent ten years in solitary confinement he relied on his science and his religion to survive. While he was denied books or writing equipment, he would keep his mind engaged by making up mathematical problems and trying to solve them, and for conversation he would recite sections of the Quran. Ultimately he used the confusion of a bombing raid during the 1991

Gulf War to escape.[8] He briefly participated in the Kurdish uprising against Saddam before being smuggled to Iran in the back of a truck. Throughout his time in exile, mostly in Tehran and later in London, he ran a charity for Iraqi refugees but never joined any of the opposition parties.

Unlike many of the other exiles who later entered government, Shahristani opposed the 2003 war. "I think it's utterly unjust [to] the Iraqi people to put them in one box with the regime of Saddam and call that Iraq, and then direct sanctions against them, or attack them," he stated. On the other hand, he was unimpressed by the antiwar movements. "For the peace marchers to demand a stop to the war without following it up with practical ways of helping the Iraqi people get rid of this dictator . . . I think they are stopping short of helping the Iraqi people."[9]

Shahristani returned to Iraq on April 7, 2003, two days before Saddam's regime officially fell. He devoted himself again to his two passions, science and religion. He tried—unsuccessfully—to establish a national academy of sciences and became an adviser to Grand Ayatollah Ali Sistani. Shahristani had well-tuned political instincts and in 2004 was tipped as a possible interim prime minister. Political scientist Toby Dodge commented at the time, "He is exactly what [UN envoy Lakhdar] Brahimi was looking for: a not too religious, not too political, not too secular, not too pro-American Shi'a who Sistani would talk to."[10] In the event, he was blocked by Paul Bremer, who feared he would not publicly express sufficient gratitude for Iraq's liberation, President Bush's most important criterion for the job.[11] Instead, he joined the United Iraq Alliance as the leader of a faction of nonaligned "independents."

Yet for all these advantages to choosing Shahristani as oil minister—a politically independent technocrat with a reputation for honesty—he had no experience in the industry: he was a nuclear chemist. Given his background, he might have been expected to take some time to familiarize himself with his new brief before making any major decisions. Instead he came into the post with a clear idea of what he wanted to do: to pass within three months an oil law to allow multinational oil companies back into Iraq.[12] Why was he so confident? Oil Ministry technocrats were far from agreed that this was the right course, as the Dead Sea meeting had shown. "Shahristani is very stubborn, very adamant about his ideas," said Muhammad-Ali Zainy, "but he seems very strong. Somehow he is supported by some power that we can't see."[13] That power was the Najaf religious establishment. Shahristani remained close to the grand ayatollah. His brother Jawad was Sistani's representative in Iran and was married to Sistani's daughter.

## The Oil Law

Few in Iraq knew about the planned oil law, but oil union leader Hassan Juma'a was working to change that. The oil workers' union had expanded to cover four provinces and was now called the Iraq Federation of Oil Unions (IFOU). "The minister spoke about a new law for investment which will be submitted to the parliament," he said three weeks later, in June 2006. "I believe this is a hasty step because the oil investment law requires long discussions and a long time. Oil belongs to the Iraqi people and not to a specific person or group. The draft law must be presented to the people."[14] The following month he explained in an article the details of what was coming. "Giving privileges such as long-term contracts to investing companies will have a negative impact on Iraq, because Iraq's resources and treasures [would be] stolen in front of the Iraqis' eyes. For decades, Iraqis [would] remain unable to respond to anything because the right of the investor is guaranteed," he wrote, referring to stabilization clauses.[15] And he feared that the arrival of foreign companies would only increase levels of unemployment, which were already around 50 percent.[16]

Through the summer of 2006 there were plenty of rumors about the oil law. It was mentioned from time to time in policy discussions about Iraq, but was it complete? Had Ron Jonkers written it? What were its contents?

It was not until early November that I started to learn some of the answers. A leaked draft was now circulating, and an Iraqi friend sent it to me. After five months of speculation and uncertainty, I read it eagerly. I quickly saw that the law did the three main jobs demanded of it: it offered international companies long-term contracts, including PSAs; it allowed the executive branch of government to agree to and sign such contracts without recourse to the parliament; and it began to shape the relative powers of the companies relative to the government. It also defined the respective roles of central and regional governments within the federal system.

As expected, the draft law stipulated that fields already producing oil would stay in Iraqi hands. (Recall that only twenty-five of Iraq's seventy-five known oilfields were producing oil. Most of the others had been discovered during the 1970s but never developed.) International companies would get the exploration areas, and the undeveloped discovered fields would be jointly managed by international companies and a reconstituted Iraq National Oil Company (INOC).* Contracts with international companies could last for up to thirty years: ten years of exploration and appraisal, followed by twenty of development and production. Three contract types were permitted: service contracts, PSAs, and buyback contracts as used in Iran, which were somewhere between the other two.[17]

Some elements of the law were less extreme than I had feared. INOC would be reestablished, with no suggestion of partial privatization as Ayad Allawi had proposed, to carry out operational and commercial roles, removing those from political interference by the Oil Ministry. And the "first priority task" was to focus on the producing fields, which would be operated by INOC. As for new fields, international companies would have to compete for contracts through bidding. Regional governments were to be consulted throughout the process, and were to provide part of the membership of federal decision-making bodies.[18]

## A Surprising Author

On December 2, 2006, while I was working late into the evening in the Platform office, a dark room with a single window beneath London's Tower Bridge, Tariq Shafiq called me. What did I think of the draft? he asked. "Well, I suppose it could be worse," I began, comparing it to some of the contracts in the former Soviet states. At least the draft Iraqi law only provided for contracts of up to thirty years—it wasn't forty. But was it wise to sign contracts lasting a generation while the country was under occupation? And many of the elements of the law that might have protected the public interest were quite vague, I added.

Shafiq began explaining the positive features of the draft. It specified that all contracts must give the maximum return to the state, that national control should be maintained. But these were precisely the features I considered too vague—the relevant section of the draft law relied heavily on the

---

* INOC had been suspended in 1987 because Saddam Hussein feared it might become a competing power base to his presidency. Most Iraqi oil experts now wanted to see INOC brought back.

word "optimum."[19] Such requirements were by their very nature subjective and could never be enforced by a court or parliament; it would be left to the judgment of the executive branch. "I have a lot of faith in this minister," Shafiq replied. "He is honest; he is thinking of Iraq's correct position in the oil industry." I was still skeptical. Then he said something that stopped me in my tracks: "I am a major party in drafting that law."

I hesitated, wondering if I had heard him correctly. Yes, he had written the oil law, he said, together with two Iraqi colleagues. They were, I would later learn, Thamir al-Ghadhban, who had run the oil ministry under Phil Carroll and later under Ayad Allawi, and Farouq al-Kasim, who had helped design the regulation of Norway's petroleum industry. Ron Jonkers of Bearing Point had not been involved: he was in Baghdad and available, and was being paid by the U.S. government to draft the law, but Shahristani had turned down his services.

"This draft is damage limitation; the alternative is far worse," Shafiq explained. The real battle, he said, was between the Kurdistan Regional Government and the federal Oil Ministry. If the KRG had its way, Iraq would be torn apart into autonomous regions, competing with each other to offer ever more generous contracts to foreign companies—what Shafiq called "wholesale PSAs." There was no possibility, he said, of saying "no foreign companies"—the government was too beholden to the Americans.

I was puzzled. In the eighteen months I had known Shafiq and the three years I had been reading his articles, he had been one of the most persuasive advocates of Iraq's homegrown capabilities. He had always praised the Iraqi oil industry's achievements and argued that so rich was the resource and so cheap the costs of its extraction that there was little need to bring in foreign companies except to assist in some technical roles. I understood his fear of Iraq fragmenting; I understood that it may have been a greater fear than that of foreign companies taking over the oil industry. But why had he felt it necessary to compromise so much?

It was not until three years later, as we reflected on events over tea in London, that it began to make more sense to me. At the UN conference at the Dead Sea in April 2006, Ron Jonkers had been very keen to talk to Shafiq. Jonkers enthusiastically told Shafiq that he had been hired to write the oil law. Shafiq was taken aback—an American lawyer, paid by the American government, writing the Iraqi oil law?

A couple of weeks later Hussain al-Shahristani, appointed but not yet announced as new oil minister, telephoned Shafiq. They had met for the first time the previous year at a conference in London, and Shahristani had been impressed by Shafiq's thinking. Would he be willing to draft the oil law? As he spoke to Shahristani Shafiq felt a sense of déjà vu. He recognized a risk, "much the same as the risk I accepted in 1964 in negotiations with the majors." On that occasion, as we saw, he brokered what he believed to be the best possible deal Iraq could achieve in the circumstances, even persuading the companies to accept Law No. 80 of 1961. But, for compromising, he had been sentenced to death by the Ba'ath Party a few years later.[20] "When Shahristani called me, I had the same thought—would this end in me being condemned to death?" On the other hand, if he declined, the law would be written by Jonkers, an American lawyer who could give foreign companies rights to Iraq's resources to the same, or even a greater, degree than the post-Soviet deals. "I said to [Shahristani], I'm not going to let the Americans write the law. They were offering to do it for free, of course. So I said I would do it for free."

There were fewer technical reasons to compromise in 2006 than in 1964—the Iraqis had run their oil industry for thirty or forty years—but in their place there were powerful political reasons. "The stresses and strains are there, from within and without. There are politicians pursuing their sectarian interests. And there are the interests of the occupier," Shafiq said. When I asked why he thought he needed to compromise so much on the role of foreign companies, he replied with a question: "What was the war all about?"

I could see now why Shafiq had made his decision, but even for him, the technocrat and pragmatist, it had clearly not been a comfortable one. There was a melancholy in his voice that I had not heard before; he was usually so practical. "We have this grand word, democracy. We don't have democracy in Iraq; we know who calls the shots. People are never consulted." In any case, he said, everyone already knew what the Iraqi people want; it was just not seen as relevant.

Shafiq told me the story of Abd al-Muhsin al-Sa'dun, who was prime minister four times during the 1920s. Sa'dun had spent much of the decade trying to reconcile the views of the British occupation authorities with those of Iraqis. That he was in and out of government so many times was an indication of the impossibility of this task—and the failure of other Iraqi governments during the period. Sa'dun had been seen as a moderate for most of his political life, but by the late 1920s he was growing frustrated at British in-transigence and resigned for the third time in January 1929 over Britain's refusal to allow the Iraqi government control of its armed forces.[21]

He returned to office for the final time later that year, after Britain finally agreed to set a date for formal Iraqi independence three years later, but he struggled to remove some of the 150 British advisers in Iraqi ministries. The position of these advisers—as in the current occupation, they were advising rather than directing—was not negotiable for the British. Coupled with the military occupation, they were the means by which the political direction of the country was controlled.[22] Unable to resolve the tensions between his two constituencies, the British and the Iraqi, at 10:30 p.m. on November 13, 1929, Sa'dun took his pistol and shot himself in the head. His suicide note read, "The people expect service; the English refuse."[23]

"But today no one in the Iraqi government shoots himself," Shafiq added as he finished the story. "He just admits his incapacity."

# 15

# The Laurel Lodge Plan

*The oil belongs to the Iraqi people. It's their asset. . . . And we talked about how to advise the [Iraqi] government to best use that money for the benefit of the people.*
—President George W. Bush, Camp David, June 2006[1]

Camp David, a naval facility in Catoctin Mountain Park in Maryland, has been a presidential retreat since 1942. While associated in the public mind with hosting negotiations between Israel and the Palestinians or its neighbors, the camp had been used for planning war more than peace: the Normandy invasion, the Bay of Pigs, the Vietnam War. On June 12, 2006, it was war again that U.S. leaders discussed. Together with his generals, the National Security Council, and many members of his cabinet, Bush had spent the day planning his message to the three-week-old government of Nouri al-Maliki. Bush's team spent "a lot of time" talking about oil.[2]

Camp David's cabins—all named after trees—are connected by mulch paths and bridleways through the woods. As Bush and his team sat around the long conference table in Laurel Lodge on June 12—a short walk or golf cart ride from the president's Aspen Lodge residence—generals and diplomats in Baghdad joined the meeting via one of the plasma TV screens on the wall. The next day Bush himself was on the plasma screen, having secretly flown to Iraq overnight for a surprise visit and his first meeting with the new Iraqi prime minister. Just the previous week al-Qaeda leader Abu Musab al-Zarqawi had been killed in a U.S. air strike on his safe house near Ba'quba, and Bush was keen to press his advantage.

So on the second day of the Camp David meetings Bush and General George Casey, commander of U.S. forces in Iraq, sat in on an Iraqi cabinet meeting in the Green Zone and announced a strategy for moving Iraq forward while Maliki did little more than agree with him. Bush insisted that it was the Iraqi government's strategy, not the United States'. "I'm impressed by the strength of your character and your desire to succeed. And I'm impressed by your strategy," Bush said to Maliki in front of the TV cameras, his words transmitted into Laurel Lodge.[3] "I discussed earlier with the prime minister, and here with his cabinet, and with members of my cabinet, the strategy necessary to have a country that is capable of answering to the needs of the people," Bush said to the cameras. And, turning back to Maliki, "I've come to not only look you in the eye, I've also come to tell you that when America gives its word, it will keep its word."

The strategy had three parts. First, to improve security by securing Baghdad, eliminating militias, and promoting reconciliation and the rule of law. Second, to "engage the nations of the region and the world in Iraq's democratic and economic development." And third, to increase oil and electricity production and "build a foundation for prosperity." Security was naturally the domain of the U.S. military, but on both economic strands too the United States would take the lead. Bush ordered deputy Treasury secretary Robert Kimmitt to work with the United Nations to develop an initiative known as the International Compact, whereby other nations would offer financial support in exchange for economic and political reforms in Iraq. And he sent energy secretary Sam Bodman to Baghdad to provide technical advice on the oil law.

## The International Compact

Robert Kimmitt had experience marshaling international pressure on Iraq. During the 1991 Gulf War, as undersecretary of state, he had been responsible for assembling the international coalition to drive Iraq from Kuwait, a success for which he was awarded the Presidential Citizens' Medal by the first President Bush. He had another qualification: he had been an investment arbitrator at the World Bank's International Centre for Settlement of Investment Disputes (ICSID), which conducts investment arbitrations. And his younger brother Mark, a brigadier, had been spokesman for Coalition operations in Iraq in 2003 and 2004.

Three days after the Camp David meetings, on July 16, 2006, the fifty-eight-year-old Kimmitt was dispatched to New York to meet UN secretary-general Kofi Annan, and then on to Baghdad to meet Iraqi officials. The International Compact idea was based on a similar process in Afghanistan and was intended as a tool to pressure the government. It had been discussed by U.S. officials since at least March, before Maliki had even been considered for the post of prime minister, although again the United States sought to portray it as the Maliki government's initiative.[4] A briefing prepared by embassy officials for Kimmitt's visit stated, "Central to the Compact will be the occasion to press the [Government of Iraq] for action on economic reform that would change positively the investment climate (particularly in the hydrocarbon [oil] sector), open the country to international trade and dismantle the remnants of the country's command economy." It instructed him, "Your public and private messages should be supportive of the Maliki government. . . . However your private message should be sharper, pressing the need for economic reform now."[5]

The two priority sectors on which the International Compact would focus were energy and agriculture, and foremost among the required reforms was passage of the oil law. In return for this and other reforms, Iraq would receive aid—some of it unpaid commitments from the 2003 donors' conference in Madrid—and further debt reductions, in particular from Iraq's neighbors, who were not members of the Paris Club of creditor nations. Effectively, it internationalized the conditions of the IMF's Standby Arrangement beyond those rich creditors. It also internationalized pressure for the oil law and other economic reforms beyond the occupation powers.

The International Compact was placed under the leadership of deputy prime minister Barham Salih, with two U.S. government officials seconded to his office to administer the process.[6] The forty-six-year-old Salih, a round-faced engineer with a shining pate and spectacles, had spent most of the 1980s and 1990s in Britain and the United States and was one of the Iraqi government's strongest advocates of the economic reforms favored by those countries. His urbane years abroad meant that, unlike most Kurdish politicians, he had never fought in the Peshmerga, earning him the local nickname "the boy." In July 2006, a U.S. embassy cable credited Salih with "a flurry of activity" on economic reform: "Watching him maneuver around the Compact, collaborating with the U.S., U.K., UN etc. in succession—one is struck by his energy level and natural political ability."[7] Tim Carney, U.S.

coordinator for economic transition, put it more bluntly: "Everybody knows he's America's man."[8]

Salih also chaired the committee tasked with reviewing and amending Tariq Shafiq's draft oil law. Ron Jonkers had been working with Salih and with Thamir al-Ghadhban on the establishment of the Energy Committee since April and now made himself available as technical expert to the committee.[9] From November onward, U.S. diplomats were invited to participate directly in the committee's meetings.[10]

## Private and Public Consultations

When Oil Minister Shahristani arrived at the U.S. Department of Energy (DOE) in Washington, D.C., on July 26, Energy Secretary Bodman spent only ten minutes with him before ushering him into a conference room. There waited a group of oilmen from Chevron, ExxonMobil, ConocoPhillips, four smaller companies, and, Bodman emphasized, two non-U.S. companies too, BP and Shell. They had come to give Shahristani their views on the content of the oil law, including, according to the meeting brief, "requirements or regulatory procedures (redlines) counterproductive to attracting and maintaining foreign investment."[11]

The company representatives emphasized the attractiveness of PSAs, together with a favorable rate of return to offset their risks. Technical service contracts—in which a state client pays a fixed fee to a contractor to carry out an agreed piece of work—would not work for them, they said. Finally, according to the meeting minutes, they "stressed that certainty and consistency in laws and stable taxing regimes are important to attracting and maintaining long-term investment."[12] It was a call for the stabilization clauses that had been used in the former Soviet states and elsewhere to insulate investors from new laws.

This was how "consultation" worked in occupied Iraq, as I would repeatedly see.

In summer 2006 I worked for a month as oil editor for a German-Iraqi organization called Media in Cooperation and Transition. MICT's dual aims were to train and support journalists in Iraq and to stimulate greater debate among Iraqis about political and constitutional issues. One of the best of MICT's Iraq-based journalists was Ziad al-Ajili, who the previous year had set up the watchdog and advocacy group Journalistic Freedoms Observatory.

That June, he interviewed Oil Ministry spokesman Asim Jihad about the new oil law. Ajili asked whether Iraqi civil society would be consulted before the parliamentary vote on the oil law. "We believe that most members of parliament are also active members in civil society institutions," Asim Jihad replied, so civil society could be considered consulted. Would there be a public debate? No. "Everything depends on the Iraqi parliament. Surely, the Iraqi parliament will look out for the interests of Iraq and its people." But what about external bodies such as the IMF and U.S. privatization advisers? This time the answer was different: "We will also seek to gain consultation in this field. As everyone knows, we will benefit from the experts' experience."[13]

So foreign experts should be consulted and the Iraqi population should not. According to a British civil servant I spoke to, U.S. and U.K. officials saw the draft oil law less than two weeks after Tariq Shafiq and his colleagues finished writing it in July 2006.[14] The same month, multinational oil companies gave their input at the meeting in Washington. Shahristani consulted the companies a second time at the OPEC meeting in Vienna in September. It was not until a year later, in July 2007, that the law was published in Iraq, in the newspaper *Al-Sabah*, and then only after a public campaign. Deputy ministers and directors general in the Oil Ministry were consulted for the first time after five months, in January 2007. And even the Iraqi parliament—which Asim Jihad said would stand in for public debate— would not see it until March 2007, eight months after its completion, when they were expected to promptly pass it into law.

At around that time I was invited to a meeting in the British Foreign Office. The building, which backs onto Downing Street, is a strange blend of the grand and the banal, the imperial ambitions of politicians and the plodding bureaucracy of the civil service. It is built around an elaborate courtyard, leading into the Grand Staircase, with colonnaded landings and marble banisters beneath a golden dome. The foreign secretary's office famously has separate doors for entry and exit, so that waiting diplomats cannot see the previous visitor departing. The working offices, however, are scruffy, mostly white-painted wood and plasterboard, much of the original decor covered over.

In one of the scruffier rooms I met Rob Sherwin, Middle East energy adviser. In his early thirties and with a degree from Birmingham rather than Oxbridge, Sherwin represented the new Foreign Office elite, from business rather than the upper classes. Before joining the Foreign Office he had

worked at Shell for nearly ten years, most recently as new business development manager for the Middle East, based in Dubai. You could say it was
work not all that different from his Foreign Office job, which was to "ensure
the U.K. meets its international energy objectives in the Middle East region"
in close partnership with senior executives from oil and gas companies. In
particular, his brief was to work for "enhanced energy sector management
and more transparent and competitive oil and gas markets."[15]

Confident, professional, and technocratic, Sherwin was keen to discuss
why Iran had failed to attract investors due to insufficiently generous contracts (he had been involved in Shell deals there), how international arbitration was standard and nothing to be afraid of, and what had gone wrong
with oil investment in Russia. I had been invited as a representative of Platform along with John Hilary of the development charity War on Want, with
whom we were working on Iraqi oil. The issues were gaining prominence—
the *Independent on Sunday* had just run a front-page story headlined
"SpOILs of War"—and the civil servants were keen to find out what critics
such as us were saying and doing.

I could see we weren't going to agree on much, so I set my targets low.
Would Sherwin agree, I asked, that given oil's dominance of the Iraqi economy there should be a full and active public consultation before proceeding
with long-term decisions?

Unfortunately not. Iraq was an occupied country, Sherwin said, and that
made people more "emotional." If Iraqis were consulted, there might therefore be a "knee-jerk reaction" against foreign investment, and that would not
be in the Iraqis' interests. "There's nothing [in the oil law] that ought to
concern anyone. The key question is how it's sold to the Iraqi people: it
would be very easy to whip up a frenzy."[16]

He asked whether I could help sell the oil law to Iraqis. I answered that
trying to convince people of a policy that was already decided was unlikely to
succeed. Instead, I said, there should be a full and genuine consultation process, with options to choose from, outlining the pros and cons of each. Sherwin disagreed. He thought the Iraqi government was in too much of a rush
to pass the law and would be unlikely to pause for lengthy consultations.

In an internal briefing two months later Sherwin wrote, "It is very difficult to gauge an accurate perception of Iraqi opinion [as] to the future development of Iraq's oil sector. However, the law will be passed to Iraq's elected
Council of Representatives and so should reflect Iraqi concerns." Borrowing

from Paul Bremer's idea of representation—where as long as there were Shi'a, Sunnis, and Kurds, all Iraqis would be considered represented—he added, "There has been Sunni representation in the drafting committee through the Minister of Planning, Ali Baban."[17]

As for the views of the Iraqis, Foreign Office minister Kim Howells commented in the House of Commons in January 2007 that "I have been to the Iraq oilfields and spoken to the men who miraculously have kept some production going. . . . Getting the oil moving again will require huge investment and expertise, but that is what will bring jobs to the thousands of young men and women in Basra who need them. I have seen all that for myself. A new hydrocarbon law is both vital and long overdue."[18] He may have spoken to some oil workers, but his opinion of the law as "vital" could hardly be seen as representative of them. Indeed, their representative organization held precisely the opposite view—but Howells (himself a former trade unionist) did not mention what the oil workers' union thought.

As so often during the occupation, the desires of the U.S. and U.K. governments and their companies were thus dressed up as those of Iraqis. The mischaracterization was reinforced by the compliant attitude of Iraq's political leaders (who, after all, had been installed or supported by the occupation powers).

## America's Man

"We know what it takes. It takes partnerships with international oil companies," said Deputy Prime Minister Barham Salih on September 10, 2006. "Iraq needs to send a strong signal to the international community about investment in oil. . . . We need to push liberalization and open our markets."[19] He was speaking at the first official meeting of the International Compact in Abu Dhabi to an audience including Robert Kimmitt and officials from the UN, the World Bank, the IMF, and other donor countries. "I'm personally in favor of PSAs," he added.

The venue could hardly have been a greater contrast to Baghdad. The seven-star Emirates Palace Hotel, whose room prices range from $400 to $11,500 a night, had opened in November 2005, and the Iraqi government was keen to try it out. Dominating Abu Dhabi's shoreline, it had been built at a cost of $3 billion—an amount just short of the annual investment budget for the entire Iraqi oil industry. The hotel flaunted wealth and excess to a degree remarkable even by the standards of the oil-rich emirate. Its website boasted that it used five kilograms of edible pure gold every year in decorating desserts and that the hotel had 1,002 chandeliers, the largest weighing 2.5 tons.[20]

At the meeting the draft of the International Compact agreement was produced. Among the goals of the oil law, the agreement listed "promoting foreign investment and private sector involvement on the basis of risk/reward pricing"—a reference to giving investors access to potentially unlimited profits, as the oil companies had urged in their Washington meeting with Shahristani, rather than fixed-fee contracts. It also called for "consistency and transparency in the application of legal and regulatory frameworks"—which would include stabilization clauses to immunize the investors from future laws—and "an international arbitration option for investment disputes."[21]

The original drafters of the oil law had included international arbitration provisions only reluctantly. Even Shafiq's 1964 negotiation with IPC—criticized by many for selling Iraq out—had stopped short of external arbitration, as the oil minister at the time saw it as a surrender of sovereignty.[22] Shafiq included it in his 2006 draft law only because it was a red line for the oil companies. "No company would accept that you [the state] have the last word on a decision," he explained to me.[23] Nonetheless, in his draft he added a note under the arbitration clause: "For consideration, some countries do not accept arbitration between a commercial enterprise and themselves on the basis of sovereignty of the state."[24] During the revisions by Salih's Energy Committee, this warning was deleted and the arbitration provisions confirmed.

Meanwhile, whereas the original draft had clearly emphasized the need to focus on producing fields first and to build up Iraqi capacity, the revised draft raised the priority attached to exploration, which would be carried out by foreign companies. It required a "comprehensive" exploration plan to be implemented "within a short time table." The result would be to dump huge acreages of potential oilfields onto the market all at once, which would then be signed away while the country was still occupied, creating a market dynamic that would lead to more profitable terms for the investors and less favorable terms for Iraq. The revised law also further limited the role of the reconstituted INOC. Whereas the first draft law had given INOC a joint role in managing oilfields that were known but not yet developed, the new version split these "greenfields" into two lists: one of fields for joint management and one of those where INOC would have a role only if it won an auction against multinational companies.[25]

And even some of the qualitative language on benefiting Iraq was coming under pressure. The Foreign Office's Rob Sherwin wrote a memo commenting on the draft law in December 2006. He expressed concern that "Iraqi ownership of the resources" could affect the ability of companies to "book" the reserves. He also disapproved of the phrase "appropriate return to the investor," as he believed there should be no limits on the returns available—they should vary with the risks the companies took, he felt. There was one point of which he approved: "Good that no mandated minimum percentages of local labour or material is included."[26]

It was at this point that lawyer Ron Jonkers finally found himself called upon. By the end of the year the committee negotiations were taking place mostly between just two of its members: Thamir al-Ghadhban and the Kurdistan Regional Government's natural resources minister, Ashti Hawrami. In December, they invited Jonkers to participate in finalizing the technical aspects of the draft. Jonkers offered to combine any comments from the British and American governments and the World Bank.[27] The following month Shahristani too said he was now "very receptive" to Jonkers's input into the wording of the draft law, as well as subsequent model contracts, once political agreement on the law had been reached.[28]

If Tariq Shafiq felt he had had to make some difficult compromises in drafting the oil law, his co-drafter Thamir al-Ghadhban was willing to go much further. "Thamir always said, 'Don't look at that draft as final.' He was being realistic," Shafiq recalled. "That draft was not perfect; it could have been improved. But I never thought it could change for the worse."[29]

## Centrifugal Force

Shafiq had been wrong about the law not getting worse. But it was not just the sweetening of terms for foreign investors that would disappoint him; there was also the question of who would negotiate and sign the deals.

The Kurdistan Regional Government had scored a significant coup in the appointment of its own natural resources minister in May 2006. Ashti Abdulla Hawrami—a fifty-eight-year-old Kurd from Halabja who had worked for the Basra subsidiary of IPC in the years immediately before nationalization—had more recently run Exploration Consultants Ltd. (ECL), an oil consultancy based in Henley-on-Thames. Former oil minister Ibrahim Bahr al-Uloum had also worked for ECL from 1997 to 2003. In early 2005 ECL had won a contract in partnership with Shell for technical study of the Kirkuk field. And just as the multinational oil companies had used such studies to get hold of geological data that would give them future advantage (as we saw in chapter 10), the appointment of Hawrami brought with it detailed knowledge of the oilfield the KRG hoped would make a future independent Kurdistan economically viable.

As for the oil law, the Kurdish parties—represented on the committee by Barham Salih and Ashti Hawrami—wanted their regional government to have the authority to sign contracts with the companies. They already had the constitution on their side and were again the most organized negotiating faction. Whereas the first draft of the oil law had given the role of negotiating and signing contracts to a new Federal Oil and Gas Council (FOGC), for which the regions would provide a third of the members, the new draft delegated contracting to the regional level (in areas where federal regions exist).[30] The role of the FOGC was reduced to reviewing contracts after a regional government (or the ministry elsewhere) had "initially signed" them. If the FOGC did not object within two months by a two-thirds majority of its members, the contracts would stand.[31] This was precisely the scenario Shafiq had wanted to avoid when he accepted the drafting job. He now foresaw a fragmented and uncoordinated Iraqi oil industry in which regions competed with each other to attract investment, each offering more lucrative terms in a race to the bottom, with the Iraqi people the losers.

Just as troubling to Shafiq was the politicization of oil industry management. In much the same way as the authors of the constitution had drafted a document to suit their political interests, so too the oil law was becoming a political football. Shafiq's draft had envisaged a small, technically focused Federal Oil and Gas Council with a maximum of nine members, but now the committee shifted its composition from technocrats to politicians, to include four ministers as well as representatives of regions and provinces.[32] The revised draft also indicated an ethno-sectarian apportionment of places on the FOGC, requiring its membership to "take into consideration a fair representation of the basic components of the Iraqi society," a phrase that had become prevalent in Iraqi politics.[33]

During late 2006, Shahristani instructed Thamir al-Ghadhban, as a member of the committee negotiating revisions, to consult his two co-authors of the draft law during the course of the negotiations. Ghadhban did so once or twice. When Shafiq and Farouq al-Kasim objected to the changes the committee was making, Ghadhban stopped consulting them. As the revisions continued, it became clear to Shafiq that his damage limitation exercise had failed.

A few months later, the tragedy of Iraq's sectarianization, which Shafiq had worked hard to reverse, would touch him personally. In April 2007, his brother was murdered at an unofficial Jaysh al-Mahdi checkpoint in Baghdad.

# 16

# The Surge

*I think it's important that Iraqis not get the wrong message, which is that the United States is getting set to leave. Because if that's the message they get, then I think increasingly you will see Iraqis, both our friends and—as well as our adversaries—start to make their calculations against the day they presume we will be gone, rather than making their calculations in a manner to help us stay.*

—Ryan Crocker, U.S. ambassador to Iraq, 2007[1]

By autumn 2006 U.S. officials were getting nervous. In May Shahristani had promised an oil law within three months. Though it had progressed quickly in the first months of the new government, it was now apparently stuck. Worse for the Americans, copies of the draft law had started to leak out, and the more Iraqis knew about it, the harder it would be to pass. Getting it enacted quickly became a U.S. priority.

On October 24 General George Casey and Ambassador Zalmay Khalilzad held a joint press conference in the Green Zone, the first performance of a soldier-diplomat double act that would punctuate the next two years. U.S. and Iraqi flags hung behind Casey and Khalilzad as they took the stage, though there were no Iraqis on the podium. Khalilzad looked assured as he read out a hastily prepared speech. Although the event was held in the Green Zone, which had far more reliable power than the rest of the city, he continued talking as the lights went out, his only acknowledgment being an apology that he could no longer see the reporter he was talking to. He had learned the knack of ignoring Iraqi power cuts.

The press conference came after a series of urgent strategy reviews involving Bush, Rumsfeld, and the generals in Washington. Khalilzad announced a new approach: the United States would be holding the Iraqi government to specific targets and deadlines. "Iraqi leaders must step up to achieve key political and security milestones on which they have agreed," Khalilzad insisted. First among these was enacting an oil law, which was "of critical importance," he said.[2]

Passing the oil law was now portrayed as the Iraqi government living up to its responsibilities, comparable to providing for security. "It's their country," noted Rumsfeld. "They're going to have to govern it."[3] Over the coming months U.S. officials would tie passage of the oil law ever more tightly to improving security.

## Toward a New Strategy

The war effort was now in real trouble back home, as many Americans believed U.S. forces were getting bogged down. The level of violence had worsened significantly during 2006, the number of militia attacks increasing from 75 per day in January to 180 in October.[4] Iraqi civilian deaths had doubled during the course of the year to nearly three thousand per month, according to the estimates of Iraq Body Count.[5] And since the bombing of the al-Askari shrine in Samarra in February, Iraq had descended into a bloody sectarian conflict.

Between the U.S. presidential election of 2004 and the midterm elections two years later, the Iraq War switched from a political asset for Bush and the Republicans to a liability. Leading Democrats wanted a phased withdrawal of U.S. troops—a view supported by most Americans—while the Bush administration was still insisting on "staying the course."[6] The Democrats won the 2006 midterms handsomely; the next day Donald Rumsfeld resigned as defense secretary. Even if it was not generally accepted that the occupation was making things worse in Iraq, most Americans now believed it couldn't make things better. Nonetheless, many analysts believed that if U.S. troops pulled out, the struggle to fill the resulting power vacuum would lead to even greater bloodshed. Democrats were nervous that if they succeeded in forcing a pullout, they would be blamed for any subsequent violence, which might affect their prospects in the 2008 presidential election.

Much American criticism of the Bush administration still started from the premise that the Iraqis were too backward to be helped. It was widely assumed that if there was to be a solution in Iraq, or even an improvement, it would have to come from a U.S. initiative rather than from Iraqis themselves. But the American public had had enough of a failing intervention. Many believed the Bush administration had not approached the problem with enough forethought or that Iraq was just too difficult a country to govern. In any case, the issue now was the exit strategy: how and when to end the war "responsibly" with the minimum of bloodshed.

The bipartisan Iraq Study Group, chaired by former secretary of state James Baker and veteran congressman Lee Hamilton, was tasked with proposing a way out of the quagmire. The principal recommendation of the group's December 2006 report was a phased withdrawal of troops. However, with an aim "to improve the situation and protect American interests," the group's recommendations were peppered with realpolitik options to ensure that key U.S. political objectives were achieved along the way.[7]

Economic development, the report stated, was central to a solution, and this would require investment, especially in the oilfields, which could come only from multinational oil companies. So the report effectively endorsed the role of Ron Jonkers, Sam Bodman, and others by recommending, "As soon as possible, the U.S. government should provide technical assistance to the Iraqi government to prepare a draft oil law that defines the rights of regional and local governments and creates a fiscal and legal framework for investment. Legal clarity is essential to attract investment." The group further recommended that the "United States should encourage investment in Iraq's oil sector by the international community and by international energy companies."[8] Along with most in the U.S. and British establishments, the Baker-Hamilton report did not acknowledge that there was any scope for an Iraqi political debate as to how, let alone whether, to bring in foreign companies. The option of keeping the Iraqi oil industry in the public sector was never considered. The report suggested, "The President should restate that the United States does not seek to control Iraq's oil."[9] But with Iraqi political leaders apparently unable to sort out their country, it became possible to pressure them to get on with the jobs they, supposedly self-evidently, needed to do.

## The Surge and the Benchmarks

In parallel with the more public Baker-Hamilton study, a number of strategic reviews were taking place within the U.S. military and political establishment. One of these was carried out in the National Security Council, coordinated by political officer Meghan O'Sullivan, who was now Bush's top adviser on Iraq and would write him a three- or four-page memo on Iraq every day.[10] O'Sullivan's review proposed a "surge" in U.S. troop numbers to reassert military control—an option that was simultaneously being pushed by several key generals. Their idea was that by achieving security, Iraq's leaders would have an opportunity to make the political deals that would form the foundation of longer-term peace.

The problem was, O'Sullivan explained to me, "all we were doing was helping create a better environment for them to make the tough decisions; it didn't necessarily mean that they would be able or willing to translate that environment into political gains. At the end of the day, we couldn't do the politics for them. We were very aware that this was the weakness of the strategy, that ultimately we weren't the people who could definitively deliver success."[11] She believed the strategy might work, she said, because she believed there were Iraqi politicians who were willing and able to make deals.

But it seems there were other ways the weakness could be addressed. While O'Sullivan was keen to stress that the United States couldn't force the Iraqi politicians to do anything, Khalilzad's approach of targets and deadlines suggested that pressure might be applied. Another option was to make sure that the right politicians were in power, those who would want to pursue the objectives the United States sought. In November 2006, O'Sullivan drafted a memo—signed by her boss, National Security Adviser Stephen Hadley, and shown to the *New York Times*—on how to focus the political process toward achieving key objectives. The memo proposed "a new political base among moderate politicians from Sunni, Shi'a, Kurdish and other communities," which the United States would "actively support Maliki in helping him develop . . . We would likely need to use our own political capital to press moderates to align themselves with Maliki's new political bloc."[12] The anti-U.S. parties in Iraq could be excluded, while these "moderates" could get through some of the business of government, including the oil law.

Later that month, Kurdistan region president Masoud Barzani made a rare trip to Baghdad and spent a month there in discussions on the establishment of this "moderate front," along with fellow U.S. allies Jalal Talabani of the Patriotic Union of Kurdistan, Adil Abdul-Mahdi of SCIRI, and Tariq al-Hashemi of the Iraq Islamic Party.[13] Various permutations were discussed, labeled the Executive Council, the Gang of Four, 3 + 1, or 3 + 1 + 1, where the 3 referred to Presidency Council members Talabani, Abdul-Mahdi, and Hashemi, and the 1s were Barzani and/or Maliki. While O'Sullivan had hoped the "moderates" would bolster Maliki, some of them preferred to use their collaboration to limit Maliki's power. Several meetings took place without Maliki, and others believed the front to consist of the other four leaders' parties plus Maliki, but not his Da'wa Party.[14] Discussions continued for some months.

One other event heightened the sense of opportunity for a change of direction: on December 30, 2006, Saddam Hussein was hanged in Baghdad. He had been sentenced to death for the massacre of nearly 150 people, mostly Shi'a, in the town of Dujail in the 1980s. His trial for the al-Anfal genocide campaign against the Kurds was still ongoing, and numerous other crimes had not even been touched upon. Iraq's new rulers had been so eager to get Saddam out of the way that they failed to achieve true justice or closure.

Less than two weeks later, in a televised address on January 10, 2007, Bush announced his "New Way Forward." Most attention focused on the "surge," the sending of an additional 28,000 troops to Iraq. The strategy in fact had two parts. A second, equally important element continued the approach begun by Casey and Khalilzad in October, using the opportunity created by the surge to press Iraqi leaders to achieve a series of political benchmarks. The benchmarks were designed, it was claimed, to foster longer-term reconciliation.[15] Khalilzad spelled out the United States' expectations in meetings with Iraqi leaders the day after Bush's address. While Bush's strategy contained eighteen benchmarks in all, there was one that would claim most of the administration's attention, as we shall see: passage of the oil law.

Almost the entire political establishment in the United States had recently been calling at least for a timetable for withdrawing the troops, but for the Bush administration to accept those calls and leave Iraq in such a dire situation, with none of the U.S. objectives achieved, could only have looked like defeat. The surge was a final toss of the dice, a last chance to turn the war around for an administration that had nothing more to lose.

Some in the United States had proposed coercion by the opposite route. The Iraq Study Group acknowledged, "The Iraqi government cannot now govern, sustain, and defend itself without the support of the United States," and recommended using the threat of reducing U.S. support to push the government to achieve the benchmarks. "If the Iraqi government does not make substantial progress toward the achievement of milestones on national reconciliation, security, and governance, the United States should reduce its political, military, or economic support for the Iraqi government."[16]

So why did Bush opt for the surge? It may be that he felt Maliki too had little to lose. Unless the United States could reassert control, which it had lost over much of the country, all it could offer through its continued support was the opportunity for Maliki to rule a failed state, so the threat of withdrawing that support was a weak one. Through military escalation and an attempt to reassert control over the country, the United States might be in a position to threaten the survival of the Maliki government if it needed to, without abandoning the whole Iraq project.

The surge was almost unanimously seen as a means to bring peace to Iraq. Even harsh critics of the war generally accepted the U.S. government's stated aim at face value and attacked the surge for being likely to fail in achieving the goal of reduced violence rather than questioning its possible other purposes. In fact the surge was a means to impose a particular political settlement on Iraq, of which the oil law was part. No doubt some U.S. officials believed that was indeed a route to peace, but clearly it was also a route to achieving U.S. political objectives.

Meghan O'Sullivan explained the administration's reasoning. "Iraq's state was so fragile that something that was highly conditional, meaning a threat to withdraw forces unless the Iraqi government did x, y, or z," would create difficulties if the Iraqi government was unable or unwilling to comply. "The United States would be forced to act on its conditionality or on its threat; and that would have potentially fatal consequences for the process of building the Iraqi state and for American interests in the region."[17]

Over the coming months U.S. efforts focused on pressuring the Iraqi government to get the oil law and other benchmarks passed. The taboo issue of *how* to reshape the Iraqi oil industry was squeezed out by the pressing question of *when*.

## The Deal at Dukan

During early 2007 Ambassador Khalilzad threw all his efforts into securing agreement on the draft oil law, working as hard as he had in pushing through the constitution in 2005. He had been nominated by President Bush as ambassador to the United Nations and was soon to leave Iraq. Khalilzad's approach was informal but urgent; his style was to do deals in leaders' homes over many cups of tea. At the same time he needed results. "Iraqi leaders understand that the patience of the American people, the patience of the leadership of the political forces in the United States, is running out," he warned in January 2007.[18]

Khalilzad raised the oil law in his regular meetings with Iraqi leaders, sometimes several times a day. As of mid-January, he became more hands-on and held a series of meetings dedicated to facilitating progress on the law—"intensive personal diplomacy," as he described it in a cable back to Washington. He met Shahristani on January 15 and Barham Salih on January 23; on January 24 he attended the meeting of the Salih-chaired oil law committee. On January 28 he met Salih, Shahristani, and Ghadhban; on January 29 Talabani; and on February 3 and 4 he traveled to Irbil for further meetings with Salih, Ghadhban, and Barzani. Then he met Talabani again on February 10, Maliki on February 16, and Salih and Maliki on February 20 and 22.[19]

The breakthrough came at a meeting at Jalal Talabani's summer retreat in the mountains an hour's drive from Sulaymaniya on February 24. His holiday house sits by Lake Dukan, the largest lake in Kurdistan, formed in the 1970s by the damming of the Lesser Zab, a tributary of the Tigris. Control of the dam had been a vital strategic goal of the Kurdish insurgency against Saddam Hussein in the 1980s, and the valley was a stronghold of Talabani's Patriotic Union of Kurdistan. Dukan was now Talabani's equivalent of Bush's Crawford ranch—he used it both as an escape from the stresses of Iraqi politics and also to host Iraqi and foreign dignitaries. It was here that he had held a summit meeting with longtime Kurdish rival Masoud Barzani in April 2003, to agree to work together in the new Iraq.

Khalilzad met the two Kurdish leaders at Dukan in a final attempt to persuade them to accept the draft text of the oil law. The outstanding issue was what would happen to existing contracts signed by the KRG (such as with DNO and Peter Galbraith) and any others it wanted to sign in the meantime. The solution Khalilzad oversaw was highly unusual: a "cover letter" for the draft law, which stipulated a sustained fast pace. The law and its attachments (such as appendices and model contracts) must be submitted to the parliament by March 15; then, if it was not passed by May 31, both national and regional governments would still have the right to sign contracts as if the law had passed. This latter point was a striking, and unconstitutional, assault on the powers of the parliament. The cover letter also confirmed the purpose of the law: "the development of this important sector in a manner that motivates private investments, transfer of skills and technologies, which requires legislative and political stability"—stability that would not exist if the 1967 laws requiring parliamentary approval of contracts remained in force. It described the law nonetheless as a "lofty national endeavour which we present as a gift to all Iraqis."[20]

Once they had agreed on the cover letter, Khalilzad telephoned Maliki to secure his approval. The next day, Khalilzad met Maliki in Baghdad to confirm his approval of the deal and to persuade him to bring forward by a day a cabinet meeting scheduled for February 27, in order to formalize the agreement as quickly as possible. On February 26 the text was formally approved in a meeting of the Iraqi cabinet, again brokered by Khalilzad, along with a resolution that endorsed the cover letter.[21]

Khalilzad celebrated his success in an editorial in the *Washington Post*. Under the law, he wrote, "oil will serve as a vehicle to unify Iraq and will give all Iraqis a shared stake in their country's future. . . . It provides the legal framework to enable international investment in Iraq's oil and gas sectors, a break from the statist and overcentralized practices of the past."[22] With the draft now approved by the cabinet, Khalilzad believed he would be leaving Iraq with the oil battle all but won. "Given that all the major parliamentary blocs are represented in the cabinet, prospects for the draft legislation becoming the law of the land are excellent," he proclaimed.[23]

# 17

# A Line in the Sand

*We strongly reject the privatization of our oil wealth, as well as production sharing agreements, and there is no room for discussing this matter. This is the demand of the Iraqi street, and the privatization of oil is a red line that may not be crossed.*
—Statement of Iraqi trade unions, December 2006[1]

The Sweifieh district of Amman seems an unlikely place to start a rebellion. One of the newest parts of Jordan's capital, its traffic-clogged streets are lined with shops offering Western clothes, perfume, and jewelry—a good spot for chic Ammanites to spend their Friday afternoon.

Fifty yards down the hill from the polished shopping area, in an unmarked concrete office block on a dusty, rubble-strewn street, was the Middle East base of the Solidarity Center, the international arm of the United States' AFL-CIO labor federation. By late 2006 the center was hosting a new group of Iraqis every couple of weeks. They were trained in workplace organizing, international labor standards, and campaign communications. It was a more organized version of the work Ewa Jasiewicz had done with the oil workers in Basra in the early years of the occupation, providing the Iraqi unionists with skills, knowledge, and resources and connecting them with the international labor movement.

On December 10, 2006, the Solidarity Center invited me to a workshop where eighteen Iraqi union leaders would discuss what was happening to Iraq's oil and how it would affect them. Sitting around a long conference table with a plastic Iraqi flag at one end were leaders of all five of Iraq's trade union federations, each of them representing many thousands of workers.

The newspapers don't even tell us such groups exist. But as for their demographics, if the papers were to be believed, the meeting could easily have descended into chaos. There were Sunni and Shi'a, Arabs and Kurds, the devout and the fiercely secular. And with all the unions' roots going back decades, they had had widely differing experiences under Saddam, under the Kurdish parties, and under the occupation: from co-optation and favoritism to marginalization and repression. Some of the unions had been all but wiped out by Saddam, living on only in the hearts and furtive whispers of the workers.

Hassan Juma'a was there with three colleagues from the Iraq Federation of Oil Unions from Basra. In union meetings on oil Hassan always stood tall. All of the unions were concerned about the future of Iraq's oil and all had sections representing workers in the industry, but Hassan represented far more oil workers as the head of the only sector-specific union federation and knew the subject better than any of his colleagues.

The General Federation of Iraqi Workers (GFIW) had six of its leaders at the meeting. It had been formed by the merger in 2005 of two reformed remnants of a Saddam-era union with the union federation associated with the Iraq Communist Party. Now claiming 800,000 members, it was Iraq's largest union federation and represented workers in all sectors of the economy, with a diverse range of political views.

The smaller Federation of Workers' Councils and Unions in Iraq (FWCUI), aligned to the Workers' Communist Party, had three members present. With fewer than 10,000 members spread across all sectors, it more resembled a cultural or political organization than a trade union. But with secular, democratic, and progressive views, it represented a key segment of left-wing Iraqi society, especially in Baghdad. The organizers of international union events such as this generally insisted that all delegations included at least one woman. Most of the women rarely spoke, but the Workers' Councils were a striking exception, with women some of the toughest activists.

Finally, there were five leaders from the two Kurdish federations, from Irbil and Sulaymaniya. Everything in Kurdistan comes in twos. The federations planned to merge when the two political parties of Barzani and Talabani did, but it was taking some time; it eventually happened in 2010. The trade unions were genuine, but their room for maneuver was constrained.

There were people from the two ruling parties monitoring them and operating within them, so they had to be careful.

I gave my usual presentation about the new oil law and PSAs, making some of the points that have appeared in this book. It was met with dejected faces. Had I bored them? Why was no one reacting, not even asking a question? "We thought the situation in Iraq was bad," one of them eventually explained, "but we didn't realize it was this bad."

I'd given the same message plenty of times before: to antiwar activists, to British and European policy makers, or to anyone else who would listen. I'd warned of the perils of locking Iraq's economy into long-term contracts of the type the oil companies wanted. But this was a different audience. The unionists had lived through nearly four years of the country's latest war and occupation. Electricity, water, and public services had collapsed long before, and now the sectarian violence was at its bloodiest. And I had just told them that things would get worse, as Iraq was set to surrender control of its economy too. If it did, it would make their struggle so much harder, as decisions would not even be made by Iraqis. I tried to think of an appropriate thing to say.

To my relief, Hassan Juma'a spoke next. He knew more about the oil law than almost anyone outside the Iraqi and U.S. governments and brought with him documents revealing the amendment of the oil law by the committee led by Barham Salih (which we looked at in chapter 15). Because of Hassan's extensive connections at all levels of the Oil Ministry and the South Oil Company—built through the successes of his union—he was an exception to the general rule that it was easier for outsiders like me to find out what was happening to Iraq's oil than it was for Iraqis.

Unlike me, Hassan knew how to talk about these issues to fellow unionists. "This law aims to produce profits for foreign companies through long-term contracts like PSAs, but at the expense of the Iraqi people," he explained. "This law would make the Iraq National Oil Company the sick man." INOC was a source of pride to many Iraqis, but the draft oil law (amended since Tariq Shafiq's first draft) reduced its role to that of a competitor with foreign companies, rather than the guardian of the nation's wealth. "Maliki promised the oil law wouldn't be ratified without consulting you. Unfortunately, that's not what they're doing now," Hassan said. And that got the unionists talking.

They spoke of their fear that foreign oil companies would bring in foreign workers, leaving Iraqis unable to provide for their families. They worried that services such as on-site medical teams at oil facilities would be cut. And they knew of the multinational oil companies' reputation for union busting and feared the companies would break any attempt by workers to defend their rights. Several of them raised wider fears too. If oil revenues went to foreign companies, how would the government be able to rebuild Iraq's infrastructure and public services? And what would be the consequence of putting yet more Iraqis out of work?

But that afternoon the mood gradually changed to defiance. The trade unions would not fear the law; they would fight it. "We have technical people; we just need equipment and training. We don't need thieves to send us back to the Middle Ages," said Kareem Abdalla Hamza from the GFIW to nods from around the room. Like so many Iraqis, he had experienced the country's tragedies firsthand: his son was murdered in sectarian violence at a checkpoint.

I wondered whether there would be at least some disagreement between the Kurdish unionists and their Arab colleagues. Commentators had been consistently asserting that the only controversies about Iraqi oil were whether contracts with foreign companies would be signed by the national government in Baghdad or by regional governments and how the revenues would be distributed across the country. For instance, when Kurdish-British journalist Michael Howard interviewed me, he cut me off when I started talking about the privatization issue. "No one is interested in that. The talk is all about who can sign the contracts." Among politicians, I knew, he was right. Certainly it was the only issue raised by the Kurdish political parties.* And whether in newspaper reports or international conferences, that was where the debate was taken to be. But at this meeting the issue did not arise.

"The Kurdish situation is completely different," began Sadeeq Ramadan Hasan, a leader of the Kurdistan General Workers' Syndicates' Union, "but we speak in the name of Iraq, not Kurdistan, because we are an integral part of Iraq. We only ask for federalism." Kurdish workers stood alongside their Arab brothers, he said; like them, "we are completely opposed to privatization, and have been since 1958." Everyone around the table applauded—their fellowship as trade unionists was far more important than any ethnic or religious differences.

---

* A few years later, he became an adviser to Ashti Hawrami.

The next day the unionists began drafting a statement. "Should a neutral person help facilitate the drafting?" I asked Shawna Bader, one of the Solidarity Center organizers. "Don't worry," she replied. "They'll be fine." She was right. Very quickly they produced a consensus document compellingly clear in its analysis and demands. How embarrassing that I had doubted they would! I'd fallen for the picture of Iraq painted by newspapers, by U.S. officials, by international organizations—that it is only outsiders who can forge agreement among Iraqis.

"Given the vital importance of oil to the economy," the statement demanded "the right of the Iraqi people to read the draft oil law under consideration. The Iraqi people refuse to allow the future of their oil to be decided behind closed doors." And they left no doubt where they stood on the issue. "Iraqi public opinion strongly opposes the handing of authority and control over the oil to foreign companies that aim to make big profits at the expense of the people. They aim to rob Iraq's national wealth by virtue of unfair, long-term oil contracts that undermine the sovereignty of the State and the dignity of the Iraqi people."[2]

As the statement was read out, there were nods of agreement and determination. And with that, the campaign to stop the oil law began.

## Unions Organize Against the Law

In the weeks following the meeting, while Ambassador Khalilzad was busy trying to secure political agreement on the oil law, the unions began to organize with the opposite goal, in spite of growing risks to their safety. On January 11, 2007, eight members of the FWCUI were kidnapped on their way to a press conference billed as criticizing the oil law. Four of them were later released, four found dead. Trade unionists were taking a huge risk in speaking out on a strategic subject in which so many powerful and dangerous interests were involved.

On January 17 the GFIW met with Barham Salih to protest the law.[3]

On February 6 the IFOU held a conference on the law at the South Oil Company's cultural center, where I had attended the privatization conference in 2005. To an audience of five hundred oil officials, trade unionists, political leaders, and civil society groups, Hassan Juma'a warned that the statement in the constitution that oil and gas are the property of the Iraqi people would "remain but ink on paper if the oil law and oil investment law being presented to the parliament are ratified—laws which permit production sharing contracts, laws without parallel in many oil producers, especially the neighboring countries. So why should Iraqis want to introduce such contracts in Iraq, given that applying such laws will rob the Iraqi government of the most important thing it owns?"[4]

Most of the other speakers were academics from the University of Basra's Arabian Gulf Studies Center, which co-sponsored the conference. According to economics professor Nabil Marsoumi, "This law would lead to almost exclusive foreign domination of all oil fields. . . . The contracts [it proposes] are expressly privatization under another name."[5]

The final statement, signed by the conference participants, was quite clear in its assessment of PSAs: they "would put the Iraqi economy in a straitjacket and would compromise Iraqi sovereignty as happened in the past. This type of agreement favors the interests of foreign companies over all matters of national interest."[6] The participants appealed to members of parliament to defend that national interest and to the government to consult with Iraqis before putting anything in place.

Hassan was more direct in his conclusion: "If those calling for production sharing agreements insist on acting against the will of Iraqis, we say to them that history will not forgive those who play recklessly with our people's wealth and destiny, and that the curse of heaven and the fury of Iraqis will not leave them."[7]

The conference was attended by representatives of all the main political parties. At the end of the day countless participants thanked the IFOU's leaders for the courageous stand they were taking on the issue. The union was now a major player on the national stage.

## Oil Experts Say No

In Baghdad, one of the first and most active campaigners against the oil law was a chemist and former technocrat named Fouad Qasim al-Ameer. In January 2007, he obtained a leaked copy of the latest draft of the law—as amended by Barham Salih's committee—and circulated it through the *al-Ghad* website. Within less than a month, he had written a fifty-page study on the law and its legal, economic, political, and historical context.[8] He argued that the investment needed for Iraq to increase its oil production was well within the capacity of national budgets; if more capital were required, it could easily be borrowed. As for the sense of urgency to pass the law, he believed it lay in the Bush administration's desperate need to achieve the occupation's core purpose, while its efforts to control Iraq were rapidly collapsing. But from an Iraqi perspective, he insisted, it would be disastrous to decide the fate of future generations "under the rule of the occupation, with insecurity, poverty, and corruption spreading like wildfire."

As the draft law was circulated, many oil experts grew worried about its contents. As no one had sought their advice or opinion, in early February a group organized an urgent meeting in Amman to discuss the law. Dhia'a al-Bakkaa, whom we met in chapter 4 trying to defend the State Oil Marketing Organization from looters in April 2003, and Mohammed al-Jibouri, the former head of SOMO who was forced out of his post under Ibrahim Bahr al-Uloum in 2003, were the co-chairs. Former oil minister Issam al-Chalabi and three former Oil Ministry directors general helped them organize the meeting.

On February 17, 2007, sixty Iraqi oil experts attended the meeting at the Amman Meridien. They included senior Oil Ministry officials (thirty had been directors general) and six former ministers. Many had been involved in the Iraq National Oil Company at its inception in 1964 or had worked for the Iraq Petroleum Company before that. These men were widely respected in Iraq for their role in building the country and its economy.

Bakkaa was mainly concerned about fragmentation of the oil industry under the new law. "There's no legal, engineering, or administrative experience in most of the governorates [provinces]," he told me. "Mainly it is in the Ministry of Oil. That makes it easy for international oil companies to manipulate the governorates when they are given contracts independently from the center." He was sympathetic to nationalistic reasons for rejecting PSAs, but like Tariq Shafiq he saw little prospect of keeping the oil industry in Iraqi hands. "If you have no choice, and the other guy is robbing half of what you have, you are compelled to accept it, as long as you keep the other half," he said.[9]

Shafiq was at the meeting too, now opposed to the law he had himself drafted. While he still wanted to see an oil law of some sort, even as damage limitation, it was not this one, after eight months of politicized revisions. He wrote in a paper he presented to the meeting,

Without a central unified policy there will be differences and competition between INOC (producing and marketing its export oil to provide

the state's income) and the regions and governorates (prioritizing exploration for additional reserves that will not be required for many years to
come), as well as friction and resentment between the haves and have-
nots amongst the various regions and governorates. . . . A stampede for
exploration and development contracts at this particular juncture of
Iraq's political and economic development would be viewed as mortgag-
ing the reserves of future generations.[10]

Faleh al-Khayat was fundamentally opposed to the law. "The draft law is
very dangerous, [and] shouldn't be issued at this time," he told Hassan
Hafidh, one of the best-connected journalists reporting on Iraqi oil, who
was at the meeting.[11]

In a letter to the Iraqi parliament, the experts made many of the same
comments as their working-class colleagues had made in Basra, albeit in
more diplomatic language. "We were hoping the public and organizations of
civil society as well as oil experts could be able to review the draft in order
to make the required corrections before presenting it to the parliament to
discuss the enactment. Yet, we think the process has been accelerated during the current complicated conditions of Iraq," they wrote. It made little
sense to them to pass a law before constitutional amendments had been
made, especially as most of them saw the oil provisions in the constitution
as problematic because they fragmented the Iraqi oil industry by devolving
too much power to the regions. Their central call was to slow down the process. Iraqi oil would best be developed in a phased way, rather than all at
once, and "long-term contracts . . . with international companies are better
avoided until the security situation improves." Finally, they wrote that if any
contracts were considered, they should be reviewed by the parliament, as
had been the case in Iraq since 1967.[12]

The Oil Ministry and Shahristani were taken by surprise, according to
Issam al-Chalabi, who explained, "They hadn't realized this subject could
unite people."[13] Shahristani responded with vitriol. "There is a blackmailed
propaganda campaign against the draft law which is being launched by certain parties who don't want Iraq to achieve progress and who want to make
this government a failure," he said to the media.[14] Speaking to U.S. diplomats,
Shahristani dismissed the oil experts as Ba'athists and Arab nationalists, and
confidently predicted that with the oil law soon to be passed, the ministry
would hold an auction of producing oilfields in the second half of the year.[15]

Issam al-Chalabi now set about organizing a larger gathering, this time inviting politicians. On March 9 he chaired a meeting of 240 people at Amman's Four Seasons hotel, broadcast on several Iraqi and Arabic television channels. During the six-hour meeting, many oil industry experts presented their views, including Bakkaa, al-Chalabi himself, and Khayat.

The Association of Muslim Scholars was there, having three days earlier added a religious dimension to the oil law critique. The AMS's one-page statement argued that as long as Iraq was occupied, the oil law would necessarily fail to reflect the Iraqi people's interests.[16] Like other critics of the law, the AMS noted that it would reverse the popular Law No. 80 of 1961 (which under the revolutionary government of Abd al-Karim al-Qasim, as we saw in chapter 2, had ended the Iraq Petroleum Company's monopoly on Iraq's oil futures) and the nationalizations of the 1970s. The association also echoed the oil workers in warning parliamentarians not to side with the occupation over the Iraqi people. "We caution the political parties—especially those that are active in pushing for this law, and which are known to the sons of our people—that they are moving in the wrong direction," the statement concluded. "They today seek to strike deals with the occupier that would squander the biggest national wealth possessed by the Iraqis. We caution them that the Iraqi people are watching all these scenes and will not allow anyone to trade in its resources. The Iraqi people will not forgive any person who squanders its resources."

Saleh al-Mutlaq, the secular head of the National Dialogue Front whom we met in chapter 7, was one of the first parliamentarians to publicly criticize the law. Speaking at the conference, he said, "We have no need for foreign companies. We are experienced enough to reap the fruit of our wealth. . . . We don't want a new law that will further divide us. We need a law that will unite the Iraqi people."[17] When I met him in 2009, he talked about the Iraqi achievements of the 1970s. "I know very well how the Iraqis used to be enthusiastic about developing their abilities and skills to drill the oil. . . . After more than thirty years, we're going back again to hand over our oil to foreign companies and to limit our human abilities. . . . Iraqis think that they have given a huge sacrifice during the nationalizations, when they starved in order to keep their fortunes. So it's not easy for them to give it away after they made these sacrifices. Maybe there is another generation that will come and will act differently. But this generation is very special in the way it was raised."[18]

Usama al-Nujaifi, a former minister of industry and prominent member of

Ayad Allawi's party, the Iraqi National List, was also critical of the oil law, speaking of the twin threats of a divided Iraq and foreign control: "The oil law project in the form as sent to parliament is very dangerous, and in it is the partition of Iraq and the dissipation of its riches." It would lead to "control [by foreign] companies over Iraq's wealth." He called for discussion of the law to be postponed until Iraq was fully sovereign and the occupation had ended.[19]

With a group of parliamentarians now expressing what would be a popular view across Iraq, Issam al-Chalabi noted that "this is what caused Shahristani to be really nervous."[20]

# 18

# The Ticking Clock

*I did hear it's almost complete. I've heard that it's complete before. And this time
I hope it really is almost complete. As in complete.*
— Condoleezza Rice on the Iraqi oil law, February 2007[1]

With the campaign against the oil law growing in Iraq, its U.S. advocates
were anxious to see it passed before that opposition got any stronger. A new
team was arriving in Iraq to implement Bush's New Way Forward. Ryan
Crocker was now point man on the oil law, taking over from Khalilzad as
ambassador in late March 2007, just after the fourth anniversary of the war.
He had led the process of selecting Paul Bremer's Iraq Governing Council in
summer 2003 and so, like Khalilzad, had close relationships with Iraq's political leaders. While Crocker had expressed concerns in his 2002 "Perfect
Storm" memo about the consequences of going to war, now he was a strong
advocate of the continued occupation, warning of even worse consequences
should the troops withdraw.[2] General David Petraeus, a rising star in the
military establishment, had replaced George Casey as commander of the Coalition forces in January 2007. U.S. government press officers tied the surge
closely to Petraeus's personality. It would be harder for critics to attack the
character and judgment of a soldier than those of a politician.

Petraeus liked to describe a Baghdad clock and a Washington clock, moving at different speeds. The Baghdad clock was moving too slowly, according
to Petraeus, because the Iraqi government was failing to "get on with the job."
Meanwhile, the Washington clock was moving too fast, as the Democrats in

Congress—responding to the views of most Americans—were pressing for the withdrawal of U.S. troops. Petraeus's job was to slow down the Washington clock—to persuade Congress and others to keep more troops in Iraq for longer, until U.S. objectives were achieved. Crocker, meanwhile, would aim to speed up the Baghdad clock, and "steer, push, prod and pound the table" to get the Iraqi leaders to pass the oil law and other benchmarks.[3] Four days after Crocker arrived in Baghdad, he visited Barham Salih for dinner and warned of Bush's frustration that the oil law had not yet been sent to the parliament. Salih suggested that some "kicking of butts" was needed.[4]

In Ryan Crocker, a marathon runner and fan of hard rock bands such as Nine Inch Nails and Alice in Chains, there could hardly have been a greater contrast in style with Khalilzad's energetic conviviality. Perhaps no less "activist" than his predecessor, the more introverted Crocker's approach was at least calmer. Khalilzad had irritated some with his high public profile—Meghan O'Sullivan's December 2006 memo had pleaded for colleagues to "encourage Zal to move into the background and let Maliki take more credit for positive developments."[5] And whereas Khalilzad was a signatory of the Project for a New American Century's infamous letter calling for regime change in 1998 and a close political ally of Donald Rumsfeld and Paul Wolfowitz, Crocker was a career diplomat, more pragmatic and less ideological. With the neocon brand now toxic, Crocker was seen, like Petraeus, as a far wiser man for the job. Crocker's realism was perceived by the more impatient in Washington as negativity, for which President Bush teased him with the nickname "Sunshine."[6] When Bush awarded Crocker the Presidential Medal of Freedom in January 2009, one of his last presidential acts, he described him as "America's Lawrence of Arabia," a comparison that Crocker himself would have known better than to make.[7] Somehow he had escaped public blame for helping create—through the Governing Council—Iraq's sectarian political mess.

Petraeus and Crocker quickly integrated their efforts, from their weekly six-mile jogs together around Camp Victory to a unified political strategy. According to journalist Linda Robinson's book on the surge, *Tell Me How This Ends*, Crocker and Petraeus would use a good cop–bad cop routine in meetings with Maliki and other Iraqi leaders. "If you don't agree to do this, you're going to have to deal with him," Crocker would say, pointing at Petraeus.[8] The general was a fearsome character. In one story, a few days after he was shot through the lung in 1991, he argued with a doctor who insisted he should stay in the hospital. To convince him otherwise, Petraeus asked him to remove the tubes and then gave him fifty push-ups.[9]

There was no shortage of U.S. advisers in the Oil Ministry. In late 2007, the Ministry of Oil engagement team consisted of nineteen embassy staff and ten from the U.S. military. The U.S. government also provided an Iraqi Oil Training Program and a National Capacity Development Program (Tatweer, which had trained more than 1,700 Iraqi oil officials), not to mention the training and engagement activities of the oil companies themselves.[10]

Getting the law passed by the Iraqi parliament was now the U.S. government's top priority, and Crocker's efforts were reinforced by the big guns of the administration. On surprise visits to Baghdad by members of Bush's national security team, it was the oil law that dominated discussions. During biweekly video conferences with Maliki, Bush warned that U.S. patience had grown thin. He repeatedly pressed Maliki on the oil law, angry that Maliki had reported achieving a deal several times but none had materialized.[11]

## The International Compact Is Signed

Zalmay Khalilzad did not stop working on Iraq when he ceased to be ambassador to the country in March 2007. As he took up his new post as ambassador to the United Nations, negotiations had just been completed on the contents of the UN-administered International Compact for Iraq.

The compact document, completed on March 16, was a bureaucrat's dream. It established an Executive Committee, a Secretariat, a Consultative Group, a Coordination Group, and a Strategic Review Board, as well as government, government-donor, and donor-donor working groups in each of five thematic areas (governance, economic reform, security, energy, and social services), supported by a series of sub–working groups. This institutional structure was equipped with a Joint Monitoring Matrix, detailed action plans, performance indicators, and financial information systems. The Joint Monitoring Matrix listed 40 goals, 55 benchmarks, and 143 indicative actions.

What did all this mean? In short, it firmed up and elaborated the benchmarks of Bush's New Way Forward and established a structure through which people from donor countries and international institutions would work closely with Iraqis to deliver them on tight deadlines. In other words, the Iraqi government would now be micromanaged.

Passing an oil law to promote foreign investment was just one of the fifty-five benchmarks, but it was the one that was constantly talked about. In an op-ed in the *Washington Post* on the day the compact document was finalized, Deputy Treasury Secretary Kimmitt again highlighted the law, which he said "sends a strong signal of economic liberalization to the world."[12]

On May 3 Kimmitt and Khalilzad joined Condoleezza Rice and Crocker in Sharm el-Sheikh, a popular tourist resort on Egypt's Red Sea coast, for the official launch of the International Compact. During a press conference on Rice's plane en route to the meeting, Kimmitt commented, "We've had a pretty significant rise in the number of approaches that we've gotten from American oil companies." But they were waiting for an oil law to determine "with whom they should be contracting, what the rules of the road are, and importantly for them what the dispute resolution mechanisms are." Many commentators had assumed that the oil companies were nervous about the danger to their employees in Iraq but, according to Kimmitt, "What they've said to us is, 'Look, Iraq is a tough place to do business, security is a real concern, but we drill oil in a lot of places where security is a concern. What we really need to know is what the rule of law is, what the rules of the road are for investment.'"[13]

In return for Iraq's commitment to meet the benchmarks, the countries present at Sharm el-Sheikh committed $38 billion in debt relief and aid. China and Saudi Arabia both agreed to the Paris Club debt relief terms, which were tied to the IMF's Standby Agreement. Other countries offered aid. The World Bank offered $2.5 billion in loans. The package provided a powerful financial incentive for Iraq to comply.[14]

The United States' new embrace of the United Nations contrasted starkly with the unilateralism of the invasion, when the neoconservatives had reigned supreme. Khalilzad explained the advantages of multilateralism in the *New York Times*: "In the role of mediator, [the UN] has inherent legitimacy and the flexibility to talk to all parties, including elements outside the political process." He added that, through the International Compact, "the influence that the United Nations has over the release of any assistance will give its envoy significant leverage to encourage compromises among Iraqi leaders."[15]

## Democracy and Occupation

In a representative democracy, so the theory goes, a government is forced to act in the interests of its people by the threat that they will replace it at the next election if it strays too far. What keeps politicians in line, therefore, is their interest in not losing their jobs. In Iraq's case, however, the electorate was only one part of the calculation. There was another constituency to which Iraqi politicians also had to respond in order to stay in office: the U.S. government. And on its primary objectives—oil privatization and the continuation of U.S. political and military influence—the Bush administration was fundamentally at odds with the Iraqi population, the same political dynamic Prime Minister al-Sa'dun and others had faced under the British occupation in the 1920s.

Iraqi politics were shaped by the need to serve these twin constituencies and to adapt to the shifting balance of power between them. In 2007 it was the Americans who had the upper hand. They kept the Iraqi government in office and could remove it if they chose, albeit at a political cost. For most of his tenure Maliki had led a government in name only, with neither control of territory nor political legitimacy in the eyes of the population. The majority of the country was held either by sectarian or criminal militias or by U.S. forces. Meanwhile, most Iraqis did not feel represented by their government, which was not meeting their most basic needs: security, electricity, water, jobs. It was often said that the government of Iraq in fact governed only a few square miles of Baghdad, enclosed behind thick concrete walls and protected by American weaponry.[16]

This political reality led to an awkwardness of language on the part of U.S. politicians and officials, who had to qualify their demands with often unconvincing disclaimers that they were really pressuring the Iraqi government on behalf of Iraq's people. As President Bush described one of his conversations with Maliki, "I reminded the government that that oil belongs to the Iraqi people, and the government has the responsibility to be good stewards of that valuable asset and valuable resource. . . . It's up to the Iraqis to pass a hydrocarbon law, which they're now debating. It's . . . for the Iraqi government to decide what to do with the people's asset."[17]

Prime Minister Maliki clearly understood the situation. In March 2007 his aides told the Associated Press that he had been warned that the White

House would no longer support his government unless he succeeded in getting the oil law passed by the end of June. They added that Maliki, knowing he could not survive without that support, interpreted this as a threat to force him from office.[18]

## Antiwar in Washington?

The strength of the threat to Maliki was reinforced by the political dynamic on Capitol Hill in Washington, where moves made by the Democrats, whether consciously or not, served to increase pressure on the Iraqi government to pass the oil law.

On the day of her nomination as Speaker of the U.S. House of Representatives following the November 2006 midterm elections, Nancy Pelosi said that ending the Iraq War was her number one priority.[19] However much the Democrats were lampooned by the Bush administration for their "cut and run" policy, that position was closer to the views of most Americans, who saw little to be achieved in Iraq and much to be lost. The Bush administration was looking thoroughly isolated in its determination to continue the war until "victory" was achieved. Even leading Republicans would defect on Iraq policy. That summer Senator Richard Lugar, a senior Republican loyalist representing Indiana, criticized the Bush administration's handling of the war and called for a reduction in the military effort. He was followed over the next month by three more Republican senators: Pete Domenici of New Mexico, George Voinovich of Ohio, and Susan Collins of Maine.

There was a curious symmetry between the political dances of Maliki and Bush. While Maliki was trying to balance U.S. and Iraqi constituencies, Bush's policies were shaped by simultaneously trying to achieve objectives in Iraq and bolster his political position back home. Under the U.S. Constitution, the president is responsible for foreign policy and the military, but it is Congress that authorizes the money to pay for it. The way for Congress to end the war, therefore, was to deny the president the funds to continue. The major political confrontation following the Democrats' 2006 victory was the 2007 Supplemental Appropriations Bill, which was needed to approve continued funding of operations in Iraq and Afghanistan. In late March 2007, a month after the Iraqi cabinet had approved the draft text of the oil law, both houses of Congress approved a bill that required U.S. troops to begin to be drawn down immediately unless the administration could demonstrate

progress on the benchmarks, among which they specifically named enactment of the oil law.[20] In any case, all troops would have to be withdrawn by
April 2008. President Bush vetoed the bill.

The second version of the bill—this time approved by Bush and enacted
into law—maintained and even intensified the pressure on the benchmarks
while removing any commitment to end the occupation. It formalized eighteen benchmarks, including enactment of an oil law. But instead of threatening a troop withdrawal, it mandated cutting off aid and reconstruction funds
to Iraq if satisfactory progress on the benchmarks was not made. Combined
with the conditional debt reductions (governed by the IMF's Standby Arrangement) and the similar deal in the UN's International Compact, the direct effect of this act was to provide another economic incentive for the Iraqi
government: future income was now dependent on passage of the oil law.
The act's indirect effect, however, was even more powerful. American officials could, with some honesty, warn Iraqi politicians that in the absence of
progress on the benchmarks, political realities back home would force a
troop reduction and hence the likely collapse of the Iraqi government. Indeed, without spelling out the consequences of failure in so many words, the
act stated that the future U.S. strategy in Iraq would be conditional on meeting the benchmarks.[21]

To defer disagreements in Washington over whether "victory" was even
possible in Iraq, the act also required General Petraeus and Ambassador
Crocker to report to Congress in September 2007 on the success of the
surge and progress on the benchmarks. That would be the make-or-break
moment for the strategy and for the whole occupation. For those hoping to
synchronize the Baghdad and Washington clocks, there was now a clear
deadline six months away, to which both clocks would count down.

## The "Revenue-Sharing Law"

How could such pressure be justified? The United States was liberator, not
colonizer, or so its politicians said, and its goal was to bring democracy. Forcing the Iraqis to hand control of their oil to multinational companies didn't
really fit this narrative. The solution, as ever, was to deny that oil privatization
was a policy decision at all; instead it was portrayed as a self-evident necessity.
And whereas the United States as occupier could not legally take control of
Iraq's natural resources, it did have a legal and moral duty to provide security.

Iraqi oil workers, oil experts, and the Sunni ulema (clerics) were all strongly opposed to the oil law; tapping into public opposition to foreign control, a growing body within the Baghdad parliament was also against it. Probably aware of the unpopularity of their plans, U.S. officials now rarely talked about democracy in Iraq, the narrative that had dominated 2004 and 2005, just as weapons of mass destruction and Saddam Hussein were the foci in 2002 and 2003. Now the talk was all about "reconciliation." The oil law was described as a peace-building measure, which the United States could then claim as justification for pressuring the Iraqis to enact. At times the U.S. administration tentatively argued that with investment in oil, Iraq's warring communities would see a common advantage in peace and security—that they would all benefit from the wealth.[22] The idea that investment could bring peace was labeled in U.S. military handbooks "Money as a Weapons System."

More often, though, the oil law was referred to as being about the fair sharing of revenues. According to this view, Iraq's oil is located in the "Shi'a south" and "Kurdish north" of the country, while the violence was being driven by the Sunnis' fear that they would lose out because they lived in the oil-poor center and west of the country. The oil law, it was said, would ensure that all of the country's sects got their fair share of oil revenues.

This notion, however, was profoundly flawed. Even if parceling out ownership of the country's wealth on the basis of religious identity had been a sensible prescription, the division popular with Western analysts rested on a fictional account of the country's geology and demography. Basra province alone contains 59 percent of Iraq's known oil, and the two neighboring provinces of Maysan (Amara) and Dhi Qar (Nasiriya) a further 12 percent.[23] The city of Basra, while predominantly Shi'a, contains a significant Sunni minority now estimated to constitute 10–15 percent of Basrawis, though there had been many more Sunnis in the city before 2003. Meanwhile, the Middle Euphrates region contains Shi'a Islam's two holiest cities, Najaf and Karbala, the power base of Shi'a communal identity, but holds no significant oil. The three provinces of the Kurdistan region contain just 3 percent of Iraq's known oil reserves. In contrast, Salah ad-Din and Mosul, provinces with mixed (though Sunni Arab majority) populations, contain twice this amount between them. The "Kurdish north" oil is in fact located in Kirkuk Province (12 percent), which the Kurdish parties claim but whose mixed population consists of Turkomans and Sunni Arabs (and others) as well as Kurds. Finally, the predominantly Sunni though sparsely populated Western Desert, while containing little *known* oil, is generally considered the most promising area of the country for new fields and where the most important exploration blocks are located.

In any case, it was simply not true that the issue of revenue sharing was driving the violence, nor that it was a matter of major dispute between political parties.* All of the parties agreed that devolved revenues should be shared between provinces and regions in proportion to population. President Bush himself would later admit that revenues were in fact already being evenly distributed without needing an oil law.[24]

Ignorance of Iraqi realities is not unusual. What was remarkable was that the law became widely known as the "revenue sharing law." One could only conclude that the many journalists and commentators who adopted this name hadn't read the draft law. Revenue sharing is mentioned in just four sentences of the thirty-three-page law, in Article 11, which states simply that the government must write a *separate* law to govern revenue distribution.[25] For example, Reuters reports on Iraqi oil often included the sentence "In February Iraq's cabinet endorsed a draft oil law regulating how wealth from the country's vast oil reserves will be shared by its ethnic and sectarian groups."[26] The *New York Times* referred to "long-promised and never-delivered legislation equitably sharing the nation's oil revenues among all Iraqis."[27] The BBC reported, "Iraq's cabinet has approved a draft oil law which aims to equitably share revenues from its oil revenues among the country's ethnic groups."[28] The law did no such thing. Almost all other Western media, however, reported it in the same way.

There can be no doubt that the U.S. administration was mischaracterizing the law. In early March 2007 the White House announced, "Iraq's Council of Ministers approved a national hydrocarbon law that provides for an equitable distribution of oil revenues throughout the country." The draft law approved by the Council of Ministers in February is widely available:[26] it allows long-term contracts to be signed with foreign companies and does not relate to revenues, except the requirement in Article 11 for a separate law to be prepared. The first draft of that revenue-sharing law was written only three months after that White House statement, in June 2007.

---

* The only political disagreement about revenues was whether they would be paid into a central bank account and subsequently allocated or paid directly into provinces' and regions' accounts. The Kurdish parties, based on historical experience, did not trust the federal government to give them their share and pushed for the latter option.

The distorted Western idea of reconciliation was illustrated by the United States' deepening alliance with the SCIRI party. SCIRI had been at the heart of sectarian cleansing and the establishment of torture centers through its control of the Interior Ministry and police in 2005 and 2006. It had been a key party in writing the divisive constitution, and it supported the creation of a Shi'a region in the south, which would lead to the breakup of Iraq into three ethno-sectarian regions. Yet a founding member of the party, Akram al-Hakim, had the job of minister for national reconciliation. U.S. diplomats said they were told (unsurprisingly) that his "heart is not really in it."[29]

In a striking taking of sides in March 2007, U.S. deputy commanding general Ray Odierno briefed SCIRI leader Abdul-Aziz al-Hakim on the U.S. capture of a leading member of his archrival Muqtada al-Sadr's Jaysh al-Mahdi, including the evidence against him (which, incidentally, related to attacks on U.S. troops rather than sectarian fighting). In return, Hakim was asked for advice on "how best to dispel misinformation about the hydrocarbon law."[30] At around that time, a U.S.-SCIRI strategic dialogue was established, with a joint committee on security, economic, and political issues. Following a visit to the White House, Abdul-Mahdi told U.S. diplomats he felt "a true sense of friendship and partnership" with Bush.[31]

The major axis of violence remained between Shi'a and Sunni, but the ethno-sectarian disputes over oil were between Arabs and Kurds. Yet U.S. embassy cables in July 2007 began to consider the possibility of passing the law with Shi'a and Kurdish but not Sunni parties' support, like the constitution—clearly, the oil law was more important to them than the reconciliation they claimed to seek.[32] And even in relation to the longer-term risk of escalation on the Arab-Kurd axis, a bigger and more explosive issue was the disputed territories such as Kirkuk, including the referendum on their status, as we shall see in chapter 20. When Crocker met the UN special representative Ashraf Qazi in May 2007, he told Qazi the United States would support the UN on that issue but "the priority of the U.S. [government] was the hydrocarbon law."[33]

## The Dukan Deal Starts to Fracture

With Maliki now fearful for his job, the sense of urgency was growing. To ease the oil law's passage, fifty parliamentarians traveled to Dubai on April

17, 2007, led by deputy speaker Khalid al-Attiya, an ally of Shahristani, to discuss the law.

The text had already been altered in order to get its main provisions passed in the most politically expedient way. Following the December 2006 trade union meeting, which had issued a statement describing PSAs as a "red line that may not be crossed," the drafting committee had renamed PSAs "exploration risk contracts" (EPCs) and "development and production contracts" (DPCs). Whereas "PSA" is a well-understood oil industry term, used in many countries, "EPC" and "DPC" were new inventions, existing only in this draft Iraqi oil law. Most analysts believed they were code for PSA. One Iraqi Oil Ministry official involved in the drafting and reviewing of the law told Dow Jones reporter Hassan Hafidh that the term had been changed "to avoid media fuss."[34]

As we saw in chapter 15, the redrafted oil law had also adjusted the membership of the Federal Oil and Gas Council to a more political and sectarianized composition. While portrayed as a reconciliation measure by U.S. officials, the law now served to entrench Iraq's divisions. And Kurdish politicians still wanted more concessions toward their vision of Iraq as a loose collection of distinct ethno-sectarian regions.

At the Dubai meeting Ashti Hawrami, the Kurdistan region's natural resources minister who had approved the revised draft in February, now turned against the law. His objection was to annexes that he said were being presented for the first time in Dubai. The annexes set out which fields would be developed by INOC, overseen by the Ministry of Oil, and which by multinational companies, overseen by regional governments (where they existed). "The annexes as they are written now will not be accepted by the KRG," warned Hawrami. "If I don't get the lion's share of fields [in the KRG region], then it's a bad law. If the law dilutes regional control, then it is unconstitutional. This law has to be in harmony with the constitution and if it isn't, then it must be thrown in the trash."[35]

Robert Gates, who had taken over from Rumsfeld as U.S. defense secretary, was not impressed. With only five months until General Petraeus and Ambassador Crocker reported to Congress on the success of the surge and benchmarks, "It is very important they [the Iraqis] make every effort to get this done as soon as possible," Gates said on a surprise visit to Baghdad two days after the Dubai meeting. "The clock is ticking."[36]

Thamir al-Ghadhban believed a compromise could easily be found. "There is nothing political in it at all. It is only the names of oil fields," he said later. He was willing to drop the annexes from the law and leave those issues for resolution later—the same approach of deferment that had got the constitution through in 2005. "And if it is required by parliament that we present to them annexes then we could do it. In a day or two we could agree on this," he added.[37] But there were other forces in play.

Most U.S. commentators blamed the stalling of the oil law solely on this dispute between Kurdish parties and their predominantly Arab counterparts, a narrative that fitted the characterization of Iraqi politics in a purely ethno-sectarian frame. In reality, both disputes—over decentralization and over foreign investment—were critical; it was their *combined* effect that was blocking the oil law, in four ways.

First, the resolution of disputes between the parties in the oil law committee took time, a delay that allowed leaks of the draft oil law to emerge in October 2006. This gave opponents of the privatization agenda a chance to organize. Without the disagreements over decentralization, it is likely that the law would have been passed within weeks of its drafting, before anyone knew what was happening.

Second, and related, the parties most supportive of the principle of long-term foreign investment and PSAs disagreed about the division of responsibility between national and regional governments. This prevented them from forming a united front to drive the law forward over the objections of civil society groups and opposition parties.

Third, the Kurdish parties had a plan B in any case: to sign their own deals in the absence of a federal law and to interpret the constitution as empowering them to do so. Although they may have preferred the long-term endorsement of a federal law and the stability that would give them, the unilateral alternative had the appeal of allowing the KRG to pursue a policy and strategy that entirely suited its agenda. With this option available, there was little incentive for the Kurdish parties to compromise significantly in the federal oil law discussions, even if that meant derailing the law. Conversely, as public and parliamentary opinion moved against the oil law and some of the details of the law shifted in response, plan B eventually became their preferred option.

Fourth, the nationalist opposition to foreign control of Iraqi oil broadly corresponded with that against decentralization of the country. A popular theory in Iraq—reinforced by observing the U.S. approach to the oil law—was that the occupiers had a twin strategy of dividing the country and taking control of its oil. The anti-decentralization and anti-privatization arguments were thus lined up together in opposition to the oil law.

In the face of growing hostility to the law, on May 9, 2007, Dick Cheney made a surprise visit to Baghdad. It was the third high-level meeting in three weeks, following Gates's visit on April 18 and Rice's attendance at the Sharm el-Sheikh conference on May 3. Never mind the growing public and parliamentary disquiet; Cheney delivered the usual message that the government has "got a job to do. They've got to meet those requirements in terms of being able to govern themselves, deal with the tough issues they've got before them in terms of reconciliation and an oil law and so forth. I pushed very hard to make certain they understand that."[38]

But he also had a more immediate mission: to cut short Iraq's parliamentary recess, which was scheduled for all of July and August. With the emerging likelihood of a September progress report to Congress and with a tough job to drive the oil law through the Iraqi parliament, the few remaining weeks of legislative time did not look like enough. While Cheney was in Baghdad, Iraqi national security adviser Mowaffaq Rubaie announced—in Washington—that the Iraqi government had persuaded the parliament to cut its recess to one month, possibly less.[39] As Cheney put it, "any undue delay would be difficult to explain."[40]

# 19

# Imposing the Law

*I've made it clear to the Prime Minister and Iraq's other leaders that America's commitment is not open-ended. If the Iraqi government does not follow through on its promises, it will lose the support of the American people.*

—President George Bush, January 2007[1]

At around 8:00 a.m. on Monday, June 4, 2007, Hassan Juma'a and other leaders of the Iraq Federation of Oil Unions arrived at the distribution terminal by Basra refinery, nine miles west of the city. The newly trained soldiers of the Iraqi army's 10th Brigade surrounded the terminal with more than thirty Humvees.[2] The reason for their presence stood facing them: fifteen hundred protesting workers. "The atmosphere here is full of tension," Hassan said to journalists, but "this will not stop us because we are defending people's rights."[3] In places the standoff turned into fistfights, and the soldiers raised their weapons. A squad of soldiers tried to grab the head of the trade union section in the distribution company, a man named Jawad Kadhim. His colleagues stood in front of him and said, "Either you take us all or you leave us all."

The workers had shut off the flow of fuel through two 14-inch pipelines to Nasiriya, Diwaniya, and Hilla. The next day they would escalate the protest, closing two 48-inch and one 32-inch pipeline, cutting off gas supplies to power stations, petrochemical, fertilizer, and steel plants, and the supply of fuel to Baghdad. And after that the union planned to extend the strike to the rest of the oil industry, including production and exports.

In one of the most decisive acts of his first fifteen months in office, Prime Minister Nouri al-Maliki had sent in the troops with a declaration that he would "strike with an iron fist anyone that would tamper with the public order or carry out evil schemes undermining the state's higher interests."[4] Maliki issued arrest warrants for the union leaders, including Hassan Juma'a, on a charge of "sabotaging the economy." He accused them of serving the agendas of Iraq's neighboring countries, a dangerous accusation in the context of Iraq's sectarian killing.[5]

The protest had been a month coming, since the IFOU called the strike on May 5. As in many strikes, a range of issues was raised. The union made sixteen demands, including settlement of unpaid bonuses from two years previously, land on which oil workers could build houses, and medical treatment for employees, especially those who worked in areas contaminated with depleted-uranium munitions. But one demand singled this strike threat out for particular attention: in a letter to Maliki, the union insisted that it, along with other civil society groups and experts, should be given the opportunity to study the oil law.[6]

On May 16 Maliki personally met Hassan Juma'a to negotiate a resolution. During a ninety-minute meeting in Baghdad, Maliki said that he did not have the expertise to discuss the oil law himself but agreed that civil society groups should have a role in the debate.[7] Meanwhile, Maliki agreed that the outstanding bonuses would be paid and that the other issues would be resolved by a commission comprising representatives of the union, the prime minister's office, and the South Oil Company. But the truce did not last. In early June Salah Aziz, head of the state-owned fuel distribution company, declared he would not abide by the prime minister's agreement with the IFOU. According to the oil workers, Oil Minister Shahristani supported Aziz.[8] The distribution workers reacted by going on strike on Monday, June 4. Now their demands were supplemented by a call for Aziz to be sacked.

At 1:00 p.m., as the standoff at the terminal continued into the withering heat of a Basra afternoon, General Ali Hamadi arrived with the arrest warrants, but the police guarding the oil facilities stopped him from carrying out the arrests. With flammable gases in the air, any shooting could lead to an explosion. Hamadi, overall commander of security forces in Basra, had been appointed by Maliki the previous year for his independence from local political parties and factions. But it was his independence that would undo the clampdown on the workers. During several hours of meetings with the union leadership that afternoon, he became persuaded of their case and reported it back to the government. He asked Hassan Juma'a to suspend the strike for a week while he tried to convince the government to change its position; if he failed, he promised, he would resign and join the protest.[9]

One person directly involved in the events told me there was another factor behind the general's decision to compromise: the Basra head of the Jaysh al-Mahdi, Muqtada al-Sadr's militia, warned that if the troops harmed the unionists, his fighters would burn down the houses of the army officers. The person who told me was no sympathizer of the Jaysh al-Mahdi but believed on this occasion they were on the right side.[10]

There was international pressure too. A statement by the AFL-CIO demanded that "the Iraqi government pull back its security and military forces and cease its menacing threats to arrest and attack these workers immediately. . . . We urge the Iraqi government to return to the bargaining table."[11] AFL-CIO president John Sweeney wrote to Secretary of State Condoleezza Rice, urging her to use diplomatic channels "to convey to the Iraqi government that military intervention is not the way to resolve this dispute."[12]

At 6:00 p.m. Safa ad-Din as-Safi, the justice minister, arrived to negotiate with the IFOU, accompanied by General Hamadi. It took until midnight to reach agreement, but the strike was suspended for seven days to give the government a chance to implement what Maliki had agreed to on May 16.

During that week workers' representatives visited religious leaders in Najaf. They reported that Grand Ayatollah Ali Sistani, the highest Shi'a authority in Iraq, had "reprimanded" the oil ministry for the unconstructive line it had taken—a significant action, given that the minister was close to Sistani.[13]

The following Monday the IFOU declared victory, and the agreement with Maliki was implemented. "The workers' will is indestructible," said the union's victory statement. "The workers can achieve what they want by the means available to them and their strength. And the oil workers are very strong, because they have a legitimate right."[14]

## A Message from the Military

On June 12, 2007, the day after the oil workers declared victory, one of America's most senior commanders visited Maliki to discuss the oil law.

Commander of U.S. Central Command (Centcom) Admiral William Fallon was one of the last Vietnam veterans still in the U.S. military, and the memory of Congress cutting funds for that war in 1975, when he believed more could have been achieved militarily, still rankled. He feared a repeat experience. He told journalist Bob Woodward, "We don't want to be in a position where we've now thrown away three or four years' worth of hard work and we're now walking out. . . . [We need to find] a position where the American people and the Congress feel that we are exercising due diligence."[15]

Fallon's meeting with Maliki came just three months before Petraeus and U.S. ambassador to Iraq Ryan Crocker would report to Congress on whether the surge strategy had been a success. "Is it reasonable to expect [the oil law] to be completed in July?" Fallon asked the Iraqi prime minister. "We have to show some progress in July for the upcoming report."[16]

Before taking on Centcom, Fallon had never set foot in Iraq, although he had flown missions over the country from a carrier in the Gulf in the 1991 war. But he was used to strong-arming states that diverged from his expectations. In his previous post, as head of the U.S. Pacific Command, he had been enraged when the Philippines kept in custody a U.S. Marine who had been convicted of raping a local woman. Under the 1998 bilateral military agreement between the countries, the Marine should have been kept in U.S. custody. Fallon responded by canceling a joint military exercise with the Philippines military and withdrawing aid from a typhoon-hit area of the country in 2006.[17]

Throughout mid-2007 there was an implicit understanding that if no progress on the oil law was achieved, Maliki might be removed from office. However, for the most part the generals—Rick Sanchez, George Casey, and David Petraeus—had restricted their comments to military issues: the security situation, control of territory, training of Iraqi forces. The ambassadors—John Negroponte, Zalmay Khalilzad, and Ryan Crocker—dealt with the political and economic issues. Crocker, the current ambassador, knew far more than Fallon about the oil law, on which he had been working constantly since he took up the Baghdad posting in March 2007. Fallon's competence was military, his command covering the Middle East, Central Asia, and the Horn of Africa.

Crocker was present at Fallon's meeting with Maliki. That the man in uniform rather than the man in a suit delivered the message about the oil law could be seen as shifting the tone from negotiation to threat. The eu-phemisms of advice or encouragement would no longer work; this was an order. The impact of the meeting was further increased by inviting *New York Times* reporter Michael Gordon to attend.[18] As David Broder at the rival *Washington Post* commented, "From an administration known for its secrecy, this deviation means only one thing: So desperate is the need to push Maliki into action that even the *Times* becomes a lever."[19] The effect of putting the U.S. demands into the public domain was to encourage new voices, inside and outside Iraq, to speak out against Maliki and to open space for other potential Iraqi leaders to intervene.

Three days after Fallon's meeting with Maliki, on June 15, the last of the five surge brigades arrived in Iraq, and Operation Phantom Thunder began. Two of the new brigades (around ten thousand soldiers) were deployed in Baghdad and three (about fifteen thousand) in the areas around the city—what General Petraeus called "the throat of Baghdad."[20] To pacify Iraq, U.S. forces would cut Baghdad off from the rest of the country, surround it with a belt of U.S. control, and then seize the city through a show of force in the streets. The imagery of overwhelming force echoed the "shock and awe" campaign of the original invasion.

Ever since the surge was announced in January, U.S. forces had been con-ducting "shaping operations"—setting up new bases, gathering intelligence, and disrupting key enemy centers, along with a dramatic increase in aerial bombardment, with consequent civilian casualties. During the course of 2007, U.S. and British planes dropped 1,447 bombs on Iraq, compared with 229 in 2006.[21] Operation Imposing the Law had begun in February, taking control of Baghdad neighborhood by neighborhood. Seventy-five combat out-posts and joint security stations were set up, projecting U.S. military force directly into the heart of the city.[22]

The troop escalation was accompanied by a warning that the United States was not going away. On May 30 White House spokesman Tony Snow had said the aim was ultimately to get U.S. forces into an "over-the-horizon" role, like the one they had in South Korea, where thousands of troops had been stationed for more than fifty years for the purpose of "maintaining stability and assurance."[23] The following day Defense Secretary Gates also referred to Korea, saying that establishing a long-term garrison was preferable to what had happened in Vietnam, "where we just left lock, stock and barrel."[24]

Meanwhile, the United States stepped up the diplomatic pressure. At the request of General Petraeus, Bush dispatched Meghan O'Sullivan back to Iraq for three months to work with Ryan Crocker in ensuring the benchmarks were met.

## Iraq's Democracy

In warning Iraq's parliamentarians not to sell out the country's future, both the IFOU and the Association of Muslim Scholars had probably recognized that Iraqi politics was shifting. The former exiles who arrived back in 2003 had had no political base but were able to succeed in the 2005 elections through appeals to sectarian and ethnic identity, and subsequently they came to dominate Iraqi politics, along with the well-organized Kurdish parties. As we have seen, Iraqis did not think in such terms, but the sectarian parties drew their power from the support of the occupation. During the course of 2007, while those parties broadly continued to pursue agendas consistent with that of the United States, other groups saw an opportunity. In the case of oil, so great was the gap between official policy and what most Iraqis believed it should be that the less powerful parties—those that had been less close to the occupation—started to use oil nationalism as a populist issue. As a result, opposition to the oil law spread quickly in the parliament.

At the March 2007 meeting with the oil experts, Saleh Mutlaq's secular National Dialogue Front, with eleven of the 275 seats in the parliament, had come out against the oil law, as had Usama al-Nujaifi, a leading member of Ayad Allawi's Iraqi National List, which had twenty-five seats.

In April the Sunni Tawafuq (Accord Front), with forty-four seats, issued a statement calling for the law explicitly to rule out PSAs and thereby challenging the oil law drafters' linguistic sleight of hand, which had simply renamed them.[25] Tawafuq's statement also called for the law to strengthen the Iraqi national government's role in managing the oil industry. Planning Minister Ali Baban—a member of the Iraqi Islamic Party, the largest of the three parties that made up the Tawafuq grouping—had been a member of the oil law committee and had endorsed the draft law when the cabinet approved it in February.[26] But by late July he was one of the leading opponents of the law, threatening to resign "one hour" after its passage if it was not changed.[27] He objected both to giving regions the right to sign contracts and to the offering of PSA contracts. Throughout the summer much of the U.S. lobbying effort focused on Baban, urging him to "take a more constructive approach," as his opposition—given his role in drafting the oil law—became a point around which opposition crystallized.[28] The impact of the public campaign can be seen both in Baban's change of position and by reading U.S. embassy cables from the period on the WikiLeaks website—time and again Iraqi MPs said they wanted to support the United States on the oil law, but it had become politically impossible for them to do so.

Another person who had changed his position was Thamir al-Ghadhban. Having supported PSAs since he first led the Oil Ministry in the weeks following the invasion and having been their major advocate on the oil law drafting committee, in April 2007 he admitted, "There is a sensitivity to this issue. I am not enthusiastic for this or a backer of production sharing."[29]

In May Vice President Tareq al-Hashemi, leader of the Iraqi Islamic Party, also condemned PSAs. "We disagree with the production sharing agreement," he said. "We want foreign oil companies, and we have to lure them into Iraq to learn from their expertise and acquire their technology, but we shouldn't give them big privileges."[30]

Nujaifi strengthened his opposition through the summer. He warned—with some justification—that U.S. pressure to achieve the benchmarks was widening sectarian divisions rather than bringing about reconciliation. In July he resigned from the parliamentary oil and gas committee to protest the intense pressure from the United States. In a press statement, he said he wanted to "keep my hands clean of this law . . . that will destroy the future of the country."[31]

Separately, two of the parties in the Shi'a United Iraq Alliance were also moving against the oil law. In June the Basra-based al-Fadhila (Virtue) party, which had fifteen seats in the parliament, echoed the call for delaying the law until after the constitution had been amended.[32] And the strongly anti-occupation party loyal to Muqtada al-Sadr—which held twenty-nine seats—forcefully attacked the law in July, calling for companies "whose governments are occupying Iraq" to be explicitly excluded from any oil contracts. "The most serious problem with the law is the production-sharing agreements, which we categorically reject," said Nassar al-Rubaie, spokesman for the parliamentary Sadr Current. PSAs would "undermine Iraq's sovereignty in the short run and will strip it of its sovereignty in the long run," he added.[33] Significantly, Maliki ally Haidar al-Abadi said in a May 2007 radio interview that Grand Ayatollah Sistani had warned Iraqi MPs against rushing the legislation the U.S. Congress was demanding, and asked them to focus instead on Iraqis' immediate needs.[34]

Between them, the National Dialogue Front, Tawafuq, Iraqi National List, Fadhila, and Sadr Current had 126 seats in the parliament.[35] The parties allied with the United States—the Kurdistan Alliance, the Islamic Supreme Council of Iraq (ISCI),* and Da'wa—had 113. To pass the law required 138 of the 275 total MPs to vote in favor. Even if the decentralization dispute was resolved and the Kurdistan Alliance supported the oil law, *and* if all of the remaining members of the UIA (excluding the Sadr Current and al-Fadhila) and some of Allawi's Iraqi National List joined the pro-law camp, *and* if they overcame the parliament's chronic absenteeism, at best only a very slim majority could be achieved. And that too was unlikely, as individual members of the Shi'a parties were looking set to rebel. For example, one of the most senior members of Da'wa, Ali al-Adeeb, son of one of the founders of the party, said in early August that the law should not be passed until the occupation had ended, and in the meantime INOC should develop and manage the oilfields.[36]

The oil law struggle was helping consolidate a change in Iraqi politics. Whereas in 2005 the parliament's configuration had been largely tripartite—Shi'a, Sunni, and Kurdish blocs—now it was coalescing into two groupings that cut across those lines. On one side were what Iraqi blogger Raed Jarrar called the "nationalists," who held traditional Iraqi views of national unity and centralized power and were most opposed to the ongoing occupation and to U.S. political agendas, including privatization. Against them were ranged the pro-occupation "separatists," who favored strong federalism with powerful regional governments defined by their ethno-sectarian identities and foreign investment in the form advocated by the United States.[37] The separatists held the most important positions in the Iraqi government, including the posts of prime minister and his deputies. The nationalists had at various times been inside or outside the government.

The first major indication of this new political landscape had come in October 2006, when the government, driven by the two Kurdish parties and SCIRI, proposed a bill allowing provinces to form new regions. The bill was

---

*The renamed SCIRI had dropped "Islamic Revolution" from its name to imply more distance from Iran.

also supported by most of Da'wa, some of the independent members of the Shi'a UIA, and some of the Iraqi National List. The other parties—notably Tawafuq,* the Sadr Current, the National Dialogue Front, and al-Fadhila— bitterly opposed the regions law and boycotted the parliamentary session, hoping to deny it a quorum. The bill nonetheless scraped through, with either 138 or 140 votes, a majority of either one or three; no one's quite sure, as the vote was decided by a show of hands and there is no record of who was present. Some opponents allege that in fact there were fewer than the 138 required for a quorum; others say some supporters were dragged in to vote at the last minute.

The oil law provoked almost exactly the same split, but, in contrast to the regions law, now the separatists were divided between Kurds and Arabs. And with nationalist sentiment now stronger, the anti-law camp looked set to secure a parliamentary majority.

## A Growing Campaign

Oil Minister Hussain al-Shahristani was not finished with trying to break the IFOU, which was thwarting the objective he had declared within hours of becoming minister over a year earlier: to pass an oil law. On July 18, 2007, Laith Abd al-Husain al-Shahir, director general of the Oil Ministry's legal department, wrote to all of Iraq's oil companies to instruct them not to cooperate with unions by providing them with offices or equipment. He pointed out that "unions enjoy no legal status to work in the state sector," a direct reference to Saddam Hussein's Law No. 150 of 1987.[38]

It was another illustration of the paradox of Shahristani—or of the gap between the man and his public persona. He had made his name as a human rights advocate, the founder of a civil society organization, and a former detainee of Saddam's regime; now he was using the dictator's laws to crush a group that had dared to express a view different from the government's. Sometimes when former human rights advocates or trade unionists are appointed to government, they show a contrary zeal that goes far beyond

---

* Jarrar classifies Tawafuq as separatist, although it has often voted with the nationalists and been alternately in government or in the opposition. This is best explained by the fact that its constituency is mostly nationalist, but its politicians' instincts are mostly separatist.

the approach of their colleagues, perhaps for fear of being seen as soft. I wondered whether this impulse might have affected Shahristani.

Again Thamir al-Ghadhban, who remained a major negotiator on the oil law behind the scenes, took a more conciliatory line than Shahristani. Asked about the attack on the union, he said, "I'm not directly involved in this matter. OK, I worked in Basra for sixteen years and I know those people. I know most of them if not all of them; they are sincere people, they are dedicated, they work hard and they contributed and they mean well. . . . Of course the minister has the right to make whatever decisions he thinks are right, no doubt about that, but also I think it is wise of labor organizations not to go into political issues. I believe they should concentrate on their social issues, their rights to improve the conditions of the workers in Basra. . . . [But] I remember seeing a video by Hassan Juma'a and I found him a very serious person, sincere and polite. He expressed his opinion. I didn't see a problem with that really."[39] Still, the decision lay with the minister.

The IFOU relied heavily on cooperation with the state-owned companies, and the minister's attack promised to hit them hard. Hassan Juma'a was in no doubt as to the reason for Shahristani's hostility—it was because the union had led the campaign against the oil law and against privatization. "We have never had a problem with previous ministers, and they had never had a problem with the unions. I do not believe that the [clampdown] is over our broaching the subject of worker's rights," he said.[40] However, the confrontation ended in stalemate. The union continued to operate, although without many of the resources it previously had relied on. But neither the arrest warrants nor the illegality order was rescinded. The union was left in a precarious position and came under increasing pressure over the following months.

While the union had played a key role in sparking opposition to the oil law, that opposition now went far wider. Just weeks before the Petraeus-Crocker reports to Congress, the month of July 2007 saw an explosion of protest from the Association of Muslim Scholars (AMS), the unions, and oil experts, as well as several new groups.

On July 4, the AMS issued a fatwa on the oil law. According to the teachings of the Prophet, it stated, water, pasture, and fire can be owned neither by individuals nor by the state; rather, they are the common property of the umma (the nation of all Muslims), over which the state has the role of guardian. But under conditions of occupation, the fatwa ruled, the state has neither the legitimacy nor the ability to take care of resources on behalf of the people. "A person who has no real authority, no free will," it explained, "is not entitled to sign on behalf of the umma a contract or covenant, when his country is under occupation of the marauding military forces, or his country encountering unstable conditions in which people cannot express their free will openly." Therefore, the signing of any contract would be haram (religiously forbidden), and the contract "considered to be null and void from a shari'a [Islamic religious law] and a commonsense point of view."

The fatwa also pointed out that oil experts had criticized the law and insisted that it not be passed without their approval. In conclusion, it warned, any member of parliament who voted for the oil law "will be damned with the wrath of God and must bear the consequences of the crime of collaborating with the enemy in stealing common wealth."[41] Although there had been many statements and communiqués, this was only the scholars' fifth fatwa in the four and a half years of its existence. According to AMS spokesman Bashar al-Faydi, because the association issued fatwas so rarely, it had a lot of impact when it did.[42] The AMS directed its two thousand imams across Iraq to discuss the fatwa in their Friday sermons, which took the message to a large popular audience.

Fouad al-Ameer, who had obtained the leaked draft oil law at the start of the year, had meanwhile followed his February critique with three further studies. Combined into a book, these now circulated in Baghdad, significantly increasing public understanding of the issue. Many were read by MPs and contributed to the growing parliamentary opposition to the law. Al-Sabah published criticisms of the law by oil experts in Amman and others, and in July the newspaper reproduced the draft oil law in full, revealing its contents to the Iraqi general public for the first time.

In late June Subhi al-Badri of the Federation of Workers' Councils—the smaller, secular union federation aligned with the Workers' Communist Party—established the Anti–Oil Law Front with support from the IFOU and several Baghdad-based civil society groups. The front organized its first demonstration on July 7 beneath Baghdad's famous Liberty Monument, which celebrates the 1958 revolution, in Tahrir (Liberation) Square in the heart of modern Baghdad. The Anti–Oil Law Front, Badri said, would be another element in the people's struggle against the oil law, "the law of slavery and servitude."[43]

Then on July 16 hundreds of workers from all unions marched through Basra, carrying a black coffin labeled FREEDOM. "If this [oil law] is endorsed by the parliament it would abolish sovereignty and hand over the wealth of this generation and the generations to come as a gift to the occupier," said their statement. "This law in fact destroys the achievements of the Iraqi masses and especially the Law number 80 of 1961 and the nationalisation of 1973."[44]

The next day the oil experts wrote a second letter signed by 108 people, including eight former ministers, and addressed to all members of parliament: "We call upon the President and the members of the Council [of Representatives] to take a memorable historic stand that will be remembered, in protecting the interests of the whole Iraqi people and in defending the rights of its sons in their present and future times."[45] This time they emphasized legitimacy and democracy. They complained that their February comments had been ignored, along with those of the unions and others. They wanted a proper debate on the oil law, rather than seeing it rushed through, and repeated that it made little sense to pass the law before the proposed constitutional amendments. They argued again that individual contracts should require the approval of the parliament. Finally, they called again for decision making to be coordinated at a central level, and they expressed concern at moves by the Kurdistan Regional Government toward signing its own contracts.

Building on the experts' second letter, yet another grouping came out in August against the oil law. Representing a broad swath of Iraq's middle classes, 419 Iraqi "intellectuals and professionals, including academics, doctors, writers, engineers, lawyers, economists, diplomats, journalists, former ministers and senior officials," signed a petition to the parliament, condemning PSAs and calling for a referendum on the law.[46]

Internationally too the campaign against the oil law was starting to become a cause célèbre. Six Nobel Peace Prize winners condemned the inclusion of the oil law benchmark in the U.S. Congress's Supplemental Appropriations bill. "A law with the potential to so radically transform the basic economic security of the people of Iraq should not be forced on Iraq while it is under occupation and in such a weak negotiating position vis-à-vis both the U.S. government and foreign oil corporations," said their July statement, given after Antonia Juhasz, an activist with Oil Change International, brought the law to their attention. The Nobel laureates went on, "The Iraq Oil Law could benefit foreign oil companies at the expense of the Iraqi people, deny the Iraqi people economic security, create greater instability, and move the country further away from peace. . . . It is immoral and illegal to use war and invasion as mechanisms for robbing a people of their vital natural resources."[47]

In Britain, I was (through Platform) part of a campaign coalition called Hands Off Iraqi Oil.[48] Antiwar groups held demonstrations across the country against U.S. pressure for the oil law. Some 145 members of the British parliament—nearly a quarter of all MPs—signed a motion "express[ing] concern that the British Government, in its involvement in the drafting of Iraq's new oil laws, has sought the views of international oil companies regarding the possible types of contracts that the Iraqi government should offer." The motion insisted that "decisions on the Iraqi oil industry should be made by the Iraqi people without outside interference" and that the British government disclose its attempts to influence Iraqi oil policy.[49]

## In the Shadowy Corners

Time was running out for the U.S. advocates of the Iraqi oil law. Having invested everything in the September deadline, they were becoming desperate. They tried to buy more time. On July 22 Ambassador Crocker met Maliki to ask for the parliamentary recess—already cut from two months to one—to be canceled altogether or shortened to two weeks, a call Maliki endorsed. But the parliament refused, to the fury of U.S. politicians and commentators. To them the Iraqi politicians were lazy and had insulted the noble sacrifices of the U.S. armed forces. No one considered that maybe the Iraqis simply did not want to do what the U.S. administration was pushing for. "Our brave men and women continue to patrol the hot streets of Baghdad in full battle gear. They will get no vacation," fumed Senator Robert Byrd, a Democrat from West Virginia and the U.S. Senate's longest-serving member. "They continue to risk their lives in the sand and the heat, supposedly to give the Iraqi politicians 'breathing room' to build a political consensus. Those politicians are now on vacation."[50]

The tone warned of the hostility that would greet admissions of failure in the September report to Congress. In Iraq the pressure remained constant even as the odds on success grew longer. Condoleezza Rice tried to remain optimistic. In an interview with CBS she pointed out:

The political leadership of these very powerful parties, which really are the key to getting legislation that can be passed, are working. They're not on vacation. The prime minister, the presidency council—which represents these very powerful party interests—are trying to work to see if they can forge a compromise on some of this legislation that then can pass the parliament. And I do hope and do believe that when that legislation is ready, the parliament will be ready to pass it.[51]

Rice was right about the relative insignificance of the Iraqi parliament. As Wael Abdel Latif, an MP from Allawi's Iraqi National List, lamented, "We know the democracy being practiced in Iraq has nothing to do with the parliament." Decisions, he said, were made in "shadowy corners."[52]

Still, time was tight, and the United States' only hope now was to secure a political deal on the oil law during the recess, clearing the way for a vote in the days following the parliament's return. The approach recognized the new political dynamic and tried to tweak it to U.S. advantage. The grand plan was to form a new pro-U.S. government coalition comprising the parties that Raed Jarrar had labeled the separatists. For all its officials' talk of getting beyond narrow sectarian agendas in Iraq and of desiring a more national political discourse, the United States chose to work with and support the parties with the strongest sectarian or ethnic agendas, just as it had during the drafting of the constitution. Indeed, when former prime minister Ibrahim al-Ja'afari told Meghan O'Sullivan that some of the nationalist parties, along with some members of Da'wa, Tawafuq, and the Kurdistan Alliance, had established an explicitly anti-sectarian coalition, she warned him against doing anything that would unsettle Maliki's position.[53]

The two Kurdish parties were straightforward, as they had always been U.S. allies. They were already aligned with ISCI, the strongest U.S. ally among the Shi'a parties. The prime minister's Da'wa Party naturally would have to be involved, so the Shi'a United Iraq Alliance would be split, jettisoning the Sadr Current and al-Fadhila, its two nationalist parties. Finally, the Iraq Islamic Party, the most opportunistic and sectarian of the parties in the Sunni Tawafuq coalition, would be brought in. This was the approach O'Sullivan and Stephen Hadley had proposed in October 2006. Not only would it help deliver a parliamentary majority (if the members of those five parties obeyed their leaders), allowing the oil law and other benchmarks to be achieved, but a coalition comprising Shi'a, Sunni Arabs, and Kurds—and hence supposedly representative—would look like a step toward reconciliation and therefore play well back in the United States.

The negotiations were coordinated by Crocker and O'Sullivan. On August 13, following frantic efforts to get the parties to the table and to prepare an agenda, a three-day summit began in Baghdad to forge this new government coalition. Present were the leaders of the five separatist parties, two Shi'a, two Kurds, and one Sunni Arab: Maliki, Hakim, Barzani, Talabani, and Hashemi. The parties called themselves the Front of the Moderates, borrowing the United States' favored language for its allies in the Middle East, the unacknowledged irony being that these were precisely the Iraqi parties with the most radical ethno-sectarian agendas.

But the move failed. Tareq Hashemi of the Iraqi Islamic Party recognized that he had the kingmaker role and demanded more cabinet posts for his party as the price of his support. He would, after all, be taking the biggest risk by aligning himself against the rest of the Sunni parties. His price was too high; instead, the other four parties cemented their own alliance.[54] Ambassador Crocker could not contain his annoyance at the breakdown of the talks. "The major problems confronting the country, the reasons that brought the leadership together are the kinds of thing that are going to have to be solved by Shi'ite, Sunni and Kurds," he said. Noting the limitations of the four parties that remained, he grumbled, "This is a Kurdish-Shi'ite grouping. It certainly seems to me that by itself it is not going to be able to get at some of these core difficulties."[55] (Furthermore, without Hashemi's party, there was no chance of marshaling a parliamentary majority.)

In fact, the situation looked even worse than if the initiative had never been tried. After months of talking reconciliation, after all the efforts of Zalmay Khalilzad to "bring Sunnis into the process," the collapse of the grand coalition highlighted the sectarian differences between the parties the United States was promoting. It also entrenched the government-opposition dynamic and appeared to push resolution of the oil law and other issues out of reach.

As always, the U.S. government and mainstream media commentators had their own version of the story. For them the failure to establish a coalition of moderates and to pass the oil law Iraq so clearly needed were an indication of the inherent sectarianism of Iraqis. Maliki was now in a very weak position, effectively leading a minority government since the resignations of the Sadr Current, the Iraqi National List, and Tawafuq. But the attempt to push through the unpopular oil law, widely seen as both dividing Iraq and handing its riches to foreigners, had in fact contributed to the delegitimizing and hollowing out of his government.

With the benchmark approach in tatters, another regime change looked like a real prospect. "I think there's a certain level of frustration with the leadership in general, [its] inability to . . . come together to get, for example, an oil revenue law passed or provincial elections," President Bush complained. "The fundamental question is: Will the government respond to the demands of the people? If the government doesn't respond to the demands of the people, they will replace the government." The unspoken subtext—that U.S. forces would be the ones to enact that supposed will of the Iraqi people—echoed so loudly from Bush's comment that he had to quickly disclaim, "That's up to the Iraqis to make that decision, not American politicians."[56] (In fact, the Iraqi people were against the law. The "people" who demanded the law and could replace the government were the people in the U.S. administration.)

While officials later insisted that Bush's remarks were not intended to weaken Maliki's position, Ambassador Crocker gave another warning on the same day: "We do expect results, as do the Iraqi people, and our support is not a blank check."[57] Yet as the nationalist parties coalesced around an antisectarian agenda, the U.S. embassy repeatedly warned them not to undermine Maliki.[58] It seems U.S. diplomats were interested only in pressure from their own allies, even if they were sectarian parties.

Now there were feverish rumors about who would replace Maliki, with the most popular theories advancing either Vice President Adil Abdul-Mahdi, the pro-U.S. member of the ISCI, or former prime minister Ayad Allawi. Speculation about Abdul-Mahdi postulated a parliamentary vote of no confidence. On the other hand, Arab newspapers and television were rife with talk of a U.S.-supported military coup to reinstall Allawi. Meanwhile, Allawi was working hard to reposition himself as the candidate of choice and had hired U.S. public relations firm Barbour, Griffith & Rogers (led by Bob Blackwill, Bush's 2004 envoy to Iraq) to promote him stateside.[59]

Other U.S. politicians took Bush's hints further and openly called for Maliki's removal. Chairman of the Senate Armed Services Committee Carl Levin, returning from a two-day visit to Iraq, announced to reporters, "I've concluded that this is a government which cannot, is unable to, achieve a political settlement. It is too bound to its own sectarian roots, and it is too tied to forces in Iraq which do not yield themselves to compromise."[60] He called on the Iraqi parliament to vote Maliki out of office and replace him with "a less sectarian and a more unifying prime minister and government."[61] (He was right about the sectarian nature of the government, although in an ironic way: Maliki himself was not its most sectarian member—the ISCI party of alternative Adil Abdul-Mahdi was more so.) Levin's words were echoed two days later by Democratic presidential candidate Hillary Clinton.

The media too were starting to write off Maliki's political future, referring to him as "beleaguered" and his government as "fragile" or "shaky." "My sense, he is toast in the not-too-distant future," commented Jack Cafferty of CNN.[62]

# PART FOUR

# Oil Companies on the Front Line 2007–2011

# 20

# The New Iraq

*If Kirkuk had no oil, no one would fight over it.*
—Qader Aziz, KRG president's envoy on Kirkuk referendum, 2008[1]

The road south from Dohuk winds between dusty hills, their crumbling sandstone alternately pale yellow, ocher, and maroon. Scrubby bushes dot their slopes, and the occasional shepherd leads his goats along rough pathways. The road passes a Peshmerga checkpoint before it finally breaks out of the hills into the Mosul plain. A turning to the left takes the traveler through the town of Ba'dree, where sheep, grassless, wander along the edge of the main street. The route continues to Ba'dree's better-off neighbor Shaikhan, a town troubled by religious tensions between Islamists and the Yezidi minority. Behind these two towns lies Jebel Semroot. A sign by the road warns off unauthorized vehicles; a second prohibits unauthorized weapons. It was on this hill, or rather beneath it, that the march of the world's superpower was finally stopped.

On September 8, 2007, two days before Petraeus's and Crocker's reports to the U.S. Congress, the Kurdistan Regional Government announced that it had signed a PSA for oil development rights over an area of three hundred square miles centered on Semroot. The beneficiary was Hunt Oil, a mid-size, privately owned company based in Dallas.

Oil Minister Shahristani declared the deal illegal, as only the national government had the right to sign oil contracts.[2] "For people who are shouting that this is illegal, our advice to them is, 'Shut up,'" hit back KRG natural resources minister Ashti Hawrami.[3] This most undiplomatic of rows marked the collapse of the deal brokered by Ambassador Khalilzad at Dukan: there was now no prospect of agreement on the oil law even among the U.S. administration's allies in the Iraqi government.

## Mission Unaccomplished

The Hunt Oil contract didn't kill the United States' oil law project so much as certify it dead. As we have seen, even if the pro-U.S. parties had resolved their differences, they could not have marshaled a parliamentary majority to pass the law. And the more people found out about the oil law, the more opposition to it had grown. The deal with Hunt was rather an indication that the KRG had recognized the law would not pass and so had decided to proceed without it. And with all U.S. efforts focused on September, the failure to meet the deadline released the pressure. There would not now be an oil law for a long time.

The unions, the experts, and others had won a remarkable victory in their campaign against the oil law. Their achievement indicated not only the unpopularity of the U.S.-sponsored legislation but also the capacity of Iraqi civil society to organize, even in the most difficult of circumstances. The United States, on the other hand, despite military escalation, persistent threats, and economic inducements, had failed to achieve its primary goal of the last eighteen months. The U.S. government naturally continued to portray the oil law as stalled because of ethnic and sectarian disputes, a characterization that was almost unanimously accepted by the media. In private, officials expressed a different frustration. A cable from Ambassador Crocker in early 2008 complained that foreign investment in Iraq's oil had been "subject to ultranationalist hype about foreign exploitation."[4] That ultranationalist hype in fact represented the view of most Iraqis.

The U.S. officials pushing the oil law had privately resigned themselves over the previous weeks to the fact that the law was unlikely to pass on time. The talk in late August 2007 of toppling Maliki may have been as much an outpouring of frustration, or the unstoppable follow-through of a long bat swing, as a genuine threat. A coup d'état was not a viable option. The whole point of the oil law—approved within the constitution by an elected government and parliament—was to give investing oil companies legal cover. A parliamentary putsch would not have worked either. It would have again taken months to form a new government, especially as there was no obvious alternative to Maliki. Both Adil Abdul-Mahdi and Ayad Allawi had limited support among Iraqis, in part because they were seen as too close to the United States. Maliki may have recognized that his position was safest as long as the United States still needed him to pass the oil law.

In the event, under the intense pressure of the benchmarks, fault lines had opened into deep fractures between the United States' Iraqi allies. Worse still for the oil law advocates, the cracks were spreading into the U.S. administration itself—between those who were glad that private companies were finally operating in Iraq and others who saw this development as an obstacle to the real prize of Iraq's giant and supergiant oilfields in the south.

The American media speculated as to whether the U.S. government had approved the Hunt deal. Was the administration in fact undermining its own policy of an oil law and reconciliation? After all, Ray Hunt, the company's chairman and CEO, was a close friend of George W. Bush. The truth was that the administration was divided. Official U.S. policy was supposed to favor centralized management of Iraq's oil. A U.S. embassy official complained, "We think that these contracts have needlessly elevated tensions between the KRG and the Iraqi government."[5] During negotiations on the oil law in 2006, the U.S. Treasury had supported a "national system which is unequivocally controlled and operated by the federal government,"[6] echoing the policy agreed at the Camp David meeting that summer. Even before the war the Pentagon's Energy Infrastructure Planning Group had recommended, "All policy issues are guided by the underlying principle that Iraqi petroleum resources belong to . . . the nation as a whole, not to any regional entity."[7]

But for others in the U.S. government, after four years of setbacks and enforced realism in Iraq, the siren call of quick-buck capitalism was too sweet to resist. Hunt had obtained a PSA after all, the type of contract oil companies desperately wanted and was proving so difficult to obtain in the rest of Iraq. Not only that, the Kurdish parties had always been U.S. allies, the Peshmerga had fought alongside the Americans, Kurdistan was stable, and Kurdish leaders were inviting the United States to establish air bases in the region. BuyUSA.gov, the breathless website of the U.S. Commercial Service, was especially enthusiastic about the "Other Iraq," as the KRG branded itself. "Boom without the bang" was one of the website's less tasteful headlines. Many in the State Department too had broken with the official policy, telling Hunt managers that the United States had no policy either for or against such deals.[8] For the next six months U.S. efforts were in disarray.

## The Other Iraq

On October 8, 2007, the KRG signed another four PSAs. On November 7, seven more. And on November 13, five more. All had been quietly negotiated without any competition.[9] These seventeen contracts, signed in just over two months, covered more than half the land area of Kurdistan. Companies such as BP, Shell, and ExxonMobil held back, leaving the field to junior players in the oil industry, relatively obscure companies such as Perenco, Norbest, and Gulf Keystone. The majors could always buy them out later if the gamble paid off.

From a Kurdish perspective, using PSAs served the two chief drivers of the region's politics: distrust of Baghdad and the dream of ultimate independent statehood. For most intents and purposes, Kurdistan was already an independent state. It had its own flag, its own constitution, and in some countries its own diplomatic representation (such as its "ambassador" to the United States, Qubad Talabani, son of Jalal); most important, the Peshmerga controlled the territory and Iraqi army units were not permitted to enter. But Kurds had little oil expertise themselves, having been kept out of the Iraqi oil business by decades of Arab favoritism. So if they were to have an oil industry and an independent economy, they would need foreigners to run it. Meanwhile, a belligerent neighbor, wanting to prevent an example being set for its own Kurdish minority, would be less willing to invade a Kurdistan populated by American and other nations' oil companies.

Ashti Hawrami was a paradoxical figure. A fifty-nine-year-old with combed-over white hair, he was one of Iraq's leading oil professionals, respected by many for what he had achieved in running the consultancy ECL. As engineer Falah Khawaja put it, "I can vouch—anywhere—Ashti is apolitical. No politics. He had not even met any of the Kurdish parties, representatives, even in London, never. He was a businessman. That came later. He was a professional. I wish he'd remained a professional, because Ashti is good. His company was bought for so many millions. ECL started with a small company called Geopec. He developed it. The guy was good. For me, I am proud of Ashti as an Iraqi."[10]

To the oil companies that came to Kurdistan and those who met him at international conferences, his approach was clear and met their needs: deals were based on a model contract that contained production sharing terms common in small to medium oil transactions. Hunt Oil had signed the contract within three months of being approached, in June 2007, by a private Kurdish company.[11] Many lauded the KRG for Hawrami's professionalism. "Congratulations and our compliments, this is a modern petroleum law that covers all relevant points," said a representative of one major oil company, praising the Kurdistan region's own oil and gas law. "Here in the USA the documents are seen to be fair, modern and thorough in all aspects" was another comment.[12] In the U.S. embassy cables released by WikiLeaks, he is almost always referred to as "Ashti"; most other Iraqi politicians are called by their surnames.

Yet his personality was hardly pragmatic in the manner one might expect. Since his arrival in the KRG in 2006, he had been maximalist in his demands from the federal government, more so even than KRG president Masoud Barzani. He did not hold back from publicly hurling insults, especially at Shahristani: "His views are irrelevant. . . . Dr. Shahristani should concentrate on making a positive contribution to the country, rather than undermining the constructive work that the KRG is carrying out."[13] Or on another occasion: "His old slogan of 'illegal and illegitimate' is becoming very boring. This message and his 'blackmail list' of companies are unproductive and embarrassing for Iraq as a country. No one is paying any attention about what he saying."[14]

Mahmoud Othman, one of the most respected independent Kurdish politicians, characterized the dispute to me. Hawrami is a "very smart businessman, a very good expert in oil, but not a politician. To be oil minister you need to be a politician. Shahristani knows nothing about oil, but he is a politician. One of them has the experience of being a politician and the other the expert—together they make one person!"[15]

If Baghdad suffers from too many decision makers, Kurdistan has too few. In Baghdad even routine tasks involve negotiating several layers of bureaucracy, shuttling between desks to get the required signatures, forms, receipts, and authorizations. In contrast, while researching this book two years after the deal, I tried to get permission from the KRG to visit the Hunt Oil site and to interview someone from the Ministry of Natural Resources.

Both requests received the same answer: "You have to ask Ashti." The minister was at a press conference, however; was there someone else who could give permission? "I don't know; you have to ask Ashti." Could I attend the press conference? "Ask Ashti."

## No-Man's-Land

I stopped to talk to two Kurdish men, Sardar and Sinar, sitting by the road in Shaikhan. I asked them about their hopes for what oil would bring them. "We don't even have chairs. We don't have services," answered Sardar. "When you look around, it's all mud. We sit on the mud. There are no gardens or trees. They don't care about us." Hadn't oil brought jobs? No, he replied, apart from very few security guards hired locally. "The workers don't come from here—maybe Dohuk or Sulaymaniya, I don't know. It's all based on *wasta* [connections]. It's who you know. It's not for poor people. Oil in Iraq is never for the people; it's all for the government."[16]

But which government? Now, that was the problem. "This is what you call a disputed area," Sardar explained. "Dohuk didn't accept my son for high school because they said he was from Mosul [Ninawa province]. Mosul didn't accept him because he is from the KRG. So he has been working three years as a laborer."

Semroot and Shaikhan were legally outside the Kurdistan Region, whose border was marked by the checkpoint we passed on our way there. But since 2003 the Peshmerga had spread south and west to claim much greater areas of territory. Hunt Oil officials were well aware of the administrative geography. On September 5, three days before the contract was announced, Hunt's regional manager, David McDonald, told U.S. officials that the "Dohuk area" of operations consisted of administrative districts of Ninawa province. But, he said, "this is a significant opportunity that outweighs the legal ambiguity," for the reason that drilling for oil in the area was "like shooting fish in a barrel."[17]

While the politicians and bureaucrats argued, the area was stagnating. "Sometimes the government doesn't build something and blames the KRG. The KRG blames the central government," said Amr, a local businessman, whom I met in a coffeehouse in downtown Shaikhan. In no-man's-land people received services from neither authority. As for the arrival of the oil drillers, Amr said, "Of course it's going to worsen the problems. It will increase the conflict between the political parties because oil is the source of their funds."[18]

## Territorial Dispute

The destabilizing role of oil is seen especially in Kirkuk, the most important of the "disputed territories." When the Turkish Petroleum Company (soon to be renamed IPC) first struck oil in 1927, it was in the southernmost of the field's three connected oil-bearing domes, so called because of the shape of the cap rock. Eighty years later two of the domes, Baba and Avanah, still provided the vast majority of northern Iraq's oil production. But the northernmost of the three domes, Khurmala, had never been developed despite several abortive attempts in the 1980s, the 1990s, and most recently 2005.

Falah Khawaja was sent north in spring 2007 to complete the half-built facilities, on behalf of the State Company for Oil Projects (SCOP). "There was a lot of piping there," he recalled. "Equipment, not all of it. We built the yards for it, we started tendering for laying the pipelines, and we had a good team. We started erecting the equipment once we had a civil engineering contract."[19] This time it looked like the work might get completed. That was until four or five months into the work, when the KRG called with a warning that this was disputed territory and SCOP had no right to work there. Then the Peshmerga arrived and ordered Khawaja's team to stop work and leave the site within forty-eight hours. "I never enter into disagreements with anybody holding a gun," Khawaja told me. So, although he believed the order was illegal, he notified his superiors in the Oil Ministry and told his men to move out. "We were driven out of Khurmala."

On November 6, 2007, three weeks after the eightieth anniversary of the first gusher from the Kirkuk field, the KRG awarded the Khurmala Dome to its own, newly formed Kurdistan National Oil Company to develop instead. The company hired by SCOP in 2005, the Iraqi-Turkish engineering firm Kar Group, had since switched sides, and with the equipment SCOP had paid it to deliver and build, it was now working for the KRG. For a while, Shell joined it as a partner, but pulled out in December 2007 for fear of being blacklisted from other projects in the rest of the country.[20]

These two incidents—awarding Hunt Oil drilling rights outside the KRG's territory and forcing Khawaja's team to stop work on the Khurmala Dome—marked a worsening of tensions over the "disputed territories."

The Kurdistan Region of Iraq is legally defined as the area autonomously governed at the time the war began in 2003 (and dating back to 1992), and comprises most of the three provinces of Irbil, Dohuk, and Sulaymaniya, plus smaller parts of Ninawa (Mosul), Kirkuk, and Diyala (Ba'quba). Yet the Kurdish parties wanted a much larger area. During negotiations on the federal structure of Iraq in 2005, KRG officials proposed a region including nearly all of Kirkuk province and about half of Ninawa and Diyala provinces, which would increase the region's area from around fifteen thousand square miles to about twenty-seven thousand.[21] These areas are ethnically mixed, containing Kurds, Arabs, Turkomans, Assyrians, and others.

The territorial disputes date back to a March 1970 agreement between the newly installed Ba'ath government and the Kurdish national movement, led by Mulla Mustafa Barzani, the hero of the Kurdish liberation struggle and father of Masoud, current president of the region. The so-called March Manifesto formally recognized the Kurdish nationality, established cultural and linguistic rights, and created a semiautonomous Kurdish-administered region. However, as expert on Iraqi politics Reidar Visser has pointed out, the agreement contained the seeds of future trouble, since it defined the new region as that with a Kurdish majority population, to be determined by an official census. With demography the basis for resolving political control, the Ba'ath Party adopted a policy of Arabization.[22] It expelled hundreds of thousands of Kurds and other non-Arabs from areas over which it wanted to retain control and incentivized Arab settlers to relocate in their place. Non-Arab families who remained faced restrictions on employment and on the ownership of property. Place-names were Arabized and Arab men were offered rewards for marrying Kurdish women as a means of ethnic assimilation.[23] These changes were compounded by a series of genocide campaigns code-named al-Anfal ("spoils of war") in the latter years of the war with Iran, in which three thousand villages were razed, often using chemical weapons. Some 1.5 million people were displaced by al-Anfal and up to 180,000 killed.[24]

After 2003 the Kurdish parties dominated the local authorities in the ethnically mixed areas—helped by the Sunni Arab boycott of the 2005 provincial elections—and began what they saw as a reversal of the previous demographic reshaping. They provided building materials and cash payments to encourage Kurds to resettle in the Kirkuk area in rapidly erected new towns. Controlled by the parties and their militias rather than by an independent property claims commission, the new changes were shaped more by politics than by justice, however, and did little to help reconciliation. In December 2006 the UN reported that non-Kurdish residents of Kirkuk faced increasing threats, intimidation, and detention, often in KRG facilities.[25] The names of streets, villages, buildings, and schools were changed from Arabic to Kurdish.[26] Meanwhile, Kurdish families living in other areas controlled by the KRG were pressured into moving to Kirkuk.[27] According to the U.S. forces' Kirkuk Resettlement Office, it was possible that as few as 25 percent of Kurdish returnees were genuine displaced persons; the others came to profit from the incentives or for political reasons.[28]

As so often, oil was playing an incendiary role. Attempts by the KRG to secure oilfields, towns, or territory with the Peshmerga were further ratcheting up the tension. "There is no hard line drawn somewhere that says this is KRG-controlled territory and these are disputed territories; it is all gray areas," Hawrami said, defending his deals outside the KRG area. "We provide the security; administratively we run the towns and villages in that area. It is and has always been under control of KRG, under our security." He went on: "Say it transpires later on we were wrong for some reason . . . well, the contract is an Iraqi contract anyway and whoever controls that region can administer the contract. It is no problem." It was the same point the United States had consistently made: there was no political dimension to the nature or terms of contracts, which were purely technical issues, determined by the market or by experts and advisers. The only political element was the struggle between ethnic or religious communities. And, like the U.S. government, Hawrami was using a denial of contested issues to divert flak from his own political maneuverings while laying the groundwork for increased tension between those communities.[29] There were now increasingly frequent skirmishes between Peshmerga and Iraqi forces along what the International Crisis Group referred to as the "trigger line."[30]

In contrast to the politicians, the inhabitants of the "disputed territories" have been consistently the most moderate voices seeking a solution: after all, they have lived in mixed communities for many years and continue to do so.[31] Living on the ethnic front line tends to dampen passions, as the "other" becomes human rather than objectified, and the place becomes home rather than a political or strategic asset. Those ordinary Iraqis remain caught in the middle. As Sardar told me in Shaikhan, "The money goes to the KRG or central government; it doesn't go to us."

## Oil and Unity

Events in Kurdistan were encouraging many Iraqis to take a more unified stand on oil policy. Many of the same groups that had opposed the oil law now criticized the KRG's contracts, including oil experts, the IFOU, and the Association of Muslim Scholars. In January 2008 opposition political leaders drafted a statement criticizing the Kurdish deals, which was signed by the leaders of parties holding 150 of the 275 parliamentary seats.[32] And Shahristani was their standard-bearer. The oil minister said in an interview, "My attitude vis-à-vis the Kurds has unified the disparate colors of the Iraqi political spectrum. Groups of various affiliations call and visit to express their support."[33]

Although these criticisms had been initially sparked by the fear of Iraq breaking up, they soon also encompassed opposition to PSAs, which were now seen as part and parcel of what was wrong with the KRG approach. Again, the two principal issues in Iraqi oil politics—the extent and form of foreign investment in the sector and the degree to which power is devolved to regional or provincial governments—merged in the opposition to the KRG deals. Even Shahristani began to hint that PSAs were part of the problem with the KRG's approach, although his objections were a reaction to the political climate (and hence the popular campaign) rather than any principled position on his part.[34] When he announced in February 2008 that the Iraqi national government would also award contracts without an oil law, a U.S. diplomatic cable reported that he had told companies, "Iraq will work to find a way, without calling it a production sharing agreement, to come up with a model contract which balances risk and reward."[35] A year later he reversed his position and declared himself open to PSAs again.[36]

Iraq's shifting political terrain was also changing the role of the United States. Ironically, the pro-U.S. KRG's oil contracts may have unwittingly hastened the twilight of the occupation, as they highlighted the United States' failure to ensure passage of the oil law, in which it had invested so much political capital. And with elections in Iraq less than two years away, local factors began to outweigh U.S. ones in determining who held power in the government. Politics began to shift away from the sectarian system installed in 2003 toward a more nationalistic configuration that would reflect the views and desires of most of the Iraqi population.

Perhaps, then, it was unsurprising that the United States continued to support the most sectarian, most regressive, and least democratic Iraqi politicians. Throughout 2008 several Iraqi political parties pushed hard for a firm date for provincial elections and a law to regulate them. It was broadly the same coalition that had opposed the oil law: secularists, Sadrists, parts of the Sunni Tawafuq bloc, and some parts of Da'wa. The grouping became known as the July 22 Coalition, after the date that it succeeded in achieving parliamentary approval of an election law. The law was vetoed, however, by two of the three members of the Presidency Council: U.S. allies Jalal Talabani and Adil Abdul-Mahdi. The ruling parties had consistently worked to obstruct new elections, which would reduce the disproportionate power they had gained in 2005. Even as U.S. leaders pressed for the elections, they remained allied to the parties that preferred the status quo.

## Anything You Can Do . . .

On the day the Hunt Oil contract was announced, the news quickly passed through the Hyatt Regency hotel in Dubai, where oil companies and Iraqi officials were meeting at a conference titled Iraq Petroleum 2007. Not to be outdone, Shahristani said that the federal Oil Ministry in Baghdad would soon be offering contracts too, under preexisting Saddam-era laws if necessary. "If for any political reason the [oil] law is delayed, we'll go ahead and start discussions with international oil companies. . . . The Ministry of Oil is entitled to sign any contract that is for the best benefit to the country," he stated.[37] But, he indicated, oil companies wouldn't be getting everything they wanted: the ministry now had a strong preference—most likely as a result of the public campaign—for fixed-fee service contracts rather than PSAs.

John Heavyside, business manager for BP in Iraq, thought differently: "We want to take risks and get incentivized to perform better; service contracts don't really allow us to do that. It's what we all want, all the international companies here. Production-sharing agreements offer a win-win situation. They are equitable and offer lucrative returns and benefits to both the state and investing companies."[38] On the other hand, given the scale of Iraq's oil bounty, oil companies could not afford to miss out, whatever the form of contract. "We simply must be there," said one executive.[39]

The following month, the Oil Ministry began a twin-track process of working toward an auction of Iraq's major oilfields while bringing in companies through two-year "bridging contracts" in the meantime. Direct negotiations

began with ExxonMobil, Chevron, BP, Shell, and Total for the bridging contracts, focusing on the fields for which they had provided technical advice
during the snuggling-up time of 2004–5. And companies were invited to
apply in January and February 2008 to be prequalified for participation in
the auction. More than a hundred applied, and thirty-five were successful.

## A Tightening Grip

In March 2008, Prime Minister Maliki launched an all-out attack on Basra,
which he named Charge of the Knights (Saulat al-Fursan), to reclaim the city
from militias. It soon became clear that the target was not all militias but
rather just the Jaysh al-Mahdi of Muqtada al-Sadr. Militias associated with
the Hakim family's Islamic Supreme Council of Iraq (ISCI) were left unmo-
lested. But immediately the operation ran into trouble, as nearly a thousand
members of the Iraqi forces refused to fight, many going over to the other
side.[40] Those who remained faced fierce fighting. "We supposed that this
operation would be a normal operation, but we were surprised by this resistance," said Defense Minister Abdel Qader Jasim.[41] According to a U.S. intelligence official, "the smell of fear was palpable" among Iraqi commanders and
political leaders in their Basra headquarters.[42] The Sadrists mocked the operation, calling it "Charge of the Mice" (Saulat al-Fa'ran).[43] U.S. forces
stepped in to save Maliki from military disaster. "Frankly, it was the special
forces and the close air support that saved the day," Maliki admitted.[44]

The United States allowed him to claim the credit, however, for two reasons. First, whereas the Iraqi public would not have supported a sustained
American operation against Iraqis, it would welcome an effort by its own
government to stamp out criminal militias. Second, while U.S. leaders had
achieved some military success in the surge, they were keen also to show
political progress, and Maliki's supposed leadership of the operation gave
them that. Sadr, on the other hand, found it harder to portray the Jaysh al-
Mahdi as an anti-occupation force, and with blood on its hands from sectarian killings, it was no longer a useful political base anyway.

Just six months after Maliki had been written off as incapable of governing Iraq, the operation showed him to be a far cannier politician than most
Iraq watchers had believed. By attacking his former Shi'a supporters (the
Sadrists had supported him within the United Iraq Alliance and thereby
given him the prime ministership), and by doing so with limited U.S.

involvement in the public eye, he began to look more like a national politician than a sectarian one. Not only did this distinguish him from other Iraqi allies of the United States, but it made Maliki a political force in his own right, allowing him to portray himself as a strong and competent leader who could bring security, stability, and order to the country.

Oil Minister Shahristani echoed Maliki's success by consolidating his control over the southern oil sector. That summer he removed Jabbar al-Luaibi from his post as director general of South Oil Company as well as the head of the South Gas Company. The *Middle East Economic Survey* commented, "Shahristani's move is, in all likelihood, intimately connected to the fundamental political power shifts taking place and should be seen in the context of Baghdad's attempt to gain full control of Iraq's oil industry sector and push through its program of restructuring and opening up to foreign investment."[45] Luaibi was not opposed outright to foreign involvement in the Iraqi oil industry but was known to be skeptical of the long-term contracts proposed in the oil law. He favored instead five-year deals to get the industry back on its feet. And at least some in the U.S. occupation would not have disapproved of his removal. For example, Charlie Ries, head of economic affairs at the American embassy in Baghdad, said, "I don't believe South Oil is a one-man show."[46] As early as 2004 a report from the British embassy had referred to "the Jabbar question" and noted, "The US want him reined in."[47]

At the same time as he was removing Luaibi, Shahristani tried again to break the IFOU. In late May 2008 he announced that twenty-two union leaders at the Basra refinery would be transferred away from Basra, where the union was based and where their homes and families were, to new jobs at the Daura refinery. Shahristani must have known that Daura was one of the most dangerous areas in Baghdad. Alaa Sabah al-Basri, the deputy head of the refinery union, told me, "Daura was a killing yard. . . . When we first arrived in Daura, people said, 'Are you militias?' We said, 'No, we're from the union.' They said, 'It's a crime to send you, because you can be killed here.'"[48]

Naftana, an informal British-Iraqi pro-union committee of which I was a member, described the transfers as "somewhere between constructive dismissal and a death sentence."[49] On June 17, 2008, Naftana organized a protest when Shahristani came to speak at a conference in London. To his credit, the minister invited me and my fellow Naftana member Sabah Jawad to speak to him about our concerns. Sabah explained the background of the union and pointed out that it had even supported the minister's stance against the KRG's contracts. "Please do not transfer these people," he said. "They are good people."

Shahristani was unmoved. His tone was calm, almost regal, but his words were dark. "These self-appointed individuals do not represent workers and are not elected," he said. "They are involved in corruption and militias." Again I was struck by the paradox of Shahristani: an intellectual with no apparent ax to grind who nonetheless repeatedly insisted that the trade unionists were militias. And no amount of detail we gave him about the union's elections, including the fact that an SOC lawyer had observed them, seemed to register. "They are not trade unionists; they are not elected," he repeated. Even if he had been right—and Sabah and I assured him he was not—the correct course of action would have been to pass his evidence to police or prosecutors and let the courts resolve the unionists' guilt or innocence. As a former human rights activist, Shahristani must have known this.

Simon Steyne of the British Trades Union Congress complained to the International Labour Organization, describing the transfer as "a move calculated to disrupt the union's activities and put them in danger" and suggesting that the obsession with the oil law was "no doubt a reason for [the Iraqi government's] unwillingness to allow free trade unions in the sector."[50] Michael Eisenscher wrote to the Iraqi ambassador to the United States on behalf of U.S. Labor Against the War, arguing, "No democracy can ever be established in Iraq unless and until its workers enjoy the full range of core labor rights recognized by the ILO. . . . Iraq must completely erase all vestiges of its authoritarian and repressive past if it is to earn the respect of the world community." Eventually the international pressure was effective. After two months at Daura refinery, its DG Dathar al-Khasshab agreed that their transfer was unfair and moved them to Samawa refinery in the south. After two more months there, the union leaders were sent to the Iraq Drilling Company for six months, then finally back to the Basra refinery.

## Hope and Fear

The shift from identity-based to nationalist politics was confirmed in the provincial elections of January 2009. Maliki had rebranded himself as a nationalist politician and won in nine of the fourteen provinces that held elections. The rival ISCI, which had no option but to continue to portray itself as the voice of the Shi'a, was trounced: from dominating almost all

Shi'a-majority provinces since 2005 as well as Baghdad, it came first in none of them and remained in ruling coalitions in only two. In Baghdad, ISCI's share of the vote fell from 54.9 to 5.4 percent.[51]

Three related currents were emerging in the new Iraq, one positive and two not. At last the sectarian conflict seemed to be passing, and the discourse of Iraqi politics was shifting from the interests of particular communities to those of the nation. On the other hand, a strengthening government was beginning to show autocratic tendencies, as seen in its attacks on trade unions. Meanwhile, escalating tensions over the disputed territories warned of a potential for new conflict, with oil playing an exacerbating role. The U.S. administration was slow to catch on to the changes and spent much of 2008 on the back foot in Iraq, even as in the United States the consensus verdict on the war moved from abject failure to recovery. A year previously there had seemed little hope for the country; now, to everyone's surprise, that had changed.

# 21

# Overwatch

*Overwatch: n. A tactical technique in which one element is positioned to support by fire the movement of another element by observing known or suspected enemy locations and engaging the enemy if he is visible.*

—U.S. Army Field Manual[1]

In the United States the benchmarks were all but forgotten. President Bush had faced political disaster in September 2007 when Petraeus and Crocker reported to Congress: the Government Accountability Office stated that only three of his eighteen benchmarks had been met. To avert that disaster, the administration had made one of its most effective tactical moves of the war. A week before the scheduled report to Congress, Bush made his third surprise visit to Iraq, but instead of traveling to Baghdad to talk about benchmarks, he flew to the desert province of al-Anbar in the west for a photo shoot with tribal leader Sheikh Sattar Abu Risha. Bush's visit was a clear signal that the benchmark strategy had been abandoned. Five days later the KRG signed its contract with Hunt Oil.

Sheikh Sattar was one of the leaders of the Sahwa (Awakening) movement, a tribe-led grouping that had switched sides from the resistance to the United States. Since becoming prominent in al-Anbar, al-Qaeda had increasingly alienated the tribes, in particular by encroaching on the traditional authority of the sheikhs and their control over roads, infrastructure, and the black market. In 2005 some sheikhs turned against al-Qaeda and sought U.S. protection, which was granted in a few localities. Petraeus decided to formalize and expand the alliance with the Sahwa, and agreed to provide weapons and salaries for its fighters. The Sahwa drove al-Qaeda out of much of al-Anbar, with the U.S. military reporting a 62 percent fall in high-profile attacks—characteristic of al-Qaeda—between March and December 2007.[2]

Bush's visit to al-Anbar was designed to shift the surge's goalposts away from "reconciliation" toward "security." And despite tough questioning from some congressional Democrats, the switch succeeded. With the rebranding of the objective, the surge now looked like a success. This suited all the main U.S. political players: it was a victory in Iraq for the Republicans and an opportunity to end the war for the Democrats. Then-senator Barack Obama said the surge had "succeeded beyond our wildest dreams."[3] News editors knew that their readers and viewers no longer wanted to read or hear about more violence in Iraq, any more than their bosses wanted to pay for expensive Baghdad bureaus. And, best of all, the story now had a Hollywood-style hero: the good man (Petraeus) who had taken on a challenge against all the odds, the maverick who had bucked everyone's advice and eventually won. In February 2009 Petraeus would perform the coin toss for the Super Bowl, further establishing him in American popular culture. Sheikh Sattar, on the other hand, did not benefit from Bush's photo opportunity. Ten days later he was assassinated by al-Qaeda with an improvised bomb outside his house in Ramadi.

Petraeus was certainly shrewder than his predecessors. U.S. forces had previously tended to see all Iraqis as enemies, and so kicked their doors down and dragged them off to prison, often with no evidence of any wrongdoing. Petraeus aimed to do what should have been obvious in a counterinsurgency campaign—avoid creating resentment among the majority of the population.

Violence had indeed diminished significantly by 2008. According to U.S. military figures, civilian deaths were down from a peak of more than 3,500 per month in December 2006 to about 700 per month in March 2008.[4] How much of this was due to Petraeus or the surge? Most analysts believed there were two main reasons behind the short-term reduction in violence: the al-Anbar tribes' decision to fight al-Qaeda and Muqtada al-Sadr's August 2007 declaration of a unilateral cease-fire, both of which removed many belligerents from the conflict.[5] In both, U.S. forces played a role, but the primary drivers were Iraqi. The al-Anbar tribes had turned against al-Qaeda in 2005 and first collaborated with the United States more than a year before Bush ordered the surge, but Petraeus was wise enough to capitalize on the shift. Sadr's cease-fire was probably partly influenced by the presence of an overwhelming U.S. force that he could not match militarily, but a more important reason was that by mid-2007 the Jaysh al-Mahdi was seen as a killer of fellow Iraqis rather than as a credible resistance force.* In the meantime, the cease-fire gave Sadr the opportunity to address his two greatest weaknesses, bolstering his religious credentials through study in the Iranian holy city of Qom and purging the elements of the Jaysh al-Mahdi outside his control.[6]

So militarily the surge had played a supportive role in reducing violence. But almost nobody asked whether its true aims were all so altruistic, nor examined the desirability of the new political settlement it tried to impose on Iraq. In these political terms the outcome of the surge was more complex. On one hand, it was a partial victory for the United States: the broadly pro-Western government had been shored up and the resistance largely broken. Unions, despite their success against the oil law, were facing increased repression. On the other hand, while the makeup of the government was ideologically favorable, the United States had rapidly declining influence over it. The surge had failed to deliver either the benchmarks, especially the oil law, or the Americans' preferred political settlement, a coalition of the most sectarian parties, between which U.S. diplomats could broker policies. Instead, political debate in Iraq was being influenced increasingly by domestic factors and thus taking a more nationalist direction.

Petraeus repeatedly stated that the progress brought by the surge was reversible. The reason it was consolidated rather than quickly reversed was a longer-term political and societal shift—ironically *in opposition to* U.S. policy. Iraqi nationalism grew in the parliament in reaction first to the overt pressures of the benchmarks and then to the unilateral actions of the KRG. Whereas the anti-sectarian parties had previously united unsuccessfully in October 2006 in an attempt to stop the law allowing the formation of new regions, the oil law struggle marked their first major success. And the more organized and articulate parliamentary opposition may have been what pushed Maliki into a more overtly nationalist position, for fear that he would otherwise lose ground electorally. Once a window opened, Iraqis

---

* The triggering incident for the cease-fire was not a confrontation with the United States but a battle with Badr/ISCI-dominated units of the Iraqi police in Karbala during a religious festival in which at least fifty were killed. The incident in the holy city may have been the last straw for an Iraqi public frustrated with the Jaysh al-Mahdi's massive killing of Iraqis.

quickly rejected the alien sectarian politics and discourse the United States had created.

## Unwelcome Guests

Since before the war President Bush and his senior officials had insisted that they had no interest in Iraq's oil or in keeping forces in Iraq beyond the immediate needs of supporting democracy or stability. So surely the administration would not object to having that insistence written into law? In the 2008 Defense Appropriations bill Congress inserted a clause stating that no funds could be used either to establish permanent U.S. bases or "to exercise United States control of the oil resources of Iraq." A subtler president probably would have accepted those restrictions and left their interpretation to semantics. After all, the United States had had "temporary" bases in South Korea for more than half a century, and PSAs termed foreign companies simply "contractors" to a state company that was in charge. But Bush, when signing the act into law, issued a "signing statement" that he would not be bound by the restriction, as it could "inhibit the President's ability to carry out his constitutional obligations" to protect national security.[7]

Bush's signing statement showed that he had failed to grasp how Iraqi politics was changing. In early summer 2008 his administration was forced to abandon a renewed push for the oil law when even the continued presence of U.S. troops came under question and diplomatic resources had to be diverted to that issue. As with earlier diplomatic crises, Meghan O'Sullivan was dispatched to Iraq to help with the negotiations. The UN mandate would expire at the end of 2008, and unless a bilateral agreement was signed with the Iraqi government, U.S. forces would then have to leave. So negotiations began on a so-called Status of Forces Agreement (SOFA) to establish the legal authority for an ongoing troop presence and to determine its powers and responsibilities.

As we saw in chapter 16, when Bush decided to order the surge, the U.S. public debate had been all about an exit strategy. Americans had disagreed about how and when, not whether, to withdraw from Iraq. The Baker-Hamilton Iraq Study Group, which occupied the center of gravity in the debate, had left open the possibility of a surge, but only as a means to withdraw while achieving U.S. political objectives along the way. To remove a hook from a fish's mouth, you first have to push it in farther. That, however, was not how the Bush administration or the military were thinking. Thomas Ricks's *The Gamble*, the highest profile of a run of books celebrating the success of the surge, concluded that now U.S. forces would have to stay in Iraq much longer in order to hold on to its achievements.[8] The surge strategy had in fact been presented to a review by the Council of Colonels* in late 2006 under the heading "Go long."[9] In the closing months of the Bush administration, that strategy was confirmed: rather than creating the conditions to allow the United States to leave, the surge had created the conditions for it to stay.

In March 2008 a team of U.S. lawyers began the SOFA negotiations in Baghdad with a bold set of demands: powers to conduct missions without Iraqi government approval and to detain prisoners independently of the Iraqi courts, immunity from prosecution for both U.S. military and contractors, and the use of fifty-eight long-term bases.[10] The Iraqi negotiators quickly rejected these demands, which were hardly consistent with the notion of a sovereign Iraq. The idea of immunity for contractors was especially unpopular after a Blackwater team had gunned down seventeen unarmed Iraqis with impunity in Baghdad's Nisoor Square in September 2007.

U.S. officials had been confident of concluding an agreement by July 2008, but in early June Iraqi negotiators reported "almost all points [were] under dispute."[11] Maliki may still have felt he needed U.S. protection, but to capitulate on major sovereignty issues would risk his continuation in power as much as the loss of U.S. military support. A year earlier the United States had been the most important determinant of whether a politician would stay in power. Now with elections coming and U.S. influence waning, the Iraqi constituency was growing more important. To work for Maliki, the SOFA therefore would have to be portrayed as a victory for Iraqi sovereignty.

As negotiations progressed, the U.S. team was forced to concede on several of its key aims. It accepted deadlines of June 2009 for the withdrawal of U.S. forces from Iraqi cities, a referendum on whether to accept the SOFA (a "no" vote would require U.S. troops to leave within a year), and the end of 2011 for the withdrawal of all troops from the country. These were major concessions by an administration that for five years had steadfastly refused

---

* A group of officers set up by General Peter Pace, chairman of the U.S. Joint Chiefs of Staff, to review strategy in Iraq.

to consider withdrawal timetables. However, there was still strong Iraqi parliamentary opposition to an agreement, possibly because with an election coming the politicians knew they would be punished by voters if they agreed to extend the occupation. As with the oil law the previous year, U.S. embassy cables obtained and released by WikiLeaks showed that many Iraqi politicians—even Maliki himself[12]—wanted U.S. forces to stay but could not afford to say so publicly, illustrating again the gap between parliamentary and public opinion.[13]

In October 2008 General Ray Odierno, who had recently taken over from Petraeus as U.S. commander in Iraq, presented the Iraqi government with a three-page list of consequences it would face if it failed to approve an acceptable SOFA by the end of the year, including an end to $6.3 billion in aid and $10 billion a year in arms sales. The United States would also stop sharing intelligence, providing air defense, protecting the coast and oil export terminals, guarding the borders, and training the military. It would no longer maintain the military hardware it had supplied or provide secure air transit to Iraqi officials. It would stop operating air traffic control and thereby close down Iraqi airspace. It would not hand over the Iraqi prisoners it held, and it would stop employing 200,000 Iraqis.[14] The SOFA's companion draft Strategic Framework Agreement (SFA) asserted, "The temporary presence of US forces in Iraq is at the request and invitation of the sovereign Government of Iraq and with full respect for the sovereignty of Iraq."[15] Odierno had just given a stark reminder of how limited that sovereignty still was.

Still, the United States had at least as much to lose politically as Iraq did materially if the SOFA was not signed. In the event, the United States conceded the last of its demands—contractor immunity—and the agreement was signed on November 17, 2008. Whereas the defeated Republican presidential candidate John McCain would have found a way to keep troops in Iraq, deferring the agreement would have given the newly elected Barack Obama an opportunity to end the occupation, blaming its sudden end and all the consequences on his predecessor. By securing the continued occupation, the form and timing of any withdrawal would now be entirely Obama's responsibility.

Maliki, meanwhile, had achieved almost all of his demands, and because he portrayed the document as a withdrawal treaty, his nationalist image was further strengthened.

## *The New War*

In reality, the SOFA was neither the withdrawal agreement Maliki claimed nor the long-term extension of the occupation antiwar critics feared. Rather, it marked a transition from the intense and unstable military phase to a new equilibrium. Whatever the Bush administration's hopes, it never would have been feasible—politically, economically, or militarily—to continue the larger, overt military presence over the long term, nor could the United States maintain its initial levels of control or influence over the country. General Odierno's threat list, and the fact that a SOFA was signed at all, showed that the United States did still have significant influence. On the other hand, the fact that the agreement contained a withdrawal timetable showed the limits of that influence.

In 2002 future oil minister Ibrahim Bahr al-Uloum had hinted at the link between the two national security priorities Bush had sought to protect in his signing statement: oil and bases. Speaking at a conference of the American Enterprise Institute, he had suggested that troops should remain as a "sort of life insurance for continuing the social and political changes . . . it's [also] a great incentive for attracting the international oil companies."[16] But how to square the long-term benefits to the United States of staying with the pressures to leave? The answer was not to go away but to remain in the background, as guarantor rather than as up-front implementer—much as an aircraft carrier in the Persian Gulf protects the flow of oil without expecting to be engaged in frequent combat. Hence the agreement to withdraw from cities the following June. Stepping back from the front line would address the most politically significant problem back home: the loss of American soldiers' lives. Meanwhile, less visibility would reduce Iraqi anger at the on-going occupation. General Petraeus called the new phase "overwatch."

Like much in the recent occupation of Iraq, there was a parallel in the British experience eighty years earlier. From Iraq's formal independence in 1932 until the 1958 revolution, Britain maintained bases in the country as well as a privileged position as supplier of military hardware, intelligence, and funds. Having effectively ruled Iraq during the 1920s, Britain's military and political role had moved into the background at independence, with the exception of 1941, when it reoccupied Iraq to remove a pro-German government. Instead, the primary Iraqi-British struggle over subsequent decades was between the Iraqi state and British oil companies in the form of the Iraq Petroleum Company. The front line was legal, economic, and technical. The British military was present only as a last resort—"life insurance," in Bahr al-Uloum's words.

In 2008 this new struggle with oil companies was just beginning, as we shall see in the next chapter. The United States would still be present until contracts were actually signed, but once they were, the battle over the coming decades would again become legal, economic, and technical, with the U.S. military in overwatch, ready to provide supporting fire if called upon. As Hassan Juma'a put it the first time I met him in 2005, "There are two stages of this war: first, the military occupation, then the economic war."[17]

## Private Armies

In September 2007 U.S. diplomats asked oil companies if they needed improved security conditions before they could invest in Iraq. "We would prefer it," they replied, "but we can always buy security."[18] Along with the lawyers on the contractual front line and the U.S. military in overwatch, then, there would be a third foreign echelon in the new Iraq, the oil companies' own private security forces.

Around the world, oil companies typically protect their installations and activities through a combination of host country military forces and private security contractors. In 2008 private military and security companies (PMSCs) were already doing major business with oil companies in Iraq. Their services ranged from armed physical security to setting up front offices in order to give the oil companies a presence in the country without risking their own staff. It was a lucrative business: in early 2009 I learned that a one-way "secure taxi" ride from Baghdad International Airport to the Green Zone—a journey of less than half an hour—cost $2,000.

Since 2003 PMSCs had constituted the largest armed foreign force in Iraq after the Americans, numbering up to 48,000 operatives by 2006.[19] Many companies had been formed since the start of the "war on terror" in 2001; one company that does have a prior track record is ArmorGroup, now part of G4S, the world's largest security company. During the 1990s, a precursor of the company called Defence Systems Limited (DSL) provided security for BP's oil extraction operations in the Casanare region of Colombia and its export pipeline. After a two-year investigation, reporters Michael Sean Gillard and Melissa Jones alleged a close connection with local police and military units implicated in torture and disappearances, including sharing intelligence on critics of the oil project, although BP strenuously denied the allegations.[20] Around the world private security contractors did not stop at defending installations from physical attack but went out proactively to neutralize any threat to their clients' interests. Could Iraq expect similar practices? With its recent history of death squads and extrajudicial detention, under both Saddam and the occupation, it was a worrying possibility.

The PMSC industry has worked hard to distance itself from the unregulated dogs of war of the 1990s. These days PMSCs present themselves as successful corporations, with shiny offices, balance sheets, and a public relations team. But on the ground things looked rather different. In 2005, a "trophy video" appeared on a website apparently run by Iraq-based employees of Aegis, another PMSC that, like ArmorGroup, has marketed itself heavily to oil companies in Iraq. To a soundtrack of Elvis Presley's "Mystery Train," the two-and-a-half-minute film shows footage shot through the back window of an SUV traveling along "Route Irish" to Baghdad International Airport.

*Train train, coming 'round, 'round the bend . . .*

Gunfire rattles whenever a vehicle appears behind. Some swerve off the road. One car veers into the back of a parked taxi, and no one emerges from it after the crash, suggesting the driver and any passengers have been killed.[21] The killing is indiscriminate, and the tone of the video suggests the perpetrators enjoy it, want to brag about it, and have no fear of the consequences.

*Train train, coming 'round, 'round the bend . . .*

A statement from Aegis did not deny that the video was genuine but claimed without any supporting details that "all of the circumstances, when seen in context, were within the approved and accepted Rules for the Use of Force, [and] no crime had been committed."[22] An investigation by the U.S. Army also found no evidence of criminality.[23] However, according to the *Irish Echo*, Rod Stoner, an Aegis employee who was in the vehicle when the video was shot, said that neither he nor anyone else in the vehicle was contacted in the course of either investigation.[24]

*Well it took my baby, but it never will again . . .*

The incidents shown on the video were far from unusual. Captain Adnan Tawfiq of the Iraqi Interior Ministry told the *Sunday Telegraph* he had received compensation claims regarding fifty or sixty such shootings by traveling private contractors. "When the security companies kill people they just drive away and nothing is done. Sometimes we ring the companies concerned and they deny everything."[25] The apparent rationale for such behavior is to eliminate all risk—a vehicle approaching a convoy from behind might contain explosives—regardless of the impact on civilians. Such attitudes boded ill for how they might behave when called on to protect oil companies. Arguably the last thing Iraq needed with its recent history of sectarian and criminal killings was a new set of interests guarded by trigger-happy gunmen.

## Continuity We Can Believe In

On February 27, 2009, new U.S. president Barack Obama took the stage at Camp Lejeune, a Marine base in North Carolina. "Let me say this as plainly as I can. By August 31, 2010, our combat mission in Iraq will end," he told thousands of watching Marines. But a "transitional force" of between 35,000 and 50,000 troops would remain in Iraq after the end of combat operations to train and advise the Iraqi military, carry out counterterrorism operations, and protect ongoing U.S. military and civilian activities. At around a third of current troop levels, it was hardly a full withdrawal, and with definitions of terrorism having expanded under Bush to encompass almost any act hostile to the United States, the mission did not look all that limited either.

Obama's announcement was better received among Republicans than among Democrats. Obama's election rival John McCain said he supported the plans, as did Republican congressional leaders. On the other hand, the Democratic leaders of the House and Senate, Nancy Pelosi and Harry Reid, expressed dismay.[26] Yet no one should have been surprised. Throughout the election campaign Obama had been careful not to commit to withdrawing *all* U.S. troops from Iraq, even while saying that he would end the war. In fact, his campaign pledge had been only to withdraw "combat troops." Few voters picked up on that detail.

One striking endorsement of Obama's plans came from Gordon Johndroe, Bush's former national security spokesman, who commented, "The specific timing is only slightly different [from what Bush had planned] but consistent with the goal of helping Iraq become self-sufficient in providing its own security."[27] The difference was that Bush had not chosen to accept a withdrawal timetable but had been forced into one by the increasingly assertive Iraqi government in the SOFA negotiations, whereas Obama had always opposed the war and sought to wind it down. But on the Iraq policy itself, his choices after taking office clearly indicated continuity with the last two (post-Rumsfeld) years of the Bush administration. His personnel retentions included not just defense secretary Robert Gates but also Centcom commander David Petraeus, Iraq commander Ray Odierno, Joint Chiefs chairman Mike Mullen, and National Security Council Iraq/Afghanistan adviser Douglas Lute (who had succeeded Meghan O'Sullivan in May 2007). These retained Bush appointees had worked hard since the election to shape the details of Obama's policy in a way that maximized the ongoing troop presence.

The same evening as Obama's announcement, Gates, pressed by journalists, said he believed the United States should have a continued presence even after the SOFA deadline at the end of 2011 to train, equip, and provide intelligence for the Iraqi military.[28] Although Obama rejected the idea of permanent bases in Iraq at the height of his election campaign in 2008, he had previously floated the idea in a pre-campaign speech of November 2006, when he suggested, "Drawing down our troops in Iraq will allow us to redeploy additional troops to northern Iraq and elsewhere in the region as an over-the-horizon force," the same concept as Petraeus's overwatch. "In such a scenario it is conceivable that a significantly reduced U.S. force might remain in Iraq for a more extended period of time," he added.[29] That idea now seemed to be back on the table.

A few months later, when the deadline approached for the referendum on the SOFA, a U.S. embassy cable reported, "To block or delay a referendum while avoiding the counter-productive impression that we are lobbying against it, Embassy is focusing intensely on senior leaders, urging delay or cancellation, while taking a quieter approach at lower levels. In public, we stress our full commitment to the [SOFA] and all its terms."[30] The comment recalled the plan in the U.K. Energy Strategy for Iraq in 2004 (see chapter 8) to "push the message on FDI [foreign direct investment] to the Iraqis in private," but with "careful handling to avoid the impression that we are trying to push the Iraqis down one particular path."

Furthermore, in a reprise of the 2007 U.S.-Iraq relationship, Obama saw an American role in pressuring Iraqi leaders to reach a political settlement.

"We can serve as an honest broker in pursuit of fair and durable agreements on issues that have divided Iraq's leaders," he said. Vice President Joe Biden went further, telling House Democrats the administration would be "very deeply involved" in brokering a political settlement. "We're going to have to get in there and be much more aggressive in forcing them to deal with these issues," he said.[31]

Americans who opposed the Iraq War may have been relieved at Obama's election, but many Iraqis were appalled at the prospects raised by his choice of running mate. Biden had long advocated dividing Iraq on ethnic and sectarian lines. In September 2007 he had proposed to the Senate what became known as the partition bill, which passed by a vote of 75–23. This nonbinding bill called for the U.S. government to encourage Iraq's devolution into three semiautonomous ethno-sectarian regions, with a much-weakened central government in Baghdad. A poll at the time found that only 9 percent of Iraqis (including Kurds) favored "a country divided into separate independent states" and only 28 percent preferred "a group of regional states with their own regional governments and a federal government in Baghdad," whereas 62 percent favored "one unified Iraq with a central government in Baghdad." Two percent considered "the separation of people on sectarian lines" a good thing, and 98 percent thought it was a bad thing.[32]

In some ways the ethno-sectarian frame through which the Obama administration (and especially Biden) viewed Iraq was even more regressive than that of the late Bush administration and risked halting or reversing the decline of sectarianism over the previous year.[33] This was seen in the administration's choice of ambassador to replace Ryan Crocker: Christopher Hill. Hill later wrote of Iraq, "Americans, not unlike many people outside the Middle East, regard the struggle in Iraq as one pitting those who supported democracy against those who somehow supported the dictatorship ["dead-enders," as then secretary of defense Donald Rumsfeld described them at a Pentagon press conference]. But, for many people in the region, the Iraq War involved something else: the transfer of power in what had been a Sunni-led country to the Shia majority. Shia-ruled Iraq has not been well received in the Sunni Arab world." (In fact, neither view was shared by many outside the U.S. administration and media.) He thus referred to Iraq as "the black sheep of the Arab world" and warned that "many Sunnis chafe at life under a prime minister who leads a Shi'a-based party."[34]

But since September 2007 the U.S. administration had been forced to accept a decline in its influence in Iraq. Even the maximal exertion of military power through the surge had failed to achieve the benchmarks, including the oil law. Obama reverted to the pre-surge notion promoted by the Baker-Hamilton group—that the threat of withdrawing support (rather than escalating military engagement) could put pressure on Iraqi leaders. In his election campaign he had said that in his administration the U.S. military "will continue efforts to train and support the Iraqi security forces as long as Iraqi leaders move toward political reconciliation." He specifically mentioned "oil revenue sharing."[35] Now the U.S. military began pointing out to journalists that the Iraqi government still needed them for intelligence, air defense, training, and weapons supplies, among other things.[36] The ongoing dependence echoed the list General Odierno had highlighted when pressuring the Iraqi government to sign the SOFA. But in direct contrast to Bush's benchmarks in 2007, U.S. pressure would operate behind the scenes and avoid embarrassing Iraqi leaders by making them look like puppets. "It has to be seen here as doing it quietly," said a State Department official, "so that you are not doing things for the Iraqis, the Iraqis are doing things for themselves but with your help and we remain in the shadows. . . . It's a very delicate choreography."[37]

In any case, Maliki was enough of a pragmatist to know the boundaries. Speaking in London on April 30, 2009, he said, "The development of the private sector is not only an Iraqi desire. . . . We feel responsibility towards the rest of the world to provide oil and stabilize markets for producers and consumers."[38] This was quite different from the messages he gave out in Iraq.

# 22

# Talking Business

*There is tremendous interest in what is on offer. The quantity of reserves on offer is unheard of, it's huge.*

—Oil company executive, February 2009[1]

Press conferences are not usually secretive occasions. But the invitation to the Oil Ministry's event in October 2008 admonished attendees, "Please do NOT share this detail with anyone other than those that 'need to know' within your organisation."[2] It came at the end of a long day of Oil Ministry talks with representatives of thirty-five multinational oil companies at London's Park Lane Hotel, at which Shahristani had outlined the contracts he would offer in an auction in June 2009. The winners would manage six of Iraq's largest oilfields and two gasfields for the next twenty years.[3] These fields between them contained 40 percent of Iraq's known oil reserves and accounted for virtually all its current production. With the vast majority of Iraq's economy up for grabs, it's little wonder the ministry was nervous.

The day was almost as significant for the multinationals as for Iraq. Forty billion barrels of oil—licensed all at once—was the largest volume of known oil to go on the market in the history of the industry. Most oil contracts—including those obtained by companies when they first moved into the major oil-producing countries of the Middle East in the early twentieth century—have been for exploration, to search for uncertain quantities of oil. Previously the largest amount of *known* oil to be contracted at once was 4 billion barrels in the Azeri-Chirag-Guneshli fields in Azerbaijan, awarded in 1994, just a tenth of what was now on offer in Iraq.[4] And this was only the start. A week earlier Shahristani had told Marc Wall, the U.S. embassy's coordinator for economic transition, that he planned another auction every three months until all seventy-five of Iraq's known fields had been awarded.[5]

I spent the morning hanging around with a gaggle of journalists, rushing to talk to anyone who came out of the meeting. I was soon to leave my job at Platform to write this book, and this was my first day's work as a freelance reporter. Several journalists commented that they'd never experienced such paranoia. At one point, three of us went back into the hotel for another cup of coffee. A security guard, knowing that we were there to report on the meeting, rushed to stop us. "I am asking you to leave the hotel," the man said, to our bewilderment. "I don't have to give you a reason."

The moods of the company men said a lot about what was going on. Two representatives of the Japanese firm Inpex seemed quite lost. "It's a lot of information," one noted. "Very quick," added the other. The two smokers—it was the smokers we got to talk to—from the China National Petroleum Company (CNPC) were more relaxed. They'd renegotiated their 1997 contract with Saddam Hussein's government for the al-Ahdab field seven weeks earlier and so knew the drill. "We expect it will be similar."

Then there was the Shell delegation, which marched in formation through the hotel with a sense of purpose as focused as a group of military police with an arrest warrant. Shell had recently signed a heads of agreement (an outline of commercial terms) that gave it the exclusive right to negotiate a full contract for gas development. If the deal was completed, Shell would get twenty-five-year exclusive rights to collect "associated" gas—the gas that occurs naturally in oilfields and was currently flared off (burned) rather than being collected, since the oil was the higher priority—from all of Basra province's oilfields and to develop Basra's non-associated gasfields.[6] "We call this a monopoly on Iraqi gas. . . . Shell will seize everything," the Iraqi parliamentary oil and gas committee warned in a statement in November 2008.[7]

Few would disagree that it made more economic and environmental sense to collect associated gas than to flare it, but Shell had deftly maneuvered itself to become the only company in the running to take over this potentially very profitable by-product. When Shell agreed in 2004 to advise

Iraq on its Gas Master Plan, most had assumed that the company was advising on a plan that the Iraqis would choose how or whether to implement. But now Shell was in line—without competition—to carry out this same plan. In light of the controversy, it eventually took Shell's Mounir Bouaziz three years of monthly visits to Iraq, including numerous meetings with ministers, plus hundreds of millions of dollars of investments by the company in community and industrial projects, to finalize the deal, and even then in reduced form (for gas from just three oilfields).

To Issam al-Chalabi, the deal made no industrial sense: a $2 billion project had been completed during his term as oil minister in the late 1980s to carry out precisely this work, and by 1990 Iraq had the capacity to collect 95 percent of its previously flared gas.[8] The point was echoed by energy economist Muhammad-Ali Zainy, who now also advised the parliamentary committee. "This is really a project that is already there, and the machines are there," he told me. Even if the compressors had been damaged or destroyed, Iraqi officials could have had new ones installed within about nine months.[9] As late as 2005 Jabbar al-Luaibi of the South Oil Company had estimated that only $100 million of investment was needed to get currently flared gas to power stations.[10] Ironically, Shell's best-known arrangement involving associated gas was in Nigeria, where the company still flared it all off despite numerous government and court orders since the 1960s to cease the practice and instead collect it. Shell itself had long set a deadline of 2008 to phase out all flaring in its Nigerian operations; the company blamed its failure to meet it on security problems and on the government's failure to fund its share of the necessary investments.[11]

But giving the project to Shell not only was unnecessary but also would undermine Iraq's ability to meet its own gas needs. Zainy pointed out that the new arrangement specified that all the gas would be sold at international prices. Shell's major interest was in trading gas in the region.[12] What would this mean for Iraqi industries that used the gas in fertilizers, petrochemicals, and electricity generation? Other countries in the region traditionally supplied gas to their industries at cost, but if Iraqi industries paid many times that price for gas feedstock they would never be able to compete with cheap foreign imports. Charging international prices prioritized exports over domestic needs. Within Iraq, where most people still got at best a few hours of electricity a day, this made people especially angry.

## Who's in Charge?

Finally we were allowed into the press conference as the oil men—more than two hundred of them—sloped off to West End bars. The Oil Ministry team briefed us on the details of the planned auction. Companies would place bids specifying how much they expected to increase a field's production and how much they would be paid for doing so. Whichever company offered to increase production the most at the lowest price would win each contract.

This sort of transparency and competition was not what the companies had hoped for. After the collapse of the oil law in September 2007, Shahristani had tried to bring in BP, Shell, ExxonMobil, Chevron, and Total—without competition but based on advisory work they had done earlier—to provide interim technical expertise and procurement for the fields that were now being offered in the auction. Just as Shell had moved straight from the Gas Master Plan to the deal for associated gas in southern Iraq, the companies had hoped that these two-year bridging contracts would be subsequently converted to long-term contracts to develop and manage the fields once an oil law was in place.[13] But after a whole year of negotiations, the Oil Ministry had announced in September 2008 that the deals would not be done. "One of the obstacles is that companies wanted a guarantee from the Oil Ministry that they would be awarded the longer-term contracts and the ministry cannot do that," one Iraqi negotiator told Dow Jones.[14] The Iraqi campaign against the oil law and the subsequent decline of U.S. influence had strengthened Shahristani's ability, and political need, to resist the companies' pressure.

"It is in some ways disappointing," Shell's exploration and production boss Malcolm Brinded reflected to oil reporter Ruba Husari.[15] But without the legal protection of an oil law, he said, it was "tremendously important that it's seen in the interest of the country," as that would reduce the chance of future governments tearing up the contracts. With no new oil law, the 1967 legislation requiring parliamentary approval of oil contracts was still in force. As a result, contracts awarded solely by the executive branch had no legal basis and would last only as long as companies maintained cooperative relationships with the government.

So aside from failing to provide the guaranteed shoo-ins, how did the contracts to be offered at the June 2009 auction match up to what the oil companies wanted? As ever, the devil was in the details. They weren't PSAs, which would have given the companies a share of the oil produced. Instead, companies would be paid fixed fees on each barrel produced and have their costs reimbursed. This would not necessarily make them less profitable than PSAs. Just as a PSA can allocate anything from 1 to 99 percent of the "profit oil" to the company, the per-barrel fee could be 10 cents (unprofitable) or 10 dollars (laughing all the way to the bank) in these new contracts. Where the contracts differed from PSAs was that the payments to companies were more predictable. In a PSA, if things go very well with the project the company can receive windfall profits. Oil companies call this prospect "upside." But under these Iraqi contracts the companies would get the same fee per barrel whatever happened. Any bonanza, such as from a high global oil price, would go to the government—and this was another success of the civil society campaign in opposing PSAs.

On the other hand, neither were they technical service contracts, as the Oil Ministry claimed. That term usually refers to contracts of at most a few years, awarded to specialist service companies such as Schlumberger or Halliburton, to carry out specific services such as drilling or installing equipment while the state runs the industry and makes the decisions. In contrast, the new contracts were for managing operations jointly with a state-owned Iraqi company, which would own 51 percent of the venture.

The foreign companies would be insulated from future Iraqi laws by stabilization clauses, and any disputes would be arbitrated under the rules of the International Chamber of Commerce. Having access to international arbitration had consistently been a top priority for the companies, as we have seen, and they still wanted more guarantees. With no oil law passed, there was a danger that an international arbitration tribunal might rule that contracts were not valid. Shahristani's arguments for the legality of what he was doing were hardly very persuasive. The constitution did not require parliamentary ratification of contracts, he pointed out. He rightly said that the constitution was legally superior to mere laws, but wrongly added that the constitution therefore canceled any law's requirement for ratification of contracts. In fact, the constitution did not specify either way, but it did state that a new law would be required to govern the oil sector. When Shahristani was pressed on this in an interview on al-Jazeera, he said that the government *had* legislated, in that it had written a law (even if the parliament had not approved it).[16]

To be confident a tribunal would accept jurisdiction in a dispute, companies also wanted an international investment treaty in place. In other words, contracts were all very well, but the companies wanted a tougher legal framework to protect them at both national and international levels.

## Kimmitt's Last Stand

Two weeks after the meeting in the Park Lane Hotel, Deputy Treasury Secretary Kimmitt arrived in Baghdad on a C-130 transport plane from Kuwait. It was just days before the U.S. presidential election, and the Bush administration was keen to secure its legacy in Iraq. Accompanying Kimmitt was deputy commerce secretary John Sullivan, a lawyer who had served as deputy general counsel for George H.W. Bush's reelection campaign in 1992. The two men had come for an event with Iraqi ministers and officials at the Rasheed Hotel in the Green Zone: the Dialogue on Business and Investment Climate.

John Sullivan used the occasion to call for six steps to reassure investing companies. Among them were passing the oil law, ratifying a trade and investment agreement with the United States, and setting up a framework "to clearly guarantee recognition of international arbitration awards and the right to submit investment claims to international arbitration." For the latter, he suggested the New York Convention.[17] All this would give the oil companies three layers of legal protection. First, the oil law would ensure the validity of any contracts, repealing the requirement for the parliament to approve them. Second, a bilateral investment treaty would enable an arbitration tribunal to accept jurisdiction in any dispute. Third, as we saw in chapter 13, the New York Convention would allow the winner in arbitration decisions to seize assets of the losing party in any of the 140 countries party to the convention.

On his return to Washington, Kimmitt sent a three-page letter to Nouri al-Maliki spelling out what was expected. "The Dialogue on Business and Investment Climate in Baghdad has highlighted steps Iraq can take to strengthen its investment climate, including passage of the hydrocarbons law, issuance of regulations for the investment law, and adoption of procedures to allow international arbitration of disputes."[18]

In March 2009 the U.S. Department of Commerce, under its Commercial Law Development Program (CLDP), gave a four-day training workshop for Iraqi officials in Amman on "negotiating and implementing durable contracts," the first of four planned workshops. And in July, CLDP offered a one-year intensive training course for twenty Iraqi practitioners on commercial law. CLDP's primary aim was to "pave the way" toward Iraq signing the New York Convention, on which it held a workshop for Iraqi officials in November 2009.[19] The Department of Interior's Minerals Management Service also gave a four-day course on international regulation, licensing administration, and dispute resolution in Irbil. And the U.S. embassy in Baghdad continued to provide assistance, advice, and training to the Oil Ministry on commercial and contractual issues.[20]

It was not just the U.S. government that was pushing the Iraqis for more favorable legal terms for investment—Dan Witt intensified his activities on Iraq, too. ITIC had organized one seminar for Iraqi policy makers in 2005 in Beirut and one in 2007 in Amman, and it had piggybacked on a government-sponsored Iraqi tour of the United States in 2006, but there was nothing in 2008. In 2009 ITIC organized two workshops, in Amman and Istanbul, focusing on the structure of taxation within the oilfield auctions and promoting stabilization clauses.

And in April a team from the Iraqi Oil Ministry's Development and Training Directorate traveled to the United Kingdom to meet potential training providers, among them BP. Foremost among the areas the team raised with the company for development were commercial and negotiating skills.[21] It was striking that the ministry team felt a deficiency in such skills just two months before they would be required to agree on twenty-year contracts; striking too that it asked one of the companies with which it would be negotiating for help. It did not bode well for the ministry's bargaining power when it found itself sitting across the table from BP and other companies.

## The Demise of the Iraqi Oil Industry

These various attempts to toughen up the legal framework were the U.S. government's final efforts to help the oil companies. As we saw in the previous two chapters, by late 2008 U.S. influence in Iraq had declined significantly, and with the military moving into overwatch, it was the oil companies that were now on the front line.

To secure favorable contracts from the Iraqi government the companies would have to fight their own battles. But without pressure from an occupying power, why should a relatively sovereign Iraqi government deal with them? True, Iraq had missed out on the significant oil industry technological

developments of the 1990s, such as directional drilling and 3-D seismic sur-
veying, but these were hardly essential given that Iraq's oil reserves were so
prodigious and easy to extract. In 1979 Iraqi production had reached more
than 3.5 million barrels per day without any of these technologies, and, as
we have seen, Iraq had some of the best technical specialists in the world—
with the ability to hold their industry together with chewing gum and baling
twine, as the Texan CPA advisers liked to put it, and plenty of improvisation.
In any case, technology could always be bought from service companies.

But since 2003 things had changed. During the first two years of the occupation many of Iraq's best experts had been removed and replaced on a
party and sectarian basis. Over the following years, many of the remaining
experts either left the country or fell victim to Baghdad's worsening violence.
In June 2006 Muthanna al-Badri, DG of the State Company for Oil Projects,
was kidnapped in Baghdad while driving home from work. The following
month North Oil Company DG Adil Qazzaz, who had worked in the company for thirty-six years, was seized by unknown gunmen, also from his car.[22]
Neither was seen again. By summer 2006 officials estimated that about two-
thirds of the top one hundred Iraqi oil managers of 2003 were no longer in
their jobs.[23]

In June 2008 Shahristani tried to reverse some of the losses. Many of the
best Iraqi experts were now based in Amman, and the minister asked them
to meet him at the embassy. But it was too little too late. None went back to
Iraq with him. Most of Iraq's technical capacity had been lost by the time
Shahristani became minister, but he bore some of the blame as well, as he
marginalized those who remained who could challenge his authority. And
he rarely consulted his officials. Luay al-Khatteeb, the former Shell external
affairs officer, put it down to Shahristani's personality. "He thinks keeping a
distance is ethical," he said. Certainly few politicians in Iraq were considered as incorruptible as Shahristani. But Khatteeb believed he went to the
extreme of not communicating with anyone. "He will continue to be an Iraqi
expat till the day he dies. As an exile, he was not a sociable person. When he
returned to Iraq, he lived in the Green Zone. He lived in isolation, whether
he was in power, in prison, in exile, or in study."[24]

While policy making in Baghdad had largely fallen victim to de-
Ba'athification and political divisions, South Oil Company had shown what
could be achieved in the field with Iraqi know-how and commitment. SOC
boss Jabbar al-Luaibi was widely respected in Basra and credited with

having restored production to nearly 2 million barrels a day during the chaotic first eight months of the occupation, while KBR and the U.S. Army Corps of Engineers had proved mostly ineffectual. His great skill was in negotiating the complex politics of Basra so that politicians, tribes, and militias supported rather than obstructed the work of SOC.

Since April 2004, however, Iraqi oil output had flatlined and had yet to exceed prewar levels of 2.5 million barrels a day. In 2009, a year after he lost his job, Luaibi gave a rare interview in which he explained why. When Luaibi asked for ministry approval of equipment purchases, it often took months to get any response. In one case SOC put out a tender to replace tanks at the Buzurgan field, at a cost of $3–4 million, as the old, corroded tanks were restraining production by 30,000 barrels a day. It sent the contract to Baghdad for approval, but the ministry did nothing for a year before finally asking SOC to retender. With the price of oil over $100 per barrel, Luaibi pointed out that the delay had cost around $1 billion. "It's not a question of communication," he said. "It's the whole system that needs to be restructured."[25]

The problem Luaibi identified could be seen throughout the Iraqi Oil Ministry. The Oil Ministry spent only half of the capital budget allocated to it in 2007, and the previous two years it had spent less than 5 percent.[26] No wonder the industry was stagnating.

What were the prospects of recovering Iraq's human capacity? For Faleh al-Khayat, the post-2003 losses "can never be recovered. You can never get Radhwan Sa'adi again in Iraq, with his experience of forty years in the oil industry, with his background as a PhD geologist from Swansea University. You don't re-create these people. You cannot replace Abdullah al-Tikriti, you cannot replace Nur al-Ani, you cannot replace these people."

Falah Khawaja, the engineer the Peshmerga drove out of Khurmala, is one of the few who remain upbeat about the Oil Ministry's future. He was head of the manpower division of the ministry from 2004 to 2006, during which time he sent more than a thousand employees abroad for training. "The manpower division stopped the rip-off," he said to me, taking a subtle dig at the subtitle of the *Crude Designs* report I wrote in 2005. "OK, we lost two generations, but we hope in five years we'll create the new cadre who'll resume Iraqi technical capacity."

Was the training effective? Apart from Khawaja, I found few who thought it was. Given the politicization of the Oil Ministry, training had become a favor to loyal staff—it was no longer based on need or ability, nor integrated with on-the-job career development. "You can send people on training, but without follow-up and assessment of the impact on their performance, and then holding them accountable for that improvement in their job performance, people will not develop themselves," said Hazim Sultan, whose person-centered approach to management we saw in chapter 2. "Training became a privilege, a chance to go outside the country. . . . The attitude became 'It's my turn.'"

For me these were sobering conversations. In the six years I had been working on Iraqi oil issues at Platform, I had criticized plans for handing the oilfields over to foreign companies, in large part because Iraq simply didn't need to do so. With its own impressive expertise, Iraq could comfortably have maintained sovereign control of its resources and kept all of the revenues generated from them. Did Iraq no longer have that option? Had the war boosters' self-serving claims—that there was nothing in Iraq but dictatorship—in fact come to pass? Had an industry proudly built over decades, to which my friends had devoted their lives through wars, sanctions, and hardship, been reduced to a blank sheet?

## Consultations in Istanbul

It was not only the loss of indigenous expertise that weakened the Iraqi government's negotiating position. Iraqi institutions had been torn apart by political divisions, the country remained unstable, the constitution still had not been reviewed and finalized, and Iraq was still occupied by 140,000 U.S. troops. These were hardly auspicious circumstances in which to sign twenty-year commitments governing the vast majority of Iraq's economy. The drop in the oil price from a high of $147 per barrel in July 2008 to just below $40 by the end of the year had also changed the balance of power. The government had cut its budget three times, from $80 billion to $58 billion, and now urgently needed more oil revenues without having to make any investment itself. The oil companies knew this and knew it gave them an opportunity to get a disproportionately favorable deal. The terms of the contracts would be determined by the relative bargaining power at the time of signing but would last well beyond that.

In December 2008 plans were announced for a second auction in late 2009, which would award contracts for some of the largest fields that had been discovered but not yet developed. The two auctions between them would put three-quarters of Iraq's oil reserves up for sale.[27] The oil companies would not get their contracts completely without competition as they had hoped, but the way the bidding was structured minimized competition between them. Given that the oilfields were some of the largest in the world, if the ministry had tendered just one or two of them, competition between the companies would have been fierce. Instead, by doing it all in two auctions, companies could bid for only the fields that most interested them. And knowing broadly what their rivals wanted, there could be mutual understandings (whether spoken or not) on how the fields should be carved up. Shell's (unnamed) regional adviser for the Middle East had made a similar point to British government officials in early 2006: Iraq's oil market was so big there was "room for everyone."[28]

As before, it was the multinational oil companies—not the Iraqi people or even the country's parliament—who were consulted on the plans. In February 2009, the Oil Ministry held a workshop in Istanbul for the companies to make their comments on the deals that were to be offered to them. Despite the odds now being thoroughly stacked in their favor, the emboldened companies played hard to get. "We are still very interested," said one senior executive. "But from what we see of the fiscal terms offered, there is not a lot of profitability in it and, if that is the case, then we cannot do it. . . . With the price of oil where it is at the moment, I do not believe they can push [for such terms] that hard."[29]

The form of the contract changed quite fundamentally following the Istanbul workshop. Most important, the state share in the joint venture was cut from 51 percent to 25 percent and the state partner reduced from "co-operator" to simply a financial partner.[30] While in the Park Lane Hotel the shared powers had been portrayed as an important part of the compromise, now the foreign companies would be firmly in charge. Other clauses further reduced the state role. The exclusive right to explore for new, undiscovered reservoirs (at different depths below the surface) was transferred from the state company to foreign companies, giving the latter considerable upside potential.[31] Inspections by regulators could now be only on a prearranged basis, rather than via spot checks.[32] And any incurred costs that the state partner disputed (for example, if it considered them inflated for tax purposes) would still be paid first and later resolved, rather than being held until resolution.[33]

## "Nobody Touches the Producing Fields"

During the second half of 2008 and early 2009 there was relatively little nationalist opposition in Iraq to the planned oilfield auctions. Incorrectly dubbing the contracts "technical service contracts" looked like it was paying off for Shahristani. Only some of the Iraqi oil experts saw the implications of the plans—after all, the contract language was sufficiently complex to deter quick readings or a simple summary. Most of their concerns focused on the first-bid round—the auction of the fields already producing oil. If Iraqi companies were operating these now, why was external management needed?

"Nobody touches the producing fields," warned Faleh al-Khayat, when I asked him about the forthcoming auction. "These are the safety net of the Iraqi people. These are the fields that will prevent Iraq losing sovereignty. It will keep the free will of the Iraqi government to act: it would always have the safety of 3 million barrels per day under its belt. It will not go hungry, its people. . . . I think it is not only a crime, it is very close to treachery to give the producing fields." He banged his walking stick on the ground. "Is the system stable enough, secure enough, legitimate enough to award such contracts for twenty years? While the constitution needs revisions—everybody says so—and while everybody is waiting for the next election to have a more representative government, this government goes and awards these fields!"[34]

Khayat wrote a series of articles for Iraqi newspapers to explain why he was so concerned about the contracts. "We are trying to save Iraq from twenty years' hook around its head," he said of his campaign, miming a noose, when we met in Amman. Under the proposed contracts Iraq's share in the investment would be just 25 percent, meaning that decision-making authority would be held by the foreign companies. Meanwhile, Khayat wrote, the Iraqi state companies would be reduced to "sub–holding companies that remotely manage their shares" in the fields. And as foreign companies awarded their service contracts to other international firms in the name of competitiveness and efficiency, "we shall quickly revert to the time when we were hiring foreign contractors to implement simple projects such as installing ten kilometers of pipeline, and the gradual elimination of the national ability to run the oil industry, which was built through decades of effort and investment."[35]

There were also concerns about timing, especially about auctioning all the fields in two closely spaced batches. In what would be the fastest-ever addition to world oil capacity, everyone would be rushing to hire seismic and drilling teams at the same time. The price of oilfield services would shoot up, while the quality went down.[36]

The principal argument for bringing in foreign companies was that because Iraq had lost so many of its own people, this was its only option for rebuilding its oil industry. But while Iraq was short of engineers, geologists, and chemists, it had an even greater deficit of lawyers, accountants, and economists. A contract is effective only if it is well drafted and overseen. If there was no effective regulation, companies would simply do whatever was most beneficial to themselves rather than what Iraqis wanted or needed. Almost unanimously, the experts I spoke to warned that the Oil Ministry didn't have enough good people to negotiate, regulate, and oversee the projects.

## Shahristani Attacked from Both Sides

For nearly eighteen months after the KRG signed with Hunt Oil, Shahristani had led the fight against legitimizing the KRG's contracts, and several Kurdish politicians believed that if he could be removed, their position on oil would be firmly established. The Kurdish parties may have had the constitution on their side (after all, they wrote it), and in any case the KRG could sign contracts and allow foreign companies to extract the oil (since it controlled its territory through the Peshmerga). But there was a fundamental weakness in their position: since the Kurdistan region is landlocked, its oil could only be exported overland. And if the oil couldn't go through the rest of Iraq (because the Baghdad government would take control of it), it would have to go through Turkey, Syria, or Iran. All three countries were unwilling to accept oil without a legal export license from the Iraqi government.

The KRG calculated that once its oil was ready for export, a cash-strapped Iraqi government would back down in order to get its majority share of the revenues. But that strategy would work only if (as had seemed likely) security fears and political divisions prevented the Iraqi government from developing—and gaining income from—fields in the rest of Iraq. To the KRG, Shahristani's bid rounds were a direct threat to their oil gains. In early 2009, therefore, they attacked Shahristani's competence, forging a brief and unlikely alliance with the nationalist camp criticizing him from opposite end of the spectrum. A report was produced in January and a symposium took place in Baghdad in February, led by America's man, the Kurdish deputy prime minister Barham Salih. Maliki, hedging his bets, gave tacit support to the symposium.

It was perhaps the most incoherent phase in the oil struggle. The legitimate criticism that could be made of Shahristani was that his Oil Ministry had not managed oilfields well: oil production had flatlined at between 2 and 2.5 million barrels per day in the three years he had been in office. This was partly because of Shahristani's antagonism toward his own professionals and partly because Shahristani's ministry had been too preoccupied with foreign investment and had not devoted sufficient attention to Iraqi capacity. For these reasons, the symposium focused on technical issues such as field management, drilling, and water injection, and it attracted the support of those who believed in indigenous Iraqi skills and were skeptical about bringing in foreign companies. The Kurdish parties driving the process actually wanted more foreign investment, though; Salih even wanted to reverse the opposition to PSAs.[37] Yet straddling the two different sides made the plan messy: Salih began to talk of bringing in investment from a favored short list of American, European, Russian, and Chinese oil companies—even though more extensive contracts, if bid competitively, would take more time compared to the process that was already under way, and the most obvious problems were in the shorter term. The companies themselves stayed focused on the concrete offer of the auctions—further indication that they had indeed now stepped up to the front line.

Under pressure, Shahristani offered Maliki his resignation and considered canceling the auction. Even his patron, Grand Ayatollah Sistani, refused to meet him on a visit to Najaf.[38] Now that Shahristani was being attacked both by the pro-investment Kurdish parties and by the nationalists and oil experts, it looked like his days were numbered.

When Maliki declined his resignation, Shahristani instead moved to stifle dissent, reprimanding Ministry of Oil staff who had contributed to the technical report. In May, he removed Kifah Numan, Jabbar al-Luaibi's protégé who had taken over from him as head of South Oil Company only a year previously. Numan had written to the oil minister warning against the auction and the impact contracts would have on SOC.[39] Again, it seemed, Shahristani wanted to assert his own control over the company at the expense of technical competence and continuity. In Numan's place was installed Fayadh Nima, a Da'wa Party member.

## Leave It to the Women

In June 2009, two weeks before the auction, another critical voice appeared in Parliament. Shatha al-Musawi, an independent (nonparty) member of the UIA coalition and a member of the parliamentary Finance Committee, called for an extraordinary session to discuss the contracts being offered.

Then forty-two years old,[40] Musawi was a Shi'a Islamist and one of Iraq's most active parliamentarians.[41] She had repeatedly criticized the country's political leaders, starting with a passionate complaint in the parliament's first meeting in March 2005 about the delay in forming a government.[42] "Iraqi women in the Parliament are more serious, more devoted, more present and more interactive than men with the public issues," she later told the *New York Times*.[43] It was true that many parliamentarians never bothered to turn up; many of them did not even spend much time in Iraq.

One of her best-known parliamentary interventions was when she challenged the former speaker Mahmoud Mashhadani in May 2007 for laughing while she spoke of the plight of Shi'a victims of sectarian cleansing in Diyala province. Mashhadani dismissed her criticism with the comment "Leave it to the women," causing other parliamentarians to speak out against him.[44] He adjourned the session without consulting his deputies (in breach of protocol) and threw a punch at another parliamentarian who reprimanded him for walking out.[45] In September 2007, Musawi made the famous rebuke to Maliki, "What progress are you talking about, Mr. Prime Minister?"[46] And following the disputed Iranian election in June 2009, she was one of the few Iraqi Shi'a politicians to openly criticize the Ahmadinejad government.[47]

Now she was getting involved in oil issues for the first time. She had learned of the importance of the auctions from watching an interview with Issam al-Chalabi on television. After that, she had made some inquiries and had spent several hours with oil experts in Baghdad. "They said Iraq had spent around $8 billion to rehabilitate these fields," she explained. "They said it is not reasonable, after all this money and all the development undertaken, that foreign companies should take these fields."[48]

She gathered signatures of fifty parliamentarians to call Oil Minister Shahristani for questioning. But the parliament's speaker, Ayad al-Samarra'i, referred the matter to the oil and gas committee, and the issue was sucked back into party politics.

## A Campaign from Within

Concerns about the auction intensified on June 14, 2009, with an intervention from new South Oil DG Fayadh Nima. SOC was responsible for nearly 80 percent of Iraq's current oil production and the planned local partner for three of the eight contracts on offer. Nima gave an interview to Reuters in Cairo in which he warned, "The service contracts will put the Iraqi economy in chains and shackle its independence for the next 20 years. They squander Iraq's revenues."[49] The same article reported that a petition opposing the contracts had been signed by more than one hundred SOC engineers.

Nima had been in his post barely a month, and most had assumed he would toe the ministry line. He had even been considered for the post of deputy minister. But on June 8 he chaired a meeting of SOC's heads of departments and top experts, all of whom were strongly against the first bidding round. Not only were the contracts illegal, but SOC could increase production much more effectively by itself, they felt. A program to increase output was actually under way.[50] Nima and the SOC engineers believed they could double production in two years, if only given the authority and funding by the Oil Ministry.[51] Alternatively, the ministry could award five-year engineering, procurement, and construction contracts while retaining Iraqi management of the fields.

They did not oppose the second round, for fields that had not yet been developed. But the first round of contracts, for fields already in production, would lead "to the disintegration of our company as well as the weakening of its financial and technical control over production at a time when our company's fields are the main source of national income." By handing over its largest fields—Rumaila, West Qurna Phase I, Zubair—SOC was set to become largely irrelevant. Far from helping rebuild the Iraqi oil sector and develop its technical skills, this transfer could wipe out what remained of its human and institutional capacities.

Until this point the oil workers' union had kept fairly quiet. While it still had strong support from the workforce and from international unions and federations, the oil union had been significantly weakened by Shahristani's order to state companies not to cooperate with it and by transfers of workers around the country, which were becoming Shahristani's weapon of choice. But now that SOC management had come out so strongly against the contracts, the workers finally felt they could express their views. On June 21 the union issued a statement warning that "the licensing round will cause the oil industry to regress to the 1960s, when foreign oil companies used to manipulate and exploit the Iraqi people's oil resources." The Iraqi economy would "be at the whim of the interests of foreign companies." Noting the views of experts that Iraq could more effectively develop the fields itself, the union called on Maliki to overrule Shahristani and cancel the auction.[52]

Even within the ministry in Baghdad many were warning against the first round of contracts, but Shahristani was not to be deflected.[53] As Dhia'a al-Bakkaa, the former SOMO head who co-chaired the February 2007 experts' meeting against the oil law, put it, "He doesn't even trust the Iraqi oil cadre. His adamant approach is not leadership . . . not listening to other logical views. He surrounded himself with yes-people . . . and the people who said no to his policy were sidelined or pushed out."[54]

# 23

# Under the Hammer

*And you see from the schedule they are dying to sign the fields before the elections, they are scheduling to sign in December 2009. And Greg, the amount of reserves in these fields . . . is not a small chicken that is going to be divided. This is really big stuff.*

—Faleh al-Khayat, August 2009[1]

On Sunday, June 28, 2009, a heavy sandstorm hit Baghdad. The streets filled with thick, grainy fog. Those who dared to venture outside covered their mouths with scarves. The palm trees fluttered restlessly. More than a hundred oil company executives had been due to land at Baghdad International Airport but were turned back because of the weather. The oil auction, planned to start on Monday, was pushed back a day.

On that Tuesday U.S. troops would leave Iraq's cities after six years, the same day the oil companies would arrive in the country's oilfields for the next twenty. Most of the attention was focused on the departure. Prime Minister Maliki had declared a public holiday for National Sovereignty Day. People danced in the streets, waved flags, decorated their cars with plastic flowers. It was "a big joy" to one Baghdad resident, "like a wedding" to another.[2]

"We hope it's going to be a good day," said Mike Daly, the head of exploration and access at BP. The lean geologist grinned confidently into the TV camera. "So far the government has laid on a splendid occasion and we are hopeful."[3] He wasn't talking about the celebrations in the streets outside.

## The Auction

The oilfield auction, held in the al-Zawraa Hall of the Rasheed Hotel on the edge of the Green Zone, was more like a game show than a business transaction. Company representatives walked to the front of the room, showed their envelopes to officials at the green-draped table, and then inserted them in a large glass box as cameras flashed.

The Rumaila field—BP's target—was first on the block. The company had been providing technical advice on the field since 2005 and now knew it well. Only an ExxonMobil-led consortium was bullish enough to put in a challenge. But then came a surprise: neither company's bid was accepted by the Oil Ministry. The ministry would pay remuneration (the profits companies would receive) of no more than $2 per barrel, well below BP's bid of $3.99—in partnership with the China National Petroleum Corporation— and ExxonMobil's $4.80. The minister asked the companies if they would accept the $2 per barrel offer. Both called their head offices to confer. The assembled oilmen and government officials waited, wondering if they had wasted their time on trying to do a deal between two sides that were so far apart. An hour later the answers came back: ExxonMobil said no, BP said yes. It was a strange turn of events. As Issam al-Chalabi commented to me a few weeks later, "When a market trader immediately halves his price, I'm unlikely to trust him!"[4]

On the seven other fields the companies' bids far exceeded the ministry's maximum, in some cases by as much as a factor of ten, and no contract was awarded. For the oil companies it was a "fiasco"; most of the international media saw the auction as a dismal failure.[5]

Shahristani had needed to look tough. Now few could accuse him of selling out. Conversely, no Iraqis other than the Kurdish politicians dared say he should have been more generous, especially given the nationalist turn in Iraqi politics. But the maximum bidding fees seemed designed for show rather than for getting the best deal. According to one company official involved in the bidding, the limit was "obviously political. You know, to send the message that Iraq is not going to give its oil away. These numbers aren't commercial. They are round. They are small and they are very simple."[6] Another pointed out, correctly, that "clearly a field such as Kirkuk is much more costly to develop than Zubair, yet the [maximum offered] fee was the same [$2 a barrel] for both."[7]

As for only awarding one field, the longer-term problem for the Iraqi oil industry was not so much the result as the fact that Shahristani had staked everything on the auction. Keeping the fields in Iraqi hands, on the grounds that the oil companies demanded too much profit, might otherwise have been a fallback option. But, having neglected the industry for so long and stalling public investment in the hope that foreign companies would take over, the ministry now had the choice of either writing off a year or going back to the companies with hat in hand. Neither route was politically appealing.

Chevron, which along with Shell had invested more than its rivals in relationship building, did not bid at all, even on the West Qurna field, where it had worked on technical studies with Total. The company's chairman and CEO, John Watson, told U.S. Deputy Energy Secretary Daniel Poneman that he feared "Iraq's bad terms will help set a precedent in other areas"—after all, these were service contracts, not PSAs.[8] The U.S. embassy reported that Chevron's decision not to bid was also based on "careful consideration of political and contractual risk,"[9] a reference to the lack of an oil law.[10]

## Running Their Own Lives

That evening, as the results of the bid round became clear, President Obama announced that Vice President Biden would supervise U.S. Iraq policy. Two days later Biden was on a plane on his way to Baghdad. Stepping out of his quarters—a silver Airstream trailer in the hold of a cargo plane—he revealed that, alongside the drawdown in troop numbers, the administration's aim was to facilitate agreement between Iraq's leaders on pressing issues of reconciliation such as the oil law.[11] If the message sounded familiar, so too did its justification. Asked whether the U.S. administration saw Iraqi progress as unsatisfactory, he replied, "Well look, I think the Iraqis are unsatisfied. They have not settled the boundary dispute in the north, the UN is working very hard with them; there's a lot to settle. They do not finally have an oil law, which everyone acknowledges is going to be necessary . . . [but] we're getting down to the wire here now, on settling all those issues that the Iraqi people know have to be settled, and that the Iraqi leaders know have to be settled."[12]

However, he was upbeat about his prospects. "I am optimistic because I do think that the Iraqis have become interested in their nationhood," he said. "They've become interested in the idea that they run their own lives."[13] That comment, with awkward wording that could have come from George W.

Bush, might have made sense to certain out-of-touch Americans. To Iraqis it must have sounded bizarre. Also like Bush, Biden had misjudged the Iraqi mood and received a harsh rebuke. According to the prime minister's spokesman, Maliki explained to Biden that "these are domestic issues and that the Iraqis are the ones who do that and who assume responsibility for it. Interference of non-Iraqi sides in these issues will create complications and problems that we are better without."[14]

In Iraq Biden copied Meghan O'Sullivan's formula and met the same leaders of the ethno-sectarian parties that she had tried to promote in 2007, but O'Sullivan herself had come to take a dim view of that approach. Now a Harvard professor, she possessed the luxury of being outside government. "Only within a political system where substance has some hope of being separated from identities are such conflicts likely to be resolved," she wrote in a critique of Biden's visit.[15]

Biden was undeterred. Two months later he was back in Baghdad to call for more economic reforms, including legal protections for investors.[16] He also warned Iraqi leaders not to be tempted to press oil companies too hard on terms, arguing that in the long run Iraq would be better off seeking terms that were profitable for foreign companies in order to attract more investment.[17] This was the argument that BearingPoint had made in its 2003 report for Rob McKee and Dan Witt's ITIC had made in 2004. Again the Obama administration was showing rather more continuity on Iraq policy than its election promises had suggested.

## Pressing Ahead

The auction—and the BP/CNPC contract—was not without its critics. Muhammad Bashar al-Faydi of the Association of Muslim Scholars, for instance, told me a few weeks later, "We consider that such contracts are null and void under the bayonets of occupation. We have warned the current government against such contracts. We told them, 'You are making a fatal mistake. No one will forgive you for what you are doing to the Iraqi population.'"[18] However, the influence of the AMS had declined since the surge. Its leaders had been repeatedly arrested and their houses and offices raided by U.S. and Iraqi forces. Now most lived outside the country.

IFOU leader Hassan Juma'a said, "These contracts are illegal. The government is wasting the national wealth by giving up a large producing oilfield to foreign companies when the Iraqi national workers could have done the same." He feared especially that BP would deny workers the right to freedom of association. Faleh Abood Umara, general secretary and one of the four founders of the union, wrote to BP, warning that the contract was illegal and threatening strikes and protests if it started work.[19] On July 17, 2009, the Oil Ministry stated that it would protect foreign companies from any action by trade unions. "The Oil Ministry stresses its rejection of threats and provocation toward anyone: the government, the ministry, foreign firms," Oil Ministry spokesman Asim Jihad said.[20]

On August 16 Shahristani repeated the tactic he had used in 2008, personally ordering the transfer of four union leaders in the drilling company to new jobs in the gas-filling plant at Taji in Baghdad. The four had led a strike on June 24, calling for reinstatement of the union (canceling the 2007 order), reactivation of canceled allowances, and postponement of the auction. The union also heard from its sources in the Oil Ministry that transfers were planned for another nineteen union leaders from across the industry.[21]

A few of the experts in Amman, including Faleh al-Khayat and Issam al-Chalabi, suspected the contract was not all it seemed, but with Shahristani having beaten BP and CNPC down to $2 a barrel, their fears gained little traction in the public mind outside Basra, where there was some opposition from community leaders and sheikhs.[22] In late July Shahristani removed Fayadh Nima from the leadership of the South Oil Company. According to documents obtained from the British government, Nima had refused to meet with BP because of his and his SOC colleagues' objections to the contract.[23] Shahristani replaced him with Dhia'a Jaafar, a Da'wa Party loyalist and Maliki ally who had won a seat on the provincial council in the 2009 elections—SOC's fourth director general in fourteen months. The U.S. provincial reconstruction team in Basra noted that Jaafar was "favorably disposed toward the United States in general, and U.S. oil firms in particular."[24] Nima was made an adviser in the ministry—"put in the freezer," according to one former colleague.[25]

Six weeks after the auction of producing fields, Shahristani was keen to press on with the next phase: licensing the largest undeveloped fields, which he aimed to award and sign shortly before elections took place in early 2010. On the block this time were ten contracts covering fifteen oilfields, including the supergiant Majnoon, West Qurna Phase II, and East Baghdad. The approach seemed to be to push ahead quickly before political factors could change the government's course. At a press conference in Istanbul I asked

Shahristani whether such twenty-year commitments would have more legitimacy if awarded by the new government after elections. "Well, I don't think
many people argue within Iraq about the need to develop our oil resources as
quickly as possible, since the country is in need of funds for reconstruction,"
he replied. "And in the Ministry of Oil we have always tried to proceed as
quickly as possible . . . and not politicizing it, not taking too much note of the
political discussions outside the ministry. . . . And it just happens that the
second bid round will mature at about the same time" as the elections.[26]


## Northern Exposure

Exports were now flowing from two fields in Kurdistan: DNO's Tawke and
Turkish company Genel Enerji's Taq Taq. Shahristani had permitted exports from these two fields because their contracts were signed before the
February 2007 agreement on the draft oil law, whereas he saw later contracts, beginning with the Hunt Oil deal in September 2007, as acts of bad
faith by the KRG. After Shahristani agreed to export licenses, exports had
begun on June 1, 2009. The opening ceremony—at which Kurdish leaders
Jalal Talabani and Masoud Barzani turned a plastic valve wheel spray-
painted gold, with dramatic opera music in the background—was attended
by a smiling Zalmay Khalilzad. The former ambassador was conspicuously
present too at a ceremony on July 18, 2009, to mark the first oil flowing from
the Khurmala Dome, the northernmost part of the Kirkuk oilfield, from
which the Peshmerga had driven Falah Khawaja in September 2007.

It is not unusual for U.S. politicians and officials to go into business after
leaving office. But Khalilzad's presence at the two KRG events highlighted
the U.S. dilemma that official policy mostly favored a centralized Iraqi oil
industry, while Kurdistan was where much of the business was. The former
ambassador had set up a strategic business consultancy, Khalilzad Associ-
ates, to help companies deal with governments in Iraq, Afghanistan, and
elsewhere in the region.[27] He was not shy about exploiting his previous public roles; each page of the consultancy's website showed a photo of him with
a different world leader. In 2009 he had been a paid adviser to the KRG's
board of investment. In May 2010 he was appointed to the board of the
Emirates-based company RAK Petroleum, a major shareholder in DNO.[28]

Khalilzad was not the only former U.S. official attracted to the black gold
in Kurdistan's hills. Another was Jay Garner, the retired general who had

briefly administered Iraq before Paul Bremer and had also overseen U.S. relief to the Kurds following the 1991 Gulf War. In 2008 he helped the Canadian company Vast Exploration obtain a PSA for the Qara Dagh block in the south of the region, after which he was made a director of the company. "The State Department has forgotten the Kurds were our allies during the war, and the Arabs were not," he told journalist Anthony Fenton. "If the State Department had any sense they would make the [KRG] the model and have the rest of Iraq follow that model."[29]

Ron Jonkers, the investment lawyer hired through BearingPoint to draft the oil law in 2006, had gone north as well, along with many of the lawyers working with the rush of minor oil companies that had arrived there since the Hunt Oil deal in September 2007. Jonkers made it clear where his loyalties lay: "No country, let alone a subnational unit, has accomplished so much, so fast, so efficiently and with so little expenses by the government." His enthusiasm for the KRG's developments was matched by his disdain for Baghdad's efforts. As he saw it, everyone had lost out from the continued commitment to centralized decision making: "Iraq must learn from its past if it does not want to remain in the past."[30]

The deal to allow KRG exports didn't last, however. Shahristani insisted that since the companies had no agreement with the Iraqi government, it had no responsibility to pay them. This was unacceptable to the KRG, which otherwise would have to pay the companies itself. With the payment issue unresolved, exports were stopped in October after less than five months.

## Another Auction

On December 11, 2009, Baghdad was in lockdown for the second oilfield auction. This time, in a display of confidence, the auction was held in the Oil Ministry, on the other side of the Tigris from the Green Zone, so the executives would have to travel. However, they would pass mostly through the grounds of the Ministry of Interior, all the surrounding roads were closed, and each had a full detail of private security guards.

This auction, held in the auditorium in the center of the ministry complex, went much more smoothly than the first. The stage was covered with plastic flowers, along with fourteen Iraqi flags with well-polished gold eagles perched atop their flagpoles. At the front of the stage was the large glass box in which the bids would be placed. It was the kind of high kitsch only Iraqis can pull off. When the minister declared the bidding open, his staff would "open the door," pulling aside a braided cordon. Confident oil executives would then stride up to the technical team's table to the right of the stage to submit their envelopes for inspection. Once these were accepted, they would step onto the stage to insert their envelopes in the glass box, to applause from the audience, and then sit in a special reserved row at the front, where a camera focused on their faces and relayed the images to a screen behind the stage. It made me think of the line to get to the hot seat in *Who Wants to Be a Millionaire?* After fifteen minutes the ministry people would "close the door" and the auction would end.

The first field on the auction block, at 10:29 a.m., was the 12.6-billion-barrel Majnoon, near Basra. Shell's Mounir Bouaziz marched up to the front table at 10:30. After putting his envelope in the glass box, he sat grinning confidently in the bidders' row. At 10:33 a representative of Total went up, more visibly nervous. This was the field for which Elf Aquitaine—now part of Total—had agreed on (though not signed) a contract with Saddam Hussein during the 1990s. And Total had provided technical advice to the ministry over the last few years, along with Chevron. Then came a sales pitch from Shahristani, his head freshly shaved from his recent hajj. The Majnoon field was 100 percent Iraqi, he told the punters—no difficulties with neighboring Iran. Eleven reservoirs, only the southern part explored. "It should be the ambition of all oil companies to bid on Majnoon," chipped in Natiq al-Bayati, director general of the contracts department. At 10:40 a.m. Shahristani announced, "There's only three and a half minutes to go. All companies should proceed now if they want to bid." There were no more takers. Again we saw the consequence of offering too much at once: each field would attract at most a few bids, as companies focused their attention on key targets rather than competing with each other for the same prizes. Shell won, partnered by the Malaysian Petronas, beating Total on both fee and production target. Bouaziz walked back to his colleagues with a swagger.

After announcing the award of Majnoon to Shell, Shahristani immediately declared open the bidding for Halfaya in Maysan province, another supergiant field and the one for which BHP had arranged wheat shipments in the 1990s. Bids would close in fifteen minutes. CNPC won this time, again in a consortium with Petronas (which would have stakes in four contracts by the end of the auction) and Total. Next, Qayara.

Beneath the glitz the rapidity of the process was quite shocking. These fields, which accounted for the vast majority of Iraq's future economy, were going under the hammer at fifteen-minute intervals. This was not development; it was a revolution. What was going through Shahristani's mind? Did he have any doubts? If he did, he didn't show them.

On the second day of the auction Lukoil (supported by Statoil) regained the contract to develop the supergiant West Qurna Phase II, which it had signed in the 1990s but Saddam had voided in 2002, and which it had chased relentlessly ever since. Next, Gharraf: fifteen minutes. Petronas itself won that one, backed up by Japex. Then the Badra field, then Najma.

In all, seven of the ten contracts were awarded. Again only the large fields attracted any competition; three smaller ones received one bid each. The fields ultimately awarded in the two rounds accounted for nearly 60 percent of Iraq's reserves. Much of what remained was in the large, technically difficult fields of Kirkuk and East Baghdad, precisely the areas where Iraq arguably most needed international technical expertise.

The auctions were an impressive piece of political theater. By creating the intrigue of a competition, they distracted attention from the bigger political issues. The story became "Which company will win?" rather than "Is this good for Iraq?" At the same time, the remuneration fees sounded low, so perhaps Iraq had done well after all. On the other hand, at the second auction the Oil Ministry set its maximum remuneration fee higher than the received bids in all the larger fields and so missed the opportunity to haggle. This confirmed the reading of the first auction—that the ministry had opted for the politically resonant $2 per barrel for all large fields regardless of their prospectivity or difficulty. The fact that the companies voluntarily bid lower than that showed that what sounds like a low price is not necessarily as low as it seems.

After the last fields were awarded, Shahristani declared the auctions a success. Oil Ministry officials congratulated each other and posed for photos. During Shahristani's press conference at the end of the day, an amateurish marching band interrupted him as it shuffled through the hall. A single trumpeter played the tune for seven marchers in ill-fitting white nylon uniforms with braids and gold epaulettes. "This is a celebration!" enthused the minister.

I felt only sadness. I thought of Hassan Juma'a and the struggle of the oil workers. Of Faleh Khayat and the old experts in Amman, and their efforts to calmly explain what was needed for the Iraqi oil industry. Of Tariq Shafiq and his cautious attempt to make the best of a bad situation. Was this what the war had been for? It certainly had not gone the way the Americans had expected. It had taken longer, there was still no oil law, and the companies had competed for service contracts rather than being handed preferential PSAs. It was also mostly Iraqis who had ultimately made the decisions, but with a radically weakened oil industry and state.

As I stepped out into the ministry car park, two Iraqi Hueys—the helicopters instantly recognizable from a hundred Vietnam war films—buzzed low overhead. Iraqi soldiers stood by their Humvees. I glanced at their tan boots and baggy fatigues, their body armor and excess gear giving them the top-heavy look of American football players. The uniform looked all too familiar.

# 24

# A Dirty Business

*[Oil operations] in Iraq, one of the most corrupt countries in the world, should be looked at as a thriving environment in which to cultivate an excessive level of corruption.*

—Munir Chalabi, political analyst, September 2011[1]

During the period between the two auctions it was clear something was going on behind the scenes. The Iraqi government had aimed to sign the Rumaila contract with BP and CNPC within a month, but discussions dragged on for more than four months, until November. In theory, all elements of the contract were fixed in the model contract, apart from the remuneration fee and target peak rate of production, both submitted in the auction bids. "It should have been signed in two weeks, no negotiations," Issam al-Chalabi said to me in August. "There's a model contract; you give me two figures. But they're negotiating."[2] Two years later, cables released by WikiLeaks showed that BP employees had revealed their true plans to the U.S. embassy on the day of the auction. Asked how they were able to reduce their remuneration fee offer by half, they said it would "just be the start of a hard negotiating process" on the terms of the actual contract.[3]

The unsuccessful bidders from the first auction also made a lot of trips to Baghdad during this period. In October consortia led by ExxonMobil and Eni announced that they would accept the ministry's maximum price on the West Qurna I and Zubair fields. They had walked away in June when the ministry offered $1.90 and $2, respectively, compared to their bids of $4 and $4.80. Like BP, they had halved their price. What changed the companies' minds?

Shahristani said the contract terms were unchanged.[4] But the companies, when speaking to their investors and to the industry press, gave a different account. "I would say we've negotiated hard with the Iraqi government and the Ministry of Oil and we've come to an arrangement that we're happy with and they're happy with," said Rob Franklin, president of ExxonMobil Up-stream Ventures, to Ben Lando of *Iraq Oil Report*.[5] Alessandro Bernini, chief financial officer of Eni, told financial analysts in a conference call that "we accepted $2 because, basically, the fiscal terms are different now."[6] The changed final terms at a fee of $2 were equivalent to the earlier model contract at $4.50.

But it was BP that had done the hard bargaining.[7] BP, after all, had been in a strong position as the only company to have accepted a deal. If it had walked out, the ministry would have been left with nothing. A U.S. embassy cable reported BP's comments on the dynamics of the negotiations, which went on for more than eight full days during five rounds. Shahristani—who, remember, is not an oil expert—conducted the negotiations himself, mostly without any support from ministry staff. He kept both South Oil, which would work with BP, and the contracts and licensing division of the ministry out of the discussions. While his staff and experts were absent, he was "un-expectedly receptive to contract changes" proposed by BP.[8] When ministry officials raised concerns about any aspect of the contracts, which happened frequently between negotiating sessions, Shahristani overrode them.[9]

To close observers, it was clear by October or November 2009 that the terms had in fact been changed. But how?

At the launch of the first bid round in Park Lane in October 2008, Shahristani had promised that "the final form of the contract that has been approved by the cabinet will be made available [to the Iraqi public] immediately. We would like to be as transparent in this process as we can."[10] In December, nearly two months after the Rumaila contract was signed with BP and CNPC, I asked Abdulilah al-Amir, Thamir al-Ghadhban's deputy as oil adviser to Maliki, when it would be published. The contract wasn't quite complete, he said. "It needs some small formalities, but after that it will be. All contracts will be." On the Oil Ministry website? I asked. Yes, he replied.[11]

And the same month Shahristani said on al-Jazeera, "These oil contracts have been as transparent as any process in the world. . . . A copy of the contract is available, I can send it to you by e-mail tomorrow; a copy is available to any Iraqi citizen and I invite him to come to my office and ask for a copy, and it will be given to him."[12] But at the time of this writing, November 2011, none of the signed contracts has been published or made available to Iraqi experts who have asked to see them.

There are strong arguments for publishing such contracts, not least to avoid corruption. Publishing contracts is now considered oil industry best practice and is routinely done by several countries.[13] The IMF recommends full publication of contracts, as does the U.S. Treasury Department.[14] Iraq's draft oil law, approved by the cabinet in February 2007 but never enacted by the parliament, would also have required publication of contracts, along with various financial data and other information.[15] But now the Oil Ministry was unwilling to publish—perhaps for fear of what would be revealed.

## A Leak Gives the Answer

About a year later, on a trip to Amman, I got hold of a leaked copy of the final version of BP's Rumaila contract. Careful comparison of this version with the original model contract, the basis of the June auction, revealed technical changes of wording that, although small, would have profound implications.

The most important change from the pre-auction model contract is in Article 12.5, which determines what happens if oil production is later restricted in order to comply with OPEC quotas or otherwise manage the Iraqi economy. In the original model contract, the cost of such production restraint was to be shared, in the form of delayed revenues to both government and companies. Companies would be allowed to produce the curtailed amount of oil later on.[16] In the renegotiated contract, however, another compensation option is added: payment of lost revenues. With this approach, BP/CNPC would be paid *whether or not* they produced oil. The government would have to pay BP/CNPC for the oil they didn't produce, as well as for the oil they did!

By definition, this payment could not come out of oil revenues; instead it would come out of other budgets. Faleh al-Khayat estimated that if a quota restrained production by 6 million barrels a day, then not only would Iraq have to reimburse the companies for their investment in idle capacity—

which he estimated at $60 billion—but it also would have to pay them compensation of $3.2 billion per year.[17] And this fact would create a strong incentive for the government not to impose any restriction in the first place, for fear that it could not afford the compensation. The result could be overproduction, a dramatic weakening of OPEC, and a collapse in Iraqi revenues. It could effectively transfer the power to determine rates of production and depletion—a key tool in managing an oil-dependent economy—from the government to companies such as BP. So the addition of those five words, "or payment of lost revenues," to the contract could have an enormous impact on the future Iraqi economy.

The issue of OPEC restrictions was a vital one. The production increases now under contract would, if achieved, take Iraqi oil production from its current level of 2.5 million barrels a day to 12 million barrels a day by 2017 (or higher if Kurdistan deals were included), a fivefold increase. In the space of a few years, this would add about 10 percent to world production capacity—an unprecedented change. And at the time of the second auction, the prospect of this increase and its effect on the oil price caused dissent from some unlikely quarters, when even supporters of foreign investment questioned the scale of the ministry's plans.

"I do think that Iraq should think twice before dumping excess capacity in the market or even maintaining excess capacity," commented Thamir al-Ghadhban. "Because that would exert a downward effect on the price of the barrel. It will be counterproductive and it will hurt Iraq."[18]

Another new critic was Fadhil Chalabi, the eighty-year-old director of the Centre for Global Energy Studies (and cousin of Ahmad Chalabi), who had consistently advocated for multinational oil companies taking the lead role in developing Iraq's oil; as a member of the State Department's Future of Iraq Project in 2002 and 2003, he had called for radical models of privatization (see chapter 3). Yet, speaking at a London conference three days before the second auction, he now warned of "the collapse of OPEC and the quota system, and a free-for-all situation where the collapse in the price will be huge. . . . From the point of view of [the] economic interests of Iraq, what Iraq can gain through more volume it will lose through collapse of the price."[19]

Would Iraq be forced to leave OPEC, as neocons and libertarians had fantasized before Phil Carroll stomped on their plans in 2003? At least Iraq would be sure to pressure OPEC for lower prices, as the British government had intended.

## Heads I Win, Tails You Lose

Five other small technical changes to the contract wording further shifted the balance of power, and of economic benefits and costs, between BP/CNPC and Iraq.

Also in Article 12.5, an extra item was added to the list of circumstances in which the companies would be compensated: the risk that Iraqi pipeline and export infrastructure would not expand sufficiently to cope with the increased production—a significant likelihood given the currently decrepit state of Iraqi infrastructure and the government's difficulty in authorizing any investment to repair it. Most experts estimated that, given the constraints, a more realistic target for Iraqi production would be about 6 or 7 million barrels a day, half the contracted amount. The original model contract provided a mechanism for the companies to help expand the infrastructure themselves, charging their expenditures to the government as "supplementary costs." But following BP/CNPC's renegotiation this risk was shifted entirely to the Iraqi side, with the companies now entitled to be paid any revenues lost as a result of infrastructure bottlenecks. Just as with OPEC quotas, the companies would be paid whether or not they produced oil.

In Article 9.20, Iraqi powers of oversight were weakened. As is normal in oil projects around the world, the contracts required Iraqi approval of major project expenditures. This approval is important to combat corruption, prevent cost inflation from depriving the government of revenues, and ensure that development meets the national interest. But whereas the model contract had required approval of any expenditures above $50 million, the renegotiation upped this threshold to $100 million and set a time limit of forty-five days for South Oil Company to make any formal objection; if it did not, its approval would automatically be assumed. Given the devastating loss of Iraqi human resources since 2003, there was a significant chance that commissioning expert advice could take time, raising the danger that expenditures could pass through without being properly examined.

Third, Article 31.4 determined the "force majeure" provisions: what would happen if an unforeseen event such as natural disaster or war affects production. This was the issue Faleh al-Khayat raised in chapter 6 as a disadvantage of using foreign companies (which stop work in such an event) compared to a nationalized industry (which must find a way to continue).

The model contract had shared the risk of lost income in such circumstances between the two sides via delayed revenues—not unreasonably, since such events could be seen as neither's fault. The renegotiated contract, however, shifted these risks entirely onto the Iraqi side, so BP/CNPC would be fully compensated from Iraqi public budgets, thus making the government liable for "acts of God."

Finally, Article 22.4 was changed so as to specifically exclude BP/CNPC from any liability if its production practices caused any geological damage to the oil reservoirs. In oil production, it is important to consider the impact of extraction on the dynamics of the oil reservoir: if oil is extracted too quickly from a certain zone, it could reduce reservoir pressures, resulting in less oil being extracted over the full life of the field. This happened in the 1990s, when Iraq had to extract oil as quickly as possible without investing in facilities such as new wells or water injection, because of the sanctions. One of the arguments commonly made for bringing in the Western multinationals was that they had greater technical skills in such reservoir management. Yet the change BP negotiated in the contract incentivized maximizing production only over the twenty-year life of the contract; only the Iraqis would be concerned about geological damage constraining production after the fields reverted to public ownership.

As for transparency, the auctions started out well, with a literally clear process during which bids were placed in a glass box in front of TV cameras. But contracts were revised after they were awarded, such that the allocation of risks, and thereby the economics of the project, were fundamentally different from those set out in the pre-auction model contract, on which companies had based their bids. If those final terms had appeared in the model contract, different amounts might have been bid and the results of the auction transformed.

## A Good Deal?

The mainstream view of the auctions was that the Iraqi government had won and that the companies would struggle. BP and CNPC "were beaten down—it looks pretty marginal at $2," reported the *Independent on Sunday*.[20] And when Eni and ExxonMobil agreed on contracts, it was said they had "cave[d] in to Baghdad's tough payment terms,"[21] having "withdrawn their earlier resistance to what the industry saw as unreasonably low payments for helping Iraq."[22] But there were indications things wouldn't be as tough for the companies as the media suggested.

As a general rule, a 10 percent rate of return is considered marginal profitability for a project of moderate risk, 15 percent is comfortably profitable, and 20 percent highly attractive. If risks are low, companies can accept single-digit returns. BP chief executive Tony Hayward told *Petroleum Intelligence Weekly* in early October 2009 that he anticipated rates of return of between 15 and 20 percent from the Rumaila field.[23] Later that month Eni's Alessandro Bernini told investors that the company's investment in the Zubair field would not lower its global average return of between 20 and 30 percent.[24] Meanwhile, there was no risk of not finding oil—the fields were well known and had been producing oil for decades—and many of the technical risks had shifted onto the Iraqi government thanks to BP's renegotiation. Deutsche Bank predicted returns of 22 percent for BP's Rumaila, 19–20 percent for Eni's Zubair, and 19 percent for ExxonMobil's West Qurna I.[25] Peter Wells, director of geological consultant Neftex, estimated rates of return of 15–20 percent on Majnoon and 15 percent on West Qurna II, even if the companies achieved only 1.2 million barrels per day of production rather than the agreed-upon 1.8 million.[26] With the upside added in the February Istanbul road show—that the foreign companies would get access to new reservoirs not yet found—these numbers could go even higher.

So how does this square with the low-sounding $2 a barrel? Under the terms of the contract, that money is all profit, since companies' costs would be fully reimbursed. And given the number of barrels—up to 2 million per day—the profit multiplies very quickly. On top of reimbursement of costs, BP and CNPC would earn profits from Rumaila of up to nearly $700 million per year *after tax* (though this amount would decline in later years of the contract).[27] That sounds a lot more impressive than $2 a barrel.

For fields as large and as cheap to develop as Iraq's, payback of investments could be very quick indeed.[28] And the companies had succeeded in negotiating the contracts so as to front-load their returns. After a threshold production target had been achieved, the government would reimburse each individual investment within months of it being expended. Once reimbursed, the cash could be reinvested. So even if a project required a total investment of $20 billion, the companies would never have to expose more than about $2 billion of capital, because it was constantly recycled. One oil company executive told me that, for the larger fields at least, all of the foreign companies' investments would have been repaid within four or five years.[29] After that, they would consistently enjoy a net profit, and overall profits would accumulate very quickly. An Iraqi oil expert commented, "People were trying to say that Iraq doesn't have the money to develop its own capacity, so we need the IOCs. But BP will get their money back within months, so where's the big investment?"[30]

This is why the rates of return are high even for remuneration fees of just $2 per barrel. For all the political tricks of the small, round per-barrel number, the contracts could be highly profitable for the multinational oil companies.

For the Iraqis it looked less promising. In December 2009 Tariq Shafiq pointed out that the contracts did not oblige the companies to purchase Iraqi goods or services, so much of the required materials would come from abroad. And while the contracts required a percentage of the workforce to be Iraqi, they did not specify local workers' levels of management or technical expertise. "The present policy lacks plans to develop the next Iraqi generation capable of ensuring supervision or audit of the future Iraqi oil industry," he concluded. "It lacks plans to 'Iraqi-ise' the management of the operations during the . . . contract life."[31] Iraq had been de-skilled since 2003, and the new contracts would do little to reverse that process. The contracts might have helped rebuild the country's skills base if the Iraqis had been given a 51 percent stake—which the international companies had successfully lobbied against in Istanbul in February 2009—and had switched to the principal management role halfway through the contract, with the international companies transferred into a technical support role (as happens in Iran). Instead, Shafiq lamented of the Iraqi oil industry, "the state's role has been relegated to a minority shareholder."

A former Iraqi oil official observed, "If the uplift in production had been done slowly, one contract at a time, then Iraq could have learned from its mistakes, improving the contracts iteratively as it went along."[32] Instead everything was signed away at once.

## Opening the Taps

The scale of the proposed development was unprecedented not just in Iraq but in the world. Over the coming years more than $100 billion would be invested, according to an Oil Ministry spokesman,[33] and perhaps as much as $200 billion when related infrastructure was included.[34] (Iraq's GDP was around $65 billion in 2009.) Reuters estimated that BP/CNPC's Rumaila field alone would require tens of drilling rigs, 60,000 tons of steel, and more than 21 million cubic feet of concrete.[35] It is difficult to imagine the impact of such rapid investment even in a country with developed infrastructure and effective institutions. In an Oil Ministry too divided and dysfunctional even to approve purchases worth a few million dollars, what likelihood was there of it effectively overseeing activity on this scale?

Still, Shahristani was in no mood to stop. In March 2010 the Ministry of Oil awarded a twelfth contract, to two Chinese companies, for the three fields in Maysan province that had not been awarded in the first auction. A third auction took place in October 2010 for three gasfields, even though there would be plenty of associated gas from the twelve oilfields already awarded. And then a fourth auction was announced, scheduled for March 2012, this time for exploration blocks. Even before the second auction, Dhia'a Jaafar, the Da'wa loyalist installed in SOC to replace Fayadh Nima, had worried about the scale and pace. "This is enough!" he declared. "We're not sure we can absorb any more right now. It is too much work and capacity for SOC to handle."[36]

During any industrial development, effective government regulation is essential to ensure that working conditions are safe for employees, prevent damage to the environment, prevent corruption and bribery, ensure that taxes are paid, and so on. In the absence of proper oversight, development will become a free-for-all, to the cost of local people and the state itself. This was where Iraq seemed to be headed. The prospect was a barely regulated gold rush, where each company raced to extract what it could before hitting infrastructure bottlenecks or before the political situation turned sour.

An executive at one of the companies told me in summer 2010 that even after the joint management committee had started meeting to make decisions on his company's project, the Iraqi members of the committee, apart from the chairman, had not seen the contract.[37] They were responsible for representing the state's interest in the project but had no means of checking what was expected or required of the company.

The impact of this lack of knowledge—combined with the reduced oversight capacity resulting from BP's renegotiation—was seen when BP and

CNPC awarded drilling contracts in March 2010. Three contracts were signed, worth about $500 million total, to drill forty-nine wells—around $10 million per well, costs that would be covered in full by the Iraqi government.[38] But the going rate for such wells in the easy desert conditions of the region, such as in Kuwait and Saudi Arabia, is usually between $2 and $4 million, and never more than $6 million, per well (depending on specifications, depth, geology, and accessibility).[39] And the contract for twenty-one of the forty-nine wells was with a Chinese company called Daqing Petroleum, which happens to be a subsidiary of CNPC. The result is that the Iraqi government pays more than it should, while CNPC (and perhaps also BP, through its partnership agreement) reaps extra profits from the cost reimbursements—a classic transfer pricing scam.

The potential for heavily overpriced subcontracts and the lack of institutional oversight mechanisms or expert knowledge of what things should cost meanwhile created ripe conditions for corruption. In 2009 Transparency International ranked Iraq the fifth most corrupt country in the world.[40] The U.S. State Department's 2009 human rights report on Iraq warned, "Anticorruption institutions were fragmented, and their interaction was hampered by a lack of consensus about their role, partly due to a lack of effective legislation as well as to insufficient political will to eliminate widespread corruption."[41] This problem dated back to the Coalition Provisional Authority, which not only failed to account for billions of dollars of Iraqi money that it handled but also dismantled the Board of Supreme Audit (BSA), Iraq's principal anti-corruption agency.* Arrogantly believing it knew better than Iraqis how to structure Iraqi institutions, the CPA established two new entities, the Commission on Integrity and the Inspectors General, neither of which is properly functioning to this day, due to inadequate powers, lack of capacity, failures of coordination, or government interference.[42] The CPA later reinstituted the BSA, but without many of its powers or resources.

A little over a year after Eni began work on the Zubair field, the anticorruption branch of the Milan public prosecutor's office announced that it was investigating allegations of bribes paid to Eni managers by construction

---

* The CPA's reason was that it considered the BSA a Ba'athist body, notwithstanding the fact that it had been established in 1927, thirty-six years before the Ba'ath first came to power.

companies seeking contracts. The Italian newspaper *Corriere della Sera* reported that, following raids of company offices and executives' homes, prosecutors believed they had uncovered a complex bribery scheme involving mobile phones with untraceable Lithuanian SIM cards.[43]

Meanwhile, there had been talk since 2003 of installing meters to measure oil flows, a job that should not have taken more than a few months. At various stages this work was to be carried out by Halliburton, Shell, BP, or Iraqi companies. But auditors reported that by the end of 2008 the metering system was still only 33 percent complete. As a result, the auditors could not confirm the accuracy of government financial records.[44]

## Lawless Islands

Kurdistan's oil industry looked, if anything, more irregular. On September 18, 2009, it emerged that the Norwegian stock exchange had fined DNO for failing to disclose sufficient information on the sale of a large number of its shares in late 2008 to a single buyer linked to one of its projects. The financial newspaper *Dagens Næringsliv* revealed that it was KRG natural resources minister Hawrami who had purchased the shares.[45] The KRG was quick to insist that there was no corruption involved and that Hawrami had—in his official capacity—bought the stake on behalf of Genel Enerji, which was trying to expand and consolidate its Kurdistan position.[46] Genel and DNO were the only two companies actually producing oil in Kurdistan thus far (others were still exploring or developing). Hawrami's intervention in itself would be odd—for the government to buy stakes in companies investing there and to facilitate commercial transactions between the companies. Whatever the truth, it damaged the KRG's reputation among international companies, raising suspicions that things might not be as they appeared. At around the time, the same newspaper also exposed Peter Galbraith's undeclared financial interest in the DNO deal.

Five months later another scandal struck when the chief executive of Genel was handed a record fine by the U.K. Financial Services Authority for insider trading in the shares of Heritage, another small KRG investor with which Genel was in the process of merging.[47] In 2011 Genel was taken over by Vallares, a financial vehicle partly owned by Tony Hayward, who became Genel's chief executive. In the midst of the 2010 *Deepwater Horizon* disaster that would force him out of his position as BP chief executive, Hayward had famously said, "I want my life back." He achieved that with the take-over, making an estimated $22 million on the deal.[48]

While oil companies were happy with the PSA model contract in Kurdis-tan, it was unclear how such companies obtained contracts in the absence of any competitive bidding process—presumably it was by making contact with the KRG, often through an intermediary such as Galbraith. John Hamilton, a journalist specializing in Middle East business at Cross-Border Information, observed that the terms of the contracts were, oddly, all the same—although different blocks have different prospectivity for oil, and you would expect the more promising blocks to offer less generous terms. He commented to me, "The Kurdistan oil industry is like a piece of Africa transported to the Middle East."[49] Indeed, much of Ashti Hawrami's work for the ECL consultancy be-fore he became minister had been in Africa, including in the kleptocracy of Equatorial Guinea, where ECL drew up the oilfield licensing regime and was found by a U.S. Senate committee to have channeled funds for young Equato-rial Guineans to study in overseas universities mostly to children and relatives of government officials.[50] Now many of the oil companies coming to Kurdis-tan were those whose major experience was in Africa.[51]

Like the federal government, the KRG was reluctant to publish its con-tracts, although the KRG's own regional oil and gas law requires details of contracts to be made available to the public.[52] When I asked in 2006 about the minister's stated commitment to transparency, a KRG official replied, "I think that the point about transparency in the article related to transpar-ency of officials and procedures, rather than providing full public access for what are essentially confidential commercial contracts. I am not sure of any company in any region that would wish to have such access granted."[53] In September 2011, the KRG finally published its contracts on its website, as a means to pressure the federal Iraqi government to endorse them.

Many of the KRG's contracts contained a highly unusual provision allow-ing the government to transfer its stake—up to 25 percent of the project—to private sector companies of its choice.[54] This is an open door to corruption, although officials claimed its purpose was to be able to bring in more profi-cient firms later.[55] Denise Natali, an American academic based in Kurdis-tan, told the *Middle East Economic Survey* (*MEES*) in June 2008 that "one cannot get a major contract without going through the political parties." Both ruling families had their own companies. *MEES* reported that Hawrami had so far blocked them from getting stakes in oil production, however.[56] Many rumors persisted. Michael Rubin, a neoconservative advocate of the war who had been disillusioned by his time in Kurdistan, alleged that the Kurdish leaders Barzani and Talabani have amassed respective personal fortunes of $2 billion and $400 million since 2003.[57] There was a blurring, he wrote in *AEI Middle Eastern Outlook*, between the institutions of regional government, business interests, and the two families.

Then there was smuggling. On July 8, 2010, Sam Dagher of the *New York Times* exposed the illicit trucking of potentially hundreds of thousands of barrels of crude oil and refined products from the Kurdistan region into Iran. This was no covert operation: more than a thousand tankers crossed the border each day, forming long lines at the three border posts. A senior KRG official had told Dagher anonymously that the proceeds were going to the two Kurdish governing parties and affiliated companies, and that officials and politicians in Baghdad were also involved. For ordinary Iraqis it was an insult that while the country still suffered fuel shortages, its politicians were profiting from fuel smuggled out of the country. "The people are being scammed, but by whom we do not know," Hamid Mohammed, one of the truck drivers, said.[58]

Iraq had built no significant refineries since 2003, so it had to import gasoline and other refined fuels even as it exported unrefined crude oil. The Iraqi government allocated a share of the imported fuel to the KRG, just as it allocated a share of export revenues. What Dagher had uncovered was that KRG officials were reexporting some of that fuel (purchased by the Iraqi government) and keeping the revenue, whether for the KRG or for themselves. When the federal cabinet called in KRG officials for questioning by the Oil Ministry, they refused to attend. "I have nothing to say about Shahristani's demand except that we have our own government and parliament and we make our own decisions," said Ashti Hawrami.[59]

"Kurdistan is like an island with no rule of law when it comes to oil," commented Abdullah Malla-Nuri, an opposition member of the KRG regional parliament.[60]

# 25

# Winter and Spring

*Our problem with our politicians is they have no idea about democracy, and they think as Saddam thought. The same!*
—Farouk Muhammad Sadiq, secretary of Iraq Federation of Oil Unions,
Basra, December 2009[1]

In mid-December 2009, shortly after the second auction, I visited the oil workers in Basra. They were more anxious than I'd seen them before. "All of the government is now against the union," said Muhammad Zaki of the petrochemical union. "They don't want to let the union work as part of democracy. There are many orders from the ministry to stop us working, especially the leadership, who are very active. They want to break us."[2] A week before the auction Nouri al-Maliki had written to the heads of oil companies, ordering them not to deal with the unions. Oil Minister Shahristani had said as much before, but an order coming from the prime minister had added weight.

Faleh Abood Umara, the union's general secretary, was due to report to the police station two days after my visit and was visibly worried. He was accused of inciting protests and criticizing ministry policies, in breach of Article 435 of the Penal Code, which prohibits "insulting a person."[3] I asked if he was concerned. "I don't care about them," he replied nervously. "We expected everything when we started the union: arrest, death, losing our jobs."[4]

Over the following months the union's conflict with the government continued to escalate. In late February and early March 2010 workers at the

Basra refinery held a series of strikes and sit-ins and a large demonstration on March 18. They called for wage increases, payment of owed allowances from the previous three years,* formal recognition of unions, and more effective measures against corruption. The Oil Ministry responded with the tactic it had used before: on April 1, it again transferred four refinery union leaders from Basra to Baghdad.

In March the South Oil Company announced in an internal memo that all industrial action was banned and that any participants in future action would be prosecuted. The same month Hassan Juma'a was called before the Commission on Integrity—a body that supposedly existed to prevent corruption—on charges of "abusing the economy" by disseminating information and statements about foreign investment in the oil sector. If convicted, he faced up to three years in jail.[5] Faleh Abood Umara was arrested the same month and held for two days in a Basra police station on the orders of the Oil Ministry.[6] Over the following two months union offices were forcibly closed in the tanker company, oil institute, and refinery, under Saddam's Law No. 150 of 1987.[7]

## A Daunting Message

At this stage, it might have been tempting to think that the United States had achieved what it came for: contracts were signed, production was set to increase rapidly, and heavy pressure would be placed on OPEC. However, without either an oil law or parliamentary ratification of contracts, the results were still provisional, as the legislation from 1967 was still in force. U.S. diplomats noted in May 2009 that "Shahristani is virtually alone (of [the Ministry of Oil's] top management) in believing that the first round bid contracts will not require [parliamentary] approval."[8]

Shortly before the second auction, Shatha al-Musawi, the parliamentarian we met in chapter 23, took a case against BP/CNPC's contract for the Rumaila field to the Federal Supreme Court. If successful, it would have set a precedent that made all such contracts unlawful.

Along with some other MPs, Musawi had previously been trying to bring

---

* Remuneration of workers was according to a complex system that included allowances for postings away from home, night shifts, or dangerous work.

Shahristani to the parliament to be questioned about the contracts. Prime Minister Maliki made an effort to block the attempt, writing a letter to the speaker of the parliament in late October marked "confidential, urgent and personal" in which he suggested that two recent large bombings in Baghdad were targeted at the oil auctions and implied that parliamentary questioning of the minister should be considered in a similar light. "Questioning Shahristani sends a daunting message to all companies which are eager to enter our oil market, and questioning the minister at this time would be in harmony with the destructive forces' objectives," wrote Maliki.[9] It was a chilling, if bizarre, indictment of Iraq's new democracy that the government considered parliamentary scrutiny "in harmony with" acts of terrorism. Maliki also threatened MPs with corruption investigations or arrest if they did not drop their demands to question ministers.[10] In the event, the blocking tactics failed. However, when Shahristani appeared before the MPs, Musawi found his answers "not adequate" and in some cases inconsistent. "I found out that the parliament is not capable of following such a case," she concluded. "That's when I decided to go to court."[11]

The Iraqi government was determined not to allow the case to succeed. In February 2010, Thamir al-Ghadhban told U.S. diplomats he predicted that even if the lawsuit was "100 percent right," the court would find a way to avoid invalidating the Rumaila contract in order to best serve the public interest. Indeed, the judiciary had little independence from the government, and in 2010 the Supreme Court found in favor of Maliki in several controversial decisions.[12] For example, it ruled that the right to form a government would fall to the largest party at the time parliament sat, rather than at the time of elections, so although Maliki came in second, a post-election merger with other Shi'a parties put him in front. The court reinterpreted another article of the constitution to find that several independent bodies, including the Independent High Electoral Commission and the anti-corruption Commission on Integrity, were in fact answerable to the executive branch of government. It ruled that the parliament could not propose legislation, only approve bills proposed by the executive.[13] As for Ghadhban, he would have preferred parliamentary ratification for the stability it would bring— and earlier had seen it as legally necessary[14]—but said any attempt would be gridlocked by ideological differences and political infighting and therefore impractical.[15]

The court did find a way to block Musawi's case, as Ghadhban had predicted. In late April 2010 it ruled that she must pay 300 million dinars (about $250,000) to fund the costs of the case, returnable if she won. While this was a considerable challenge, she turned to fellow parliamentarians for the solution. Several political blocs agreed to support her and help her raise the money: the Sadrists, al-Fadhila, the Kurdish parties, and Ayad Allawi's grouping.[16] These blocs all disagreed with the existing government about oil, but they had widely differing ideas as to what they'd do instead, from the Sadrists and Fadhila, who suspected the contracts were too generous to the foreign companies, to the Kurdish parties, who saw them as too centralized and not generous enough.[17] Where the parties all agreed was that the parliament should review the contracts.

Musawi's challenge betrayed the fragility of the oil companies' position. Whatever the outcome of her case, it was clear the companies would have great difficulty defending their contracts if future governments tried to amend or cancel them. So pressure resumed for an oil law, this time to retrospectively legalize the contracts. "Iraq's petroleum regime is incomplete. Therefore legal questions will remain until this is resolved," said oil and gas lawyer J. Jay Park at a conference on Iraqi oil in London in December 2009. The contracts on their own were not sufficiently legally secure for investors. Turning to Iraqi legislators, he said, "Iraq's constitution requires that a petroleum law be passed, so just do it!"[18]

As national elections approached in March 2010, there was renewed talk of the oil law being passed by the new parliament. In a way, backdating the contracts' legality would be the worst of both worlds for Iraq and doubly beneficial for the companies. It is a basic rule of business investment—and of gambling—that the higher the risk of losing, the greater the reward one demands for winning. Companies had insisted throughout the process on highly profitable contracts because of the political risks of not having an oil law. If an oil law was now passed confirming the legality of their contracts, thereby removing the last remaining risk, it would enshrine this profitability at a much higher rate than if they had been signed *after* the law.

Shahristani said he hoped the new parliament would also bring ratification of the Trade and Investment Framework Agreement with the United States, the first step toward a bilateral investment treaty that would allow company disputes with the Iraqi government to be arbitrated outside the country.[19] But first there was the matter of forming a government.[20]

## Politicians' Seats

Most observers had been cautiously hopeful before the vote, before becoming pessimistic once more upon seeing the results. To an extent, with Allawi's secular bloc and Maliki's intermittently nationalist party winning 91 and 89 of the 325 seats, respectively, the result continued the trend away from sectarianism indicated in the previous year's provincial elections. But there were other forces at play. First, it was immediately interpreted in the United States on the basis of sectarian logic anyway, labeling Maliki's party Shi'a (largely accurately) and Allawi's Sunni (largely inaccurately).* Commentators had to twist their logic to fit the result into their frame. Former ambassador Christopher Hill puzzled, "The real problem for Allawi is that he's a Shi'a. So for a Shi'a who's essentially representing Sunni to be one of the three leadership positions, the question is what box is he checking?"[21] So despite the relative success of the less sectarian parties, the post-election bargaining took a decidedly sectarian turn.

Before the elections Iran had encouraged a major new round of de-Ba'athification organized by Ahmad Chalabi that excluded 561 candidates, most of them secular nationalists, thereby clearing the way for the sectarian parties. The barred candidates included Saleh al-Mutlaq, who had been one of the first parliamentarians to oppose the oil law in 2007 and a leading voice against many of the most sectarian government policies since 2005. According to Iraq expert Reidar Visser, the de-Ba'athification campaign was aimed precisely at reversing the cross-sectarian alliances that had started to develop after the provincial elections.[22]

Western commentators had predicted that Shahristani's successes in oil policy would win his party many votes.[23] The results did not support that view: he received a mere 6,364 votes in his Baghdad constituency, compared to the 37,379 threshold he needed to be elected outright. He regained his seat only because Maliki received 622,961 votes, with those above the threshold being reallocated among his party.[24]

The clearest message of the results was a rejection of the post-2005 political establishment, with the exception of Maliki himself. Only 62 of the 275

---

* About a third of Allawi's winning candidates were Shi'a, including Allawi himself, and his party won several seats among Shi'a sections of the electorate. However, the fact that it also won most of the votes of the Sunni community led U.S. commentators to label it Sunni.

incumbent MPs were returned to the parliament, and several ministers, including the ministers of interior and defense, lost their seats. The Sadrists, who had been in opposition most of the time since 2005, gained 39 seats, while their coalition partner ISCI, the most powerful party in 2005, was punished with only 18.* The Sunni Islamists, who had dominated the Sunni vote in 2005, were trounced with just 6. Even the Kurdistan Alliance of Jalal Talabani and Masoud Barzani saw its seat count decline, from 53 out of 275 to 43 out of 325. Yet despite the mandate for change, political leaders worked hard to cling to their positions. To the anger of voters, political leaders went to neighboring countries immediately after the election for help in consolidating their power.†

Months dragged on after the elections, as politicians continued to haggle over which of them would get the ministries. In the system the United States had created, politicians were unresponsive to the desires of Iraqis, and power was negotiated by horse trading in the Green Zone rather than with the population. The effect had been to give the United States power over politicians while isolating them from the population. But the ultimate result was that when U.S. power eventually declined after 2007, it was Iran that stepped into the vacuum. There could have been no worse outcome for the bungling architects of the war and occupation than to greatly empower their archenemy—and the realization of this may have lain behind an increasingly bellicose posture toward Iran during 2011.

Shatha al-Musawi had decided not to stand in the election, frustrated at the weakness of the parliament's ability to hold Iraq's leaders to account. "I am not ready to lie to people claiming that we have a democracy," she said.[25] "The gentlemen are currently not the least bit interested" in Iraq's problems. "All they are interested in is whether they will be in the same positions after the election and whether they will control the same budgets."[26] The principal political parties had colluded to weaken parliament, she said to me in August 2010. "Most of the governmental institutions are working without law and violating the constitution every day because they decided not to have an effective parliament." She added, "We have really a dictatorship"—a striking condemnation, given that she had been impris-

---

* That the two former enemies were now coalition partners was an indicator of how quickly relations can change in Iraqi politics.
† Iran supported the Shi'a alliance of the Sadrists and ISCI and pushed Maliki to join them. Turkey and several Arab states supported Allawi.

oned and her father murdered by Saddam Hussein's regime when she was a teenager.[27]

It would appear that her criticisms of the parliament were well founded. The parties that had supported her court case stepped back from it as they jostled for power, fearing that their involvement might damage their prospects of winning key ministries. And without that support she could no longer raise the court's deposit. Two months later Iraqiyya announced that the outgoing government's oil and gas contracts were illegal because they had not been ratified by the parliament.[28] The timing revealed the opportunistic nature of Allawi's support: at that stage, it was too late to obtain a ruling from the court, but as politicians got closer to forming a government, it could be seen as a useful bargaining chip and a good reason for the government not to want Iraqiyya to be in opposition. Musawi had also lost the support of the oil experts advising her. All were still working in the industry and had been warned by the minister not to cooperate with her. In early August her lawyer quit as well. Musawi was now living in Irbil with her husband, also a former MP. "I don't think it is a good idea to go to Baghdad," she told me.

## A Spark of Hope?

Iraqis remained unhappy with their leaders. This unhappiness manifested itself in June 2010, when demonstrations took place across the country in protest at the continuing failure to provide more than a few hours of electricity per day, seven years after the fall of Saddam. The mobilization could perhaps be seen as a precursor of the uprisings that would take place throughout the region the following spring. Electricity generation had suffered the same handicaps as oil production: bomb damage from 1991, decay under sanctions, looting in 2003, botched repairs by unaccountable U.S. contractors, and intermittent attacks by saboteurs. And in electricity, too, skilled technicians and managers had been replaced with party loyalists and sectarian quotas, and political divisions prevented decisions being made or money spent.

The protests began in a sweltering Basra on June 19, when an early summer heat wave took temperatures above 120 degrees Fahrenheit and brought several thousand demonstrators onto the streets. They carried a coffin representing electricity. One man climbed onto the coffin and wept to show his grief at the lack of services. Police fired into the crowd, killing at least one. Two days later a thousand people demonstrated in Nasiriya. Some carried chairs to symbolize Iraq's politicians squabbling over their seats in government rather than working to solve the country's problems.[29] Police fired water cannons at protesters who tried to storm the provincial council building. A few hours later the electricity minister, Kareem Waheed, resigned.

Oil Minister Shahristani became acting electricity minister to replace Waheed, as protests spread to Kut, Hilla, Baquba, and Baghdad. In one of his first acts, on July 20, 2010, he issued a ministerial order to prohibit all trade union activities and any official communication with the unions. The next day, on his orders, police raided the offices of the electricity workers' trade union and confiscated computers, documents, and furniture. He promised "immediate legal action" under terrorism legislation against any who resisted the clampdown.[30] "Any employee who gets a salary to do a specific work is not allowed to do any other activities under any name, whether it is a union or humanitarian . . . or whatever [it] is called," he said.[31]

The uncompromising ferocity of Shahristani's assault on the electricity unions provoked a strong response from the international trade union movement. The AFL-CIO wrote to Prime Minister Maliki, "By organizing unions and bargaining for improved working conditions, Iraqi workers are trying to practice internationally recognized rights long denied to them by decades of dictatorship. . . . Your government continues to implement antiunion labor laws which originated in a far less democratic and less hopeful era of Iraqi history."[32]

The increasing attacks on unions ended the success of the Iraqi government's campaign of divide and rule against the unions. Previously its favoritism toward the General Federation of Iraqi Workers had succeeded in creating competition between the union federations, to the extent that only two of them attended a pan-union conference in March 2009. But Shahristani had targeted electricity unions from two of the federations—the GFIW and the Federation of Workers' Councils and Unions in Iraq—who now organized joint demonstrations against the minister.[33] And Shahristani's involvement prompted the oil workers' union federation to express its solidarity. "What is really good here is that it seems this order has brought together different federations working now together," said Hashmeya Muhsin Hussein, head of the GFIW-affiliated electricity union.[34]

There was now a growing international campaign for Iraq to recognize labor rights, and the efforts of U.S. and international unions were further spurred by the series of clampdowns on Iraqi unions during summer 2010. While the Iraqi government was following Saddam Hussein in trying to snuff out civil society organizations that might criticize it, international solidarity restrained some of its fiercest attacks. Recognizing this, in May 2010 the government banned trade unionists from traveling overseas without permission. At its annual meeting the same month, the executive committee of the International Federation of Chemical, Energy, Mine and General Workers' Unions passed a resolution stating that it "condemns all of these Iraqi government acts against trade unions," adding, "We are appalled that seven years after the fall of Saddam Hussein's regime, workers in Iraq are still without legislative protection of their fundamental rights at work."[35]

Throughout the summer the international campaign continued to expand, especially through the behind-the-scenes efforts of Michael Eisenscher of U.S. Labor Against the War. Eisenscher told me he felt the increased repression was succeeding in weakening the Iraqi unions. "I think this was very consciously done in anticipation of the end of occupation, and the need for the Iraqi government to establish control over a sector that would be a locus of resistance and popular organization against the government."[36]

I told him I thought that sounded pessimistic.

"I don't see it as pessimism," Michael replied. "I see it simply as an assessment of the balance of forces. It's only pessimism if you draw conclusions that nothing you do makes a difference. And we don't draw that conclusion." Indeed, USLAW had—remarkably—continued to grow since 2003. It held a conference call of the steering committee every month, and continued to sign up new organizations even in late 2011. "There was a certain level of demoralization that took place in the peace movement after the war started. You know, there was this huge global movement, holding demonstration after demonstration, including some very large ones, and nothing prevented the war—so there was a kind of letdown and a period of disorientation. Many people were intimidated into silence or withdrew. But that did not happen in USLAW," Michael explained.

In July the U.S. national antiwar movement's annual conference passed a resolution objecting to the ongoing attacks on unions and calling on antiwar activists to pressure Congress, the Obama administration, and through them the Iraqi government to respect the rights of Iraqi workers.[37] Similar resolutions were passed by trade unions as they entered their annual conference season, beginning the following month with the Communication Workers of America and the American Federation of Teachers.[38] And in September, twenty-one members of Congress wrote to Maliki demanding the passage of a new labor law and the cancellation of post-2003 anti-union measures.[39]

The IFOU now began to make some headway against the latest transfers of four refinery workers to Baghdad. According to Ibrahim Radhi, the leader of the refinery union, pressure from international unions persuaded the ministry to transfer them back south after about seven weeks, to work in the Rumaila field, about fifty kilometers west of Basra. Meanwhile, they initiated a court case, demanding to be returned to their old jobs at the Basra refinery. In August the court ruled in their favor: they could now return to their homes and families and to their jobs in Basra, the union's headquarters.[40] It was the first success in the year of intensified repression since the oil contracts were awarded. "They tried to take this action against us to paralyze the union," Ibrahim told me, "but as unionists, we don't really care what the minister says or does. This is our mission: we will do everything for workers."

## Fixing a Hole

Partial resolution of Iraq's electoral impasse finally came in November 2010, not because the politicians themselves showed any maturity or sense of the national interest, but because the Supreme Court ordered them to form a government, following a successful case brought by four civil society organizations. Still, the key post of defense minister was not filled until August 2011, and at the time of this writing the interior minister has not been appointed at all, more than eighteen months after the election. Shahristani was promoted to deputy prime minister responsible for energy, while his former deputy Abdul-Karim al-Luaibi became oil minister. Meanwhile, the secular Saleh al-Mutlaq—in spite of being barred from the election— became another deputy prime minister.

Maliki opted for a fudged government of national unity. He could have formed a majority government in coalition either with Allawi's Iraqiyya bloc or with a combination of the Iraqi National Alliance grouping of the Sadrists and ISCI and the Kurdish parties. Each had their redlines, but by partially dealing with them all Maliki could avoid being held for ransom by any—

instead it would be a persistently dynamic pattern of wheeling and dealing to keep each happy.

Along with the trade unions' position, the entire future of the oil industry remained contested. Whatever their view of the bid rounds, Iraqi oil experts were almost unanimous in criticizing the production levels the contracts set, as we saw in the previous chapter. Producing 12 million barrels a day was unrealistic, given the state of Iraqi infrastructure; and even if it were achievable, it would crash the oil price and leave Iraq worse off. During the course of 2011, the Oil Ministry finally seemed to accept this view.

The new oil minister, Abdul-Karim al-Luaibi, announced in early May that he intended to renegotiate the contracts and lower the production targets to more feasible levels. But the companies declared that they would expect to be compensated for any change, and shortly afterward the ministry stepped back from the proposal. If the companies' refusal to accept an achievable level of production seemed odd, the reason could be found in BP/CNPC's contract renegotiations of 2009. Thanks to those changes, the Iraqi government is obliged to pay the companies at the rate they bid in the auction, even if oil market considerations or infrastructure constraints prevent them actually delivering those levels of production. From the companies' perspective, it doesn't matter whether their target rates are achievable or not; they get paid anyway. Hence they would be unlikely to accept being paid according to a lower target rate. In other words, while the Oil Ministry had erred in accepting such high production targets, the contract renegotiation with BP now prevented the ministry from correcting its error.

The government seemed not to notice it still had one potential card up its sleeve, however: the issue of the contracts' legality. So while the companies might point to their contracts and argue that the government has no right to change the production targets without compensation, the government could point to the law and argue the contracts don't give the companies any rights at all until ratified by the parliament. However, such an about-face would have been politically uncomfortable for the government, to say the least.

Once again an oil law was pushed, and once again politicians divided over who would control the spoils. In summer 2011, in fact, *two* oil laws were proposed: one by the Oil Ministry and one by the parliamentary oil and gas committee. The former, building on the nationalist political gains of 2007 and 2008, strengthened the central government's role compared to the 2007 draft. The committee's version, through an alliance of Kurdish parties and Allawi's bloc (whose anti-Maliki ambitions trumped the nationalist policies for which its supporters had voted), did the opposite and empowered the regions. Notably, both drafts—including the committee's, which reflected party politics more than parliamentarianism—would remove the parliament's power to review and ratify contracts, repealing the 1967 law.

As had happened in 2008, a U.S. administration that would have liked to deploy its resources to pressure for the passage of the oil law was distracted by the question of whether it would keep troops in Iraq, as the Status of Forces Agreement was due to expire at the end of the year. In April 2011 Admiral Mike Mullen, chairman of the Joint Chiefs, visited Iraq to press the lobbying effort. Taking care to get the positioning right, he asked the Iraqi government if it would like to invite U.S. troops to stay, but warned it would need to decide soon. No, thank you, Maliki replied: "The [Iraqi] military and the security forces have become able to take the responsibility, to maintain the security and to work with professionalism and patriotism."[41] Well, Iraqi leaders should decide soon, Mullen repeated.[42]

For Meghan O'Sullivan the oil contracts were an important reason for an ongoing U.S. military presence. In a *Washington Post* op-ed titled "Why U.S. Troops Should Stay in Iraq" she echoed Faleh al-Khayat's 2003 analysis of the United States' strategic interests:

> Most compelling, there is the role that Iraq may play in averting a major global energy crisis in the coming years. . . . If demand continues to outgrow supply, it will be only a few short years before global spare capacity of oil—one of the indicators most closely tied to prices—gets dangerously low, and jittery markets push prices up and up. . . . Iraq is one of a very small number of countries that could bring oil online fast enough to help the world meet this growing demand at a reasonable price. In fact, major energy institutions and international oil companies are already assuming that Iraq will significantly increase its oil production in the coming decade.[43]

While Iraqi politicians could not afford to be seen to request that U.S. troops remain in Iraq, privately they hoped that the Americans would stay. In July 2011, Maliki agreed to keep a number of military "instructors"[44]—a term that he believed would allow an agreement to be struck without the political difficulty of going to the parliament for approval.[45] Some U.S. administration officials suggested the number should be around 10,000,[46] while the Iraq commander General Lloyd Austin III (who had replaced General Odierno) wanted 20,000.[47] The following month, Iraqi political leaders agreed to begin negotiations over the precise terms of any agreement.

## Springtime in Baghdad

In 2011 the IFOU, battered by the relentless attack of the previous eighteen months, made further progress, as the charges against Hassan Juma'a and Faleh Abood Umara were dropped. In April, Hassan reflected in an open letter on eight years of occupation. "Instead of aiding Iraqis' struggle for freedom, equality and democracy and to get rid of the iron grip of a repressive past, the pretext of democracy and freedom brought us religious fighting, fanaticism and a sectarian quota system. As for the suffering of the Iraqis the occupation made the moist clay much muddier" (an Arabic saying). Yet events around the region were giving renewed cause for optimism. "The winds of change are affecting the homeland and the Arab World so this will . . . contribute to the strengthening of unity and to lay the foundations of democracy in Iraq and the Arab World."[48]

On February 25, 2011, Iraq held its own "Day of Rage," in which around three thousand people protested in Baghdad's Tahrir Square, with ten thousand protesters in Basra and thousands more in another sixteen cities across the country. The protests in Iraq were less widely reported than those elsewhere in the region—perhaps because Western journalists struggled to make sense of how Iraqis could be protesting against a government they had elected the previous year. The reason is that, as we have seen, the United States refused to "let a thousand flowers bloom" and instead steered Iraq's political evolution so that only pro-U.S. politicians had a chance of succeeding in elections. Those politicians had no interest in providing services such as electricity or water and were keen to "treat ministries like private bank accounts," as the International Crisis Group put it.[49] Iraq's Arab Spring protests actually were most persistent in non-Arab Sulaymaniya, where demonstrators camped in the main square for three months—reflecting the fact that the most authoritarian and least democratic forces in post-Saddam Iraqi government are the Kurdish parties.

Iraqi politicians were caught unawares, and the protests achieved some quick victories. Two provincial governors—in Basra and Hilla—were forced from office. Maliki agreed to halve his salary and announced that he would not seek a third term. The government, meanwhile, transferred $1 billion budgeted for military aircraft to social programs.

For Meghan O'Sullivan, who now serves as an adviser to Hess Corporation as well as teaching the geopolitics of energy at Harvard, the democracy protests spelled bad news. "Popular pressure on the Maliki government is more likely to be deleterious to energy developments than it is to be beneficial," she warned.[50]

As the government came to grips with the situation, it adopted a cunning two-track approach. Maliki announced that he was giving the Iraqi government one hundred days to rectify the problems and provide services, which appeased the moderate protesters and bought Maliki some time. Meanwhile, he used violence to crush the hard core and deter others. Pro-government thugs attacked protesters in Baghdad's Tahrir Square with sticks and knives while the police stood by. Offices of organizers were raided, and journalists who reported on the protests were arrested and had their equipment seized.[51] After the hundred days expired with no meaningful change, weekly protests resumed in Tahrir Square, with the number of people turning out generally a few hundred and sometimes a few thousand, but the momentum had been lost for the time being.

Interunion collaboration strengthened during 2011 as the government declared that the leaders of the GFIW—the one federation it had said it intended to recognize—had no standing to represent workers, and that the government would itself form a new leadership for the federation. The British Trades Union Congress threatened to block the Iraqi government delegation from participating in the next meeting of the International Labour Organization if it continued, prompting the government to postpone the move.[52] The GFIW was joined by the FWCUI and its offshoot the General Federation of Workers' Councils and Unions in Iraq (GFWCUI) in a protest against government interference in unions in Baghdad in April. The same month, GFWCUI, the oil workers' IFOU, and other unions held a joint protest at the Rumaila field over BP's failure to pay overtime and allowances for working night shifts. And the GFWCUI also protested in June when the government transferred Kirkuk Oil Union president Jamal Abdul Jabar, a GFIW member, to the other side of the country.

## *Exeunt*

Shatha al-Musawi had lost her court case on a procedural issue, not an interpretation of the substantive law. Unless an oil law was passed, the oil contracts remained technically illegal. So if a future, more representative Iraqi government decided those contracts weren't in the national interest, the oil companies would have no *legal* means to stop the Iraqis from tearing them up. They would, however, have economic and political means of pressuring that government—indeed, a major reason for keeping troops in an "over-the-horizon" role was to provide "a sort of life insurance" through the influence they projected. But the situation changed on October 21, 2011.

"Today, I can report that, as promised, the rest of our troops in Iraq will come home by the end of the year," President Obama announced from the White House. "After nearly nine years, America's war in Iraq will be over."[53]

In the manner of the slow-motion moments before a car crash, the final withdrawal of troops felt at the same time both unexpected and entirely inevitable. It was unexpected in that Obama and Maliki each had an exposed flank, and needed the troops to stay—Obama for fear of attack from Republicans who would accuse him of squandering all the gains made by soldiers' sacrifices, and Maliki because U.S. support would strengthen his shaky grip on power. More broadly, the U.S. and Iraqi governments both had longer-term strategic interests in maintaining the troops' presence: the United States in order to influence a strategically vital country and protect its oil industry, and Iraq to shore up a government widely seen as illegitimate.

On the other hand, in both countries large majorities of the populations wanted the troops to leave, and that public opinion had played a role in both Obama's and Maliki's electoral successes. The specific sticking point in discussions was the insistence by American lawyers that troops should be immune from Iraqi law: in the event of any crime committed by U.S. troops, the accused would be tried in the United States, not Iraq. In early October Iraqi leaders declared that immunity was off the table. From a U.S. perspective, it was a sine qua non: the world's military superpower could not possibly accept foreign jurisdiction over its troops in Iraq, let alone the precedent it would set internationally. Furthermore, the entire political narrative of honorable American soldiers trying to help lazy, barbarous, or ungrateful Iraqis would make the possibility of conviction politically explosive. From an Iraqi perspective, there was no way politicians could possibly accept such immunity after the country's experiences since 2003, including torture at Abu Ghraib, targeting of civilians and use of banned munitions in Fallujah, mass murder of civilians in Haditha, and gang rape and murders in Mahmudiya. And because U.S. influence in Iraq had declined since the failure to achieve the oil law in 2007, it could not overcome these Iraqi demands. In these respects, failure to achieve an agreement was inevitable.

The withdrawal came many years too late, leaving a reinforced Iraqi political system in which the corrupt could thrive, which was structurally incapable of providing services for the population and which was showing increasing moves toward authoritarianism to stay in power. Nonetheless, the departure of the U.S. military released a major brake on Iraq's political development toward a more representative, more Iraqi system. So the economic war would be fought by the companies on their own, without the military in overwatch. At long last, Iraqis would be able to shape their own future.

# 26

# Another Regime Changed

*Regardless of the talents of the Libyan people, they will need substantial inter-*
*national help. Societies that have endured decades of oppression rarely flourish*
*quickly once the dictator is gone. . . . Security, often provided by outsiders, is*
*needed to build sustainable political institutions.*

—Meghan O'Sullivan, April 1, 2011[1]

In April 2011, a month into the Anglo-French-American intervention in
Libya, British foreign secretary William Hague was asked in an interview
why the military had been deployed in support of democracy in Libya but not
in Côte d'Ivoire, where at the time long-standing ruler Laurent Gbagbo was
clinging to power after losing an election and dragging the country into civil
war.[2] In principle Hague supported democracy in both countries, he said:
the difference was that Britain had *interests* at stake in Libya. First of these
was that Britain and its European allies were anxious to prevent increased
flows of refugees—Libyans and other Africans—into Europe. Second,
Hague feared the establishment of terrorist training camps in the desert.
Third and most important, he believed that the West's failure to intervene
would have "terrible economic consequences [for] the price of oil. . . . We
can't stand aside."[3]

It seemed like a remarkable admission, in light of how strenuously a
war motive had been denied in Iraq. But he was not the only one now saying yes to "blood for oil." In the United States, business magnate Donald
Trump—who made a brief but ultimately abandoned pitch for the Republican

presidential nomination—argued for seizing Iraq's and Libya's oil. "In the old days," he explained, "when you had a war, to the victor belong the spoils. You go in. You win the war and you take it."[4] Right-wing commentator Ann Coulter agreed: "Of *course* we should go to war for oil. . . . We need oil. That's a good reason to go to war."[5]

One might wonder if the Iraq War had made cynical motivations again acceptable. Or perhaps it was Iraq that was the anomaly: previous decades had not seen such squeamishness about admitting an oil motive for war. Author Michael T. Klare recounted in his book *Blood and Oil* how the acknowledged centrality of oil in U.S. foreign and military policy went back to Franklin D. Roosevelt's meeting with King Ibn Saud in 1945, through the Cold War containment doctrines of Presidents Truman, Eisenhower, and Kennedy, and up to the Carter Doctrine of 1980, Reagan's establishment of the Central Command, and Defense Secretary Dick Cheney's justification of the 1991 Gulf War.[6]

So was Hague right that Western intervention in Libya might prevent an increase in the price of oil? Was oil really part of the strategic reason for the war? As in Iraq, the answer was yes, but not in the most obvious way.[7] There were important differences from the Iraq War: a UN resolution, a movement in Libya calling for the military action, and a multilateral approach in which the United States played only a supporting role. And whereas the Iraq War had been planned for years, the war in Libya happened very quickly. In terms of oil, one difference was scale: although Libya has the largest reserves in Africa, they were not game-changing like Iraq's, which are three times their size. Another difference is that, since the West's 2004 rapprochement with Muammar Qadhafi, the oil multinationals were already operating in Libya.*

But even if Libya were not a strategic pivot for the industry to the extent that Iraq was, it produced enough oil to have an impact on the price. If Qadhafi had slaughtered Benghazians in March 2011 as he threatened, the international community would likely have felt compelled to impose sanctions, shutting out Libya's 1.7 million barrels a day of production.[8] This would strain oil markets and hence push up the price of oil at a time when

---

* Although the companies grumbled about unprofitable contractual terms and some analysts suggested those terms were restraining the levels of foreign investment, there was no serious prospect of a post-Qadhafi regime renegotiating those deals.

the world economy was especially fragile. The short-term problem was one of quality: Libya was Europe's principal supplier of sweet (low-sulfur), light crude, and many refineries do not have the facilities to process heavy or sour crude.[9] In the medium term, there could be a quantity problem too, as global oil demand was rising at around 1 to 2 million barrels a year, and the industry's spare capacity of 5 million barrels per day would be depleted before long.

There was another strategic driver of military action: claiming ownership of the Arab Spring while rehabilitating the notion of humanitarian intervention. Since Iraq that notion—an important element in the West's toolbox for managing international affairs—had been discredited.* And after France had offered troops to protect Zinedine Ben Ali from Tunisian demonstrators, and both Britain and the United States had backed Hosni Mubarak against the Egyptian democracy protesters in Cairo's Tahrir Square, those powers needed to do something to reposition themselves on the side of democracy. Conversely, the domino effect of the Arab uprisings was creating a region-wide instability that posed a major strategic threat. By participating in a revolution in a country lying between two that already had overthrown their dictators, the West gained an opportunity not only to reclaim credibility as a force for good but also to steer the unfolding of the Arab Spring. As British prime minister David Cameron said in a speech to the UN shortly after Tripoli fell, "The international community has found its voice in Libya."[10]

In the case of Iraq, it would be too simplistic to say the United States went to war in Iraq for oil and constructed a lie about weapons of mass destruction to allow it to do so. Recalling Faleh al-Khayat's analysis in chapter 3, the WMD were part of the rationale, but in the context of a need to expand Iraqi oil production. Similarly, many in the U.S., U.K., and French governments were genuinely motivated by Qadhafi's threat to Benghazians, but the context was of likely sanctions disrupting the oil market. Both cases followed a general pattern in the Middle East: the West's concerns about security or human rights are always refracted through the lens of oil.

---

*The official reason for the Iraq War was the security threat posed by weapons of mass destruction, but humanitarian issues were added as a supplementary argument, especially when the WMD turned out not to exist.

## Creating the New Regime

The other big question hanging over Libya was what would happen after military operations. Meghan O'Sullivan's former mentor Richard Haass, now chair of the Council on Foreign Relations, opined, "What is also likely is that Libyans will not be able to manage the situation about to emerge on their own."[11] Writing in an article in the *Financial Times* titled "Libya Now Needs Boots on the Ground," published the day in August Tripoli fell, he gave a lengthy checklist for the things that "must" be done. As for the United States, he urged that a few thousand troops be sent, since "leadership is hard to assert without a presence."

When Libyan leaders rejected a foreign military presence, other channels of influence had to be found. The U.K.-led International Stabilisation Response Team (ISRT) warned Libyans that if

> the emerging leadership does not have the confidence of the international community, international re-engagement could be . . . delayed. Any such delay would have a spiral effect on financial viability, popular confidence and the ability of the international community to support security efforts. International wariness of the new [Libyan government] could also undermine efforts to develop UN Security Council support.[12]

The Western powers effectively held Libya's purse strings—both directly in the form of frozen assets and indirectly through their ability to withhold endorsement of the new political leaders for the purpose of oil sales.

The United Nations was another channel of influence. The UN mission, with 146 international staff members, was to be led by Europeans, not Africans or Arabs.[13] While it was being set up in October, Ian Martin, its British-born special representative, actively consulted several Western ambassadors, but not Chinese representatives or members of the African Union.[14] He argued that the Security Council mandate taken up by NATO did not end with the fall of Qadhafi, and so NATO would continue to have powers and responsibilities in Libya. This was a remarkable twist of logic, given that the mandate was to protect civilians; the Western powers had decided that it justified regime change because it was Qadhafi who posed the threat.

The UN would work with the World Bank and the International Organization for Migration, with the former taking on responsibility for economic issues. The World Bank's vision for Libya had been set out a few years earlier: remove restrictions on foreign ownership of land and sectoral restrictions such as in banking, reform the labor code "to provide necessary flexibility to business operation," and replace the progressive corporate tax rate with a low flat rate.[15] And the UN too was quite capable of seeing what it wanted to see. Its post-conflict plan asserted, "The country's development had been handicapped by its command economy. . . . [State investments, price controls, and subsidies] stifled the private sector to a point of near nonexistence and resulted in below-potential economic growth, stagnant living standards [and] fragile macroeconomic conditions."[16] This was despite its acknowledgment that "Libyan reality is one of nearly universal access to a range of services and of low poverty levels" and of "favourable macroeconomic outcomes."

Even without the United States directly able to select leaders, as in Iraq, the control over Libya's resources and international legitimacy must have helped the rise of pro-Western politicians. Foremost among these for much of 2011 was the urbane Ali Tarhouni, who held the oil and finance portfolios while the fighting was under way. After Qadhafi was toppled, Tarhouni kept these briefs but also became acting prime minister and security chief. He had left Libya in 1973 and had been an economics professor at Washington University since the mid-1980s. On a visit by David Cameron and French president Nicolas Sarkozy in September, Tarhouni declared, "This is a lovefest. We're just telling them that we love them."[17] He left the government in November 2011, himself complaining of too much outside—specifically Qatari—influence.[18]

Like in Iraq, the new leaders held their discussions with foreigners, not with their own people. The National Transitional Council's (NTC) road map for political transition, for example, was shared widely internationally, but barely at all among Libyans.[19] As for the shape of the political system, U.S. secretary of state Hillary Clinton made a statement that sounded ominous in light of the Iraq experience: "We will be watching and supporting Libya's leaders as they keep their stated commitments to conduct an inclusive transition."[20] The ISRT urged "facilitating participation of all sectors of Libyan society."[21] "Inclusivity" and "representation of all parts of Iraqi society" were precisely the euphemisms used to create a fundamentally divided Iraq. Of course, the dividing lines in Libya would be different: perhaps tribal, ethnic, or regional.

## Unknown Unknowns

Learning the lessons of Iraq became the mantra for the Americans and Europeans who wanted to shape Libya's future. The lesson for me, though, wasn't how to intervene better—it was not to intervene. However, as events unfolded, in spite of some similarities with Iraq, the new Libyan leaders seemed not to be so beholden to their international sponsors.

My friend and former colleague Mika Minio commented, "The National Transitional Council seems to be more resistant to 'advice' than the Iraqi government was."[22] The NTC had refused both a continued NATO military presence and the use of private military companies. "That's partly because the Iraqi government was installed by the occupation and the NTC wasn't. If they do things the Libyan people aren't happy with, they can be overthrown in the way the Iraqi government couldn't be." These conditions forced the new political leaders to compromise rather than abuse their power.[23]

I met Mika in a north London pub in mid-October, about six weeks after the fall of Tripoli and a few days before Qadhafi was found and killed. I had worked with Mika for several years and always admired both his well-tuned political instincts and his keenness to get involved in the communities where he worked. When he joined Platform in 2005, his first assignment was to attend a campaign meeting in Tbilisi; Mika flew there a week early so that he could start learning the Georgian language, including its elaborate curly script.

A fluent Arabic-speaker, he had grown increasingly interested in North Africa since mid-2008 and had tracked the involvement of oil companies there, especially Shell and BP. He had followed how the British government and royal family had lobbied for the companies' entry into the country in 2004 and 2007, respectively.[24] He had noted how, fifteen months after many protesters in Benghazi had been murdered by the regime in 2006, BP had been delighted "to pay the $350 million signature bonus towards new tanks and new rifles, or to be squirreled away in a hidden bank account," in order to get a plum exploration deal.[25] I asked him what impact this had had on Libyan politics. "It helped strengthen the regime internationally. From Qadhafi's perspective he was signing the [contracts] because it was strengthening his status. . . . For sure it weakened the hands of dissidents."

Britain's and the United States' relationships with Qadhafi over recent years might not encourage Libyans to welcome their ongoing presence, a fact that may now come to hamper the oil companies. For instance, BP's major offshore exploration project was brokered by Mark Allen, the former MI6 agent who had facilitated the rapprochement in 2003–4 (and who had highlighted the energy security advantages of attacking Iraq in December 2001). He is believed to be the author of a series of 2004 letters, found in a government building in September 2011 by Human Rights Watch, to Qadhafi's intelligence chief Mousa Kousa arranging the rendition of dissidents to Libya, where they were tortured. "This was the least we could do for you and for Libya to demonstrate the remarkable relationship we have built over recent years," one letter reportedly said. As a further potential embarrassment to Allen and BP, one of the dissidents rendered under this program was Abdelhakim Belhaj, who in post-Qadhafi Libya became head of the Tripoli Military Council.[26]

Mika showed me an eight-page 2007 article in the glossy *BP Magazine* that gushed about how safe, modern, and progressive the country feels to a businessman.[27] The implication of the article, Mika observed, is "that Libya has changed overall. There's very much a sense that overall people's lives are improving, that there are more freedoms. . . . If the public discourse is that things are changing, it's very difficult to communicate stories that things aren't changing on the human rights front."

Indeed in February 2011, BP's chief executive, Bob Dudley, announced that "we remain committed to doing business there."[28] This was the day after newspapers reported that dozens of unarmed protesters had been killed by the regime.[29]

## Learning Lessons

It was clear throughout 2011 that few in the West knew much about Libyan culture, society, or politics, although that did not stop them from pronouncing on what would be best for the country. This made me again think back to Iraq and all the disastrous policies imposed through ignorance or self-interest, and of the Iraqis I had met who gave me a view totally different from that provided by media and the government.

I reflected that if all we have is Western governments relaying their perspective on Libyans, filtered through the lens of their interests, or media reporting it with all the usual simplifications and sensationalism, a genuine Libyan voice would be absent from the "debate" about Libya's future. If we could somehow learn more about the complexity of Libyan society, it might help break down the categorial shorthands that had been so damaging in Iraq.

I thought too of the pioneering role played in 2003 by activists such as Ewa Jasiewicz. What those who went independently to Iraq discovered was a society that was extremely complex: the legacy of decades of dictatorship had left no one able to trust anyone else, and many concealed their own political agendas. By going there, Ewa and others could see people face-to-face, talk to them, and gradually build a picture of the dynamics involved and who could be trusted. It was that early, brave work that made it possible for the antiwar movement, trade unions, and others to work in solidarity with genuine Iraqi counterparts; without it, we never would have heard about Iraqis such as Hassan Juma'a.

So I felt happy that in 2011 some activists and independent journalists traveled to Libya. Among them was Mika, who planned to go there via Egypt about a month after I spoke to him. I asked him his thoughts.

The changing context does provide opportunities for companies to push for their advantage, but it also provides opportunities for social movements. As solidarity organizations, we need to try to empower those movements in the face of pressure from Europe and the U.S. . . . If we're going to work on an ongoing basis with Libyans, we need to have a deeper understanding of what people there want and the Libyan culture and context. And if everyone in Libya says, 'Get lost, we don't want support or advice from anyone including people like you,' well, that's fine too.

# Conclusion

In the summer of 2009 I lived for a short time in the Jabal Luweibdeh district of Amman, a leafy part of the old city now inhabited by artists. One of my neighbors was the Jordanian film director Madian Mostafa, who showed me his unreleased film *The Birds Don't Sing Anymore*. The film shows its protagonist, émigré Iraqi poet Ali al-Sudani, sinking deeper into depression as he observes the 2003 war on television from Amman. He feels utterly disconnected from his country. In summer 2003 he takes a taxi to Baghdad, where he has an emotional reunion with friends and family, but it does not lessen his sense of distance from Iraq, a country that is being reconstructed in a manner alien to him. On his return to Amman, Sudani tries to resolve his feelings about his nationality by painting an Iraqi flag. Halfway through the top stripe, however, he runs out of red paint. When he finds neither paint nor money in his flat, he cuts his fingertips with a razor blade, to complete the painting with his blood.

The meaning of such typically Arab symbolism is clear: while the Iraqi state is destroyed by invasion and replaced by outsiders' ideas of what it should be, the notion of Iraq and its prospects for the future live on in the Iraqi people themselves.

## A Conflict of Interests

The message of Madian Mostafa's film is diametrically opposed to the official narrative of events in Iraq. According to that version, Iraqis were too divided, self-interested, or politically immature for the Iraqi state to survive independently. Only the United States could hold the country together, prevent the escalation of sectarian violence, and broker deals between Iraqi politicians. This rationale made it impossible to talk of the "withdrawal" of U.S. troops; only "responsible withdrawal" was an option. Under the Bush administration, the United States was supposed to pressure Iraqis into "reconciliation"; under Obama, it would serve as "honest broker."[1]

It is much easier to see other people's base motives than one's own. While Western officials and commentators have keenly discussed the best policies for balancing the interests of Iraq's different factions, politicians, parties, and neighboring countries, almost none have acknowledged that the most powerful actor present, the United States itself, had motives of its own. These motives are not limited to oil, but it is quite plain that the United States has an interest in what happens to Iraq's oil. Remember oil analyst and State Department adviser Robert Ebel's words: "What did Iraq have that we would like to have? It wasn't the sand."

The government found it easy to dismiss the "blood for oil" theory by setting up a straw man in the notion that it wanted to seize the physical substance itself. The real oil interest was to expand Iraqi oil production through foreign investment, so as to relieve pressure on the oil market. In the event, the resulting instability had the opposite effect, driving prices up to record levels.

When only one U.S. company (ExxonMobil) obtained a significant stake in an oilfield contract, this was neither a disastrous failure by the U.S. government nor a disproof of its interest in oil (both were suggested by commentators) but an indicator that oil politics are not quite so simple. Of course, the oil companies were "desperate to get in there," said BP in a meeting with the British government in the run-up to war. Foreign investment had the power to open the taps, so the companies' objectives dovetailed neatly with those of the British and American governments. As we saw in chapter 1, it was denied that these meetings between oil companies and the British government took place. Indeed, throughout our story, we have heard denials of actions, motivations, and opinions that documentary evidence directly contradicts. Perhaps this is because the interests involved are very far from the altruistic (or at least indifferent) public position Western governments and companies have felt they had to take.

Many Americans consider an oil-centered foreign policy and military posture incompatible with their values, their desire to be secure and at peace with the world, and the ever more pressing need to address climate change. Such a policy and posture are costly and may even be self-defeating, as the Iraq episode shows that a more aggressive and self-interested approach breeds resentment and opposition. Why not pursue policies that ease rather than deepen oil addiction? Steve Kretzmann of Oil Change International believes the volume of oil industry dollars sloshing around Washington intoxicates politicians and prevents them from assessing the problem rationally or objectively. "The oil industry has Washington completely wired. Not only are they top lobbyists and campaign financiers, but the oil industry isn't afraid to spend unlimited amounts via third party front groups. . . . If we're ever going to fundamentally change the U.S. approach to climate change, energy independence, or foreign policy, we're going to need a separation of oil and state."[2]

## Destroy to Build

The struggles over oil policy—the lens through which we have observed the events in Iraq—illustrate in microcosm the evolution of Iraqi politics as a whole.

Take the American and British assumptions when the occupation began, that Oil Ministry officials were appointed on the basis of Ba'ath Party loyalty rather than ability and that the industry was rife with corruption.[3] We saw in chapter 6 that the Oil Ministry was in fact one of the least politicized elements of Saddam's government. Most in the industry were loyal to their country rather than to the Ba'ath regime. Before March 2003 the Iraqi oil industry functioned remarkably well, given its repeated disruption by wars and its sanctions-bound isolation from the rest of the world, and the Iraqis developed distinctive engineering skills precisely to overcome these difficulties. And while corruption had grown since the imposition of sanctions in 1990, the majority of senior technocrats were honest.

Ironically, during the first three years of the occupation every one of these presumed problems grew into a debilitating impediment. Iraqi human and institutional capacity were all but destroyed, the oil industry became strongly politicized, and corruption mushroomed. Was this all due to a mistake? Had an ill-prepared United States, intoxicated by its own military power, blundered ignorantly and arrogantly into a country it did not understand or bother to learn about? That was part of the picture, but in many respects this outcome was a little too convenient for the occupiers. The United States and United Kingdom needed to find that the Iraqi oil industry wasn't up to the job. That is what they found. For why otherwise would the Iraqis let foreign companies run their oilfields, given their history, politics, and industrial abilities?

When you examine the occupation's approach to governing Iraq, it looks very like the models employed throughout history by empires and expansionist powers to occupy and control foreign lands.

Step one: install friendly Iraqis in government who will support the U.S. agenda. As we have seen, the primary outcomes of the two prewar planning exercises on oil, in the Pentagon and the State Department, were not detailed plans for restructuring the Iraqi oil industry but proposals for who should be its future leaders. The Pentagon group favored Thamir al-Ghadhban, a respected "internal" (non-exile) Iraqi who nonetheless supported handing over management of the Iraqi oil sector to multinational companies. He was made the first "chief executive" of the Oil Ministry. His successor Ibrahim Bahr al-Uloum was a favorite from the State Department's exercise.

Step two: keep institutions deprived of resources and authority so as to maintain their dependence on the occupiers. The damage to Iraq's oil industry began with unchecked looting, but the rot spread when U.S. Army planners and engineers delegated repairs to unaccountable and often negligent U.S. contractors who failed in most of the projects they took on. The CPA denied investment funds to the Oil Ministry, and Iraqi experts and managers were demotivated by being undervalued, deprived of authority, and made to serve under the occupation forces.

Step three: preserve dominance over the long term by fomenting political divisions. Far more lasting damage was done to Iraq's Oil Ministry by politicization than by neglect or the sidelining of experienced managers. The CPA under Paul Bremer made ethnic and religious identity the ticket to power, beginning with establishment of the Iraq Governing Council in July 2003. The "invasion of the Chalabis" then purged the ministry of many of its skilled people and replaced them on a political and sectarian basis— including one replacement whose previous experience was as a pizza chef. The new ministry officials had little interest in serving national or institutional goals; everyone was now in it for themselves. In such an environment it is not at all surprising that corruption flourished. As Iraqi options for independently developing their oil diminished, a weakened Oil Ministry was forced to depend on the United States for its technical lead and ultimately on foreign investors to run the industry.

This damning view of the occupation is reinforced when we remind ourselves of what happened to the Iraqi oil industry next. During the first three years of occupation, while the ministry apparatus was effectively dismantled, Western "advisers" worked to set up a new conceptual framework for the future Iraqi oil industry in which multinational companies would play the lead role. Then, once a government was in place with sufficient legal authority to grant long-term contracts, another U.S. adviser, Ron Jonkers, was recruited to draft an oil law whose primary purpose was to reverse the hard-won nationalization of the postcolonial era. Again, it was denied that Jonkers was actually supposed to draft the law—although that was precisely what his contract said he was to do. Not only would the law give multinational companies the primary role in running the Iraqi oil industry, but it would strip the Iraqi parliament of its power to scrutinize contracts, as well as establish a powerful body of legal protections for the companies' interests. Like many of the advisers, Jonkers had a background in reshaping the laws of the former Soviet republics to the advantage of multinational investors.

When that approach was unsuccessful and Jonkers was replaced as oil law author by three Iraqis led by Tariq Shafiq, their draft was subsequently amended both to strengthen the powers of foreign investors and to pander to the interests of Iraq's ethno-sectarian politicians. Early drafts were seen by American and British officials—and even discussed with multinational oil companies—long before they were seen by members of the Iraqi parliament, much less the general public. But while the U.S. administration had hoped the law would be passed before anyone knew about it, in late 2006 its contents started to leak out. And the more Iraqis heard about the law, the stronger grew the opposition to it. For a year U.S. officials and politicians—right up to the president—cajoled and pressured Iraqi leaders to pass the law. They conditioned both aid and debt relief on its passage and even effectively threatened to remove the Maliki government from office.

## Divide and Rule

Although the Bush administration ultimately stepped back from that threat, it had been able to make it because the Iraqi government would have collapsed without U.S. military support. The government had no meaningful legitimacy or support among the Iraqi population, its institutions were fundamentally divided along ethnic or religious lines, and it operated according to the logic of self-preservation.

While Western commentators like to believe that sectarianism and corruption are simply in Iraqis' nature, the radical increase in these two diseases after 2003 grew directly from the political structures the occupation created, the Iraqi Governing Council and Bremer's rules for the January 2005 elections. Iraq's new political leaders, many of them former exiles, shrewdly took advantage of the new structures and made the rules permanent in the 2005 constitution, overseen by U.S. ambassador Zalmay Khalilzad. Meanwhile, both the Bush and Obama administrations chose as their allies the most sectarian of the parties: in particular, the (Shi'a) Islamic Supreme Council of Iraq (ISCI, formerly SCIRI), led by the al-Hakim family, and the two established Kurdish parties, along with the prime minister's (Shi'a) Da'wa Party and at times the (Sunni) Iraq Islamic Party.

Eventually the West's primordial view of Iraqi society became self-fulfilling. Beginning with the contention that Iraqi society was at heart about religious and ethnic divisions, the occupation created a political system that encouraged those to be expressed. Similarly, the consistent U.S. identification of the resistance as "Sunni" and the new government as "Shi'a and Kurdish" ultimately created those very tensions: power, wealth, and favors flowed to the latter two, while the first was harshly repressed. And al-Qaeda-style jihadists took full advantage of the new environment. Arguably, U.S. forces were the first to instigate avowedly sectarian attacks by conducting wide sweeps of Sunni areas, during which they shot or arrested anyone about whom there was doubt.

With the parties' political bases now residing in communal identity rather than ideology or policy, it was almost impossible for a sense of Iraqi national interest to develop. Iraqi politics became a zero-sum game: it could not develop dynamically because the dividing lines were fixed.

Was it planned that way? There were certainly advantages for the occupation powers, because a divided population could be ruled. If politicians had organized around policies rather than identity, a populist government might have forced an end to the occupation, which the majority of Iraqis demanded. But as long as Shi'a competed with Sunni and Arab competed with Kurd, and as long as those tensions could be stoked when necessary, there would never be a sufficiently organized rejection of the occupation, either military or political. However, to suggest that U.S. officials consciously planned the sectarianization of Iraqi politics would be to overstate both the predictability of politics and the capacity and coherence of U.S. agencies. We have seen disagreements over numerous issues in our story: whether to strengthen the Iraqi oil industry or sweep it out of the way, whether to support secular political parties or religious ones, whether to support or oppose the KRG's signing of oil contracts, and so on. Reflecting these differences as well as changing circumstances, U.S. strategy changed repeatedly. In any case, while the policies may have helped maintain U.S. dominance in Iraq in the short term, an ironic longer-run consequence of sectarianization, the promotion of unpopular politicians, and the separation of the political class from the population was to make Iran the major power on the eve of the United States' departure. Without the U.S. interventions, Iraqi nationalism never would have allowed Iranian influence to take hold.

Of course, political splits, inconsistencies, and complexities have not been unique to the Americans. Among the most perplexing Iraqi political actors are the Sadrists, who have actively pursued nationalist, even democratic politics and have reached out meaningfully to their Sunni compatriots. Yet supporters of Muqtada al-Sadr were among the worst culprits in the sectarian slaughter of 2006–7.

Nor do U.S. players divide neatly into good, pragmatic "doves" and bad, ideological "hawks," as many critics of the war have suggested. The hawks in the Pentagon were the drivers behind the greatest crime, the decision to launch a war of aggression, but the most damaging decisions during the subsequent occupation came from the supposed doves of the State Department and the CIA. Many in the Pentagon advocated a short occupation and bitterly criticized State for instigating Paul Bremer's extended rule. In a way, it was the doves' pragmatism that came to be the problem. Before the war many doves were skeptical because they foresaw the difficulties of an occupation and rejected the naïveté of certain neocons' belief that liberated Iraqis would embrace Ahmad Chalabi, the United States, and even Israel as symbols of democracy. But once the United States was committed to war, the same cautious people pushed the more divisive policies of the occupation as the means to achieve U.S. objectives. For example, the State Department's Ryan Crocker, who had suffered sleepless nights over the coming war, became the principal engineer of the Iraqi Governing Council, the starting point of sectarianism in Iraq. Meghan O'Sullivan, who had argued for containing rather than removing Saddam in early 2001, became a key advocate of the continued policy of sectarian balancing and a strong supporter of SCIRI/ISCI, the most sectarian Shi'a party.

A simplistic narrative will not do, whether based on American altruism or on hegemonic designs.

## Fuel on the Fire

The roots of the U.S. approach to governing Iraq lie not in conspiracy but in political psychology, in particular the ability of human beings to genuinely hold beliefs that serve their own interests. The American presence in Iraq since 2003 has claimed a *mission civilisatrice*: bringing democracy, economic development, and a model for how to run an oil industry effectively. From this paternalistic viewpoint, which necessarily presupposes cultural superiority, Western officials, politicians, and commentators simply could not see any Iraq besides the one they either pitied or despised. Iraqis could not be seen as citizens, with their own complex and diverse desires and opinions; instead they were portrayed as having only collective identities.

Furthermore, in spite of overwhelming evidence, U.S. officials could not publicly accept that the "insurgency's" motivation was to resist occupation, because they saw themselves as liberators, not occupiers. Any action to prevent the Americans' work, even by Iraqis, was to be seen as a serious threat to Iraqi interests as much as American ones. Hence General Sanchez's warning that "we have to work very hard" to contain the "danger" of linkages between Shi'a and Sunnis.

In much the same way, the United States could not accept that there might be a legitimate political position that opposed the apparently self-evident need for multinational companies to run the oil sector, in spite of Iraqi history, popular opinion, and the usual practice in the region. In place of a debate about foreign involvement, U.S. officials reduced the politics of oil to the question of how revenues would be distributed. Thus Ron Jonkers, the investment lawyer hired by USAID to draft the oil law, wrote, "The politics is about control of oil revenues. It is only after oil is monetized that politicians become really interested."[4] Similarly, when the U.S. provincial reconstruction team (PRT) office in Basra became aware of growing discontent over the 2009 oil auction, it speculated in a cable to Washington that local people could be concerned about reduced opportunities for corruption and smuggling once the companies arrived, or perhaps they were worried that too much of the extra revenues would go to Baghdad rather than staying in Basra. Even when quoting local accusations of "neocolonialism" or "selling out" SOC to the West, the PRT office explained them away as "interested parties jockeying for position under new rules to come, and staking out bargaining positions for still-to-be-negotiated final contract details and subcontract tendering after awards are made."[5]

In other words, in order to deflect a conflict between the U.S. oil agenda and the views of ordinary Iraqis, officials and commentators reframed the question. Oil was to be seen not as an integral part of the state and its economic policy, something about which there should be a range of views, but as simply a generator of revenue, and hence something to be competed for and, by extension, fought over.

When contracts were signed governing the majority of Iraq's oil for the next twenty years, this good news for many in the West had to be expressed as good news for Iraqis. "The glue that holds the country together is oil," Vice President Biden said in May 2010. "There's a lot of oil, the promise of it is real, there's a lot of gas, and it's all over the country. Everyone has figured out that getting a legitimate share of a much bigger pie is a pretty good deal."[6] Were its consequences less serious, the idea that belligerents would lay down their arms when they recognize that their interests are best served by sharing the wealth fairly would be laughable. Events in Iraq—as in most other oil-exporting countries—have consistently demonstrated the opposite to be the case.

Even if resolution was found to the conflict over Iraqi or Kurdish control of the oil-rich "disputed territories," the likelihood is of massive corruption and renewed conflict over the source of almost all the country's wealth. With Iraq's divided politics and ineffective institutions, oil development resembles a gold rush, where companies operate without oversight to maximize their returns before politics catches up with them. Already there is evidence of overpricing scams and bribery in the awarding of subcontracts. Contrary to Biden's assertion, the existence of oil revenue has not discouraged militias from fighting to control it; instead, it has helped them to accumulate cash, weapons, and power. The government will have a direct interest in ensuring the continued flow of oil and an incentive to silence anyone who threatens that flow. And working alongside it will be the oil companies' own armies of private military and security companies, which, despite efforts to professionalize their image, have been practitioners of unregulated violence in Iraq as in other countries.

In short, oil looks set to be a destabilizing influence on Iraq's future. Given the scale of the U.S. interests involved, leading figures in the Obama administration tried to keep their military forces in overwatch—the "insurance policy," as Ibrahim Bahr al-Uloum called it—beyond the end-of-2011 deadline for their departure. Their failure to do so can be traced back in part to the intense struggle over the oil law in 2007. Ever since the September deadline passed without a law, U.S. influence in Iraq has steadily waned.

## The Iraqi Soul

There is one cause for a more optimistic view of the future. Iraq's emergence from the dark days of 2006 and 2007—when it looked like sectarian forces would dominate the streets and the government for a generation—was primarily thanks to the Iraqi people's refusal to accept sectarianism. And although Iraq remains cursed with a dysfunctional political system, corrupt politicians, and major influence from neighboring Iran, the departure of the United States—which consistently, though perhaps unwittingly, obstructed reconciliation and genuine nation building—can only improve the chances of Iraq becoming more, well, Iraqi.

Both recent and more remote history suggest that Iraqis will not quietly allow the Iraqi state to be divided, nor reduced to a mere global gas pump. In a culture as old and rich as Iraq's, even dictatorship, occupation, and extreme violence cannot fully subdue the population. A thousand years ago Baghdad was the intellectual capital of the world—a heritage that persists today in the Iraqi soul. The country also has impressive levels of political literacy and a keenness among ordinary people to debate the issues of the day, things to which other societies (including mine, in the United Kingdom) should aspire. While recent Western commentaries on Iraq have often portrayed the country's political leaders as responsible moderates who have tried to rein in the ethno-sectarian excesses of the Iraqi population, for most Iraqis it is the other way around.

Those who created that image continue to believe they know more about Iraqis than the Iraqis themselves. In August 2010 Anne Nivat reported in the *International Herald Tribune* an Iraqi commenting, "The Americans introduced distinctions between our people that were unheard of. We were to have quotas according to our religious sect. As a result, the little discipline we had was replaced by sort of a chaos based on supposedly 'democratic' values. If that's democracy, nobody wants it." Yet Nivat, who is French, found it necessary to correct him about his experiences: "Adeeb [a Turkoman] seemed to have forgotten that under the previous regime his options were greatly limited because of his ethnicity."[7]

After 2003 an organized Iraqi civil society developed in spite of, rather than because of, the U.S.-U.K. occupation. For example, while viceroy Paul Bremer tore up much of Iraq's existing law in the name of replacing dictatorship with democracy, in June 2003 he reasserted Saddam Hussein's 1987 law prohibiting labor unions in the public sector. U.S. officials kept quiet when the Iraqi government passed and implemented Decree No. 8750 in August 2005, which allowed it to seize union funds; when it sent in troops against the oil workers' protest in June 2007; when it prosecuted union leaders; and when it raided the electricity workers' union offices in July 2010.

Perhaps this U.S. antipathy was unsurprising given the interests at stake. After all, a grassroots movement led by trade unions, oil experts, and subsequently political parties and religious groups succeeded in stopping the passage of the oil law, even when the world's sole superpower made it a top priority and sent additional troops to assert its will in Iraq.* This was an impressive and quite surprising achievement. The contracts that ultimately were signed gave away far less to investors than would have been the case without the oil law campaign. While still problematic, unlike PSAs they did not grant foreign investors the upside of potential windfall profits. In 2005 and 2006 the international oil industry (and the U.S. and U.K. governments) had been so unified in the view that PSAs were the way forward in Iraq that such agreements had looked inevitable.

The struggles over the oil law played at least some part in reasserting an Iraqi national character, not only because they created a space in which Iraqis organized together across sectarian boundaries but also because they

---

*Another factor was the disagreement between Kurdish and other pro-U.S. political parties. While Western commentators did not look beyond the pro-U.S. parties and suggested that their (ethnic) disagreement was what killed the law, in reality both factors were important. As we saw in chapters 20–22, the oil law could not have passed even if all the pro-U.S. parties had agreed, for a parliamentary majority opposed it, following the grassroots movement's campaign.

led to the rejection of PSAs signed by the KRG and to the turn away from sectarian politics in 2008. Oil is a unifying issue for Iraq's people as much as it is a divisive one for its politicians.

There have been plenty of other civil society achievements in Iraq that lie beyond the remit of this book. Public protests by the Organisation for Women's Freedom in Iraq caused a provision to be dropped from the TAL interim constitution that would have granted Islamic clerics power to adjudicate domestic disputes.[8] Work by the Journalistic Freedoms Observatory led to the establishment of an official hotline for threatened journalists in October 2008 and to more journalist access to government events.[9] A ten-month lobbying campaign by a coalition of groups in 2009 succeeded in eliminating draconian measures in the government's proposed civil society law.[10] Perhaps most significant, in late 2010 the politicians' impasse was finally broken when a coalition of four civil society groups—the Center for Iraqi Peace Support, al-Amal Society, Iraqi Association for Health Management and Development, and Women for Peace—won a lawsuit to compel them to form a government, which happened in December 2010.[11]

These achievements would be impressive in any country; in Iraq's situation they are all the more so. Yet they are rarely reported in the Western media. Before events in Tunisia and Egypt hit the headlines in spring 2011, these successes disproved the common assumption that Iraqis or Arabs lack the capacity or desire for democracy.

Now U.S. troops have left, but foreign oil companies have arrived en masse with their own private armies. The difficulties the companies' operations will cause are just starting to become apparent, but their contracts are not validated in Iraqi law and remain vulnerable to legal challenge. Another fight over the oil law is around the corner. Trade unions struggle to defend their tenuous position in Iraq; their counterparts in Europe, the United States, and elsewhere work to strengthen their efforts. Independent parliamentarians and civil society groups demand a say in their country's future. This is Iraq's economic war, the struggle of the coming years and decades.

# Acknowledgments

This book grew out of several years' work at Platform (www.platformlondon
.org). There could be few better places in the world to be employed. Platform
is an organization that values the human spirit, unlocks its greatest potential, and is fearless in challenging power. James Marriott in particular was a
constant source of advice, encouragement, and inspiration.

Oil Change International (www.priceofoil.org) shines a light on the darker
practices of the oil industry; the organization is a smart operator in trying
to wring the oil out of U.S. politics, and a supporter of this book. Thanks to
Steve Kretzmann for ideas and reflections, and for educating me in U.S.
politics.

The Joseph Rowntree Charitable Trust (www.jrct.org.uk) funded my work
in Platform from 2005. It was a difficult and risky project for them, often
with little prospect of success. I am deeply grateful for their faith in Platform and in me, and I thank them too for supporting this book with further
grants. Thanks to Nick Perks, Stephen Pittam, and the trustees.

The Barry Amiel and Norman Melburn Trust (www.amielandmelburn.org
.uk) generously awarded me a grant to write this book. I thank Willow Grylls
and the trustees.

I am especially indebted to my lawyers, Phil Michaels and Kel McClanahan, who not only helped extract documents from the U.K. and U.S. governments but also gave me renewed faith that freedom-of-information acts can
be used to great effect. My researcher Sophie Roumat's dogged persistence

won my gratitude, though perhaps not that of some recalcitrant government officials.

Reporters working overseas depend heavily on "fixers," whose skill at arranging interviews is vital though not always acknowledged. I am deeply grateful to Ahmed Fadaam, Yahya Hamied, and Shko Bakr, in Baghdad, Amman, and Irbil, respectively. Thanks also to the Iraq Federation of Oil Unions, and especially Farouk Mohammed Sadiq Ismael and Hassan Juma'a, for hosting me in Basra. Mohammed al-Kadhim was as generous as ever in arranging and interpreting a telephone interview. Thanks to Lucy Garnier for transcribing many of my interviews.

My U.K. editor, Dan Hind, was a reliable source of wisdom, and his presence gave me confidence throughout the process. I am grateful for his excitement at the subject matter and belief in the project. I also thank Kay Peddle and Will Sulkin at Random House for their very great patience and constant support. My U.S. editor Sarah Fan worked magic on the text, consistent in her ability to spot what I was trying to say and how to do so with more grace. Thank you, too, to Maury Botton and all of the team at The New Press.

I am grateful to John Hilary and colleagues at War on Want (www.waron want.org) for supporting me while I worked on this U.S. edition and for putting up with my bleary-eyed state in the mornings.

Several friends and colleagues reviewed drafts of the book or parts of it: Munir al-Chalabi, Martin Duffy, Ellie Jupp, Shawna Bader-Blau, and Tareq Ismael. Each improved the text with their comments, although I am responsible for the remaining flaws.

All those I interviewed gave up their time—often at risk to themselves or their careers—simply because they believed the story should be told.

Thanks also to others who assisted with research, contacts, or advice, including Graham Lee and Global Witness, Altaf Makhiawala, Nick Schwellenbach, Ewa Jasiewicz, Keith Fisher, Mark Lynas, David Bacon, Issam al-Chalabi, Faleh al-Khayat, Michael Eisenscher, T.J. Buonomo, Faiza al-Araji, Mary Forbes, Martha Mundy, Joyce Battle and National Security Archive, Michael Schwartz, Hayat Majali, Rafiq Latta, Abdellatif Najar, Nadia al-Sharif, Justin Alexander, Jonathan Stevenson, Ruth Tanner, Heike Mainhardt-Gibbs, Becca Fisher, Rob Sykes, Erik Leaver, Solomon Hughes, Elizabeth Palmer, Saeed Farouki, and Ralph Hötte.

As well as those mentioned above and in the text, I owe particular intellectual debts to Herbert Docena, Nick Hildyard, International Crisis Group,

Dahr Jamail, Raed Jarrar, Michael Klare, Naomi Klein, Kamil Mahdi, Sami Ramadani, Ian Rutledge, Anthony Shadid, Jonathan Steele, and Reidar Visser. In lieu of a bibliography, anything by these authors is recommended. Anthony Shadid passed away in February 2012 while reporting from Syria, a great loss both to journalism and to international understanding of the Middle East. His book on the Iraq War, *Night Draws Near*, is one of the best—a work of true compassion and courage. I also made frequent use of statistics compiled by Michael O'Hanlon and colleagues in the Brookings Institution's *Iraq Index*.

Thanks to my friends for putting up with me while writing the book, and to my brother, Doug, and parents, Paul and Colly, for endless reserves of support, both practical and emotional. And to my soul mate, Rosemary Forest: I could not have written this without you.

This book is dedicated to Guy Hughes, who was both an exceptional campaigner and a dear friend. He was the driving force behind the media success of the publication *Crude Designs*, which first took my research to a wider audience in 2005 and formed the basis of my subsequent work leading up to this book. He refused all my pleas for him to share the credit on that report. He died in a mountaineering accident two months later.

Finally, I am grateful to Iraqi friends, civil society groups, and oil experts for showing me a different side of Iraq to what we see in the papers. They gave me hope for the future.

# Notes

The following abbreviations are used in the notes (see also the List of Abbreviations on page xvii).

| | |
|---|---|
| AFP | Agence France-Presse |
| AP | Associated Press |
| BIS | (U.K.) Department for Business, Innovation and Skills |
| *CSM* | *Christian Science Monitor* |
| DJ | Dow Jones |
| DOC | (U.S.) Department of Commerce |
| DOD | (U.S.) Department of Defense |
| DOE | (U.S.) Department of Energy |
| DTI | (U.K.) Department of Trade and Industry (now Department for Business, Innovation and Skills) |
| FCO | (U.K.) Foreign and Commonwealth Office |
| FOIA | Freedom of Information Act |
| FOIP | Future of Iraq Project |
| *FT* | *Financial Times* |
| ICG | International Crisis Group |
| ICRC | International Committee of the Red Cross |
| IEA | International Energy Agency |
| *MEED* | *Middle East Economic Digest* |
| *MEES* | *Middle East Economic Survey* |
| NEPDG | (U.S.) National Energy Policy Development Group |
| *NYT* | *New York Times* |
| *PIW* | *Petroleum Intelligence Weekly* |

SIGIR      (U.S.) Special Inspector General for Iraq Reconstruction
TUC        Trades Union Congress
UP         University Press
UPI        United Press International
USIP       United States Institute of Peace
*WP*       *Washington Post*
*WSJ*      *Wall Street Journal*

## Introduction

1. George Bush, *Decision Points* (London: Virgin, 2011), 223–24; Dick Cheney, *In My Time* (New York: Threshold, 2011), 364–69.

2. "The 112 Billion Barrel Question," *International Petroleum Finance*, April 1, 2003.

3. Alan Greenspan, quoted in Bob Woodward, "Greenspan: Ouster of Hussein Crucial for Oil Security," *WP*, September 17, 2007.

4. George W. Bush, AP, August 31, 2005.

5. Condoleezza Rice, interview with AP Editorial Board, June 8, 2007.

6. Carrie Satterlee, "Facts on Who Benefits from Keeping Saddam Hussein in Power," Heritage Foundation, Web Memo No. 217, February 28, 2003.

7. Conrad Crane and Andrew Terrill, *Reconstructing Iraq*, U.S. Army War College, February 2003, 21.

8. Indeed, in February 2003 leading war hawk Richard Perle, chair of the Defense Policy Board, attacked the French government for opposing a second UN resolution authorizing war with Iraq because of its oil interests, and in the same interview dismissed notions of a U.S. oil motive. David Rose, "Top Bush Aide Savages 'Selfish' Chirac," *Observer*, February 23, 2003.

9. Interview with Steve Kroft, Infinity CBS Radio, November 14, 2002.

10. *National Energy Policy*, NEPDG, White House, May 2001, chap. 8, 4.

11. *U.K. Energy Strategy for Iraq*, September 2004, para. 10, obtained through FOIA.

12. NATO Bucharest Summit Declaration, April 3, 2008.

13. Jaap de Hoop Scheffer, "Energy Security in the 21st Century," NATO speech, October 23, 2008.

14. Hillary Clinton, speech to the Atlantic Council, February 22, 2010.

15. Nick Butler, "Iraq Needs 'Oil for Peace' Deal," *FT*, September 11, 2007.

## Chapter 1: An Immense Strategic Advantage

1. "FW: IRAQ–VIEWS OF UK BUSINESS," e-mail from Edward Chaplin, October 2, 2002, obtained through FOIA.

2. Ibid.

3. Dunia Chalabi, "Perspective for Investment in the Middle East/North Africa Region," presentation to the OECD on behalf of the International Energy Agency, Istanbul, February 11–12, 2004, 7.

4. "Worldwide Finding and Development Costs on the Rise," *Oil and Gas Journal*, June 11, 2003.

5. James Boxell, "Top Oil Groups Fail to Recoup Exploration Costs," *FT*, October 11, 2004.

6. "Oil Majors Replace Less than 100% of Reserves, Report Says," DJ, June 22, 2007.

7. Minutes of meeting of Michael Arthur with Richard Paniguian, FCO, November 6, 2002, obtained through FOIA.

8. "Oil Firms 'Discuss Iraqi Stake," BBC News, March 12, 2003.

9. Minutes of meeting of Baroness Symons with BP (Paniguian, Renton), Shell (Withrington, Graham), and BG (Bethell), BIS, October 31, 2002, obtained through FOIA.

10. Minutes of meeting of Baroness Symons with Richard Paniguian and Tony Renton, Trade Partners U.K., December 4, 2002, obtained through FOIA.

11. "FW: IRAQ—VIEWS OF UK BUSINESS," e-mail from Edward Chaplin, February 10, 2002, obtained through FOIA.

12. Interviewed by Jeremy Paxman, *Newsnight*, BBC2, February 6, 2003.

13. Peter Beaumont and Faisal Islam, "Carve-up of Oil Riches Begins," *Observer*, November 3, 2002.

14. Steve Kroft, CBS, *60 Minutes*, December 15, 2002.

15. Baroness Symons meeting minute, BIS.

16. *Energy Compass*, "Russia/Iraq—No Change," December 20, 2002; Simon Pirani, "Carving Up Iraq," October 6, 2002, http://www.zmag.org/znet/viewArticle /11588.

17. *Moscow Times*, "US Blackmailing Russian Firms in Iraq," December 11, 2002.

18. Daniel Yergin, *The Prize* (New York: Touchstone/Simon and Schuster, 1992), 152–56, 160.

19. Lieutenant General Sir Stanley Maude, Proclamation of Baghdad, March 19, 1917.

20. Sir Maurice Hankey to Balfour, 1918, cited in Helmut Mejcher, *Imperial Quest for Oil* (London: Ithaca, 1976), 40.

21. Quoted in John Keay, *Sowing the Wind* (London: John Murray, 2003), 128.

22. The small exception was the Khanaqin territories transferred from Persia in 1913—these were covered by a separate concession held by Anglo-Persian.

23. Peter Sluglett, *Britain in Iraq* (New York: Columbia UP, 2007), 107.

24. Author's interview with former Shell manager, London, July 2009.

25. T.R.H. Cole QC, Australian government commission of inquiry, "Inquiry into Certain Australian Companies in Relation to the UN Oil-For-Food Programme," November 24, 2006, vol. 3, 151 (http://www.offi.gov.au/).

26. "Draft Press Release in the Event That Project Q Goes Public," BHP, undated, released by Cole Inquiry, exhibit EXH_1171.

## Chapter 2: The Human at the Center

1. Conversation with the author, Basra refinery, May 27, 2005.

2. Chemical Safety Board, "CSB Investigation of BP Texas City Refinery Disaster Continues as Organizational Issues Are Probed," press release, October 30, 2006.

3. Unless otherwise indicated, this section is based on an interview with the author, Kingston, January 18, 2010.

4. Quoted in David Hirst, *Oil and Public Opinion in the Middle East* (London: Faber and Faber, 1966), 63.

5. Ibid., 40, 89.

6. *The International Petroleum Cartel*, Federal Trade Commission, released through Subcommittee on Monopoly of Select Committee on Small Business, U.S. Senate, 83d Cong., 2nd sess., Washington, DC, 1952.

7. Dana Adams Schmidt, "West to Keep Out of Iraq Unless Oil Is Threatened," *NYT*, July 18, 1958.

8. Cited in Hirst, *Oil and Public Opinion*, 94.

9. *Al-Mustaqbal*, October 13, 1961, cited in ibid., 98.

10. Joe Stork, *Middle East Oil and the Energy Crisis* (New York: Monthly Review Press, 1975), 107.

11. Hanna Batatu, *The Old Social Classes and the Revolutionary Movements of Iraq* (London: Saqi, 2004), 985–86; see also Said Aburish, *Saddam Hussein* (London: Bloomsbury, 2001), 55–56, 59.

12. Telegram 407 from Baghdad to secretary of state, February 9, 1963, declassified November 4, 2005, www.icdc.com/~paulwolf/iraq/Coup%20Details%20Feb%201963.htm.

13. Batatu, *Old Social Classes*, 985–90.

14. Interview with the author, January 18, 2010.

15. For a detailed account of the negotiations, see George Stocking, *Middle East Oil* (Nashville: Vanderbilt UP, 1970), 256–69. Also Majid Khadduri, *Republican Iraq* (London: Oxford UP, 1969), 236–39, 293–94.

16. See also Stocking, *Middle East Oil*, 262–63. The deal was accepted by all IPC member companies except Standard Oil of New Jersey (Exxon).

17. Interview with the author, London, July 8, 2009.

18. Interview with the author, Amman, September 3, 2009.

19. Ibid.

20. Marion Farouk-Sluglett and Peter Sluglett, *Iraq Since 1958* (London: I.B. Tauris, 2003), 147.

21. Interview with the author, September 3, 2009.

22. *Annual Statistical Bulletin 1999*, OPEC, Table 38, 46. Initial developments

were carried out by French and Russian companies not part of the nationalized consortium, but by the mid-1970s INOC was managing operations, making use only of foreign technical specialists through service agreements.

23. Tariq Shafiq, "Iraq Oil Potential," paper presented at conference on Iraqi Oil and Gas, Imperial College, London, June 27, 2005, 14.

24. United Nations statistics cited in Abbas Alnasrawi, *Iraq's Burdens* (Westport, CT: Greenwood, 2002), 103 (1980 prices).

25. Farouk-Sluglett and Sluglett, *Iraq Since 1958*, 228, 230ff.; Aburish, *Saddam Hussein*, 106ff.

26. Interview with the author, Amman, September 3, 2009.

27. Interview with the author, Amman, August 30, 2009.

28. Although Sadr was prominent within Shi'ism, Islamic economics does not differ between the sects. He never thought of his economics as distinctively Shi'a; nor did those who read, cited, or followed him (Shi'a and Sunni alike) even refer to his work as Shi'a. Rodney Wilson, "The Contribution of Muhammad Baqir al-Sadr to Contemporary Islamic Economic Thought," *Journal of Islamic Studies* 9, no. 1 (1998), 57, 59.

29. Dai Yamao, "Emergence of a New Islamic Movement: al-Sadr and Formation of Islamic Da'wa Party," paper presented to International Association of Contemporary Studies, 2nd conference, Philadelphia University, Jordan, June 11–13, 2007, 4–6.

30. T.M. Aziz, "An Islamic Perspective of Political Economy," *Al Tawhid Islamic Journal* 10, no. 1, chap. 3, www.al-islam.org/al-tawhid/politicaleconomy.

31. Wilson, "The Contribution of Muhammad Baqir al-Sadr," 53.

32. Muhammad Baqir al-Sadr, "Islam and Schools of Economics," pt. 1, first published 1979, salmun.cwahi.net/wrel/rislam/shiite/econ/econ.htm.

33. Muhammad Baqir al-Sadr, *Iqtisaduna*, vol. 2, pt. 1, 6–12, and vol. 1, pt. 2, 95–96, cited in Mohamed Aslam Haneef, *Contemporary Islamic Economic Thought* (Kuala Lumpur: Ikraq, 1995), 111.

34. Sadr, *Iqtisaduna*, vol. 2, pt. 1, 174–80, cited in Haneef, *Contemporary Islamic Economic Thought*, 120.

35. Sadr, *Iqtisaduna*, vol. 2, pt. 2, 15, cited in Haneef, *Contemporary Islamic Economic Thought*, 121.

36. Crude Oil Production, Iraq, http://www.economagic.com/em-cgi/data.exe /doeme/paprpiq (accessed September 1, 2010).

## Chapter 3: Burning Ambition

1. Zalmay Khalilzad, "The United States and the Persian Gulf," *Survival* 37, no. 2 (Summer 1995): 96–97.

2. Testimony to Senate Armed Services Committee, September 11, 1990, in Media Education Foundation film *Blood and Oil*, dir. Jeremy Earp, 2008.

3. James Mann, *Rise of the Vulcans: The History of Bush's War Cabinet* (New York: Penguin, 2004), 192.

4. Issam Nashashibi, "Zalmay Khalilzad: The Neocons' Bagman to Baghdad," *Washington Report on Middle East Affairs*, April 2003.

5. Defense Planning Guidance, DOD, FY 1994–1999, February 18, 1992, draft, 2, 8, obtained by National Security Archive, www.gwu.edu/~nsarchiv/nukevault /ebb245/doc03-full.pdf.

6. Ibid., 2.

7. Patrick Tyler, "Senior U.S. Officials Assail Lone-Superpower Policy," *NYT*, March 11, 1992.

8. Mann, *Rise of the Vulcans*, 211.

9. Dick Cheney, *Defense Strategy for the 1990s*, DOD, January 1993.

10. Zalmay Khalilzad and Paul Wolfowitz, "Overthrow Him," *Weekly Standard*, December 1, 1997.

11. *Rebuilding America's Defenses*, Project for a New American Century, September 2000, 2.

12. Irwin Steltzer, *The Neocon Reader* (New York: Grove Press, 2004), 16.

13. Unless otherwise indicated, this section is based on author's interview with Faleh al-Khayat, Amman, August 21, 2009.

14. *Energy Support for Global Missions*, Defense Energy Support Center, Fact Book FY 2003, 26th ed., 18.

15. Pakistan consumed 125 million barrels, Sweden 120 million. *Statistical Review of World Energy 2004*, BP, 9.

16. All statistics from *Statistical Review of World Energy 2001*, BP, 4, 6.

17. *Geopolitics of Energy into the 21st Century*, Center for Strategic and International Studies, Washington, DC, CSIS, 2000, Executive Summary, xix–xx.

18. Edward Morse and Amy Myers Jaffe, *Strategic Energy Policy Challenges for the 21st Century* (New York: Council on Foreign Relations, 2001), 8.

19. *World Energy Outlook*, International Energy Agency (Paris: IEA, 2001), 74–75.

20. Morse and Jaffe, *Strategic Energy Policy Challenges*, 13, 16, 46.

21. Ibid., 22, 33, 46–47.

22. *U.K. Energy Strategy for Iraq*, FCO Iraq Policy Unit, September 6, 2004, obtained through FOIA.

23. George W. Bush, "Foreign Policy," autumn 2000.

24. Presidential debate, Al Gore and George W. Bush, October 11, 2000.

25. George W. Bush, "A Comprehensive National Energy Policy," September 29, 2000.

26. Ron Suskind, *The Price of Loyalty: George W. Bush, the White House, and the Education of Paul O'Neill* (London: Free Press, 2004), 85.

27. Jane Mayer, "Contract Sport," *New Yorker*, February 16, 2004.

28. David Ignatius, "Cheney's Cheney," *WP*, January 6, 2006.

29. Stephen Hayes, *Cheney: The Untold Story of America's Most Powerful and Controversial Vice President* (New York: HarperCollins, 2007), 314, 324.

30. Dick Cheney, *In My Time* (New York: Threshold, 2011), 317.

31. Task Force documents obtained under FOIA by the Natural Resources Defense Council, at www.nrdc.org/air/energy/taskforce/pdf/034.pdf and by Judicial Watch, at http://www.judicialwatch.org/oldsite/IraqOilFrgnSuitors.pdf.

32. *National Energy Policy*, NEPDG, chap. 8, 4, 5.

33. Second attachment to letter from Richard Dearlove's Private Secretary to Sir David Manning, December 3, 2001, TOP SECRET—declassified April 2011 and released by the Iraq Inquiry.

34. *Transmittal of the Report on the US–U.K. Energy Dialogue*, U.S. Department of Commerce, July 30, 2003, sec. 1.

35. "Iraq: Conditions for Military Action," U.K. Cabinet Office, July 21, 2002, reproduced in *Sunday Times*, June 12, 2005.

36. "Decisions needed," EIPG briefing, January 30, 2003, slides 5–9, obtained through FOIA.

37. Briefing for secretary of defense, EIPG, January 11, 2003, slide 15, obtained through FOIA.

38. Work status and decisions needed, EIPG briefing, January 10, 2003, slide 10, obtained through FOIA.

39. "Declaratory policy," EIPG decision briefing for deputies, December 17, 2002, slide 6 vs. slide 3, obtained through FOIA.

40. Michael Mobbs, "How Kellogg, Brown and Root Became Involved in USG Work on Iraq Oil Matters," June 4, 2004, provided to author. See also SIGIR, *Hard Lessons: The Iraq Reconstruction Experience* (Washington, DC, 2009), 28–30.

41. "How to Spend Proceeds from Iraqi Petroleum Production," EIPG briefing for deputies, November 6, 2002, and briefing for secretary of defense, January 11, 2003, obtained through FOIA.

42. "Background Briefing on Oil as a Weapon of Terror," DOD, January 24, 2003.

43. "Repair, Production and Sale Plans—Overview," EIPG, December 18, 2002, obtained through FOIA.

44. "Organizing and Managing Iraq's Petroleum Resources," EIPG, January 10, 2003, briefing for deputies, obtained through FOIA.

45. "Planning for the Iraqi Petroleum Infrastructure," EIPG, January 10, 2003, obtained through FOIA.

46. Ariel Cohen and Gerald O'Driscoll, "The Road to Economic Prosperity for a Post-Saddam Iraq," Heritage Foundation Backgrounder, 1633, March 5, 2003.

47. Irwin Stelzer, "Iraq's Oil Mess," *American Outlook*, fall 2003.

48. "U.K. Energy Strategy for Iraq," FCO Iraq Policy Unit, September 6, 2004, obtained through FOIA.

49. Interview with the author, Washington, DC, September 25, 2009.

50. Future of Iraq Project member interview with the author, September 2009.

51. Martin Bright, "Colin Powell in Four-Letter Neo-con 'Crazies' Row," *Observer*, September 12, 2004.

52. Attributed to Colin Powell, in Bob Woodward, *Plan of Attack*.

53. Scott Shane, "Ryan Clark Crocker, a Diplomat Used to Danger," *NYT*, January 6, 2007.

54. "Eight Years On—a Diplomat's Perspective on the Post-9/11 World," *Newsweek*, September 5, 2009.

55. Candace Pontoni, "Former U.S. Ambassador Gives Talk on Current Situation in Iraq," *Whitworhian*, October 25, 2009.

56. Karen DeYoung, *Soldier* (New York: Knopf, 2006), 459.

57. FOIP briefing, November 1, 2002, slides 2–3, obtained by National Security Archive, www.gwu.edu/~nsarchiv/NSAEBB/NSAEBB163/iraq-state-02.pdf.

58. See, e.g., David Phillips, *Losing Iraq* (New York: Basic, 2006), 38. Also Ian Lockhart (UK Trade Partners), minutes of meeting with BP regarding Iraqi oil, December 5, 2002, obtained through FOIA.

59. Interview with the author, Washington, DC, September 16, 2009.

60. Oil and Energy Working Group member interview with the author, September 2009.

61. Interview with the author, Washington, DC, September 16, 2009.

62. "Post-Saddam Iraq Could Be a Supergiant Producer, Says Fadhil Chalabi," *MEES* 46, no. 12 (March 24, 2003).

63. Ebel interview with the author.

64. OEWG member interview with the author.

65. Andrew Tully, "After Hussein, How Will Iraqis Assert Control Over Their Oil?" Radio Free Europe/Radio Liberty, April 28, 2003.

66. Ibid.

67. "Iraqi Oil Policy Recommendations After Regime Change," OEWG, Oil Policy Subcommittee paper, reproduced in *MEES* 46, no. 18 (May 5, 2003), D6.

68. OEWG, Oil Policy Subcommittee, Summary Paper, April 20, 2003, 3–8, obtained by National Security Archive, www.gwu.edu/~nsarchiv/NSAEBB/NSAEBB198/FOI%20Oil.pdf.

69. Dick Cheney, speech to Veterans of Foreign Wars, Nashville, August 26, 2002; and Bob Woodward, "Greenspan: Ouster of Hussein Crucial for Oil Security," *WP*, September 17, 2007.

70. Jennifer Loven, "Bush Gives New Reason for Iraq War," AP, August 31, 2005.

71. Paul Wolfowitz, interview with Sam Tanenhaus, *Vanity Fair*, transcript, May 9, 2003, www.defense.gov/transcripts/transcript.aspx?transcriptid= 2594.

72. Interview with the author, Washington, DC, September 16, 2009.

## Chapter 4: Wiping the Slate

1. Harlan Ullman and James Wade, *Shock and Awe* (Washington, DC: National Defense University, 1996), 23.

2. Samia Nakhoul, "Baghdad a Ghost City as Clock Ticks Towards War," Reuters, March 19, 2003.

3. Michael Moseley, *Operation Iraqi Freedom: By the Numbers*, U.S. Central Command Air Forces (USCENTAF), April 30, 2003, 15.

4. Sue Chan, "Iraq Faces Massive U.S. Missile Barrage," CBS, January 24, 2003.

5. Iraq Body Count, *A Dossier of Civilian Casualties in Iraq, 2003–2005*, reports. iraqbodycount.org/a_ dossier_of_civilian_casualties_2003_2005.pdf.

6. Unless otherwise indicated, this section is based on the author's interview with Faleh al-Khayat, Amman, September 1, 2009.

7. "New Policy on Cuneiform Texts from Iraq," American Schools of Oriental Research, November 30, 2004, web.bu.edu/asor/excavations/textpolicy.html.

8. Nabil al-Tikriti, "Negligent Mnemocide and the Shattering of Iraqi Collective Memory," in *Cultural Cleansing in Iraq: Why Museums Were Looted, Libraries Burned and Academics Murdered*, ed. Raymond Baker, Shereen Ismael, and Tareq Ismael (London: Pluto, 2010), 101.

9. Zain al-Naqshbandi, *Report on the Central Awqaf Library*, signed by library director Salah Karim Husain, June 28, 2004, oi.uchicago.edu/OI/IRAQ/zan.html.

10. Saad Eskander, "The Tale of Iraq's 'Cemetery of Books,'" Iraq National Library and Archive, October 2004, www.iraqnla.org/fp/art/art6.htm.

11. Douglas Jehl and Elizabeth Becker, "Experts' Pleas to Pentagon Didn't Save Museum," *NYT*, April 16, 2003.

12. Robert Fisk, "Untouchable Ministries," *ZNet*, April 16, 2003.

13. UNESCO, "Iraq—Education in Transition: Needs and Challenges," April 2004, Table 9.9, annex 1, 50.

14. Jairam Reddy, "The Current Status and Future Prospects for the Transformation and Reconstruction of the Higher Education System in Iraq," United Nations University report, May 1, 2005, 1.

15. "Looters Ransack Baghdad Hospitals," BBC News, April 10, 2003.

16. "Daily Bulletin," ICRC, April 13, 2003.

17. "Armed Looters Attack Baghdad Hospital," AFP, April 10, 2003; "Instability Plagues Baghdad," BBC News, April 11, 2003.

18. Bill Blakemore, "Iraqi Hospitals Face Crises After Looting," ABC News, April 19, 2003.

19. "Looters Ransack Baghdad Hospitals," BBC News.

20. "Daily Bulletin," ICRC.

21. "Humanitarian Crisis Looms in Iraq Because of Breakdown of Law and Order," UN News Centre, April 9, 2004.

22. Donald Rumsfeld, DOD news briefing, April 11, 2003.

23. Paul Martin, Ed Vulliamy, and Gaby Hinsliff, "US Army Was Told to Protect Looted Museum," *Observer*, April 20, 2003.

24. Colin L. Powell, interview with Tom Brokaw, NBC News, April 11, 2003.

25. Donny George, "The Looting of the Iraq National Museum," in *The Destruction of Cultural Heritage in Iraq*, ed. Peter Stone and Joanna Farchakh Bajjaly (Woodbridge: Boydell Press, 2008), 102.

26. Charles Ferguson, *No End in Sight* (New York: Public Affairs, 2008), 118, 124–25.

27. See also Paul Martin, "British Tactics in Basra Praised," *Washington Times*, April 3, 2003.

28. Rajiv Chandrasekaran, *Imperial Life in the Emerald City* (London: Bloomsbury, 2007), 133.

29. Ibid., 185.

30. "The Idaho–Baghdad Connection," University of Idaho, College of Agricultural and Life Sciences, Programs and People, winter 2004.

31. Author interview with member of OEWG, September 2009.

32. Interview with the author, Rumaila, May 28, 2005.

33. George, "Looting of the Iraq National Museum," 97.

34. Andrew Lawler, "Impending War Stokes Battle Over Fate of Iraqi Antiquities," *Science*, January 31, 2003, 643.

35. "World Energy Outlook 2005: IEA Projects Growth in Middle East and North Africa Oil and Natural Gas Sectors Through 2030," IEA, press release, November 7, 2005.

## Chapter 5: Emergent Iraq

1. Anthony Shadid, *Night Draws Near: Iraq's People in the Shadow of America's War* (New York: Picador, 2006), 9.

2. Interview with the author, Basra, December 21, 2009.

3. Paul Bremer, *My Year in Iraq* (New York: Threshold, 2006), 19, 385.

4. *Strategy and Impact of the Iraq Transition Initiative: OTI in Iraq (2003–2006), Final Evaluation*, USAID, September 30, 2006, HDA-1-00-03-00124-00.

5. *Donor Activities and Civil Society Potential in Iraq*, USIP, Special Report 124, July 2004.

6. Haifa Zangana, "Colonial Feminists from Washington to Baghdad," *Al-Raida* 22, no. 109–10 (Spring/Summer 2005), 30–39.

7. Interview with the author, Amman, September 5, 2009.

8. Hassan Juma'a's speech at Manchester Trades Council/Greater Manchester Stop the War, November 24, 2005, edited transcript in *Socialist Worker*, December 10, 2005.

9. Tony Horwitz, "US Played an Active Role in Encouraging Revolt," *WSJ*, December 26, 1991.

10. Interview with the author, Amman, September 5, 2009.

11. Interview with the author, London, February 2005.

12. David Bacon, "Iraq's Oil Union Will Defend the Country's Oil," *Truthout*, April 5, 2005.

13. Robert Collier, "Religious Frenzy and Anger on Once-Banned Pilgrimage," *San Francisco Chronicle*, April 23, 2003.

14. Maher Chmaytelli, "Anti-US Demo Fails to Draw Large Crowd as Shiite Pilgrimage Winds Down," AFP, April 23, 2003.

15. "Iraq's Muqtada al Sadr: Stabiliser or Spoiler?" ICG, July 11, 2006, 5.

16. Faleh Jabr, *The Shi'ite Movement in Iraq* (London: Saqi, 2003), 184.

17. "Iraq's Muqtada Al-Sadr," ICG, 5.

18. Peter Beaumont, "Revolution City," *Observer*, April 20, 2003.

19. Cecile Feuillatre, "In Baghdad Slum, Religious Shiites Take Hospitals Under Their Wing," AFP, May 4, 2003.

20. Muhammad Bashar al-Faydi interview with the author, Amman, August 23, 2009.

## Chapter 6: The Coalition Authority

1. Quoted by Robert Fisk, "Iraq: 1917," *Independent*, June 17, 2004.

2. Author interviews with former Iraqi oil officials, Amman, summer 2009.

3. Interview with the author, Amman, August 21, 2009.

4. Interview with the author, Amman, August 2009.

5. Author interview with former Iraqi oil official, Amman, August 2009.

6. Unless otherwise indicated, this section is based on the author's interview with Faleh al-Khayat, Amman, September 1, 2009.

7. Interview with the author, summer 2009.

8. Author interview with former Iraqi oil official, summer 2009.

9. Author interviews with former Iraqi oil officials, Amman and London, summer 2009.

10. "Chief Iraqi Oil Official Miffed at Opec—Focusing on Boosting Output," *The Oil Daily*, May 30, 2003.

11. See also Eric Herring and Glen Rangwala, *Iraq in Fragments* (London: Hurst, 2006), 14–15.

12. Paul Bremer, *My Year in Iraq* (New York: Threshold, 2006): "I was eight thousand miles and at least a century removed from home" (16); "The bickering continued. . . . I watched in silence as the Iraqis learned hard lessons about the need for flexibility and compromise in a democratic system" (306). At times he takes on a tone that could be interpreted as racist, commenting on political negotiations with Grand Ayatollah Sistani: "Is this more Persian carpet haggling?" (272).

13. Michael O'Hanlon, *Iraq Index*, Brookings Institution, November 19, 2003, 4. Figures for May aren't available.

14. James Pfiffner, "U.S. Blunders in Iraq: De-Baathification and Disbanding

the Army," *Intelligence and National Security* 25, no. 1 (Spring 2010): 3. Specifi-cally, it applied to the top four layers of the party hierarchy, down to *firqa* (section member).

15. See, e.g., Ferguson, *No End in Sight*, 171–76.

16. Bremer, *My Year in Iraq*, 40.

17. Gordon Rudd, CPA historian, interview with Meghan O'Sullivan, December 29, 2003, obtained through FOIA; George Packer, *The Assassins' Gate: America in Iraq* (London: Faber and Faber, 2007), 124.

18. Meghan O'Sullivan, "Iraq: Time for a Modified Approach," Brookings Insti-tution, Policy Brief 71, February 2001, 1–2.

19. Meghan O'Sullivan, "The Response to Terrorism: America Mobilizes," pre-sentation at Brookings seminar, September 21, 2001.

20. Rudd, interview with O'Sullivan. Rudd was an academic given access to the CPA during its operation for the purpose of later writing an official history. He has not done so yet.

21. Memorandum from Robin Raphel to Paul Bremer (drafted by Meghan O'Sullivan), "Re: Procedures to Implement De-Ba'athification Policy," March 15, 2003, obtained by PBS, *Frontline*, www.pbs.org/wgbh/pages/frontline/yeariniraq /documents/raphel.pdf.

22. Rudd interview with O'Sullivan.

23. Unless otherwise indicated, this section is based on author's interviews with oil workers, Basra, May 2005.

24. Robin Raphel and Rick Whitaker, interview with Gary Vogler, SIGIR, May 10, 2006, obtained through FOIA.

25. *The Baghdad Billions*, BBC World Service, November 9, 2006.

26. Dave Oliver, "Restarting the Economy in Iraq," November 2003, 11, oversight-archive.waxman.house.gov/documents/20070206180618-70251.pdf.

27. Interview with the author, Amman, September 7, 2009.

28. Rudd interview with O'Sullivan.

29. Interview with the author, Houston, September 21, 2009.

30. Interview with the author, Amman, August 30, 2009.

31. Interview with the author, Amman, August 21, 2009.

32. Unless otherwise indicated, this section is based on author interviews with Falah al-Khawaja, Amman, August 30, 2009, and Faleh al-Khayat, Amman, Sep-tember 1, 2009.

33. Christian Miller, "Missteps Hamper Iraqi Oil Recovery," *Los Angeles Times*, September 26, 2005.

34. *Hard Lessons*, SIGIR, 181.

35. "Contingency Planning for Production and Sales—Status," EIPG, December 12, 2002, obtained through FOIA.

36. Michael Stinson e-mail, "RE: Emergent DFI Budget Requirements," May 2, 2004, obtained through FOIA.

37. Interview with the author, London, July 9, 2009.

## Chapter 7: Invasion of the Chalabis

1. "Deputy Ministers," e-mail from Robert McKee, February 12, 2004, obtained through FOIA.

2. Jonathan Steele, *Defeat: Why America and Britain Lost Iraq* (London: I.B. Tauris, 2008), 11.

3. Hamza Hendawi, "Iraq's New Governing Council Holds First Meeting," AP, July 13, 2003.

4. Gordon Rudd interview with Scott Carpenter, June 29, 2004, obtained through FOIA.

5. Paul Bremer, *My Year in Iraq* (New York: Threshold, 2006), 347.

6. ICRSS and Gallup polls, cited in Herring and Rangwala, *Iraq in Fragments*, 148.

7. Ryan Crocker interview with Aziz Al-Hajj of Al-Iraqiyya Television, April 19, 2007.

8. Bremer, *My Year in Iraq*, 95.

9. "Iraqi Interim Authority," Office of the Undersecretary of Defense for Policy, briefing paper for Rumsfeld, March 6, 2003, quoted in Douglas Feith, *War and Decision: Inside the Pentagon at the Dawn of the War on Terrorism* (New York: Harper, 2009), 405.

10. Gordon Rudd interview with Paul Bremer, January 7, 2008, transcript obtained through FOIA.

11. "Iraqi Imam Calls for Departure of US Forces, Urges National Unity," Al-Jazeera, July 18, 2003, 09:30 GMT, trans. BBC Monitoring, July 18, 2003.

12. "Anti-US Slogans Shouted at Shi'ite Mosque in Iraq," AFP, July 18, 2003.

13. Interview with the author, Baghdad, December 14, 2009.

14. Cited in Steele, *Defeat*, 212.

15. Feith, *War and Decision*, 372. What the Arab regimes actually feared most was an Iraq allied with Iran. Ironically, the U.S. obsession with communal identity almost certainly helped strengthen Iran's hand.

16. "Iraq in the State of the Union Speech," Raed Jarrar blog, January 29, 2008, http://raedinthemiddle.blogspot.com/2008/01/iraq-in-state-of-unionspeech.html.

17. Interview with the author, Baghdad, December 14, 2009.

18. Gary Younge, *Who Are We—And Should It Matter in the 21st Century?* (London: Viking, 2010), 6.

19. *Iraq Index*, April 16, 2004.

20. Author interview with member of OEWG, September 2009.

21. Interview with the author, Amman, November 11, 2010.

22. The case was also reported internally in Reuben Jeffrey, memorandum for the Deputy Secretary of Defense, "Allegations of Iraq Oil Corruption," May 24, 2004.

23. E-mail from Meghan O'Sullivan to author, November 16, 2010.

24. E-mail from Faleh al-Khayat to author, August 14, 2010; *Iraq Oil and Gas: A Bonanza-in-Waiting*, Energy Intelligence Research, special report, spring 2003.

25. Unless otherwise indicated, this section is based on author interview with Faleh al-Khayat, Amman, August 21, 2009.

26. Author interview with former Iraqi oil official, Amman, August 2009.

## Chapter 8: The Advisers

1. *U.K. Energy Strategy for Iraq*, September 2004, obtained through FOIA, para. 8.

2. This section is based on "Cable from London to Canberra regarding Record of Conversation: Mr Downer and BHP Billiton," Australian Department of Foreign Affairs and Trade, May 20, 2003, released by Cole Inquiry, exhibit EXH_1014, www.ag.gov.au/www/inquiry/offi.nsf/indexes/images/AWB.0269.0014.pdf.

3. Saeed Shah, "BHP 'Wanted Rifkind to Lobby US for Iraq Oil,'" *Independent*, July 5, 2006.

4. Letter from Malcolm Rifkind to Patricia Hewitt, June 9, 2003, obtained through FOIA.

5. "Management Change in the Iraqi Oil Sector," Energy Markets Unit, DTI, paper presented at meeting of interdepartmental Oil Sector Liaison Group, May 28, 2003, obtained through FOIA.

6. Key points briefing for Joan MacNaughton's meeting with Anna Borg at the IEA, U.K. Department of Energy, October 16, 2003, obtained through FOIA.

7. Paul Bremer, *My Year in Iraq* (New York: Threshold, 2006), 38. This view was echoed in March 2008 by President Bush, who commented at a speech at Wright-Patterson Air Force Base in Dayton, Ohio, "In many ways, the legacy of the tyrant continues to haunt the Iraqi economy. . . . The infrastructure for Iraq's oil sector is still owned and managed by the central government, and suffers from decades of under-investment." White House, press release, March 27, 2008.

8. Joseph Stiglitz, "Iraq's Next Shock Will Be Shock Therapy," *ZNet*, March 12, 2004; "Let's All Go to the Yard Sale," *Economist*, September 27, 2003. For a discussion, see Herbert Docena, "Shock and Awe Therapy," *Focus on Trade*, no. 110, Focus on the Global South, June 2005.

9. Irwin Stelzer, "Iraq's Oil Mess," *American Outlook*, fall 2003.

10. Ariel Cohen and Gerald O'Driscoll, "The Road to Economic Prosperity for a Post-Saddam Iraq," Heritage Foundation, March 5, 2003.

11. Interview with the author, Houston, September 21, 2009.

12. Greg Palast, *Newsnight*, BBC2, March 17, 2005; AFP, "Rift Emerges Over the Fate of Iraqi Oil," February 12, 2003.

13. "On the Record with Iraq's Top Oil Official, Thamer al-Ghadban," *Petroleum Intelligence Weekly*, June 4, 2003.

14. Carola Hoyos, "Oil Groups Snub US on Iraq Deals," *FT*, July 24, 2003.

15. Ian Lockhart (UK Trade Partners), meeting with BP regarding Iraq oil, December 5, 2002, obtained through FOIA.

16. "Views: Looking at Iraq," *Shell in the Middle East*, April 2004, 39.

17. Comment made to the author, April 30, 2009.

18. Telephone interview with the author, May 17, 2006.

19. *Annual Report 1997*, ITIC, 2.

20. Author telephone interview with Witt, May 2006.

21. *Strategic Questions for Our Future*, ITIC, undated; record of views expressed at Board and Sponsor's meetings held between December 2003 and May 2004; "ITIC to Launch Iraq Tax Reform Project," author interview with Witt; *Bulletin*, ITIC, July 2003; "ITIC Iraq Study Presented to Ministry of Finance and Ministry of Oil at Beirut Workshop," ITIC, *Bulletin*, February/March 2005, 8–10, 27, 31.

22. Author interview with Dhia'a al-Bakkaa, Amman, September 7, 2009.

23. Interview with the author, Washington, DC, September 25, 2009.

24. Institute for the Analysis of Global Security, Iraq Pipeline Watch, www.iags .org/iraqpipelinewatch.htm.

25. USAID contract with BearingPoint, effective July 18, 2003, Annex C, RAN-C-00-03-00043-00.

26. *Options for Developing a Long Term Sustainable Iraqi Oil Industry*, Bearing-Point, USAID, December 19, 2003, 4, 51.

27. Transparency International Corruption Perceptions Index, 2003.

28. *Options for Developing*, BearingPoint, 5.

29. Ibid., 4, 47.

## Chapter 9: Anti-Iraqi Forces

1. Quoted in Dexter Filkins, "Tough New Tactics by U.S. Tighten Grip on Iraq Towns," *NYT*, December 7, 2003.

2. For instance, a December 2004 poll by the International Republican Institute found that 65 percent of Iraqis preferred a larger role for the state in the economy and only 5 percent a smaller role. IRI, Survey of Iraqi Public Opinion, November 24–December 5, 2004, 44, cited in Eric Herring and Glen Rangwala, *Iraq in Fragments* (London: Hurst, 2006), 233.

3. *Iraq Index*, December 15, 2004, 40.

4. Paul Bremer, *My Year in Iraq* (New York: Threshold, 2006), 309.

5. Ibid., 314.

6. "Violent Response: The U.S. Army in al-Falluja," Human Rights Watch, Iraq report 15, no. 7(E), June 2003.

7. Dahr Jamail, *Beyond the Green Zone: Dispatches from an Unembedded Journalist in Occupied Iraq* (Chicago: Haymarket, 2007), 138–39, 165; Ahmed Mansour, *Inside Fallujah* (Moreton-in-Marsh: Arris, 2009), 142, 160. See also James Paul and Céline Nahory, *War and Occupation in Iraq*, Global Policy Forum, June 2007, 55, 64.

8. Jo Wilding, "Inside the Fire," OpenDemocracy, April 13, 2004; Rahul Mahajan, "Report from Fallujah," April 12, 2004, www.empirenotes.org/fallujah.html.

9. Bremer, *My Year in Iraq*, 362.

10. Rajiv Chandrasekaran and Anthony Shadid, "US Targeted Fiery Cleric in Risky Move," *WP*, April 11, 2004; Nir Rosen, "US Newspaper Ban Plays into Cleric's Hands," *Asia Times*, March 31, 2004.

11. *Counterinsurgency Operations*, U.S. Army, Field Manual-Interim FMI3–07.22, October 2004, Appendix E, cited in Herring and Rangwala, *Iraq in Fragments*, 176.

12. "US Brands Radical Shiite Cleric an Outlaw Amid Anti-coalition Uprising," AFP, April 5, 2004.

13. In a poll at the end of April 81 percent of respondents said their opinion of Muqtada al-Sadr was better than three months previously. *Iraq Index*, December 15, 2004, 36.

14. *Iraq Index*, December 15, 2004, 36.

15. Lieutenant General Ricardo Sanchez, CPA press briefing, April 8, 2004.

16. Dana Priest and Robin Wright, "Iraq Spy Service Planned by U.S. to Stem Attacks," *WP*, December 11, 2003; Johanna McGeary, "Taking Back the Streets," *Time*, July 6, 2004; Spencer Ackerman, "Allawi's Muscle—the CIA-Controlled Iraqi National Intelligence Service," *TPM Muckraker*, August 24, 2007.

17. Hannah Allam and Warren Strobel, "Amidst Doubts, CIA Hangs On to Control of Iraqi Intelligence Service," Knight Ridder, May 8, 2005.

18. Seymour Hersh, "Torture at Abu Ghraib," *New Yorker*, May 10, 2004.

19. Michael Hirsh and John Barry, "The Salvador Option," *Newsweek*, January 8, 2005.

20. Bremer, *My Year in Iraq*, 340.

21. Gordon Rudd, CPA historian, interview with Paul Bremer, January 7, 2008, obtained through FOIA.

22. Vivenne Walt, "The Race to Tap the Next Gusher," *Time*, April 16, 2006.

23. Javier Blas, "A New Era for Iraq's Oil," media.ft.com/cms/88df8636-0395-11dc-a931-000b5df10621.swf.

24. Farah Stockman, "Former Diplomat Denies Oil Dealings Influenced Views," *Boston Globe*, October 15, 2009.

25. *Dagens Næringsliv*, October 18, 2009, cited in Reidar Visser, "New Information in the Tawke-gate Affair: Galbraith Was Also a Paid Consultant," October 19, 2009, historiae.org.

26. Author interview with Iraqi oil official, September 2009.

27. Major General Richard Natonski, interviewed by John Way, March 16, 2005, in *Al-Anbar Awakening, Vol. 1: American Perspectives—U.S. Marines and Counterinsurgency in Iraq, 2004–2009*, ed. Timothy McWilliams and Kurtis Wheeler (Quantico, VA: Marine Corps University Press, 2009).

28. James Conway, interviewed by John Piedmont and David Crist, July 7, 2005, in *Al-Anbar Awakening, Vol. 1*.

29. Bremer, *My Year in Iraq*, 341.

30. Mansour, *Inside Fallujah*, 181.

31. Michael Howard, "US Troops Kill 300 in Najaf Raid," *Guardian*, August 7, 2004.

32. Patrick Cockburn, *Muqtada al-Sadr and the Fall of Iraq* (London: Faber and Faber, 2008), 195.

33. Adrian Blomfield, "Police Expel Journalists from Najaf," *Daily Telegraph*, August 16, 2004.

34. "Iraqi VP Raps US for 'Uncivilised' Najaf Deaths," AFP, August 6, 2004.

35. Mansour, *Inside Fallujah*, 292.

36. Article 18:6.

37. Lieutenant General Thomas Metz, "Massing Effects in the Information Domain: A Case Study in Aggressive Information Operations," *Military Review*, May/June 2006, 109–10.

38. Ann Scott Tyson, "Increased Security in Fallujah Slows Efforts to Rebuild," *WP*, April 19, 2005.

39. Daud Salman, "Slow Progress in Battered Fallujah," Institute for War and Peace Reporting, November 17, 2005.

40. Tyson, "Increased Security in Fallujah."

41. "Focus on Reconstruction in Fallujah," Integrated Regional Information Network, May 24, 2005.

42. Interview with the author, Amman, August 23, 2009.

43. "Update Notes," UN, November 11, 2004, 2; Vincent L. Foulk, *The Battle for Fallujah* (Jefferson, NC: McFarland, 2007), 223–24.

44. Dr. Salam Ismael, "Falluja—One Year On," Doctors for Iraq, December 2005.

## Chapter 10: The Hands of Iraqis

1. Interview with the author, London, February 2005.

2. "Position Profile—External Affairs Support, Iraq," Glenn Irvine International, autumn 2004.

3. Greenstock's last day in government service was March 31, 2004. "Application to Accept an Outside Appointment: Sir Jeremy Greenstock GCMG," letter from Tony Nichols of Advisory Committee on Business Appointments to Carole Sweeney of Foreign and Commonwealth Office, June 22, 2004, obtained through FOIA.

4. "Quick Readout on the Allawi Visit So Far," FCO internal e-mail, September 29, 2004, obtained through FOIA.

5. "Post-Retirement Employment," e-mail from Carole Sweeney to Jeremy Greenstock, May 24, 2004, and Greenstock reply, May 26, 2004, both obtained through FOIA.

6. Jeremy Greenstock memo, "Subject: Iraq Oil," January 29, 2004, obtained through FOIA.

7. Jeremy Greenstock, special address to Asia Oil and Gas Confernece, Kuala Lumpur, June 14–15, 2004, obtained through FOIA.

8. "Chevron Texaco to Give Oil Ministry Tech Assistance," DJ, October 20, 2004.

9. Interview with the author, London, July 10, 2009.

10. "Allawi Outlines New Iraqi Petroleum Policy," MEES 48, no. 37 (September 13, 2004): A1–A4.

11. The number is imprecise because of some variation in the definition of "field."

12. "Iraq Prepares Ground for Future Contracts,"Oil Daily, June 11, 2004.

13. "Iraqi Minister Assesses Cost of Attacks on Oil Facilities, Outlines Future Plans," interview on Al-Sharqiyah, Baghdad, in Arabic 1235 GMT August 28, 2004, trans. BBC Monitoring, August 29, 2004.

14. Interview with Ruba Husari, Iraq Oil Forum, May 6, 2009.

15. Petroleum and Iraq's Future: Fiscal Options and Challenges, ITIC, fall 2004, 8–10, 27, 31.

16. Ibid., 11, 27. For a discussion of contracts effectively guaranteeing profits, see Ian Rutledge, The Sakhalin II PSA—a Production Non-sharing Agreement, CEE BankWatch Network et al., 2004.

17. Ibid., 19.

18. Andy Rowell, interview with Dan Witt, al-Khaleej (UAE newspaper), June 4, 2006, in Arabic, English original provided to author.

19. Interview with the author, Houston, September 21, 2009.

20. Nicolas Pelham, "Oil to Be Privatised but Not Just Yet, Says Iraqi Minister," FT, September 5, 2003.

21. Walter van der Vijver, "A New Era for International Oil Companies in the Gulf," speech to Emirates Center for Strategic Studies and Research conference, Abu Dhabi, October 19, 2003.

22. Daniel Johnston, International Petroleum Fiscal Systems and Production Sharing Contracts (Tulsa: Pennwell, 1994), 39.

23. Thomas Wälde, "The Current Status of International Petroleum Investment: Regulating, Licensing, Taxing and Contracting," Centre for Energy, Petroleum and Mineral Law and Policy Journal 1, no. 5 (July 1995).

24. "Iraq Prepares Ground for Future Contracts,"Oil Daily, June 11, 2004.

25. Telephone interview with the author, May 17, 2006.

26. Dan Witt, "Iraq Project Update," ITIC, Bulletin, November/December 2004, 8.

27. Letter from Kim Howells MP, FCO, to Alan Simpson MP, March 7, 2007, held on file by the author.

28. Rowell interview with Witt, al-Khaleej, 2006.

29. Other, more established Iraqi unions were represented in Britain by a particularly factionalist individual, who had built a strong relationship with British unions.

30. Interview with Hassan Juma'a, Basra, May 26, 2005.

31. "Priorities and Concerns of Iraqi Trade Union Leaders," U.S. embassy cable, January 31, 2006, obtained by WikiLeaks.

32. Unless otherwise indicated, this section is based on the author's telephone interview with Michael Eisenscher, August 2, 2010.

33. *Meeting Face to Face: The Iraq–US Labor Solidarity Tour*, dir. film by Jonathan Levin and Michael Zweig, Center for Study of Working Class Life and US-LAW, September 2005.

34. "Joint Statement by Leaders of Iraq's Labor Movement and U.S. Labor Against the War," June 26, 2005, www.uslaboragainstwar.org/downloads/Iraqi%20USLAW %20Joint%20Statement.English.pdf.

35. Todd Boyle video of Michael Eisenscher speech, "Labor's Stake in Ending the Wars," Seattle, April 6, 2010, vimeo.com/10768556.

## Chapter 11: Now It Becomes Legal

1. Interview with the author, Amman, August 28, 2009.

2. Interim Constitution of Iraq, 1970, Article 13, published by the University of Wuerzburg's International Constitutional Law Project, www.gjpi.org/wp-content /uploads/1970-interim-constitution.doc.

3. Constitution of Kuwait, 1962, Article 152; Constitution of Iran, 1979, Articles 153, 44(2).

4. Telephone interview with the author, November 8, 2010.

5. Nibras Kazimi, "Dangerous Lineup," *New York Sun*, April 26, 2006.

6. *Iraq Index*, December 15, 2004, 31.

7. A Zogby poll in January 2005 found that 82 percent of Sunni Arabs and 69 percent of Shi'a wanted U.S. forces to withdraw either immediately or after an elected government was in place (www.zogby.com/news/ReadNews.dbm?ID=957). In August 2005 a U.K. Ministry of Defence poll found that 82 percent of Iraqis "strongly opposed" the continued presence of U.S./U.K. troops, 45 percent supported attacks on those troops, and less than 1 percent thought the occupation was improving security in Iraq. Sean Rayment, "Secret MoD Poll: Iraqis Support Attacks on British Troops," *Sunday Telegraph*, October 22, 2005.

8. James Dobbins et al., *Occupying Iraq: A History of the Coalition Provisional Authority* (Santa Monica: Rand, 2009), 44.

9. "Supporting the Iraqi Opposition," Rumsfeld memo to Cheney, Powell, Tenet, and Rice, July 1, 2002, quoted in Douglas Feith, *War and Decision: Inside the Pentagon at the Dawn of the War on Terrorism* (New York: Harper, 2009), 253.

10. Donald Rumsfeld, "Principles for Iraq: Policy Guidelines," May 8, 2005, cited in Dobbins et al., *Occupying Iraq*, 540; also 42–44.

11. Jonathan Morrow, "Iraq's Constitutional Process II: An Opportunity Lost," USIP Special Report 155, November 2005, 12–13.

12. Peter Galbraith, *The End of Iraq: How American Incompetence Created a War Without End* (New York: Simon and Schuster, 2007), 199.

13. Reproduced by Reidar Visser at www.historiae.org/galbraith.asp.

14. James Glanz and Walter Gibbs, "U.S. Adviser to Kurds Stands to Reap Oil Profits," *NYT*, November 12, 2009.

15. When Galbraith's oil interests became known in 2009, the *NYT* published an editor's note (November 13) saying that they should have been disclosed in previous op-eds, or alternatively the articles not published.

16. "President Welcomes Iraqi Prime Minister Jaafari to the White House," White House, press release, June 24, 2005.

17. *Iraq Index*, August 29, 2005, 20, 5.

18. "Shia Political Insider Qassim Daoud Worries About the Kurds and Ponders a Moderate Iraqi Path Forward," U.S. embassy cable, July 23, 2005, obtained by WikiLeaks.

19. Morrow, "Iraq's Constitutional Process," 10.

20. Telephone interview with U.K. official directly involved in constitutional negotiations, October 2010.

21. Morrow, "Iraq's Constitutional Process," 15.

22. Ibid., 16–17.

23. "Vice President Abdel Mehdi Ponders the Constitutions and How to Give Shia What the Kurds Now Have," U.S. embassy cable, June 20, 2005, obtained by WikiLeaks.

24. Joseph Biden and Leslie Gelb, "Unity Through Autonomy in Iraq," *NYT*, May 1, 2006.

25. *Iraq Index*, August 29, 2005, 33.

26. "The Making of the Iraqi Constitution and Evaluation of the Process," UN-AMI Office of Constitutional Support, unpublished, December 2005, 8.

27. Iraq constitution, 2005, Article 112.

28. Galbraith, *End of Iraq*, 167.

29. Kamil Mhaidi et al., "Open Letter on the Oil and Gas Wealth in the Draft Iraqi Constitution," October 18, 2005, www.iraqrevenuewatch.org/reading/101805 .pdf.

30. Tariq Shafiq, "Oil Industry Implications of Iraq's Constitutional Articles 108, 109 & 111 Governing Oil & Gas Assets: A Call to Reconsider," *MEES* 49, no. 23 (June 5, 2006).

31. "Pushing the Shia and Kurds to Improve the Draft Constitution," U.S. embassy cable, August 24, 2005, obtained by WikiLeaks.

32. "President Congratulates Iraqis on Successful Elections," White House, press release, October 16, 2005.

33. "Unmaking Iraq: A Constitutional Process Gone Awry," ICG, September 26, 2005, 6.

34. "Analysis and Overview of the Text of the Iraqi Constitution," UNAMI Office of Constitutional Support, December 2005, unpublished, sec. 5.3.

35. "Unmaking Iraq," ICG, 11–12.

36. Galbraith, *End of Iraq*, 201.

## Chapter 12: Iraq Divided

1. Kamil Mahdi, "Iraq's Oil Law: Parsing the Fine Print," *World Policy Journal*, summer 2007, 17.

2. Interview with the author, Amman, August 22, 2009.

3. Results at Platform, www.carbonweb.org/showitem.asp?article=294&parent=39.

4. Zena Awad, "Iraqi Trade Unionist Speaks to the *Socialist*," *Socialist*, March 19, 2005.

5. E-mail to author from Meghan O'Sullivan, November 16, 2010.

6. Bradley Graham, "U.S. to Expand Prison Facilities in Iraq," *WP*, May 10, 2005; Reuters, "US Frees 1,400 Detainees in Iraq for Ramadan," October 10, 2007.

7. Douglas Jehl and Kate Zernike, "Scant Evidence Cited in Long Detention of Iraqis," *NYT*, May 30, 2004.

8. Hannah Allam and Warren Strobel, "Amidst Doubts, CIA Hangs On to Control of Iraqi Intelligence Service," Knight Ridder, May 8, 2005.

9. Tom Lasseter, "Sunnis Claim Shiite Militia Carries Out Campaign of Threats, Murder," Knight Ridder, June 8, 2005.

10. "Shi'ite Politics in Iraq: The Role of the Supreme Council," ICG, November 15, 2007, 14.

11. Richard Norton-Taylor, "British Lawyers to Pursue Iraqi Security Forces over Killings," *Guardian*, May 20, 2005.

12. *Human Rights Report 2005—Iraq*, U.S. State Department, March 8, 2006; Andrew Buncombe and Patrick Cockburn, "Iraq's Death Squads," *Independent on Sunday*, February 26, 2006.

13. Buncombe and Cockburn, "Iraq's Death Squads."

14. Charlotte Sector, "Grim Business Is Booming at Baghdad Morgue," ABC News, June 6, 2006.

15. John Burns, "To Halt Abuses, U.S. Will Inspect Jails Run by Iraq," *NYT*, December 14, 2005.

16. Ellen Knickmeyer, "Abuse Cited in 2nd Jail Operated by Iraqi Ministry," *WP*, December 12, 2005; John Burns, "To Halt Abuses, U.S. Will Inspect Jails Run by Iraq," *NYT*, December 14, 2005.

17. Interview with the author, Amman, August 19, 2009.

18. "Iraq Shrine Bombing Was Specialist Job: Minister," AFP, February 24, 2006.

19. Marc Santora, "One Year Later, Golden Mosque Is Still in Ruins," *NYT*, February 13, 2007.

20. Ellen Knickmeyer and K.I. Ibrahim, "Bombing Shatters Mosque in Iraq," *WP*, February 23, 2006.

21. Ellen Knickmeyer and Bassam Sebti, "Toll in Iraq's Deadly Surge," *WP*, February 28, 2006.

22. For example, "Sunni Association, al-Sadr Movement Discuss al-Sadr City,

al-Hurriyah Attacks," al-Jazeera, November 24, 2006, trans. BBC Monitoring, November 25, 2006.

23. Ned Parker and Ali Hamdani, "How Violence Is Forging a Brutal Divide in Baghdad," *The* (London) *Times*, December 14, 2006.

24. Edward Wong and Damien Cave, "Iraqi Death Toll Rose Above 3,400 in July," *NYT*, August 15, 2006.

25. *Second Transparency Report*, Office of the Oil Ministry's Inspector General, June 2006, trans. and circulated by Iraq Revenue Watch, 9–10.

26. Ghaith Abdul-Ahad, "Oiling the Wheels of War," *Guardian*, June 9, 2007.

27. Ibid.

28. Stuart Bowen (SIGIR) statement, U.S. Senate Committee on Homeland Security and Governmental Affairs, August 2, 2006.

29. Oliver Poole, "Corrupt Iraq Officials 'Fund Rebels,'" *Daily Telegraph*, February 7, 2006.

30. "Iraq: Oil Update," British embassy Baghdad, eGram 17398/06, May 11, 2006, obtained through FOIA.

## Chapter 13: A Law to End All Laws

1. Interview with the author, Amman, August 21, 2009.

2. "Invitation and Agenda," UNAMI conference on oil and gas, April 4–6, 2006.

3. Canadian Petroleum Hall of Fame, www.canadianpetroleumhalloffame.ca /roland-priddle.html.

4. Taking development costs as between $3,000 and $5,000 per daily barrel and operating costs as $1 per barrel, at a price of $40 per barrel it would take 77 to 128 days' production; at $80, half this time.

5. Tariq Shafiq, "Oil Industry Implications of Iraq's Constitutional Articles," *MEES* 49, no. 23 (June 5, 2006).

6. Primarily Laws Nos. 97 and 123 of 1967. See, for example, Nori Jafar et al., "Legal Opinion Presented to Iraqi Parliament," June 4, 2009, www.iraqenergy.org /news/downloader.php?dfile=Legal%20Opinion%20on.pdf.

7. "Iraq: Preparing for the Next Government," U.K. Embassy Baghdad, eGram 18991/05, November 23, 2011.

8. See "IMF Standby Agreement Signed," Jubilee Iraq, December 23, 2005, www.jubileeiraq.org/blog/2005_12.html.

9. Ali Allawi, *The Occupation of Iraq* (New Haven: Yale UP, 2007), 428.

10. Felix Salmon, "Restructuring Debt Is Top Priority," *Euromoney*, September 2004.

11. "How the Iraq Deal Was Done," *Euromoney*, September 1, 2005.

12. *Standby Agreement with Iraq*, IMF, December 23, 2005, Appendix 1, 42, para. 36, 44, para. 45.

13. U.S. forces in Iraq, press briefing with Zalmay Khalilzad, March 24, 2006.

14. Daphne Eviatar, "Wildcat Lawyering," *American Lawyer*, November 4, 2002.

15. Nino Chkhobadze (Georgian minister for the environment), letter to John Browne (BP CEO), November 26, 2002.

16. Host government agreement between Georgia and MEP participants, April 28, 2000, Article 7.3, Article 12.1. Also Nicholas Hildyard and Greg Muttitt, "Turbo-Charging Investor Sovereignty," Focus on the Global South, *Destroy and Profit*, February 2006.

17. Nikolai Topuria, "Georgia Signs Off on BTC Pipeline After Marathon Talks," AFP, December 2, 2002; "There Will Be No Alternative to Have BTC Running in Detour of Borjomi Gorge," *Black Sea Press*, December 2, 2002; "President of Company 'GG&MW' Criticized Resolution of Georgian Powers Related to Laying of the Oil Pipeline via Borjomi Gorge," *Black Sea Press*, December 2, 2002; Natalia Antelava, "Georgia: The Costs of Oil Wealth," *Transitions Online*, December 10, 2002.

18. Paul Brown, "Human Rights Row over BP Plan to Lay Turkish Pipeline," *Guardian*, August 31, 2002.

19. For more discussion, see Greg Muttitt, "Nationalising Risk, Privatising Reward," *International Journal of Contemporary Iraqi Studies* 1, no. 2 (September 2007).

20. Unlike national courts, international investment tribunals consider only the narrow commercial issues and not the wider body of the country's law, nor questions of public interest. See, for example, Susan Leubuscher, "The Privatisation of Law," *Transnational Dispute Management* 3, no. 2 (April 2006).

21. *Bilateral Investment Treaties 1959–1999*, UN Conference on Trade and Development, 1; *World Investment Report 2006*, xix. The use of arbitration too has rapidly expanded. One of the most popular sets of arbitration rules among investors is under the International Convention on Settlement of Investment Disputes. The ICSID Centre, part of the World Bank, which oversees the use of the rules, registered more cases in 2006–10 (181) than during the previous thirty-eight years of its existence (172).

22. Anthony Sinclair, "The Origins of the Umbrella Clause in the International Law of Investment Protection," *Arbitration International* 20, no. 4, 411–34.

23. E. Lauterpacht, "Anglo-Iranian Oil Company Limited Persian Settlement: Opinion," January 20, 1954, 4, cited in Sinclair, "Origins of the Umbrella Clause."

## Chapter 14: The Pragmatist

1. Interview with the author, London, July 8, 2009.

2. Cody Lyon, "What Does Iraq's New Oil Law Say About an Invasion?" *Ohmy News*, April 8, 2007, english.ohmynews.com/ArticleView/article_view.asp?no=354797&rel_ no=1.

3. Christopher M. Blanchard, "Iraq: Oil and Gas Legislation, Revenue Sharing and US Policy," Congressional Research Service Report RL34064, December 10, 2008, 26.

4. "Terms of Reference: Ronald Jonkers, Petroleum Legal and Regulatory Advisor," USAID, December 24, 2005, obtained through FOIA.

5. "US Envoy Calls for New Iraqi PM," BBC News, March 28, 2006.

6. "Dawa Party Leader Pleased with Constitution," U.S. embassy cable, August 25, 2005, obtained by WikiLeaks.

7. Mariam Karouny, "New Iraq Oil Min Seeks Blns in Investments," Reuters, May 22, 2006.

8. Michael Bond, "Saying No to Saddam," *New Scientist*, June 27, 2004.

9. Interview by Jana Wendt, Nine Network (Australia), *Sunday*, February 23, 2003.

10. Michael Theodoulou, "Profile: Hussain al-Shahristani," *Times Online*, May 26, 2004.

11. Paul Bremer, *My Year in Iraq* (New York: Threshold, 2006), 359.

12. Karouny, "New Iraq Oil Min."

13. Interview with the author, London, July 9, 2009.

14. Ziyad al-'Ujayli, "Hassan Juma'a: No Privatisation of the Oil Sector in Iraq," Niqash.org, June 18, 2006.

15. Hassan Juma'a Awad, "The Iraqi People Are the Victims of Investment," Niqash.org, July 19, 2006.

16. Deepa Babington, "About Half of All Iraqis Unemployed—Govt. Official," Reuters, February 9, 2006.

17. 2006 Draft Iraqi Oil Law, Articles 5.9–5.11, 8.2–8.4, 6.2(c).

18. 2006 Draft Iraqi Oil Law, Articles 5.21, 5.10, 6.2(a).

19. 2006 Draft Iraqi Oil Law, Articles 6.2(d).

20. Unless otherwise indicated, this section is based on the author's interview with Tariq Shafiq, London, July 8, 2009.

21. Hanna Batatu, *The Old Social Classes and the Revolutionary Movements of Iraq* (London: Saqi, 2004), 191–92.

22. Liora Lukitz, *Iraq: The Search for a National Identity* (London: Frank Cass, 1995), 19–20.

23. Sa'dun's note went on to describe his experience of being caught between the irreconcilable British and Iraqi positions: "I have no supporter. The Iraqis who call for independence are weak and helpless and very remote from independence. They are incapable of appreciating the advice of men of honour like myself. They think that I am a traitor to my country and slave of the English. What a grievous affliction! I who sacrificed myself . . . and bore disdain and manifold humiliations for the blessed land in which my forefathers lived happily." Quoted in Batatu, *Old Social Classes*, 192. Details also in "Death of Premier of Iraq," *Times*, November 14, 1929, 14. Nonetheless, King Faisal wrote to the British High Commissioner, "The loss would be easier to bear in any circumstances other than the present, when he and his colleagues were so evidently delighted with the help the British Government was giving towards the fulfilment of the hopes of the country." Reporting that

letter, the *Times* noted drily that "a very different tone is to be observed in the vernacular Press." "New Iraqi Cabinet-Commemoration of Sir Abdul Muhsin," November, 20, 1929, 13.

## Chapter 15: The Laurel Lodge Plan

1. George W. Bush, "President's Remarks to the Travel Pool," Camp David, June 12, 2006.

2. Ibid.

3. "President Bush Makes Surprise Visit to Iraq," White House, press release, June 13, 2006.

4. U.S. embassy cables, March–May 2006, obtained by WikiLeaks.

5. "Scenesetter for Deputy Treasury Secretary Kimmitt and State Counselor Zelikow's Visit to Iraq," U.S. embassy cable, July 17, 2006, obtained by WikiLeaks.

6. Briefing for Undersecretary Tim Adams, U.S. Treasury, telephone call with Mark Malloch-Brown (UN), August 4, 2006, obtained through FOIA.

7. "Scenesetter for Kimmitt and Zelikow," U.S. embassy cable.

8. SIGIR interview with Timothy Carney, April 5, 2008, obtained through FOIA.

9. "IRMO Oil Adviser/Iraqi Hydrocarbons Law," e-mail from Lisa [surname removed], British embassy in Baghdad, May 1, 2006; "Success Story: Ministry of Oil Agrees to Project Adviser's Recommendation for the Formation of a Committee to Draft Petroleum Law," USAID, undated, both obtained through FOIA.

10. U.S. embassy cables, November 2006–February 2007, obtained by WikiLeaks.

11. Briefing for Samuel Bodman, meeting with Hussein Shahristani and oil companies, DOE, July 26, 2006, obtained through FOIA.

12. "Industry Dialogue on Iraqi Oil and Gas Sector Development," DOE, meeting notes, July 26, 2006, obtained through FOIA.

13. Ziad al-Ajili, "The Laws Will Be Clear for All," Niqash.org, June 15, 2006.

14. Meeting with Tamsin Rees and Rob Sherwin, FCO, January 11, 2007.

15. Job description, Middle East energy adviser, FCO, September/October 2005.

16. Meeting with Tamsin Rees and Rob Sherwin, FCO, January 11, 2007.

17. Rob Sherwin, "Press Lines on the Hydrocarbons Law," FCO, March 30, 2007, obtained through FOIA.

18. Kim Howells MP, *Hansard*, January 24, 2007, col. 1524.

19. Jim Krane, "Iraq Official Calls for Oil Partnerships," AP, September 11, 2006.

20. Emirates Palace Hotel website, www.emiratespalace.com/en/facts/index.htm.

21. *The International Compact with Iraq*, sec. 4.5, 21.

22. Stephen Duguid, "Technocrats, Politics and Planning: The Formulation of Arab Oil Policy, 1957–67," PhD diss., Simon Fraser University, July 1976, 145.

23. Interview with the author, London, July 8, 2009.

24. 2006 Draft Iraq Oil Law, Article 32.

25. Draft Oil and Gas Law, February 15, 2007, trans. KRG, Articles 8(F), 6(B).

26. Rob Sherwin, "Comments on Draft Iraqi Hydrocarbon Law," FCO, December 17, 2006, obtained through FOIA.

27. "Draft Hydrocarbons Law," e-mail (sender's name redacted), December 24, 2006, obtained from DECC through FOIA. It is not clear whether Sherwin's and the Treasury's technical comments were passed to Jonkers; in any case those particular provisions were not changed in the final draft.

28. "MinOil Responding to Pressures to Advance Hydrocarbon Law, but Negotiations Continue," U.S. embassy cable, January 15, 2007, obtained by WikiLeaks.

29. Interview with the author, London, July 8, 2009.

30. 2006 Draft Oil Law, Articles 5.5, 5.6.

31. Draft Oil and Gas Law, February 2007, Article 10 (D).

32. 2006 Draft Oil Law, Article 5.5.

33. Draft Oil and Gas Law, February 2007, Article 5 (C).

## Chapter 16: The Surge

1. U.S. State Department, Ryan Crocker news briefing, May 1, 2007.

2. Ambassador Zalmay Khalilzad, joint press conference, Baghdad, October 24, 2006.

3. David Cloud, "U.S. to Hand Iraq a New Timetable on Security Role," *NYT*, October 22, 2006.

4. *Iraq Index*, January 29, 2007, 20.

5. Iraq Body Count, www.iraqbodycount.org/database. Iraq Body Count counts only casualties recorded in the media or in official or NGO reports.

6. For example, "Americans Would Begin Iraq Withdrawal in 2007," Angus Reid Global Monitor, December 21, 2006, www.angusreid.com/polls/view/14168; World PublicOpinion.org, "U.S. Public Opinion in Line with Iraq Study Group's Proposals," December 5, 2006, www.worldpublicopinion.org/pipa/articles/brunitedstatescan adara/283.php?nid=&id=&pnt=283&lb=brusc.

7. James Baker and Lee Hamilton (co-chairs), *The Iraq Study Group Report* (New York: Vintage, 2006), ix.

8. Ibid., Recommendations 62–63, 84–85.

9. Ibid., Recommendation 23, 61.

10. Elisabeth Bumiller, "Adviser Has President's Ear as She Keeps Eyes on Iraq," *NYT*, June 12, 2006.

11. Telephone interview with the author, November 8, 2010.

12. Stephen Hadley, memorandum, November 8, 2006, reproduced in "Text of U.S. Security Adviser's Iraq Memo," *NYT*, November 29, 2006.

13. "Talabani, Barzani, Hashimi Meet to Discuss Moderate Coalition Participation," U.S. embassy cable, November 26, 2006, obtained by WikiLeaks.

14. "Former Iraqi DPM Discusses Moderate Front," U.S. embassy cable, February 18, 2007, obtained by WikiLeaks.

15. President Bush, televised speech on Iraq, January 10, 2007.

16. Baker and Hamilton, *Iraq Study Group Report*, 32, and Recommendation 21, 61.

17. Meghan O'Sullivan, "Memo to the New President: Managing the Iraq War," Harvard Belfer Center, January 21, 2009.

18. Rick Jervis, "U.S. Ambassador Expects Progress Within Months," *USA Today*, January 18, 2007.

19. U.S. embassy cables, January–February 2007, obtained by WikiLeaks.

20. "Hydrocarbon Law Cover Letter Agreed, Path Cleared for Cabinet Approval," cover letter, reproduced in U.S. embassy cable, February 26, 2007, obtained by WikiLeaks.

21. Iraq Council of Ministers, Oil and Energy Committee agreement, February 26, 2007, leaked by and trans. Raed Jarrar, raedinthemiddle.blogspot.com/2007/03/council-ofministerss-resulotion.html.

22. Zalmay Khalilzad, "A Shared Stake in Iraq's Future," *WP*, March 3, 2007.

23. Statement by Ambassador Zalmay Khalilzad on hydrocarbon law, U.S. State Department, February 27, 2007.

## Chapter 17: A Line in the Sand

1. Hassan Juma'a Awaad et al. (eighteen signatories), "Statement Issued by the Iraqi Labor Union Leadership at a Seminar Held from 10 to 14 December 2006, in Amman, Jordan to Discuss the Draft Iraqi Oil Law," www.carbonweb. org/showitem .asp?article=223&parent=39.

2. Ibid.

3. Shawna Bader-Blau, "Iraqi Unions vs. Big Oil," *Middle East Report* 243 (Summer 2007): 20.

4. Hassan Juma'a, speech, Basra, trans. Martha Mundy, February 6, 2007, www .basraoilunion.org/archive/2007_02_01_archive.html.

5. *Azzaman*, February 9, 2007, www.azzaman.com/index.asp?fname=2007\02\02 -09\853.htm.

6. Final conference statement, Basra, trans. Kamil Mahdi, February 6, 2007.

7. Hassan Juma'a speech, Basra.

8. Fouad Al-Ameer, "Discussion on the Iraq Oil Law," *Al-Ghad*, February 20, 2007, www.alghad.org/2007/02/20/discussion-onthe-iraq-oil-law.

9. Interview with the author, Amman, August 28, 2009.

10. Tariq Shafiq, "Iraq's Draft Petroleum Law: An Independent Perspective," *MEES* 49, no. 8 (February 19, 2007).

11. Hassan Hafidh, "Iraq Oil Technocrats: Time Not Suitable for Oil Law," DJ, February 17, 2007.

12. Ibraheem Abdul Kareem Rasheed et al. (sixty-one signatories), "Open Letter to Members of Iraqi Parliament—Iraqi Oil Experts Seminar Held in Amman," February 17, 2007.

13. Interview with the author, Amman, August 16, 2009.

14. Spencer Swartz and Hassan Hafidh, "Gaps Remain Between Iraq, Kurdish Govts on Oil Law," DJ, February 26, 2007.

15. "DCM Discusses Hydrocarbon Legislation Status with Oil Minister," U.S. embassy cable, April 1, 2007, obtained by WikiLeaks.

16. "Statement No 382 Concerning the Oil and Gas Law," Association of Muslim Scholars, March 6, 2007, trans. BBC Monitoring as "Iraqi Sunni Group Warns Parliament Against Passing Oil and Gas Law."

17. "Iraq Experts Say Draft Oil Industry Law Fraught with Problems," AFP, March 18, 2007.

18. Interview with the author, Baghdad, December 14, 2009.

19. *IraqSlogger*, "Iraqi List Deputy Bashes Draft Oil Law," March 13, 2007.

20. Interview with the author, Amman, August 16, 2009.

## Chapter 18: The Ticking Clock

1. Ernesto Londoño, "In Baghdad, Rice Acknowledges Frustrations in U.S.," *WP*, February 18, 2007.

2. See, for example, Gina Chon, "U.S. Envoy Notes Risks of Earlier Withdrawal From Iraq," *WSJ*, January 23, 2009.

3. Thomas Ricks and Karen DeYoung, "For the US, the Goal Is Now 'Iraqi Solutions,'" *WP*, January 10, 2008.

4. "Deputy Prime Minister on Hydrocarbon Laws," U.S. embassy cable, April 3, 2007, obtained by WikiLeaks.

5. Stephen Hadley, memorandum, November 8, 2006, reproduced in "Text of U.S. Security Adviser's Iraq Memo," *NYT*, November 29, 2006.

6. David Ignatius, "A Farewell Warning on Iraq," *WP*, January 18, 2009.

7. "President Bush Commemorates Foreign Policy Achievements and Presents Medal of Freedom to Ambassador Ryan Crocker," U.S. State Department, press release, January 15, 2009.

8. Linda Robinson, *Tell Me How This Ends: General Petraeus and the Search for a Way Out of Iraq* (New York: Public Affairs, 2008), 150.

9. Thomas Ricks, *The Gamble: General David Petraeus and the Untold Story of the American Surge in Iraq, 2006–2008* (London: Allen Lane, 2009), 87.

10. "Building Capacity at the Ministry of Oil," U.S. embassy cable, November 25, 2007, obtained by WikiLeaks.

11. Peter Baker et al., "Among Top Officials, 'Surge' Has Sparked Dissent, Infighting," *WP*, September 9, 2007.

12. Robert Kimmitt, "A Strong Fiscal Framework for Iraq," *WP*, March 16, 2007.

13. U.S. State Department, Condoleezza Rice and Robert Kimmitt press briefing, en route to Sharm el-Sheikh, May 1, 2007.

14. *2007 Mid-Year Progress Report*, International Compact with Iraq, July 20, 2007, 39.

15. Zalmay Khalilzad, "Why the United Nations Belongs in Iraq," *NYT*, July 20, 2007.

16. For example, "Iraq and the Kurds: Resolving the Kirkuk Crisis," ICG, April 19, 2007, 4; Gareth Stansfield, "Accepting Realities in Iraq," Chatham House MEBP07/02, May 2007.

17. Press conference of the President, White House, June 14, 2006.

18. "Al-Maliki Tells Aides U.S. Benchmark Deadline Is June 30 or His Ouster Possible," AP, March 13, 2007.

19. Nancy Pelosi, "Bringing the War to an End Is My Highest Priority as Speaker," *Huffington Post*, November 17, 2006.

20. Supplemental Appropriations Act (enrolled by House and Senate), U.S. Congress HR 1591, Sec. 1904(a)(2), (b), (c).

21. U.S. Public Law 110–28, Supplemental Appropriations Act, May 25, 2007, Secs. 1314(b)(1)(A), (c).

22. For example, Sean McCormack, U.S. State Department daily press briefing, February 26, 2007.

23. Kamil al-Mehaidi, "Geographical Distribution of Iraqi Oil Fields and Its Relation with the New Constitution," Revenue Watch Institute, 2006.

24. George W Bush, "President Bush Discusses Iraq," White House, April 10, 2008.

25. "Article 11: Petroleum Revenues" states in full: "A. According to the Constitution of Iraq (Articles 106, 111, 112 and 121(3)) regarding the ownership of Oil and Gas resources, the distribution of its revenues, and the monitoring of federal revenue allocation, the Council of Ministers must submit a draft federal revenue law to the Council of Representatives regulating these matters in adherence to the sections of this Article. B. The oil revenues include all the government revenues from Oil and Gas, royalties, signing bonuses and production bonuses of Petroleum contracts with foreign or local companies. C. The revenues mentioned in Article 11B must be deposited in an account called 'the Oil Revenue Fund' established for this purpose, and the federal revenue law shall regulate the Oil Revenue Fund and ensure its fair distribution according to the Constitution. D. Another fund must be created under the name 'the Future Fund,' and a certain portion of the Oil Revenue

Fund must be deposited in the Future Fund and be regulated by the law." Draft Oil and Gas Law, February 15, 2007, trans. KRG.

26. "Iraq Invites 15 Foreign Firms to Drill 100 Oil Wells," Reuters, April 3, 2007.

27. "Coming Soon, Maybe: An Iraqi Oil Law," NYT, February 28, 2007.

28. "Breakthrough in Iraq Oil Standoff," BBC News, February 27, 2007.

29. "Ambassador and DCM Meet with Iraqi National Security Adviser," U.S. embassy cable, October 29, 2006, obtained by WikiLeaks.

30. "DCM Engages SCIRI's al-Hakim on Detentions," U.S. embassy cable, March 28, 2007, obtained by WikiLeaks.

31. "Ambassador Discusses Debaathification Reform, SCIRI Strategic Dialogue with VP Abdel Mehdi," U.S. embassy cable, April 6, 2007, obtained by WikiLeaks.

32. "Hydrocarbon Law's Status at the Council of Representatives," U.S. embassy cable, July 14, 2007, obtained by WikiLeaks.

33. "UNAMI SRSG Qazi's May 25 Meeting with the Ambassador," U.S. embassy cable, May 28, 2007, obtained by WikiLeaks.

34. Hassan Hafidh, "Iraq Amended Draft Law Sets Out New PSA Model," DJ, January 16, 2007.

35. Simon Webb, "Iraq Oil Law to Go to Parliament, Kurds Wary," Reuters, April 18, 2007.

36. Lolita Baldor, "Gates: Clock Is Ticking on Iraq," AP, April 19, 2007.

37. Interview with MEES, September 10, 2007.

38. Dick Cheney, interviewed by Bret Baier, Fox News, May 10, 2007.

39. Margaret Warner, "Iraqi National Security Adviser Meets with US Lawmakers," PBS NewsHour, May 9, 2007.

40. Dick Cheney news conference, Baghdad, May 9, 2007.

## Chapter 19: Imposing the Law

1. President Bush, televised speech on Iraq, January 10, 2007.

2. Unless otherwise indicated, this section is based on the author's interviews with Hassan Juma'a Awad, Amman, September 5, 2009, and with Farouk Mohammed Sadiq Ismael, Basra, December 20, 2009.

3. Ben Lando, "Oil Strikers Met by Iraqi Troops," UPI, June 6, 2007.

4. Aref Mohammed, "Iraqi Oil Pipeline Workers Strike," Reuters, June 5, 2007.

5. Al-Iraqiyya newscast, "Seventeen Killed in Car Bombing; Political, Security Update," trans. BBC Monitoring, June 5, 2007.

6. Iraq Federation of Oil Unions, letter to Prime Minister Maliki, May 5, 2007, www.basraoilunion.org/2007/05/fullstrike-communique-to-iraqi-prime.html.

7. Hassan Juma'a interview with the author, Rome, May 29, 2007.

8. Mohammed al-Kadhim (Solidarity Center) interview with the author, Amman, June 12, 2007.

9. Hassan Juma'a interview with the author, Amman, September 5, 2009.

10. Author's interview with person with direct knowledge of events, December 2009.

11. "American and British Unions Back Iraqi Oil Workers' Strike," AFL-CIO-TUC joint statement, June 6, 2007, www.tuc.org.uk/inter national/tuc-13366-f0.cfm.

12. "AFL-CIO Calls on Iraq to Stop Threatening Workers in Oil Fields," AFL-CIO, press release, June 7, 2007.

13. Hassan Juma'a statement, trans. Sami Ramadani, June 11, 2007.

14. Ibid.

15. Bob Woodward, *The War Within: A Secret White House History 2006–2008* (London: Simon and Schuster, 2008), 351.

16. Michael R. Gordon, "U.S. Warns Iraq That Progress Is Needed Soon," *NYT*, June 12, 2007.

17. Thom Shanker, "Tensions Flare Over Custody in Rape Case in Philippines," *NYT*, December 22, 2006.

18. Gordon, "U.S. Warns Iraq."

19. David Broder, "Failure on Two Fronts," *WP*, June 17, 2007.

20. General David Petraeus interview, PBS, *Jim Lehrer Show*, April 4, 2007.

21. Josh White, "U.S. Boosts Its Use of Airstrikes in Iraq," *WP*, January 17, 2008.

22. Melinda Larson, "Baghdad Security Plan Seeing Many Successes," American Forces Press Service, April 9, 2007.

23. Press briefing by Tony Snow, White House, May 30, 2007.

24. David Sanger, "With Korea as Model, Bush Team Ponders Long Support Role in Iraq," *NYT*, June 3, 2007.

25. *Platts Commodity News*, "Iraqi Sunni Bloc Wants Ban on Oil Production-Sharing Deals," April 24, 2007.

26. *The Australian*, "Iraq Deal on Law to Share Oil Riches," February 28, 2007.

27. *IraqSlogger*, "Minister to Resign if Oil Bill Passes," July 20, 2007.

28. "Prime Minister Directs Minister of Planning to Help Restore Sunni Political Engagement," U.S. embassy cables, July 2, 2007, obtained by WikiLeaks.

29. Kate Dourian, "Iraq Vows to Meet May 31 Oil Law Deadline; Pledge Comes with Some Aspects of Draft Still in Dispute," *Platts Oilgram News*, April 19, 2007.

30. Jamal Halaby, "Iraq's VP Opposes Draft Oil Bill, Claims It Gives Too Many Concessions to Foreign Firms," AP, May 20, 2007.

31. "MP Najafi Warns Rushing Through Benchmarks Detrimental to Iraqi Security and Unity," U.S. embassy cable, July 12, 2007, obtained by WikiLeaks.

32. Hiba Dawood and David Enders, "The Battle for Iraqi Oil," *Left Turn*, June 10, 2007, www.leftturn.org/?g=node/679; U.S. embassy cables (obtained by WikiLeaks) show Fadhila telling U.S. diplomats in late May that the party supported the oil law, and in late July that it opposed it.

33. "Sadr Bloc Joins Sunnis in Rejecting Iraq Oil Law," AFP, July 5, 2007.

34. Radio Sawa, May 7, 2007, www.radiosawa.com/arabic_news.aspx?id= 1246588.

35. Including the two seats of al-Risalyun, which always voted with the Sadr Current.

36. "Top Iraq MP: No Oil Law Under Occupation," UPI, August 3, 2007.

37. Raed Jarrar, "False Sectarianism and the Battle for Oil," *Fellowship*, fall 2007, 18–20.

38. Laith Abd al-Husain Al-Shahir letter, trans. Martha Mundy, July 18, 2007.

39. Ben Lando, "Interview: Top Iraq Oilman Thamir Ghadhban," UPI, September 19, 2007.

40. Ali Faruq, "Head of Iraqi Oil Union: Oil Minister's Decision Is Illegitimate," Niqash.org, August 6, 2007.

41. AMS, fatwa on oil law, trans. Yahya Hamied, July 4, 2007.

42. Interview with the author, Amman, August 23, 2009.

43. "The Anti–Oil Law Frontier Stages a Mass Demonstration in Baghdad," Iraq Freedom Congress, July 5, 2007, www.uslaboragainstwar.org/article.php?id=14029.

44. "Hundreds of Iraqis Protest Draft Oil Law," AFX News, July 16, 2007.

45. Letter from Iraqi oil experts to the parliament, July 16, 2007.

46. Letter from Iraqi intellectuals to the parliament, published in *MEES* 50, no. 33 (August 13, 2007).

47. Betty Williams, Mairead Corrigan Maguire, Jody Williams, Shirin Ebadi, Wangari Maathai, and Rigoberta Menchu Tum, "In Support of the Iraqi People, in Opposition to the Iraq Oil Law," Nobel Women's Initiative, June 19, 2007.

48. The coalition comprised Platform, War on Want, Voices, Iraq Occupation Focus, Corporate Watch, and Jubilee Iraq.

49. U.K. Parliament, Session 2006–7, Early Day Motion 1180, sponsored by Katy Clark MP.

50. Robert Byrd, C-SPAN, August 1, 2007.

51. Condoleezza Rice, interviewed by Bob Schieffer, CBS, *Face the Nation*, August 5, 2007.

52. Ned Parker, "Key Laws or No, Iraq's Parliament Takes a Break," *Los Angeles Times*, July 31, 2007.

53. "Kurds Still Standing by Maliki Government—for Now," U.S. embassy cable, July 2, 2007, obtained by WikiLeaks.

54. Steven Hurst, "Iraqi Leaders Forge New Political Pact," AP, August 17, 2007.

55. Mariam Karouny, "New Iraq Alliance Formed to Back Shaky Government," Reuters, August 16, 2007.

56. George W. Bush, "Joint Press Availability with Prime Minister Harper and President Calderón," Montebello, Canada, August 21, 2007.

57. Paul Tait, "U.S. Envoy Says Iraq Making Poor Political Progress," Reuters, August 21, 2007.

58. "Kurds Still Standing," U.S. embassy cable, July 2, 2007; also "Fadila Head: Creation of New Front Imminent," July 20, 2007, obtained by WikiLeaks.

59. "Allawi Pays $300K for Anti-Maliki US Campaign," *IraqSlogger*, August 23, 2007.

60. Thom Shanker and Mark Mazzetti, "Time Has Run Out to Forge Iraqi Unity, 2 Senators Say," *NYT*, August 21, 2007.

61. "US Senators Hint Maliki Should Go if Reconciliation Fails," AFP, August 20, 2007.

62. Wolf Blitzer et al., "Major GOP Defection on Iraq," CNN, *The Situation Room*, August 23, 2007.

## Chapter 20: The New Iraq

1. Quoted in ICG, "Oil for Soil," October 28, 2008, 19.

2. *Platts Oilgram News*, "Iraq Oil Minister Denounces Hunt's PSC with Kurdistan," 85, no. 179 (September 11, 2007).

3. Jim Landers, "Hunt Oil Deal Could Help Shape Kurds' Future," *Dallas Morning News*, October 24, 2007.

4. Ryan Crocker/U.S. embassy Baghdad, Cable 2008-Baghdad-471, "Fine Tuning Our Position on Oil," February 19, 2008, obtained through FOIA.

5. "Hunt Oil Deal Creating Tension in Iraq: US," AFP, September 27, 2007.

6. "Iraq Hydrocarbons Law; Initial Comments," U.S. Treasury, August 2006, obtained through FOIA.

7. EIPG briefing for deputies, October 18, 2002, 7, obtained through FOIA.

8. "Now Open—CS Irbil! The Boom Without the Bang," BuyUSA, October 10, 2006; e-mail from David McDonald to Ken Topolinsky (both of Hunt Oil), "Notes from Meetings with US Embassy Officials in Irbil," September 28, 2007, obtained by House Oversight Committee.

9. For a discussion of the KRG contracts' terms, see Greg Muttitt, "Investor Rights vs Human Rights," *KHRP Legal Review* 13 (2008): 53–86.

10. Interview with the author, Amman, August 30, 2009.

11. Letter from Ray Hunt to Stefanie R. Osbum, Executive Director, President's Foreign Intelligence Advisory Board, July 12, 2007, www.reform.democrats.house .gov/documents/20080702154414.pdf.

12. KRG Natural Resources Minister responds to comments on draft Kurdistan Petroleum Act, August 22, 2006, web.krg.org/articles/detail.asp?rnr=95&lngnr=12 &anr=13070&smap=.

13. "KRG Responds to Dr Shahristani's Recent Statements on Oil," September 11, 2007, www.krg.org/articles/detail.asp?rnr=223&lngnr=12&smap=02010100& anr=20130.

14. Ben Lando, "Iraq Oil Showdown," *Iraq Oil Report*, May 14, 2009.

15. Interview with the author, Baghdad, December 14, 2009.

16. Interview with the author, Shaikhan, December 22, 2009.

17. Patricia Butenis/U.S. embassy Baghdad, Cable 2007-Baghdad-3071, "Hunt Oil Signs Agreement with KRG Under KRG Oil Law," September 12, 2007, obtained through FOIA.

18. Interview with the author, Shaikhan, December 22, 2009.

19. Interview with the author, Amman, August 30, 2007.

20. "Tussle for Kirkuk Oil," U.S. embassy cable, July 23, 2008, obtained by WikiLeaks.

21. For example, Bayan Sami Abdul Rahman and Brendan O'Leary, "Federalism and Oil and Gas," presentation to LSE/OSI seminar, June 29–30, 2005.

22. For a discussion, see Reidar Visser, "Disputed Territories in Iraq: The Practical Argument Against Self-Determination in Kirkuk," historiae.org, May 25, 2009.

23. David McDowell, *A Modern History of the Kurds* (London: I.B. Tauris, 2004), 340.

24. Kerim Yildiz, *The Kurds in Iraq: The Past, Present and Future* (London: Pluto, 2004), 25.

25. UNAMI human rights report, November 1–December 31, 2006, 3–4.

26. Steve Fainaru, "Kurds Reclaiming Prized Territory in Northern Iraq," *WP*, October 30, 2005.

27. Stephen Farrell, "As Iraqis Vie for Kirkuk's Oil, Kurds Are Pawns," *NYT*, December 9, 2007; David Romano, "Whose House Is This Anyway?" *Journal of Refugee Studies* 18, no. 4 (2005): 438.

28. Romano, "Whose House Is This Anyway?" 439–40.

29. Ben Lando, "Kirkuk Project Battle Heats Up," UPI, November 28, 2007.

30. "Iraq and the Kurds: Trouble Along the Trigger Line," ICG, July 8, 2009.

31. Joost Hiltermann, "Everyone Wants a Piece of Kirkuk, the Golden Prize," *National*, February 26, 2009.

32. "Iraq Factions Join Against Kurd Oil Deals," UPI, January 15, 2008.

33. Ali Jawad, "Opposing Kurds Turns Oil Minister into Hero," *Azzaman* (English), February 1, 2008, www.azzaman.com/english/index.asp?fname=news\2008 -02-01.kurd1.htm.

34. Al-Arabiya, December 13, 2007, *Iraq Markets*, trans. BBC Monitoring, "Iraqi Oil Minister Discusses Oil Law, Supply of Gas to Syria," December 29, 2007.

35. "Iraqi Minister of Oil Announces Government Will Proceed Under Draft Oil and Gas Law," U.S. embassy London, Cable 2008-London-385, February 6, 2008, obtained through FOIA.

36. Stanley Reed, "OPEC Update: Get Used to Lower Prices," *BusinessWeek*, March 18, 2009.

37. Ben Lando, "Deeper than an Oil Law in Iraq," UPI, September 10, 2007.

38.  Ewa Jasiewicz, "Black Gold Turns Grey as Western Giants Prepare to Draw from the Wells of Iraq," *Independent*, September 30, 2007.

39.  "Oil Minister Courts Enamored Oil Firms," U.S. embassy cable, October 11, 2007, obtained by WikiLeaks.

40.  Stephen Farrell and Qais Mizher, "Iraq Dismisses 1,300 After Basra Offensive," *NYT*, April 14, 2008.

41.  Aref Mohammed, "US Forces Drawn Deeper into Iraq Crackdown," Reuters, March 28, 2008.

42.  Thomas Ricks, *The Gamble: General David Petraeus and the Untold Story of the American Surge in Iraq, 2006–2008* (London: Allen Lane, 2009), 281.

43.  Stephen Farrell and Ammar Karim, "Drive in Basra by Iraqi Army Makes Gains," *NYT*, May 12, 2008.

44.  "Maliki's Military Operation in Basrah: Lessons Learned," U.S. embassy cable, April 18, 2008, obtained through WikiLeaks.

45.  "Iraq's Shahristani Reshuffles Southern Oil Leadership," *MEES* 51, no. 22 (June 2, 2008): 2.

46.  Gina Chon, "Turf War Hits Iraq's Oil Industry," *WSJ*, July 30, 2008.

47.  "RE: National Oil Company," (name removed), FCO e-mail, August 11, 2004, obtained through FOIA.

48.  Interview with the author, Basra, December 20, 2009.

49.  "Confrontation with the Unions Will Lead the Iraqi Government Nowhere," Naftana statement, June 5, 2008.

50.  "TUC Slams Iraqi Government at ILO," TUC Briefing, June 4, 2008, www .tuc.org.uk/international/tuc-14873-f0.cfm.

51.  Riyadh Mohammed, "Election Results," *NYT* "At War" blog, February 6, 2009, atwar.blogs.nytimes.com/2009/02/06/election-results-whos-up-whos-down.

## Chapter 21: Overwatch

1.  *Field Manual*, 101-5-1, MCRP 5-2A: Operational Terms and Graphics; William Safire, "On Language: Overwatch," *NYT Magazine*, October 14, 2007.

2.  *Measuring Stability and Security in Iraq*, DOD, Report to Congress, December 2007, 21.

3.  *O'Reilly Factor*, Fox News, September 4, 2008.

4.  "Multi-National Force-Iraq Charts to Accompany the Testimony of Gen. David Petraeus," DOD, April 8–9, 2008, 2.

5.  See, e.g., Dylan Matthews and Ezra Klein, "How Important Was the Surge?" www.prospect.org, July 28, 2008.

6.  Ned Parker, "Sadr Militia Moves to Clean House," *Los Angeles Times*, December 7, 2007.

7.  "President Bush Signs H.R. 4986, the National Defense Authorization Act for Fiscal Year 2008 into Law," White House, press release, January 28, 2008.

8. Thomas Ricks, *The Gamble: General David Petraeus and the Untold Story of the American Surge in Iraq, 2006–2008* (London: Allen Lane, 2009), 313–25.

9. Ibid., 103.

10. "Withdrawal from Iraq," International Institute for Strategic Studies, *Strategic Comments* 14, no. 10, 1.

11. Lauren Frayer, "Iraqi Lawmaker Says Talks over US-Iraqi Security Pact at 'Standstill,'" AP, June 3, 2008.

12. "Maliki Confidante Careful on SOFA and Disputes Importance of Sunni Arab Tribes for Security," U.S. embassy cable, August 29, 2008, obtained by WikiLeaks.

13. U.S. embassy cables, September–November 2008, obtained by WikiLeaks; e.g., "D Presses Parliamentary Speaker on Security Agreement, Minorities," October 7, 2008.

14. Leila Fadel, "U.S. Lists Services It'll Cut Off if Iraq Rejects Pact on Troops," McClatchy, October 27, 2008.

15. Strategic Framework Agreement between USA and Iraq, November 17, 2008, sec. 1, para. 3.

16. Ibrahim Bahr al-Uloum, "The Day After," speech at American Enterprise Institute conference, October 3, 2002.

17. Interview with the author, London, February 2005.

18. "Oil Minister Courts Enamored Oil Firms," U.S. embassy cable, October 11, 2007, obtained by WikiLeaks.

19. "Actions Still Needed to Improve the Use of Private Security Providers," U.S. Government Accountability Office, GAO-06-865T, June 13, 2006, 2.

20. Michael Sean Gillard and Melissa Jones, "BP's Secret Military Advisers," *Guardian*, June 30, 1997; Michael Gillard, Ignacio Gomez, and Melissa Jones, "BP Hands Tarred in Pipeline Dirty War," *Guardian*, October 17, 1998.

21. Available at s3.amazonaws.com/corpwatch.org/downloads/aegis.wmv.

22. Aegis statement regarding Trophy video allegations, February 27, 2008, posted on business-humanrights.org.

23. Jonathan Finer, "Contractors Cleared in Videotaped Attacks," *WP*, June 11, 2006.

24. Ray O'Hanlon, "Botched Investigation?" *Irish Echo*, June 14, 2006.

25. Sean Rayment, "Trophy Video Exposes Private Security Contractors Shooting Up Iraqi Drivers," *Sunday Telegraph*, November 27, 2005.

26. Peter Baker, "Iraq Withdrawal Plan Gains G.O.P. Support," *NYT*, February 27, 2009.

27. Peter Baker, "With Pledges to Troops and Iraqis, Obama Details Pullout," *NYT*, February 28, 2009.

28. "Press Conference Call with Secretary Gates," DOD, February 27, 2009.

29. Barack Obama, "Way Forward in Iraq," Chicago Council on Global Affairs, November 20, 2006.

NOTES TO PAGES 252–257

30. "Iraqi Politicians Pass the Buck as Security Agreement Referendum Law Progresses," U.S. embassy cable, June 9, 2009, obtained by WikiLeaks.

31. "Biden Warns of 'Perilous Road' Ahead," AP, February 6, 2009.

32. BBC, ABC News, and NHK poll of 2,000 Iraqis, September 2007, news. bbc.co.uk/1/shared/bsp/hi/pdfs/10_09_07iraqpoll.pdf.

33. See Reidar Visser, "Biden, US Policy in Iraq and the Concept of Muhasasa," www.historiae.org, July 6, 2009.

34. Christopher Hill, "The Arab Spring's Unintended Consequences," aljazeera .com, October 1, 2011.

35. Barack Obama campaign, Iraq webpage, emphasis added, www.barackobama .com/issues/iraq.

36. Shanker, "Campaign Promises on Ending the War in Iraq Now Muted by Reality', NYT, December 4, 2008; Bill Ardolino, "Threat Matrix," longwarjournal. org, October 18, 2009; "Gates Says US Air Force May Remain in Iraq Beyond 2011," Voice of America, December 11, 2009; Michael Gordon, "Civilians to Take US Lead as Military Leaves Iraq," NYT, August 18, 2010.

37. Jane Arraf, "To Meet June Deadline, US and Iraqis Redraw City Borders," CSM, May 19, 2009.

38. Nouri al-Maliki, keynote speech to "Invest Iraq" conference, London, April 30, 2009.

## Chapter 22: Talking Business

1. Simon Webb, "Iraq Proposes to Improve Terms for Big Oil Deals," Reuters, February 12, 2009.

2. Iraq Ministry of Oil invitation to press conference, October 10, 2008.

3. More precisely, the auction was for six contracts covering eight oilfields, and two covering gasfields (Akkaz and Mansuriyah).

4. This was the amount estimated at the time of signing. It was later upgraded to 5.4 billion barrels.

5. Ryan Crocker/U.S. embassy Baghdad, Cable 2008-Baghdad-3241, October 7, 2008, obtained through FOIA.

6. Heads of Agreement between Ministry of Oil and Shell, September 22, 2008, Clauses 3(k), 2(f).

7. Ahmed Rasheed, "Iraq Lawmakers Say Will Challenge Shell Gas Deal," Reuters, November 25, 2008.

8. Issam al-Chalabi, "Appeal for the Protection of the Oil Wealth of the Country," trans. Nadia al-Sharif, September 26–27, 2008.

9. Telephone interview with the author, December 10, 2008.

10. Meeting of Jabbar al-Luaibi with U.K. embassy team, reported in FCO e-mail, "HMA in Basra," July 3, 2005, obtained through FOIA.

11. "The Elusive Goal to Stop Flares," Shell, 2008, www.shell.com/home/content/environment_society/shell_world_stories/2008/flaring.

12. Mounir Bouaziz, "Backing Iraq's Gas Master Plan," *Shell in the Middle East,* October 2008.

13. Letter from David O'Reilly to Sam Bodman, June 20, 2008, obtained from DOE through FOIA; DOE, memo of conversation between Donny MacDonald (Chevron Iraq country manager), Al Hegburg, and others, April 23, 2008, obtained through FOIA; Simon Webb, "BP Hopes to Sign Iraq Service Contract Midyear," Reuters, April 7, 2008.

14. Hassan Hafidh, "Iraq Blames Intl Oil Firms for Scrapping of Service Contracts," DJ, September 16, 2008. Another issue was whether the companies would be paid in oil or cash, although, as one company source said, "the remuneration issue isn't a complicated one and can be solved." DJ, "Iraq Is Asking Global Oil Firms for Final Proposals," May 18, 2008.

15. Ruba Husari, "Shell's Upstream Chief Offers His Take on Iraq's Landmark Bid Round," *International Oil Daily,* November 7, 2008.

16. Jasim Azawi interview with Husain Sharistani, Al-Jazeera English, December 18, 2009.

17. DOC, Briefing Book for Deputy Secretary of Commerce John Sullivan for Dialogue on Business and Investment Climate, "Talking Points for Opening Remarks, and Talking Points to Be Raised During DBIC," November 1, 2008, obtained through FOIA. The other three points, which would not affect oil companies, were to confirm the appointment of the chair of the National Investment Commission, to provide for clear title to land for investors, and to pass implementing regulations for the investment land.

18. Letter from Robert Kimmitt to Nouri al-Maliki, undated (November 2008), obtained from DOC through FOIA.

19. "Commercial Law Development Program (CLDP) Assistance to Come to Iraq," U.S. embassy cables, July 12, 2009, obtained by WikiLeaks; "Minutes of March 18 SFA Oil and Gas Working Group meeting," March 22, 2010, obtained through FOIA.

20. "Third Meeting of Economic and Energy Joint Coordination Committee," U.S. embassy cable, June 13, 2009, obtained by WikiLeaks.

21. "Training and Development in the Oil Sector," Letter from BP to Iraq Ministry of Oil, April 28, 2009, obtained from FCO through FOIA.

22. Including in the northern division of INOC.

23. Chip Cummins, "Brain Drain Slows Flow of Iraqi Oil," *WSJ,* August 22, 2006.

24. Interview with the author, London, July 10, 2009.

25. Ruba Husari, interview with Jabbar al-Luaibi, May 20, 2009, www.iraqoilforum.com/?p=788.

26. "Iraq Public Expenditure and Institutional Assessment," World Bank, June 2008, 1:79. "Measuring Stability and Security in Iraq," Department of Defense, report to Congress, June 2008, 10.

27. "Terms Take Shape for Iraqi Bid Rounds," *PIW*, October 6, 2008. The percentage has been adjusted from that in the article to reflect changes in the list of second-round fields after it was published.

28. "FW: Meetings with Shell," [names removed], FCO Iraq Policy Unit e-mail, February 22, 2006, obtained through FOIA.

29. Richard Nield, "Oil Majors Criticise Baghdad Over New Contract Terms," *MEED*, February 17, 2009.

30. Technical Service Contract (model), April 23, 2009, Articles 9, 27.

31. Ibid., Article 5.

32. Ibid., Article 16.1.

33. Ibid., Article 20.8.

34. Interview with the author, Amman, September 9, 2009.

35. Faleh al-Khayat, "The First Round of Licenses and the Risk It Represents for the Iraqi National Oil Industry," *Arab Al-Yawm* (Jordan), June 17–18, 2009, trans. Nadia al-Sharif.

36. Author interview with Faleh al-Khayat, September 9, 2009.

37. "Iraq DPM Barham Salih on Oil, ICI and Budget," U.S. embassy cable, March 19, 2009, obtained by WikiLeaks.

38. "Oil Minister Shahristani Target of Criticism," U.S. embassy cable, January 20, 2009, obtained by WikiLeaks.

39. "First Oil Bid Round: The Greatest Show on Earth," U.S. embassy cable, June 22, 2009, obtained by WikiLeaks.

40. She argued that the law of Iraq should reflect shari'a, including the rules that permitted men to have four wives and that women should receive smaller shares of inheritances than men. She defended these positions on grounds both principled— "I like that family should be the major principle for women here"—and pragmatic: with women making up 55 percent of the population after so many men had died in Iraq's three recent wars, bigamy would reduce the amount of loneliness. Meanwhile, men had more need of inheritance because men, not women, were expected to support their poorer relatives. "We have different traditions," she said to journalists from the *New York Times*. "What is acceptable to you is not acceptable to us." Robert F. Worth, "In Jeans or Veils, Iraqi Women Are Split on New Political Power," *NYT*, April 13, 2005.

41. Ibid., Article 5.

42. Edward Wong with Zaineb Obeid, "Delay Possible on Iraq Charter as Talks Falter," *NYT*, March 30, 2005.

43. John Leland and Riyadh Mohammed, "Iraqi Women Are Seeking Greater Political Influence," *NYT*, February 17, 2010.

44. Jim Clancy, Hala Gorani, Becky Anderson, Hugh Riminton, Don Lemon, and Christiane Amanpour, "Tony Blair Announces He'll Step Down; Bush Speaks About Wars in Iraq, Afghanistan," CNN, May 10, 2007.

45. Tina Sussman, "The Conflict in Iraq: Shortages in a City; Lawmaker Gets Physical; If Not Time Off, Maybe Parliament Members in Iraq Need a Timeout," *Los Angeles Times*, May 11, 2007.

46. *Commercial Appeal*, "On the Front: Al-Maliki Sees a Better Iraq—'What . . . Are You Talking About?'" September 11, 2007.

47. Lennox Samuels, "The Turmoil Next Door," *Newsweek*, June 26, 2009.

48. Waleed Ibrahim and Ahmed Rasheed, "Iraq Oil Ministry to Push Ahead with Deal Tender," Reuters, June 16, 2009.

49. Ahmed Rasheed, "Iraq Oil Execs Rebel over Contract Tenders," Reuters, June 14, 2009.

50. Letter from Fayadh Nima to Husain al-Shahristani, June 10, 2009, reproduced in English translation in *MEES* 52, no. 25 (June 22, 2009): 26–27.

51. "Iraqi Oil: Mixed Messages from South Oil on the Bid Round and International Oil Firms," U.S. embassy cable, July 31, 2009, obtained by WikiLeaks.

52. IFOU statement, June 21, 2009, www.uslaboragainstwar.org/article.php?id=19630.

53. "First Oil Bid Round: The Greatest Show on Earth," cable via WikiLeaks, June 22, 2009.

54. Interview with the author, Amman, August 28, 2009.

## Chapter 23: Under the Hammer

1. Interview with the author, Amman, September 9, 2009.

2. Tim Cocks and Muhanad Mohammed, "Iraqis Rejoice as U.S. Troops Leave Baghdad," Reuters, June 29, 2009.

3. Channel 4 News, June 30, 2009.

4. Interview with Issam al-Chalabi, Amman, August 16, 2009.

5. "Baghdad Ambushes Upstream Investors with Fees Demands," *MEES* 52, no. 27 (July 6, 2009): 2.

6. Ibid.

7. Perry Williams, "A Crushing Blow to Baghdad's Oil Plans," *MEED*, July 9, 2009.

8. DOE, S2 meeting with John Watson, January 15, 2010, obtained through FOIA.

9. "Iraq's Oil Bid Round 2: U.S. Firms' Participation," U.S. embassy cable, December 21, 2009, obtained by WikiLeaks.

10. "First Oil Bid Round: The Greatest Show on Earth," U.S. embassy cable, June 22, 2009, obtained by WikiLeaks. Also UPI, "Exxon, Shell: Iraq Oil Law Needed for Deal," February 13, 2008.

11. "Biden in Iraq: This Is the Moment," ABC News, July 2, 2009, abcnews.go .com/video/playerIndex?id=7989627.

12. Ibid.

13. Andrew Quinn, "US Vice President Biden Visits Baghdad," Reuters, July 2, 2009.

14. Ali al-Dabbagh, interviewed by Husayn Turki, al-Iraqiyya, July 4, 2009, trans. BBC Monitoring, "Iraqi Spokesman Says Biden Told 'We Want to Solve Our Problems by Ourselves,'" July 5, 2009.

15. Meghan O'Sullivan, "Issues Before Identity in Iraq," WP, July 21, 2009.

16. Scott Wilson, "Biden Pushes Iraqi Leaders on Vote Law, Oil-Bid Perks," WP, September 17, 2009.

17. Edwin Chen, "Biden Presses for Improved Iraq Investment Climate," Bloomberg News, September 17, 2009.

18. Interview with the author, Amman, August 23, 2009.

19. Hussain Juma'a interview with the author, Amman, September 5, 2009; Aref Mohammed, "Iraq's Weakened Unions Fight Foreign Oil Firms," Reuters, July 13, 2009; Ben Lando, Nizar Latif, and Alaa Majeed, "Workers Rebel," Iraq Oil Report, July 17, 2009.

20. Khalid al-Ansary and Missy Ryan, "Iraq Vows to Shield Oil Firms from Union Threats," Reuters, July 17, 2009.

21. Author interview with Hassan Juma'a, September 5, 2009.

22. U.K. consulate Basra, notes of meeting with BP, July 21, 2009, obtained through FOIA.

23. Briefing notes for meeting with BP on July 21, 2009, FCO. Obtained through FOIA.

24. "Basra: South Oil Company Director Optimistic About the Future," U.S. embassy cable, November 5, 2009, obtained by WikiLeaks.

25. Author interview with former oil official, Amman, August 2009.

26. Hussain Shahristani, press conference, Istanbul, August 25, 2009.

27. As its website puts it, the firm "serves clients at the nexus of commerce and public policies"; www.khalilzadassociates.com/aboutus.aspx.

28. Sam Dagher, "Prospects Abound Among the Kurds," NYT, July 14, 2010.

29. Anthony Fenton, "Drill, Garner, Drill," Mother Jones, November 24, 2008.

30. Ronald Jonkers, "The Path Forward," The Oil and Gas Year: Kurdistan Region of Iraq 2009, 45–47.

## Chapter 24: A Dirty Business

1. Munir Chalabi, "Iraqi Oil: Transparency and Corruption," ZNet, September 26, 2011.

2. Interview with the author, Amman, August 16, 2009.

3. "Iraq's First Oil Bid Round Sputters," U.S. embassy cable, June 30, 2009, obtained by WikiLeaks.

4. Gina Chon, "Some Oil Firms Now Accept Iraq Terms, Minister Says," *WSJ*, November 4, 2009.

5. Ben Lando, "Exxon Exec Optimistic in Iraq Entry," *Iraq Oil Report*, February 4, 2010.

6. Eni SpA, Q3 2009 earnings conference call, October 29, 2009.

7. Simon Webb, "Lower Taxes Lure Big Oil to Iraq Oilfield Deals," Reuters, October 14, 2009.

8. U.S. embassy cable, "Oil Minister Flexible with IOC in Private," September 4, 2009, obtained by WikiLeaks.

9. "Iraq Oil: Ministry Officials Skeptical as Courting Continues," U.S. embassy cable, August 26, 2009, obtained by WikiLeaks.

10. Hussain Shahristani, speaking at press conference, London, October 13, 2008.

11. Interview with the author, London, December 7, 2009.

12. Jasim Azawi interview with Husain Sharistani, Al-Jazeera English, December 18, 2009.

13. See Heike Mainhardt-Gibbs, "Transparency of Extractive Industry Contracts: The Case for Public Disclosure," Bank Information Center, October 2007; Revenue Watch Institute, "Contract Transparency," resources.revenuewatch.org/en /backgrounder/contracttransparency.

14. *Guide on Resource Revenue Transparency*, IMF, 2007, 17; U.S. Department of Treasury, "Statement Concerning the Extractive Industries Review," JS-1841, August 2, 2004.

15. 006 Draft Oil Law, Article 36(A)(3).

16. This could be done either by extending the term of the contract or by increasing the production profile at some later date from that specified in the development plan. Either way, they would produce the same aggregate amount over the full life of their contract, but it would be worth less due to the time value of money.

17. E-mail to the author, August 16, 2011.

18. Ruba Husari, "Ghadhban Assesses Progress and Prospects in Iraq's Oil Sector," *MEES* 53, no. 9 (March 1, 2010), 25.

19. Fadhil Chalabi, presentation at CWC Iraq Petroleum conference, London, December 7, 2009.

20. David Strahan, "Thirty Contestants, Only One Winner in the Iraqi Oil Licence Gameshow," *Independent on Sunday*, July 5, 2009.

21. "Oil Revival," *Iraq Oil Forum*, October 12, 2009, www.energyintel.com/n/ Portal/oilrevival.aspx.

22. Chon, "Some Oil Firms."

23. "Tony Hayward: Getting BP Back on Track," *PIW*, October 5, 2009.

24. Eni SpA, earnings conference call.

25. Paul Sankey, David Clark, and Silvio Micheloto, *The Mother of All Oil Stories*, Deutsche Bank, October 4, 2010, 22. It is not clear whether these estimates factored in the contract changes. If compensation for nonproduced oil (due either to infrastructure limits or to OPEC quotas) were added, the returns would be even higher.

26. "Baghdad Awards 4.8Mn B/D Second Tranche of Upstream Oil Projects," *MEES*, December 21–28, 2009, 2.

27. Remuneration is $2 per barrel: 25 percent of this goes to the state partner (SOMO), and a 35 percent corporate tax is deducted. This leaves 75 percent × 65 percent × 2 = $0.975 per barrel to the companies. At peak, incremental production is targeted as 1.85 million barrels. Hence annual profit of 365 × 0.975 × 1.85 million = $658 million. This is a simplified calculation, assuming the "R" factor is below 1.0 and performance factor is 1, and before adjusting for baseline depletion.

28. For example, BP/CNPC's investment in the Rumaila field is estimated at $15 billion, spread over several years. When the field is producing at an extra million barrels a day—just over half of the targeted increase—it could repay the companies $11 billion per year at an oil price of $60 per barrel. (Up to 50 percent of revenues may be used to pay the companies' costs and remuneration; 50 percent × 365 × 60 million = 10.95 billion.)

29. Author's conversation with oil company executive with direct knowledge of the contracts, July 2010.

30. Interview with the author, Amman, November 2009.

31. Tariq Shafiq, "Iraq's Oil and Gas Challenges and Opportunities," *Iraq Oil Report*, January 6, 2010.

32. Interview with the author, Amman, November 2010.

33. Ammar Karim, "Iraq Approves Oil Deals with Foreign Firms," AFP, January 6, 2010.

34. Sankey, Clark, and Micheloto, *Mother of All Oil Stories*, 1.

35. Ayla Jean Yackley, "Iraqi Oil Deals Mean Reams of Steel, Miles of Pipes," Reuters, December 10, 2009.

36. "Basra: South Oil Company Director Optimistic About the Future," U.S. embassy cable, November 5, 2009, obtained by WikiLeaks.

37. Author's conversation with oil company executive with direct knowledge of the contracts, July 2010.

38. Rania el-Gamal, "Iraq Awards Rumaila Drilling Deals Worth $500 Mln," Reuters, March 31, 2010.

39. Author interviews with Iraqi oil experts, Amman, November 2009. For example on the Khafji field, which is shared between Kuwait and Saudi Arabia, a $300 million contract was awarded in August 2010 for drilling 151 wells [Samuel Ciszuk, "Schlumberger, Halliburton Both Likely to Clinch Services Contract for Shared Saudi Kuwaiti Khafji Oilfield," IHS Global Insight Daily Analysis, August 18, 2010]. In November 2009 Halliburton won a contract to drill up to 185 wells in

Saudi Arabia's Ghawar field ["Halliburton receives drilling contract for Saudi Arabia's Ghawar Field," Associated Press, November 6, 2009]; analysts estimated the contract was worth between $500 million and $1 billion ["Aramco to Award 500m Drilling Work in Ghawar," A1SaudiArabia.com, October 13, 2009; Rhonda Duey, "Halliburton Gets Coveted Ghawar Contract," *Hart's E&P*, November 6, 2009]. Even in Iraq itself there were some irregular variations. In August 2011 Lukoil awarded a $160 million contract to Baker Hughes to drill 23 wells in the West Qurna II field [Hassan Hafidh, "Lukoil, Baker Hughes Agree to Drill in Iraq Field, DJ, August 16, 2011], working out at $7 million per well. Faleh al-Khayat observed that if anything drilling in West Qurna should be more expensive than in fields like Rumaila, since West Qurna is in soggy marshland, farther from ports and with greater security concerns. "Was LUKoil tougher in contracting because it has to pay the cost itself and will not recover it till it achieves commercial production?" he wondered—compared to the Rumaila field where BP/CNPC would quickly recoup the cost from the Iraqi government (e-mail to the author, January 15, 2012).

40. Out of 180 countries assessed. Transparency International, *Corruption Perceptions Index 2009*.

41. State Department, *Human Rights Report*, 2009.

42. "Failing Oversight: Iraq's Unchecked Government," ICG, September 26, 2011, 13–16.

43. Luigi Ferrarella and Giuseppe Guastella, "ENI Investigated over Alleged Oil Bribes in Iraq and Kuwait," *Corriere della Sera*, June 22, 2011.

44. *Development Fund for Iraq, Statement of Proceeds of Oil Export Sales*, KPMG, independent auditor's report, December 31, 2008, 2.

45. "Hawrami Caught in the Middle with DNO," *Upstream*, September 18, 2009.

46. "Eide Keeps Mum over Kurdish Threat," *UpstreamOnline*, September 28, 2009.

47. Caroline Binham, "U.K. Hands Record Fine to Genel CEO for Inside Trades," *Bloomberg News*, February 16, 2010.

48. James Quinn, "There's No Comparison Between Running BP and Running Genel, Says Tony Hayward," *Sunday Telegraph*, September 11, 2011.

49. Conversation with the author, London, October 3, 2011.

50. "Money Laundering and Foreign Corruption," U.S. Senate Permanent Subcommittee on Investigations, report prepared by the minority staff in conjunction with the hearing on July 15, 2004, 104.

51. "Iraqi Kurdistan: Africanists Venture In," *African Energy* 215, September 9, 2011.

52. KRG Regional Oil and Gas Law, Article 52.

53. E-mail from Mia Early, Kurdistan Development Corporation, June 14, 2006.

54. KRG Model Production Sharing Contract, Article 4.5.

55. Article 55 of the KRG Regional Oil and Gas Law bars public officers (and their spouses and children) from holding shares in companies with interests in oil

and gas fields. The fear is that such interests may be acquired indirectly; covertly; or through allies, friends, and relatives.

56. "Iraqi Kurds Look to Strengthen Oil Sector," *MEES* 51, no. 23 (June 9, 2008): 3–4.

57. Michael Rubin, "Is Iraqi Kurdistan a Good Ally?" *AEI Middle Eastern Outlook*, January 2008.

58. Sam Dagher, "Smugglers in Iraq Blunt Sanctions Against Iran," *NYT*, July 8, 2010.

59. Khalid Waleed and Shorsh Khalid, "Oil Smuggling Allegations Widen Baghdad–Irbil Rift," Institute for War and Peace Reporting, *Iraq Crisis Report* 346, July 23, 2010.

60. Dagher, "Smugglers in Iraq."

## Chapter 25: Winter and Spring

1. Conversation with the author, Basra, December 19, 2009.

2. Interview with the author, Basra, December 20, 2009.

3. *Iraq Trade Union Rights Bulletin*, Solidarity Center, June 2010, 3.

4. Interview with the author, Basra, December 20, 2009.

5. *Iraq Trade Union Rights Bulletin*, Solidarity Center, April 2010, 1–2.

6. Carmen Gentile, "Union Leaders Taken to Court for Oil Sector Dissent," *Iraq Oil Report*, July 2, 2010.

7. *Iraq Trade Union Rights Bulletin*, Solidarity Center, June 2010, 1.

8. "Ministry of Oil Update on Bid Rounds, Oil Production and Shell Flared Gas Deal," U.S. embassy cable, May 1, 2009, obtained by WikiLeaks.

9. Letter from Nouri al-Maliki to the parliament, October 2009, trans. Yahia Hamied.

10. "PM Pushes Back on Parliamentary Questioning," U.S. embassy cable, June 26, 2009, obtained by WikiLeaks.

11. Telephone interview with the author, August 14, 2010.

12. "Failing Oversight," ICG, 25.

13. On the implication of these and other changes, see Fadhil al-Nashmi, "Fears That Iraqi PM Grabbing Power," Niqash.org, July 5, 2011.

14. "Oil Minister Shahristani Target of Criticism," U.S. embassy cable, January 20, 2009, obtained by WikiLeaks.

15. "Rumaila Oil-Field Lawsuit Continues but Success Unlikely," U.S. embassy cable, February 6, 2010, obtained by WikiLeaks.

16. Ben Lando, "Ex-MP Vows to Continue Rumaila Challenge," *Iraq Oil Report*, May 4, 2010.

17. "Sadr; Renegotiate Illegal Iraq Oil Deals," UPI, April 28, 2010.

18. J. Jay Park, presentation to CWC Iraq Petroleum Conference, London, December 8, 2009, 35–36.

19. "Dialogue on Economic Cooperation," U.S. embassy cable, November 3, 2009, obtained by WikiLeaks.

20. Khalid al-Ansary and Jim Loney, "Iraq Oil Law a Priority—PM Hopeful Allawi," Reuters, March 31, 2010; *Iraq Oil Report*, "Insight into Dawa Oil Thinking," April 8, 2010.

21. Christopher Hill interviewed by Melissa Block, NPR, November 11, 2010.

22. Reidar Visser interviewed by Greg Bruno, "Avoiding Crisis in Iraq's Political Minefield," Council on Foreign Relations, January 25, 2010, cfr.org.

23. For example, "Oil Deals Vital to Iraq PM's Campaign," AP, March 2, 2010.

24. Alice Fordham, "Election Shakes Up Parliament's Oil Seats," *Iraq Oil Report*, April 2, 2010. Under the election rules, each candidate's excess of votes above the 37,379 threshold would then be redistributed within their party in an order determined by how many individual votes each party candidate received.

25. John Leland and Riyadh Mohammed, "Iraqi Women Are Seeking Greater Political Influence," *NYT*, February 17, 2010.

26. Author's telephone interview with Shatha al-Musawi, August 14, 2010.

27. Ibid.

28. Maher Chmaytelli and Nayla Razzouk, "Iraq's Allawi Bloc Says Oil, Gas Licenses are Illegal," *Bloomberg News*, October 24, 2010.

29. "Iraqi Electricity Minister Resigns over Shortage," AP, June 21, 2010.

30. Iraqi Ministry of Electricity, ministerial order 22 244, July 20, 2010, English translation at www.tuc.org.uk/international/tuc-18242-f0.cfm.

31. Ben Lando, "Shahristani Clamps Down on Electricity Unions," *Iraq Oil Report*, July 26, 2010.

32. Letter from Richard Trumka to Nouri al-Maliki, August 11, 2010, www .solidaritycenter.org/Files/iraq_rlt_letter081110.pdf.

33. Majid Hameed, "Protests in Basra, Baghdad, Samarra," www.uslaboragainst war.org/article.php?id=22827.

34. Abdullah Muhsin, "Account of Police Raid on Basra Office of Electricity Union," www.uslaboragainstwar.org/article.php?id=22715.

35. "ICEM Executive Condemns Repressive Union Actions by Iraq," ICEM, *ICEM in Brief*, May 31, 2010.

36. Telephone interview with the author, October 6, 2011.

37. Resolution "In Support of Labor Rights for Iraqi Workers," submitted by Michael Eisenscher on behalf of U.S. Labor Against the War and adopted without dissent by the United National Antiwar Conference to Bring the Troops Home Now, held in Albany, NY, July 23–25, 2010.

38. Resolution "Support Iraqi Labor Rights," Communications Workers of America national convention, August 12, 2010, www.uslaboragainstwar.org/article.php ?id=22821; "Special Order on Labor Rights in Iraq," American Federation of Teachers national convention, 2010, www.uslaboragainstwar.org/article.php?id=22660.

39. Letter from Rep. Sam Farr et al. to Nouri al-Maliki, September 29, 2010,

uslaboragainstwar.org/downloads/Congressional%20Letter%20to%20Al-Maliki%20October%202010.pdf.

40. Author's telephone interview with Ibrahim Radhi, October 10, 2010. When I spoke to Ibrahim, the ministry had still not implemented the court order to return them to the Basra refinery, and so the workers were considering going back to court.

41. "Maliki Tells Mullen Iraqi Troops Can Take Over," AP, April 22, 2011.

42. Aaron Davis, "Iraq Must Decide on Lasting U.S. Troop Presence 'Within Weeks,' Mullen Says," WP, April 23, 2011.

43. Meghan O'Sullivan, "Why U.S. Troops Should Stay in Iraq," WP, September 9, 2011.

44. As so many times in the war, a linguistic change seemed to be the way to square the circle. Just as Iraqis had seen through the term PSA, forcing a new name of "exploration risk contract" to be invented, so too the word "adviser" was unavailable to explain the continued presence of the forces, as British "advisers" had been an important mechanism of control over Iraq from the 1920s to the 1950s.

45. Reidar Visser, "Of Instructors and Interests in Iraq," Middle East Research and Information Project, merip.org, August 22, 2011.

46. Karen DeYoung and Scott Wilson, "Iraqis Fail to Agree on Whether to Ask for Some U.S. Troops to Stay Beyond Deadline," WP, July 10, 2011.

47. Tim Arango and Michael Schmidt, "Iraqi Dispute About U.S. Troops Reflects Clashing Emotions," NYT, October 6, 2011.

48. Letter from Hassan Juma'a Awad, President, "In the Eighth Anniversary of the Aggression and Occupation," April 12, 2011.

49. "Failing Oversight," ICG, ii.

50. Meghan O'Sullivan, "Iraqi Politics and Implications for Oil and Energy," Harvard Belfer Center, July 2011, 5.

51. "Days of Rage: Protests and Repression in Iraq," Amnesty International, April 11, 2011.

52. "TUC Appalled by Withdrawal of Union Recognition Rights by Iraqi Government," TUC, press release, May 9, 2011.

53. Remarks by the President on Ending the War in Iraq, White House, October 21, 2011. The United States would still have the world's largest embassy in Baghdad, occupying an area of 1.5 square miles, plus enormous consulate outposts in Basra and Irbil, supported by up to 7,000 private soldiers. But their ability to shape Iraqi politics would be minor.

## Chapter 26: Another Regime Changed

1. Meghan O'Sullivan, "Will Libya Become Obama's Iraq?" WP, April 1, 2011.

2. The Times journalist could equally have chosen examples from within the region, such as the bloody reprisals against protesters by the governments of Bahrain and Yemen, both close allies of the West.

3. Camilla Long, "Juggling Gadaffi and All That Jazz," *Sunday Times*, April 10, 2011.

4. Donald Trump, interview with George Stephanopoulos, ABC News, April 19, 2011.

5. David Case, "Ann Coulter: Let's Fight Wars for Oil," GlobalPost, April 25, 2011.

6. Michael T. Klare, *Blood and Oil: The Dangers and Consequences of America's Growing Petroleum Dependency* (London: Penguin, 2005), 4ff.

7. While some members of the Libyan National Transitional Council said that contracts would be awarded preferentially to companies from countries that participated in the war (see, e.g., NTC oil "minister" Ali Tarhouni, "Libyan Rebels Will Reward Their 'Friends,'" *Petroleum Economist*, April 5, 2011; NTC chairman Mustafa Abdul Jalil, quoted in Yarislav Tofimov, "Rebels Attack Gadhafi Bastion," *WSJ*, September 16, 2011), just as Chalabi had done in Iraq in 2003, others rejected the suggestion (e.g., NTC U.K. representative Guma al-Gamaty, quoted in Vivienne Walt, "Libya's Oil Industry: Don't Expect a Quick Comeback," *Time*, September 6, 2011). In any case, this referred not to existing contracts, which would almost certainly be honored, but to future awards, and even for those preferential treatment was far from ensured.

8. See, e.g., Eric Watkins, "IEA Sees Lengthy Reduction in Libyan Oil Output," *Oil and Gas Journal*, March 21, 2011; Guy Chazan and Stacy Meichtry, "Eni Chief Blasts Libya Sanctions," *WSJ*, March 17, 2011.

9. "Daily Summary Bulletin: Oil and Gas Situation in the Light of the Libyan Uprising," European Commission, March 1, 2011, annex.

10. David Cameron, speech to the UN General Assembly, New York, September 22, 2011.

11. Richard Haass, "Libya Now Needs Boots on the Ground," *FT*, August 22, 2011.

12. "Libya," ISRT, May 20–June 30, 2011, 18.

13. Matthew Russell Lee, "In Libya, UN Plans over 200 Staff," *Inner City Press*, October 28, 2011.

14. Matthew Russell Lee, "On Libya, as UN Martin 'Did Nothing' and Needs Extension, Western Priority Meetings," *Inner City Press*, September 22, 2011.

15. World Bank, Socialist People's Libyan Arab Jamahiriya Country Economic Report, July 2006, vi.

16. UN Internal, consolidated report of the integrated pre-assessment process for Libya post-conflict planning, working draft, August 5, 2011, 12, obtained by *Inner City Press*.

17. Tofimov, "Rebels Attack Gadhafi Bastion."

18. "Libya Leaders Supported by 'money, arms, PR'- ex-Premier," Reuters, November 24, 2011.

19. ISRT, "Libya," 15.

20. "Comments from Paris Conference on Libya," Reuters, September 1, 2011,

uk.reuters.com/article/2011/09/01/us-libya-conference-highlights-idUKTRE78056 520110901.

21. "Libya," ISRT, 14.

22. Interview with the author, London, October 11, 2011.

23. See Rory Stewart, "Because We Weren't There?" *London Review of Books*, September 22, 2011, 11–12.

24. Mika Minio-Paluello, "Oil, British Foreign Energy Policy and Middle East Repression," Platform blog, February 24, 2011, blog.platformlondon.org/2011/02/24 /oil-british-foreign-energy-policy-and-middle-east-repression.

25. Ben Amunwa, "How BP Made Friends with Mu'ammar Gaddafi," Platform blog, February 24, 2011, blog.platformlondon.org/2011/02/24/how-bp-made-friends-with-mu%CA%BFammar-gaddafi-on-monday-bp-ceo-bob-dudley-dec.

26. "Documents Reveal Libya Rendition Details," Human Rights Watch website, September 8, 2011. Richard Spencer, "MI6 Worked with Gaddafi Government on Rendition Operation," *Daily Telegraph*, September 5, 2011.

27. Tony Park, "Libya: A Commanding Presence on the World Stage," *BP Magazine*, no. 4 (2007): 28–35.

28. Lisa Holland, "BP Evacuates Workers Amid Unrest," *Sky News*, February 21, 2011.

29. Nick Meo, "Libya Protests: 140 'Massacred' as Gaddafi Sends in Snipers to Crush Dissent," *Daily Telegraph*, February 20, 2011.

## Conclusion

1. Barack Obama, "Responsibly Ending the War in Iraq," speech given at Camp Lejeune, February 27, 2009.

2. E-mail to the author, October 26, 2011.

3. "Management Change in the Iraqi Oil Sector," paper presented at meeting of interdepartmental Oil Sector Liaison Group, DTI, May 28, 2003, obtained through FOIA.

4. Ronald Jonkers, "The Path Forward," in *Oil and Gas Year: Kurdistan Region of Iraq 2009*, 47.

5. "Basra: Local Dissatisfaction Grows in Final Run-up to First Oil Bid Round," U.S. embassy cable, June 29, 2009, obtained by WikiLeaks.

6. Scott Wilson, "Biden: US Troops Will Leave Iraq on Deadline," *WP*, May 27, 2010.

7. Anne Nivat, "Iraq's Troubling Ambiguities," *International Herald Tribune*, August 3, 2010.

8. OWFI feared the measure would deny women divorce and inheritance rights. Ultimately it was reintroduced into the permanent constitution in 2005, when the power of the Islamists had been consolidated and was more firmly supported by the United States.

9. "Another Interior Ministry Initiative to Protect Journalists," Reporters Without Borders, October 21, 2008; Farah Ali, "Boost for Iraqi Media Rights Campaign," *IWPR News*, August 11, 2010.

10. International Center for Not-for-Profit Law, Iraq webpage, www.icnl.org /knowledge/ngolawmonitor/iraq.htm. These measures had included criminal penalties of up to three years in jail for membership in an improperly registered organization and a government power to refuse or suspend registration and confiscate organizations' property at its discretion without needing a lawful reason.

11. Kholoud Ramzi, "Called to Account," Niqash.org, August 17, 2010.

# Index

al-Abadi, Haidar, 214–215
Abbasid Dynasty, 42
Abdul-Ahad, Ghaith, 141
Abdul-Mahdi, Adil, 78–79, 111, 120–121, 126, 128, 149, 181, 223, 224, 229, 237
al-Abdullah, Tariq (Maliki adviser), 159
al-Abdullah, Tariq (Sheikh), 138
Abood. *See* Umara, Faleh Abood
Abraham, Spencer, 6
Abu Ghraib prison, 98–99, 159, 310
Abu Ghaith (painter), 132
Abu Rabab (fireman), 11, 12
Adam Smith International, 146
Adams, Terry, 106
Addington, David, 30
al-Adeeb, Ali, 215
"advice", 45; as euphemism, xxxii–xxxiii, 90–91, 108, 150, 158, 166, 170, 212, 235, 316, 318; oil advisers, 66–67, 69–70, 73, 81, 87–94, 107, 146–147, 167, 197, 261, 262, 323; oil companies providing, 91–92, 106–107, 238, 256–257, 258, 273, 279; oil law advice, 150–154, 158, 191; political advisers, 123–124, 129, 145–146; under Britain (1917–1958), 7, 157, 165
Aegis, 250
Afghanistan, 117, 122, 124, 168, 200
AFL-CIO. *See* American Federation of Labor and Congress of Industrial Organizations
Agresto, John, 44–45
al-Ahdab field, 256
Ahmed (interpreter), 76
al-Ajili, Ziad, 169–170
Alekperov, Vagit, 6
Alexander, Justin, 115
Algeria, 150–151
Ali (architect), 131–132
Ali, Imam, 20, 54, 97, 135
Allam, Hannah, 136
Allawi, Ali, 149, 163
Allawi, Ayad, xxiii, xxiv, xxxi; and CIA, xxxiii, 136; coup rumors, 223, 229; elections, 120–122, 194, 229, 299–301; interim prime minister, xxxiii, 99–102, 163;; meeting BP, 106; oil contracts and, 163, 298, 301; oil policy, 107, 108, 109, 162, 305–306; religious identity of, 74, 299–300, 306. *See also* Iraqi National Accord; Iraqi National List; Iraqiyya.
Allen, Mark, 31, 317

al-Amal Society, 330
al-Ameer, Fouad Qasim, 190–191, 218
American Council for Cultural Policy, 47
American Enterprise Institute, 25
American Federation of Labor and Congress of Industrial Organizations (AFL-CIO), 117, 118, 185, 210, 302
American Federation of Teachers, 304
Amr (businessman), 232–233
al-Amir, Abdulilah, 283–284
al-Anbar province, 128, 138, 242–244
al-Anfal campaign, 100, 181, 234
Anglo-Iranian Oil Company / Anglo-Persian Oil Company (BP), 7, 8, 15, 154
al-Ani, Nur, 263
Annan, Kofi, 168
Anti–Oil Law Front, 218
appropriations bills, 200, 219, 245
Arab-Israeli War, 17
Arab nationalism, xxiv, 50, 77, 192
Arab Petroleum Training Institute, 19
Arab Spring, 29, 35, 307–308, 313, 330
Arabization policy, 234
Arbitration in oil contracts, 93, 145, 154, 155, 156, 167, 171, 173, 259, 260, 298
Arif, Abd al-Salam, 16–17
ArmorGroup, 249, 250
army, Iraqi, 15, 23, 41, 51, 63–64, 70, 134, 136, 137, 208–210, 230
army, U.S., 97, 242, 250. *See also* U.S. Army Corps of Engineers
Asia Oil and Gas Conference, 106
al-Askari shrine, 138–139, 178
Association of International Petroleum Negotiators, 155
Association of Muslim Scholars (AMS), xv, xxii–xxiii, 56, 75; Fallujah attack, 96, 102; oil law and contracts, 193, 217–218, 275
Assyrians, 74, 234
al-Attiya, Khalid, 205
auctions for oilfield contracts: influence on structure of, 261, 265, 275; opposition to, 266–271, 275–276, 295, 297, 326–327; plans for, 174, 192, 237–238; renegotiation of contracts, 282–284, 287; round 1, 255–256, 258, 272–274; round 2, 264, 276–277, 278–282; rounds 3 and 4, 290
Austin, Lloyd, III, 307
Australia, 9, 85

Avanah dome, 233
Awqaf Library, 42–43
Azerbaijan, 4, 93, 151, 153, 154, 256
Aziz, Qader, 227
Aziz, Salah, 209

Ba'ath Party, xxiv, xxxii–xxxiii, 192; 234; Ba'athists post-2003, 98; dictatorship, xxxiii, 21, 55, 78, 164, 234, 321; in government, 16–19, 234; membership, 42, 49, 59, 63, 67–68, 78, 79, 120; oil policy of, xxxii, 17–18, 321; opposition to, xxiii, 36, 55, 82, 112. *See also* de-Ba'athification; Hussein, Saddam
Baba Dome, 8, 233
Baban, Ali, 172, 213–214
Bacon, David, 115
Bader, Shawna, 189
Badr Corps / Badr Organization, xxiii, 55, 136, 139
al-Badri, Subhi, 218
al-Badri, Muthanna, 262
Baghdad, xxix, 23, 56, 60, 61, 102, 112, 208, 218, 241, 243, 249, 269, 276, 296, 299, 301, 302, 304, 308, 319; culture and demography, 126, 140, 186; "Day of Rage", 307–308; federal government vs KRG, 181, 188, 230, 237, 239, 253, 267, 278; history of, 7–8, 19, 42–43, 328; Iraqi government in, 209, 222, 231, 263; looting of, 42–46; oil auctions in, 272–274, 278–281, 282; opposition to oil law in, 190, 218; security plan, 167, 212; U.S. bombing of, 40–41; U.S./U.K. officials in, 62, 63, 64, 66, 86, 88, 90, 92, 111, 120, 158, 163, 166, 168, 184, 196, 197, 205, 207, 210–212, 246, 260, 261, 274, 275, 297; violence in, 80, 131–132, 137–140, 176, 239, 262. *See also* Daura; Firdos Square; Green Zone; Oil Ministry; Council of Representatives; Tahrir Square; Umm al-Qura
"Baghdad clock", 195–196
Baghdad University, 90, 147
Bahjat, Nasman, 40
Bahr al-Uloum, Ibrahim, xii, 58, 60, 175; as oil minister, 80–83, 89, 93, 109, 149; U.S. and 37, 248–249
Baker, James, 179
Baker-Hamilton. *See* Iraq Study Group
al-Bakkaa, Dhia'a, xii, 45–46, 67, 191, 271
Baku-Tbilisi-Ceyhan (BTC) pipeline, xv, 4, 151–153
Barbour, Griffith & Rogers, 223
Barzani, Masoud, xxiii, 122–123, 125, 181, 183, 186, 222, 231, 234, 277, 294, 300
Barzani, Mulla Mustafa, 234
Basra Petroleum Company, 58–59
Basra refinery, 11–13, 66–67, 73, 114, 208–210, 239, 256

Basra University, 115
al-Basri, Alaa Sabah, 239
al-Bayati, Natiq, 279
Bayt al-Hikma (House of Wisdom), 42
BearingPoint, 92–93, 151, 158, 163
Bechtel, 32
Belhaj, Abdelhakim, 317
Ben Ali, Zinedine, 313
Benchmarks, 177, 180–182, 196, 197–198, 201, 205, 213, 214, 219, 221, 223, 229, 242, 244, 254
Benghazi, 312, 313, 316
Bernini, Alessandro, 283, 288
BG Group, 5–7
BHP petroleum, 9–10, 85–86
Biden, Joseph, 126, 253, 274–275, 327
Blackwater, 96, 246
Blackwill, Bob, 223
Blair, Tony, 6, 8, 31, 105
Board of Supreme Audit (BSA), 291
Bodine, Barbara, 44
Bodman, Sam, xii, 167, 169, 179
Borjomi-Kharagauli National Park, 151
Bouaziz, Mounir, 257, 279
BP, xxxii, 9, 12, 28, 31, 94, 151, 169, 249–250, 292, 308; Azerbaijan and, 93, 151–153, 155; BP/CNPC contract, 273, 275, 276, 282–289, 290–291, 296–298, 305; history in Iraq/Middle East, 9, 15, 26, 58, 154; influencing Iraqi oil policy, 92, 105–106; in Libya, 316–317; oil contracts, 237–238, 258, 261, 272–273, 276, 282–285, 288–289; strategic interests in Iraq, 3, 4–6, 89. *See also* Anglo-Iranian
Brahimi, Lakhdar, 160
Bremer, Paul, xi, 81, 160; civil society and, 49, 50, 73, 115, 329; de-Ba'athification, 63, 64, 65, 67, 82; economy of Iraq, 75, 87; Iraqi Governing Council, 73–75, 96, 120, 121, 134; leaving Iraq, 99–100; legacy of, 172, 322, 324; occupation and, 62, 73, 95, 96, 97, 98, 101, 122; oil and, 70, 86, 87, 93; personality, 62–63. *See also* Coalition Provisional Authority
Brinded, Malcolm, 258
British-American Project, xxxii
British Council, 90
British Museum, 44
British Petroleum. *See* BP
Broder, David, 212
Brown, Chris, 111
Browne, John, 94
Bureau of Near Eastern Affairs, U.S. Department of State, 35
Bush, George H.W., 28, 51–52, 167, 260
Bush, George W., 96, 160, 178, 191, 196, 208; 2000 presidential campaign, 29; administration of, 27, 64–65, 135, 179, 197, 199, 200; energy task force, xxx, 29–30; Iraqi constitution and, 124, 129;

Iraqi politicians and, 124, 167, 199, 204, 324; Iraq war and, xxvii, 31, 40, 85; Laurel Lodge plan, 166–167; oil and, 37, 166, 196, 197, 199, 203, 223, 229, 245; surge/New Way Forward, 178, 179, 181–182, 213, 242–243; vs withdrawal of troops, 178, 181–182, 200–201, 245–246, 248, 252
Butler, Nick, xxxii
Buzurgan field, 263
Byrd, Robert, 220

Cafferty, Jack, 224
Cameron, David, 313, 315
Camp David facility, 166–168, 229
Camp Lejeune, 251
Camp Victory, 196
Carney, Tim, 168–169
Carroll, Phil, xiv, 67, 68, 70, 87–90, 92, 107
Carter, Jimmy, 312
Casey, George, 167, 177, 181, 195
Cato Institute, 87
Center for Iraqi Peace Support, 330
Center for Strategic and International Studies (CSIS), xv, 27, 36
Central Command, U.S,, 211, 252, 312
Central Intelligence Agency (CIA), 16, 31, 136
Centre for Global Energy Studies, 36, 285
Chalabi, Ahmad, 6, 34–37, 54, 57, 62, 81, 82, 136, 276, 299
Chalabi, Fadhil, 36, 285
Chalabi, Munir, 113, 282
al-Chalabi, Issam, xii, 132, 146–147, 192–194, 257, 269, 273, 322
Chandrasekaran, Rajiv, 45
Chaplin, Edward, 5, 111
Chapuk, Sondul, 74
Charge of the Knights, 238
Chayyid, Faleh, 51–53
Chemical Safety Board (CSB), 12
Cheney, Dick, xxvii, 32; energy task force, xxx, 30; Gulf War, 23–24, 312; Halliburton and, 3, 32, 92; oil and, 3–4, 29–30, 37, 86; oil law and, 207
Chevron, 15, 38, 91–92, 106, 169, 238, 258, 274
China, 9, 107, 198
China National Petroleum Corporation (CNPC), xv, 256, 273, 279, 291. See also BP/CNPC contract
Chkhobadze, Nino, 151–152
Churchill, Winston, 7, 8, 122
Clinton, Bill, 25, 28, 37, 151
Clinton, Hillary, xxxi, 224, 315
Coalition Provisional Authority (CPA), xi, xii, 44, 66, 70, 105–106, 291; governing model, 49, 63, 73, 74, 83, 95, 121, 134, 322; Iraqi Governing Council, 73–74, 81; long-term occupation, 62; de-Ba'athification, 63, 64, 67, 82

Cohen, Ariel, 87
Collins, Susan, 200
Commerce, U.S. Department of, 260
Commercial Law Development Program (CLDP), 260–261
Commission on Integrity, 291, 296, 297
Communication Workers of America, 304
Congress, U.S., 29, 30, 117, 158, 195–196, 200–201, 205, 207, 211, 215, 219, 220
Conoco-Phillips, 92, 169
constitution of Iraq: drafting of, 119–130, 145–146, 183, 221; impact on Iraqi politics, 128–130, 134, 159, 204, 297, 300–301, 324; oil contracts and, 205, 206, 259, 267; oil law and, 148, 175, 184, 189, 298; planned revisions of, 128, 192, 214, 219, 264, 266
contracts. See oil contractcs
Conway, James, 101
Corner House, 152
corruption, 93, 115, 262; culture of, 310, 321–324, 327, 328; Iraqi efforts against, 81–82; Iraqi anger at, xxiii, 70, 191, 296; militias and, 140–141; misuse of anti-corruption measures, 240, 296, 297; oil contracts with foreign companies and, 282, 284, 286, 290–294
Côte d'Ivoire, 311
Coulter, Ann, 312
Council of Colonels, 246
Council of Representatives, Iraq (parliament), 115, 128, 139, 236, 247, 265; oil law and, 161, 170, 171–172, 184, 190, 192–194, 196, 197, 202, 204–207, 213–215, 218–224, 228–229, 305–306, 323; oil contract scrutiny and, 147–148, 157, 161, 256–257, 258, 259–260, 269, 296–298, 305; politics, xxi–xxv, 120–122, 215–216, 220–224, 228–229, 237, 244, 269, 299–301
Council on Foreign Relations, 28, 314
Crawford ranch, Texas, 31, 183
Crisis Action, 116
Crocker, Ryan, xi, 35, 62, 74, 195–197, 201, 205, 211–213, 220, 228, 253, 325
Cross, Tim, 69
Crude Designs report, 116, 263

Dagens Næringsliv (newspaper), 123, 292
Dagher, Sam, 294
Daly, Mike, 272
Daoud, Qasim, 124–125
Daqing Petroleum, 291
Daura refinery, 13, 69, 88, 239–240
Da'wa Party, xxi, 20, 55, 120, 78–79, 102, 181, 215–216, 221, 324
Day of Rage, 307
de-Ba'athification, 63, 65–68, 81, 82–83, 89, 98, 119, 134, 159, 262, 291, 299
Dead Sea meeting, 145–146, 150–151, 160, 163

*Deepwater Horizon* disaster, 292–293
Defence Systems Limited (DSL), 249
Defense Energy Support Center (DESC), 25
Defense Planning Guidance, 24
Defense Policy Board, 6
Defense, U.S. Department of (Pentagon), 6, 23–25, 35, 41, 44, 57, 63, 88–89, 99, 322, 325. *See also* Energy Infrastructure Planning Group; Feith; Gates; Rumseld; Wolfowitz
Democratic Party, U.S., 178–179, 195, 200–201, 243, 251, 253
Deutsche Bank, 288
Development Alternatives International, 49
development and production contracts (DPCs), 162, 205
DeYoung, Karen, 35
al-Dhari, Harith, xxiii, 75
Dialogue on Business and Investment Climate, 260
disputed territories, 204, 232–236, 241, 274, 327
DNO (Det Norske Oljeselskap), 100–101, 123–124, 130, 183, 277, 292
Dobbs, Henry, 8
Dobriansky, Paula, 50
Doctors for Iraq, 103
Dodge, Toby, 160
Domenici, Pete, 200
Downer, Alexander, 85
Driscoll, Gerald, 87
Dubai, 171, 204–205, 237
Dudley, Bob, 317
Dujail, 181
Dukan deal, 183–184, 204–207, 228
Dundee University, 110

East Baghdad oil field, 18, 276, 279
"East Jordan", 9
Ebel, Robert, xii, 27, 30, 36–37, 39, 320
Egypt, xxviii, xxxiii, 148, 198, 313, 330
Eide, Helge, 100
Eisenhower government, 15
Eisenscher, Michael, xii, 116–118, 240, 303
elections, xxii–xxv; occupation and, 73, 100, 101, 134, 199; Iraqi parliament, 2005, 103–104, 120–122, 124, 147, 148–149, 159, 213, 324; Iraqi parliament, 2010, 236, 244–247, 266, 272, 276–277, 297–300, 304–305, 307; Provincial, 223, 234, 237, 240–241, 276
electricity generation, 33, 149, 167, 257, 301–302
Elf Aquitaine, 279
Energy Infrastructure Planning Group (EIPG), xvii, 31–34, 36, 69, 88, 92, 229
energy security, xxx–xxxi, 29, 317. *See also* oil market
Energy, U.K. Department of, 87

Energy, U.S. Department of (DOE), 31, 169. *See also* Bodman
England, Lynndie, 98
Eni oil, 92, 282–283, 287, 291–292
Enron, 28, 30
Equatorial Guinea, 293
Exploration Consultants Ltd. (ECL), 174–175, 230, 293
exploration risk contracts (EPCs), 205
Exxon-Mobil: contracts, 232, 258, 273, 282–283, 287, 320; history in Iraq, 8, 15; influence over Iraqi oil policy, 92, 169; interests in Iraq, 3

al-Fadhila (virtue) Party, xxii, 214–216, 221, 298
Faisal, King, 7, 8
Fallon, William, 211–212
Fallujah, 95–98, 101–104, 120, 135, 310
Farouk-Sluglett, Marion, 18
fatwa, xix, 102–103, 217–218
al-Faydi, Muhammad Bashar, 56, 103, 275
Federal Advisory Committee Act, U.S., 30
Federal Oil and Gas Council (FOGC), Iraq, 175, 205
federalism, 122–124, 126–130, 161, 162, 163, 175, 188, 203, 205–206, 215, 227–231, 234, 236, 253, 294
Federation of Workers' Councils and Unions in Iraq (FWCUI), 186, 189, 218, 302
fee. *See* remuneration fee
Feith, Doug, 75, 77
Fenton, Anthony, 278
Ferdinand, Franz (Archduke), 7
Ferguson, Charles, 44
Finance, Iraqi Ministry of, 111
*Financial Times*, xxxii, 314
Firdos Square, Baghdad, 42, 73
Fluor, xii, 32
force majeure, 59, 286–287
Foreign Office, U.K., xiii, 3, 4–6, 106, 111, 170–171, 172, 174
Foundation for Defense of Democracies, 50
France, xxx, xxxiii, 9, 122
Francino, Mike, 146
Franklin, Rob, 283
Free Iraqi Forces, 54
Free Officers' Movement, 15
Freedom of Information Act, xxix, 6, 158
fuel products, 33, 41, 88, 92, 140–141, 149, 208–209, 294
Future of Iraq Project, U.S. Department of State, 36–37, 45, 60, 81, 89, 109, 285

G8 group of nations, xxx
Galbraith, Peter, xii, 100, 123–124, 126–127, 130, 183, 293
Geneva Convention, 102
Gaddafi. *See* Qadhafi
Garner, Jay, 62, 277–278

gas, natural 106, 208, 239, 255, 256–257, 290. *See also* oil

Gas Master Plan, 106, 257, 258

Gates, Robert, 205, 212, 252

de Gaulle, Charles, 122

Gbagbo, Laurent, 311

Genel Enerji, 292–293

General Federation of Iraqi Workers (GFIW), xv, 186, 188, 302

General Federation of Workers' Councils and Unions in Iraq (GFWCUI), 308

George, Donny, 46

Georgia, 4, 151, 153

Germany, 7, 63, 169, 248

al-Ghadhban, Thamir, xi, 93, 159, 214, 217, 322; under Allawi, 107, 110; Energy Committee establishment, 169; Iraq occupation and, 322; oil contracts, 283, 285, 297–298; oil law and, 163, 169, 174–176, 183, 206, 214, 217; Oil Ministry leadership 2003, 34, 58, 59, 60–61, 67–69, 81, 83, 88–89

Gillard, Michael Sean, 249

Goolsby, George, 151, 152

Goran (change), xxiii

Gordon, Michael, 212

Gore, Al, 29

Government Accountability Office (GAO), 30, 242

Green Zone, 73, 76, 97–98, 112, 167, 177, 199, 249, 262, 273, 278, 300

Greenspan, Alan, 37

Greenstock, Jeremy, 105–106

Gulbenkian, Calouste, 100

Gulf Keystone, 230

Gulf War, 12, 23–27, 41, 51–52, 56, 160, 312

Haass, Richard, 64, 314

Haditha, 310

Hadley, Stephen, 180, 221

Hafidh, Hassan, 192, 205

Hagler, Graylan, 117

Hague, William, 311–312

al-Hakim, Abdul-Aziz, 120, 125, 204. *See also* Supreme Council for the Islamic Revolution in Iraq (SCIRI); Islamic Supreme Council of Iraq (ISCI)

al-Hakim, Akram, 204

al-Hakim, Muhammad Baqir, 56–57, 80, 135

Halabja, 174

Halfaya oil field, 9, 279

Halliburton, xxvi, 3, 32, 92, 259, 292. *See also* Kellogg, Brown & Root (KBR)

Hamadi, Ali, 209

Hamilton, John, 293

Hamilton, Lee, 179

Hamoudi, Humam, 125

Hamza, Kareem Abdalla, 188

Hands Off Iraqi Oil coalition, 220

Hankey, Maurice, 8

Hasan, Sadeeq Ramadan, 188

Hashem, Jihad, 40

al-Hashemi, Tariq, xxii, xxiv, 78, 214, 222

Hawrami, Ashti, xi, 174, 188n, 230–232; KRG oil contracts, 228, 235; KRG oil scandals, 292, 293; oil law, 174–175, 205

Hawza, xix, 20

Haysom, Fink, 150

Hayward, Tony, 288, 292–293

Heavyside, John, 237

Hendryx, Frank, 14

Heritage Foundation, 87

Herring, Eric, 97n

Hersh, Seymour, 98

Hewitt, Patricia, 86

High Commission for Refugees, 44

Hilary, John, 171

Hildyard, Nick, 152–153

al-Hilfi, Abdul-Jabbar, 115

Hill, Christopher, 253, 299

Howells, Kim, 111, 172

al-Huda, Bint, 21

Hudson Institute, 34

Human Rights Watch, 317

Hunt Oil, 227–231, 233, 237, 267, 277

Husari, Ruba, 258

Husayn, Imam, 54

Hussein, Hashmeya Muhsin, 302

Hussein, King of Jordan, 16

Hussein, Saddam, vii, xxiv, 42, 43; capture of, 92–93; dictatorship and violence, 21, 45, 50, 51, 54, 55, 63, 64, 78, 98, 100, 139, 149, 159, 183, 295, 301; economic policy, 35, 67; hanging of, 181; Iran-Iraq War, 21, 67, 149; Iraqi attitudes to, 64, 73; Iraqi oil field destruction by, 33, 47; Kuwait invasion by, 21, 23, 56; oil contracts under, 6, 9, 36, 85, 148, 256, 279, 280; oil interests and, xxx, 23, 27, 28–29, 31, 37; Oil Ministry under, 67–68, 85, 93, 321; oil policy of, 87, 90, 162; opposition to, 51, 120; Sunni Arabs under, 77–78; trade unions and, 49, 114, 115, 118, 156, 186, 216, 296, 303, 329; ; U.S. policy regarding, 25, 30, 51–52, 64–65, 202, 212, 325–326. *See also* Ba'ath

hydrocarbon law. *See* oil law

IFOU. *See* Iraq Federation of Oil Unions (IFOU)

Imperial College London, 59

Operation Imposing the Law, 212

improvised explosive devices (IEDs), 124, 140

Independent High Electoral Commission, 297

Indonesia, 93, 109

Inpex, 256

Institute of Petroleum, 3

insurgency, 95n, 97n, 98–99, 104, 122, 124, 135, 136, 138, 183, 243, 326. *See also* resistance

Interior, Iraqi Ministry of, 136–137, 138, 204, 251, 278, 300
Interior, U.S. Department of, 261
International Centre for Settlement of Investment Disputes (ICSID), 167
International Chamber of Commerce, 259
International Committee of the Red Cross, 136
International Compact, 167–169, 172–173, 197–198, 201
International Court of Justice, 154
International Crisis Group, 129, 235, 307
International Development, U.K. Department for (DFID), 146
International Energy Agency (IEA), 28, 31, 47
International Federation of Chemical, Energy, Mine and General Workers' Unions (ICEM), xv, 303
International Monetary Fund (IMF), 111, 115, 149–150, 168, 170, 284
international oil companies (IOCs), 237; contracts in Iraq, 89, 222, 258–259, 264, 265, 268, 272–273, 275, 278–281, 287–289; history and, 7–10, 15–18, 248, 271; influencing Iraqi oil policy, 91, 105, 133, 158, 170, 173, 265; Iraqi attitudes towards, 36, 147, 148, 187, 188, 191; Iraqi oil policy towards, 108, 127, 159, 172, 214, 219–220, 237; Kurdistan and, 230, 231, 278, 293; legal protections, 150, 153, 173, 187, 229, 260, 298, 309; in Libya, 316–317; oil law and, 160, 170, 198, 228; relationship-building, 90, 106–107, 197; role in post-Saddam Iraq, xxviii, 3–6, 36–37, 81, 88, 89, 128, 179, 237, 249, 274, 289; security and, 198, 248, 249–250, 251, 306. See also auctions; individual oil companies; International Tax & Investment Center; investment; Iraq Petroleum Company; oil contracts; production sharing agreements
International Organization for Migration, 314
International Republican Institute, 49, 126
International Stabilisation Response Team (ISRT), 314, 315
International Tax and Investment Center (ITIC), xvi, 91–92, 108, 111, 155, 261
intifada, xix, 51, 78
investment, 115–116, 147; Iraqi policy towards foreign investment in oil sector, 88–89, 107, 127, 128, 148, 159, 161, 172, 268; legal protections for, 151–157, 159, 167, 169, 173, 179, 184, 198, 228, 260–261, 275, 298; non-oil, 19, 93; oil projects and, 109, 147, 257, 266, 284–285, 288–290, 298; public investment in Iraqi oil, vii, 69–70, 90, 119, 147, 190–191, 257, 263, 264, 266, 268, 274, 286, 287, 322–323; U.S./U.K. call for foreign investment in Iraqi oil, xxx, 27–29, 31, 33, 37, 47, 85, 86, 108, 148, 149–150, 168, 172, 173,

179, 198, 228, 275, 320. See also international oil companies
Iran: Iraqi oil and, 140, 267, 279, 294; Iraqi politics, influence over, 120, 121, 122, 160–161, 215, 299, 300, 325, 328; oil nationalization under Muhammad Mossadegh, 14–15, 154; oil policy of, 93, 119, 162, 171, 289; U.S. strategic interests in, 23, 26, 28, 39, 91
Iran-Iraq War, vii, 21, 55, 67, 68, 91, 114, 149
Iraqi Association for Health Management and Development, 330
Iraq Body Count, 41, 178
Iraq Communist Party, xxiv, 16, 21, 53, 74–75, 120, 186
Iraq Drilling Company (IDC), xv, 46, 240
Iraq Federation of Oil Unions (IFOU), 161, 236; government attacks on, 208–210, 216–217, 239–240, 295–295, 304, 307; oil contracts and, 275–276, 308; oil law and, 161, 186–190, 208–210, 213, 218. See also Juma'a; oil workers' union
Iraqi Governing Council, 73–75, 80–83, 96, 120–121, 134, 195, 322, 324
Iraqi government. See constitution, Council of Representatives; Finance Ministry; Interior Ministry; Maliki; Oil Ministry
Iraq Islamic Party, xxii, 128, 181, 213, 214, 221–222, 324
Iraq Leadership Council, 120
Iraq Liberation Act (2008), 29
Iraqi List, xxiv
Iraqi National Accord, xxiii–xxiv, 136. See also Allawi
Iraq National Alliance (Sadrists + ISCI), xxii, xxv, 300, 301
Iraqi National Congress (INC), xxv, 6, 136. See also Chalabi, Ahmad
Iraq National Library and Archive (INLA), 43
Iraqi National List, 194, 215–216, 221–223
Iraq National Museum, 42, 44, 45, 46–47
Iraq National Oil Company (INOC), 16–17, 18, 37, 87, 107, 147, 162, 173–174, 187, 191–192, 205, 215
Iraqi Oil Training Program, 197
Iraq Petroleum (2007), 237
Iraq Petroleum Company (IPC), 8–9, 13–18, 26, 51, 100, 109, 148, 191, 193, 233, 248–249
Iraq Reconstruction and Development Council (IRDC), 60, 70
Iraq Study Group (Baker-Hamilton), 179, 182, 245, 254
Iraqi Turkoman Front (ITF), 74
al-Iraqiyya network, xxiv, 99
Iraqiyya political bloc, xxiv, 301
Irbil, 123, 183, 186, 234, 261, 301
Islam, xix, 42, 50, 53, 55, 56, 76–77, 79, 132–133, 330. See also Association of Muslim Scholars; Shi'a; Sunni

Islamic economics, 11 20–21, 217–218
Islamic Caliphate, 42
Islamic Revolutionary Guard, 55
Islamic Supreme Council of Iraq (ISCI), xvi, 215, 223, 238, 324
Israel, 17, 27, 76, 166, 325
Istanbul, 151, 155, 261, 264–265, 276, 288–289

Jaafar, Dhia'a, 276, 290
Ja'afar, Jasim Muhammad, 138
al-Ja'afari, Ibrahim, xxxi, 102, 120, 124–125, 136, 138, 159, 221
Jabar, Jamal Abdul, 308
Jaffe, Amy Myers, 28, 30–31
Jamail, Dahr, 96, 333
Japex, 280
Jarrar, Raed, 215, 221, 333
Jasiewicz, Ewa, xii, 112, 318
Jasim, Abdel Qadar, 238
Jawad, Sabah, 239
Jaysh al-Mahdi, xix, 76, 97–98, 139, 176, 238, 244. See also Sadrists
al-Jazeera, 96, 101, 102
al-Jibouri, Mohammed, 81–82, 191
Jihad, Asim, 170, 276
Johndroe, Gordon, 251–252
Johnston, Daniel, 110
Jones, Melissa, 249
Jonkers, Ron, xi, 151, 153, 155, 158, 163, 169, 174, 179, 278, 323, 326
Jordan, 80, 90, 131–132, 145, 153, 185
Journalistic Freedoms Observatory, 169, 330
Jubilee Iraq debt campaign, 115
Juhasz, Antonia, 219–220
July 22 Coalition, 237
Juma'a, Hassan: establishment of oil union, 51–53; international connections, 112–113, 116–117; life in Basra, 113–114; occupation, views on, 113, 134, 249; oil contracts and, 275; oil law and 161, 186–187, 189–190; oil, views on, 53–54, 105; prosecution of, 296, 307; protest and, 208–210; al-Shahristani and, 217

Kadhim, Jawad, 208
Kar Group, 233
Karbala, 54, 59, 79, 126, 135, 159, 202, 244n
al-Kasim, Farouq, 163, 176
Kazakhstan, 91, 154
Kellogg, Brown & Root (KBR), xvi, 13, 32, 34, 68–69. See also Halliburton
Khalilzad, Zalmay, xi, 62, 137; ambassador, 122, 137, 195, 196, 222; International Compact, 197–198; Iraq constitution, 125, 128, 324; Kurdistan and, 277; oil law and, 150, 177–178, 183–184, 189; surge / New Way Forward, 180, 181; U.S. strategic interests and, 23–25
Khamenei, Ayatollah Ali, 55

al-Khasshab, Dathar, 240
al-Khatteeb, Luay Jawad, 106–107, 262
al-Khawaja, Falah, xii, 20, 67–69, 230, 233, 263, 277
al-Khayat, Faleh, xii, 25–26; coalition authority and, 61–62; de-Ba'athification and, 67–68, 83; oil contracts and, 266, 276, 280, 284–286, 306; oil law and, 192; Oil Ministry and, 41, 69, 81, 84; war-for-oil theory, 58–59; WMD and, 313
Khurmala Dome, 233, 263, 277
Kimmitt, Robert, xiii, 167–168, 198, 260
al-Kindi Hospital, 43
Kirkpatrick, Jeane, 50
Kirkuk, 126, 127, 202, 204, 227, 233, 234–235
Kirkuk oil field, 13–14, 17, 19, 127, 175, 233, 273, 277, 280, 308
Klare, Michael T., 312, 333
Kousa, Mousa, 317
Kretzmann, Steve, 321
KRG. See Kurdistan Regional Government
Kristol, William, 50
Kufa Mosque, 54, 55, 75–76
Kurdistan Alliance, xxiii, 215, 221
Kurdistan Democratic Party (KDP), xxiii. See also BarzaniKurdistan General Workers' Syndicates' Union, 188
Kurds, 153; campaign for rights, 50, 80, 123, 234; ethnic / sectarian divisions and, 35, 104, 122, 126–127, 136, 138, 172, 186, 204, 205, 215–216, 253, 324–325; identity, 79–80, 234; and Kirkuk, 127; Saddam's campaigns against, 78, 80, 181, 234; trade unions, 186, 188
Kurdish parties, xxiii, xxiv, 298, 307; elections and, 120, 300, 301; Iraqi constitution and, 122–128, 159; Iraqi Governing Council, 73–75, 77; oil law and, 174, 175, 204, 205–206, 215, 306; U.S. and, 62, 122, 136, 138, 180, 181, 183, 221–222, 229–230, 278; See also Galbraith; Kurdistan Democratic Party; Patriotic Union of Kurdistan; Peshmerga
Kurdistan Regional Government (KRG), xvi; corruption and, 292–294; disputed territories and, 232–235, 327; Independence, 175; Iraqi federal government and, 163, 188, 203, 219, 231, 236, 267–268; oil contracts and, 100–101, 227–229, 230–231, 236, 267, 277–278, 293 oil exports, 267, 277, 285, 294; oil reserves, 202. See also Natural Resources Ministry
Kuwait, 16, 21, 23, 27, 51, 93, 114, 119, 167, 291

Lando, Ben, 283
Lasseter, Tom, 136–137
Latif, Wael Abdel, 221

Law 80 (1961), vii, 15–17, 164, 193, 219
Law 150 (1987), 49, 115, 156, 216, 296
Lauterpacht, Elihu, 154
League of Nations, 10
Lebanon, 35, 74
Levin, Carl, 223–224
Libby, I. Lewis "Scooter", 32
Libya, xxxiii, 28, 90, 91, 311–318
looting, 42–47, 52, 63, 68, 81, 83
Lloyd-George, David, 58
al-Luaibi, Abdul-Karim, 304, 305
al-Luaibi, Jabbar, xiii, 52, 239, 257, 262–263, 268
Lugar, Richard, 200
Lukoil, 6, 280
Lunceford, Steve, 158
Lundquist, Andrew, 30
Lute, Douglas, 252

MacLeod Dixon law firm, 155
Mahajan, Rahul, 96
al-Mahdi, Imam Muhammad, 76, 138
Mahdi, Kamil, 146
Majid, Ali Hasan (Chemical Ali), 5
Majnoon oil field, 18, 106, 276, 279, 288
Makovsky, Michael, xiii, 34, 36, 59, 88, 92
al-Maliki, Abdullah Jabbar, xiii, 48–49, 51–53, 114
al-Maliki, Nouri, xxiii, 159, 199, 268, 269, 272, 276; Charge of the Knights, 238–239; de-Ba'athification, 82, 159; elections, 299–300, 304–305; electricity unions and, 302; International Compact, 168, 199–200; oil contracts, 254, 260, 268, 271, 283, 297, 299–300; oil law and, 183, 184, 187, 197, 210–212, 229, 306; protests against, 308; sectarianism and, 159, 224, 240, 244, 299; SOFA negotiations, 246–248, 254, 306; trade unions and, 209–210, 295, 302–303, 304; U.S. and, 166–167, 180–181, 182, 196, 197, 199, 200, 220, 221, 222, 260, 275, 309; U.S. threat of removal, 199–200, 204, 210–212, 223–224, 228–229
Malla-Nuri, Abdullah, 294
Mandela, Nelson, 88
Mann, James, 24
Mansour, Ahmed, 96, 101
March Manifesto, 234
Marines, U.S., 42, 45, 47, 95, 96, 101–103, 251
Marsoumi, Nabil, 190
Martin, Ian, 314
Mashhadani, Mahmoud, 269
Maude, Stanley, 7–8
Mayer, Jane, 30
Maygoro, Eliodoro, 150
McCain, John, 247, 251
McClanahan, Kel, xxix
McDonald, David, 232
McKee, Rob, 92, 93–94, 106, 107, 275

McPherson, Peter, 44
Media in Cooperation and Transition (MICT), 169–170
memorandum of understanding (MOU), xvi, 106
Merrill Lynch, 4
Metz, Thomas, 103
MI6. See Secret Intelligence Service
Michaels, Phil, xxix
militias, 99, 131, 132, 139–141, 167, 178, 199, 238, 239, 240, 263, 327. See also Badr Corps; Jaysh al-Mahdi; Peshmerga; resistance
Minio, Mika, xiii, 316, 318
Ministry of Oil. See Oil Ministry
Mobbs, Mike, 31, 32
Mobil, 15. See also Exxon-Mobil
"moderates", 164–165, 180–181, 222–223, 235, 328
Mohammed, Hamid, 294
Mohan, Nasir Mohsin, 46
Mossadegh, Muhammad, 14–15, 154
Mostafa, Madian, 319
Mosul, 8, 81, 128–129, 202, 227, 232, 234
Moussa, Hamid, xxiv, 74
Mubarak, Hosni, 313
Mudros, Armistice of, 8
Mu'awiyah, 54
Prophet Muhammad, 54
al-Mukhtar, Khaled, 147
Mullen, Mike, 252, 306
al-Musawi, Shatha, xiii, 269, 296–298, 300–301
al-Mutlaq, Saleh, xiii, 76–77, 78–79, 193, 213, 299, 304
Mystery Train, 250

Nahr Bin Umar oil field, 18
Naftana committee, 239
Najaf, 20, 55, 80, 97–98, 101–103, 120, 126, 132, 135, 161, 202, 210, 268
al-Najm, Samir, 67–68
al-Nakib, Firas, 136–137
Nasiriya, 62, 112, 202, 208, 302
Natali, Denise, 293–294
National Democratic Institute, 49
National Dialogue Front, xxiv, 193, 213, 215–216
National Security Council (NSC), U.S., 30, 32–33, 166, 180, 252. See also Hadley, O'Sullivan
National Security Strategy (2002), U.S., 25
National Sovereignty Day, 272
National Transitional Council (NTC), Libya, 315–316
nationalism, 50, 77, 109, 213, 244, 325
nationalization, xxxii, 3, 15–19, 21, 26, 50, 51, 87, 93, 128, 154, 174, 193, 323
Natonski, Richard, 101
Natural Resources, Kurdistan Ministry of, 231–232. See also Hawrami

Neftex, 288
Negroponte, John, 211
neoconservatives, xxv, xxvii, 25, 34–35, 50, 87, 88–89, 196, 198, 294, 325
New Way Forward, 181, 195. *See also* surge; benchmarks
New York Convention on Enforcement of Foreign Arbitral Awards, 155, 156, 260–261
Nigeria, 38, 68, 257
Nima, Fayadh, 268, 270, 276, 290
Nivat, Anne, 328–329
Norbest, 230
North Atlantic Treaty Organization (NATO), xvi, xxx–xxxi, 314
North Korea, 39
North Oil Company, 262
Norway, 84, 163
al-Nujaifi, Usama, 193–194, 213
Numan, Kifah, 268

Obama, Barack, xxxii, 243, 247, 251–254, 252, 274, 275, 303, 309, 328
occupation of Iraq (post-2003), 63, 83, 138, 171, 172, 195, 307; British (post-WWI), xxx, 6–9, 97, 164–165, 248–249; decision for long occupation, 57, 62; Iraqi opposition to, xxii, xxiv, 62, 73, 75–76, 96–98, 102, 104, 113, 118, 121, 135, 247; Iraqi suspicion of motives, 53–54, 56–57, 191, 206–207; Iraqis adjusting to reality of, 41, 61–62; legal basis, 7, 87, 245–247, 306–307, 309–310, 314; mechanisms of control, xxxii, 45, 49–51, 98, 99–100, 104, 121–122, 133–135, 138, 172, 236–237, 247, 316, 321–326; misunderstanding Iraq, 77–78, 201–204, 245, 321, 324; oil and, xxx, 31–34, 53–54, 83, 110–111, 173, 210–212, 327; oil contracts signed under, 86, 89–90, 110–111, 155–156, 162, 173, 191, 193–194, 218–220, 264, 275; political dynamics of, 22, 95, 169, 171, 199–201, 213, 215, 236–237, 238–239, 244, 247, 248; strategic objectives, 22, 106, 122, 164, 172, 191, 320, 321–322, 326–327. *See also* Coalition Provisional Authority; resistance; oil law; Status of Forces Agreement; surge; withdrawal
Odierno, Ray, 204, 247, 248, 252, 254
Office of Iraqi Affairs, U.S. Department of State, xi, 35
Office of Reconstruction and Humanitarian Affairs, 64
Office of the Humanitarian Coordinator for Iraq, 44
Oil and Energy Working Group (OEWG), U.S. Department of State Future of Iraq Project xvi, 36–37
Oil Change International, xxix, 116, 219, 321

oil companies. *See* international oil companies (IOCs); individual oil companies
oil contracts, Iraqi federal government, xxxi, 90, 106, 187, 189, 249, 268, 305, 306; American companies and, 25, 28, 32, 37, 47, 214, 269, 320; bargaining position and decentralisation, 128, 163, 175, 191–192; bargaining position and technical capacity, 191, 261, 264, 266, 267, 283, 289, 290–291; bargaining position of occupied country, 110–111, 147, 161, 162, 187, 191–192, 218, 275; competition for 107, 162, 258, 265, 266–267, 268, 280, 283; form of, 3, 37, 86, 93, 106, 109, 110, 147, 162, 169, 173, 190, 205, 213, 220, 229, 231, 235, 236, 237, 239, 258–259, 265, 270, 274, 329; Iraq Petroleum Company and, 8–9, 14–18, 100, 109; legal terms of, 59, 108, 145, 150, 151–156, 161, 259–261, 286–287; legality of under direct occupation, 32, 86, 89–90, 147, 259, 260; legality of under Iraqi law, 147–148, 150, 161, 184, 198, 219, 237, 274, 275–276, 296–298, 301, 305–306, 309; plans to award, 31, 36, 237, 255–256, 264–265, 276, 290; Saddam Hussein and, 5, 6, 36, 85–86, 148n, 279, 280; transparency of, 283–284, 287. *See also* arbitration; auctions; BP/CNPC contract; investment; oil law; production sharing agreements; profitability; return; service contracts; stabilization clauses; technical service contracts
oil contracts, Kurdistan Regional Government, 123, 127, 163, 175, 183, 213, 219, 230–231, 236, 240, 293; corruption allegations and, 293–294; disputes with federal government, 188, 227–229, 231, 232–235, 267; DNO, 100, 123, 279; exports, 279; Genel Energi, 279; Hunt Oil, 227–228, 229–230, 232, 233, 242. *See also* disputed terroitories; Natural Resources Ministry
oil contracts, Libya, 312, 316
Oil for Food program, vii, 82
Oil, Iraqi Ministry of, xi, xii, 140, 147, 162, 187, 192, 197, 261, 263, 268, 322; corruption, 141, 321; contracts and, 237, 255–256, 258–259, 265, 267, 270, 271, 273–274, 278–281, 282–285, 290, 296, 305–306; deBa'athification and, 67, 73, 82–85; international oil companies and, 106, 111, 160; Iraq War and, 41–42, 43, 45, 47; Kurdistan Regional Government and, 163, 233, 294; oil law and, 151, 160, 162, 163, 170, 175, 192, 205; postwar leadership of, 58–62; senior officials of, 19, 26, 34, 58–62, 68, 89, 90, 100, 107, 146, 191, 321; trade unions and, 210, 216,

Oil, Iraqi Ministry of (*cont.*)
276, 295–296, 303–304; under Saddam
Hussein, 67–68; U.S. occupation and, 36,
60–62, 68–70, 80–82. *See also* advice;
Bahr al-Uloum; Ghadhban; Shahristani,

oil law: 148, 155, 161–163, 179, 180, 284;
consultation on, 169–172; drafting of,
151, 155, 158, 163–165, 173; Dukan deal,
183–184; experts and, 190–194, 218–219;
International Compact and, 168, 173,
197–198; Iraqi parliament and, 192,
193–194, 202, 204–205, 213–216, 219,
220–221, 237, 244–245; Kurdish parties
and, 175, 205–207; oil contracts and,
148, 150, 236, 237, 258, 259, 274, 296;
renewed attempts to pass (post-2007),
245, 266, 274, 298, 305–306; revenue
sharing and, 201–204; Barham Salih
revisions committee, 169, 173–174,
175–176, 187, 190, 205, 206; al-
Shahristani and, 159, 160, 161; the surge
and, 180–182; trade unions and, 161,
187–190, 209, 216–219, 240; U.S. failure
to achieve, 228–229, 236, 244, 254, 310,
328; U.S. September 2007 deadline, 201,
207; U.S./U.K. calls for, 148–150;
U.S./U.K. lobbying for passage, 167, 172,
177–178, 195–197, 199–201, 205, 207,
210–212, 221–224;

oil market, 15–16, 17, 25–29, 33, 34, 47, 173,
255, 285, 306, 312–313

oil price, 18, 23, 27, 28, 33–34, 86, 259,
264–265, 285, 305, 306, 311–313, 320

oil reserves, xxix, 3–4, 5, 8, 23, 26, 29,
174, 192, 202–203, 255, 262, 265,
280, 312

oil workers' union, xiii; establishment of,
48–49, 51–54; growth, 112–114, 161;
privatization conference, 114–115; protest
at Basra refinery (2003), 66–67, 112; U.S.
visit, 116–118. *See also* Iraq Federation of
Oil Unions; Juma'a

Oliver, Dave, 66–67, 69

O'Neill, Paul, 30

Organisation for Economic Co-operation and
Development (OECD), xvi, 28

Organisation for Women's Freedom, 330

Organization of the Petroleum Exporting
Countries (OPEC), 26, 33–34, 61, 86,
150, 170, 284–285

O'Sullivan, Meghan, xii, 64–65, 196, 252;
benchmarks, 213; de-Ba'athification,
64–66, 67, 82–83; Iraqi constitution and,
124–125; Libya, 311, 314; oil contracts,
306, 308; "moderates", 180–181,
221–222; SCIRI / Adil Abdul-Mahdi,
120–121, 122; sectarianism and, 134,
221, 275, 325–326; Status of Forces
agreement, 252, 306; the surge and, 180,
182

Othman, Mahmoud, 231

Ottoman empire, 7, 43

Overseas Private Investment Corporation
(OPIC), 151

Pace, John, 137

Pace, Peter, 246n

al-Pachachi, Adnan, 96

Pacific Command, U.S., 211

Palestine, 27, 64, 166

Paniguian, Richard, 4–5

Paris Club, 149, 168, 198

Park, J. Jay, 155, 298

Patey, William, 148

Patriotic Union of Kurdistan, xxiii, xxiv, 181,
183. *See also* Talabani, Jalal

Pearlstein, William, 46–47

Pelosi, Nancy, 200, 251

Perenco company, 230

"Perfect Storm" memo, 35, 195

Perle, Richard, 50

Persian Gulf oil, 25, 28, 37, 248

Peshmerga, xix, xxiii, 80, 139, 168, 227,
229, 230, 232, 233, 234, 235, 263,
267, 277

Petraeus, David H., xxvii, 195–196, 201, 205,
212–213, 242–243, 243–244, 252

Petronas oil, 279–280

Operation Phantom Fury, 102

Operation Phantom Thunder, 212

Platform (charity), xxviii–xxix, 116, 133, 151,
162, 256, 316

Plymouth Congregational United Church of
Christ, 117

Poneman, Daniel, 274

Porcupine LLP, 100

Potter, Kent, 91

Pottery Barn rule, 35

Powell, Colin, 35, 44

Presley, Elvis, 250

Priddle, Adam, 146

private military and security companies
(PMSCs), xvi, 249–251, 278, 287, 316,
328

privatization, xxxii, 36–37, 44, 59, 87–89, 92,
107, 113–115, 190, 215. *See also* oil
contracts

production sharing agreements (PSAs), 245;
author's study of, 115, 116, 153, 187;
explanation of, 109–110; Iraqi opposition
to, 147, 185, 187, 190, 213–214, 219,
236; Iraqi policy towards, 107, 111, 172,
236, 268; KRG and, 227, 229, 230, 231,
278, 293; oil companies call for, 108,
155, 169, 237; oil law and, 161, 162,
163, 205; service contracts vs,, 237,
258–259, 281, 329; U.S./U.K. call for,
37, 86, 274

profitability. 107, 108, 173, 259, 275, 288–289,
298. *See also* return on investment

Project for a New American Century (PNAC), xvi, 25, 37, 196
Putin, Vladimir, 155

Qadhafi, Muammar, 90, 312, 313, 314, 316–317
al-Qaeda, xxx, 37, 38, 50, 135, 137–138, 242–243, 324
Qarmat Ali water treatment plant, 69
al-Qasim, Abd al-Karim, 15–16, 193
Qazi, Ashraf, 204
Qazzaz, Adil, 262

Radhi, Ibrahim, 66, 304
RAK Petroleum, 277
RAND Corporation, 24
Rasheed Hotel, Baghdad, 76, 260, 273
Rashid, Amr, 42
Ratawi field, 9
Reagan, Ronald (administration), 99, 312
Regan, David, 85–86
Reid, Harry, 251
remuneration fee, 259, 273, 279, 280, 282–283, 289
Renton, Tony, 5
Republican Guard, Iraq, 99
Republican Party, 178, 200, 243, 247, 251, 309, 311–312
resistance against occupation, armed, 63, 80, 92, 95n, 104, 124, 136, 138, 139, 178, 204, 238
returns on investment, 147, 150, 162, 169, 174, 237, 288–289, 327
revenue sharing, 127, 188, 201–204, 326–327
Rice, Condoleezza, 78–79, 198, 207, 210, 220–221
Ricks, Thomas, 246
Ries, Charles, 239
Rifkind, Malcolm, 85–86, 89
Rikabi, Sadiq, 159
al-Rikabi, Fu'ad, 78
Risha, Sattar Abu, 242
Robinson, Linda, 196–197
Roosevelt, Franklin D., 312
Roosevelt, Kermit, 15
Roosevelt, Theodore, 15
Royal Air Force, 97
Royal Navy, 7
Rubaie, Mowaffaq, 207
al-Rubaie, Nassar, 214
Rubin, Michael, 294
Rumaila oil field, 17, 46, 47, 69, 106, 270, 273, 304, 308. See also BP/CNPC contract
Rumsfeld, Donald, 44, 57, 64, 121, 178, 196, 253
Russia, xxx, 9, 26, 77, 87, 89, 107, 148, 154

al-Sa'adi, Radhwan, 263
Saddam. See Hussein

al-Sa'dun, Abd al-Muhsin, 164–165, 199
al-Sa'di, Ali Salih, 78
Sadr Current, xxi–xxii, 214–216, 221, 223, 237, 298, 300, 301
Sadr movement (Sadrists), xxi–xxii, 55–56, 97, 103, 325
See also Jaysh al-Mahdi
al-Sadr, Muhammad Baqir, xxi, 20–21, 25
al-Sadr, Muhammad Muhammad Sadiq, 55
al-Sadr, Muqtada, 55–56, 75–76, 97–98, 103, 121, 139, 238, 244, 325
as-Safi, Safa ad-Din, 210
Sahwa (Awakening) movement, xix, 242–243
Salih, Barham, xii, 168–169, 172, 175, 183, 189, 196, 267–268
"Salvador option", 98–99
al-Samarra'i, Ayad, 269
Samawa refinery, 240
Sanchez, Rick, 98, 104, 211, 326
Sardar (Kurdish man), 232, 235
Sarkozy, Nicolas, 315
Sassaman, Nathan, 95
Saud, Ibn (King), 312
Saudi Arabia, 16, 26–27, 39, 93, 198, 291
Schatz, Lee, 45
Scheffer, Jaap de Hoop, xxxi
Schlumberger company, 259
Secret Intelligence Service (MI6), U.K., xvi, 15, 31, 317
sectarianism, 77; conflict, 35, 135–140, 176, 188, 238, 269; division of Iraq, 126, 205, 253; identity, 79–80; Iraqi rejection of, 133–134, 215, 223, 236, 241, 244–245, 307, 328; non-sectarian Iraqi culture, xxix–xxx, xxxiv, 74, 76, 79, 104; oil and, 202–204; politics, xxi, 74, 79, 80, 119, 120, 127, 139, 159, 175, 205, 213, 215, 239, 244, 299, 322–323; U.S. and media perceptions of, 79, 132–133, 202–204, 206, 222–224, 228, 320, 324; U.S. role in, 74–75, 98, 104, 122, 133–135, 136, 138, 196, 204, 214, 221–222, 236–237, 253, 275, 299, 324–326. See also Iraqi Governing Council; Shi'a; Sunni
Senate, U.S., 15, 23, 126, 220, 223, 251, 253, 293
September 11, 2001 attacks, 31, 65
service contracts, 162, 237, 258–259, 274. See also auctions; oil contracts; technical service contracts
Sethna, Zaab, 6
Seven Sisters, 15–16
Shadid, Anthony, 48
Shafiq, Tariq, xii; criticism of oil policy, 128, 146–147; early career, 13–14; Iraq Petroleum Company negotiations, 17; oil contracts, 280–281, 289; oil law drafting, 158, 162–165, 170, 173, 187; oil law concerns and opposition 169, 174, 175–176, 191–192, 323

al-Shahir, Laith Abd al-Husain, 216
al-Shahristani, Hussain, xii, xxii, 262, 299,
    304; as acting electricity minister,
    302; background of, 159–161; control
    over oil industry, 239, 262; international
    oil companies and, 169, 170; KRG and,
    227, 231, 236, 267–268, 277–278, 294;
    oil contracts and, 237, 255–259, 266,
    268, 269, 273–274, 276–277, 279–280,
    283–284, 290, 296–297, 298; oil law
    and, 160, 163–164, 169, 170, 174,
    175–176, 177, 183, 192, 194, 205,
    258; PSAs and, 236; trade unions
    and, 209, 216–217, 239–240, 270–271,
    276, 302
Shaikhan, 227, 232–233, 235
Sharm el-Sheikh, 198
Shell oil, 88, 89, 109, 170–171, 292; dealings
    with Saddam, 9, 85; gas contract, 106,
    256–257; history in Iraq, 8; influencing
    Iraqi oil policy, 92, 169; Kirkuk field, 175,
    233; oil contracts, 237–238, 256, 258,
    265, 279; relationship-building, 90,
    105; strategic interests in Iraq, 3,
    5–6, 28
Sherwin, Rob, xiii, 170–171, 174
Shevardnadze, Eduard, 152
Shi'a Muslims, xix, xxi–xxii, xxix, 20, 43, 269;
    culture and identity, 79–80; demography,
    126, 202; discrimination, 84; political
    parties, 73–74, 78, 120, 122, 125, 128,
    180, 215, 221–222, 238, 240–241, 297,
    299, 300; religious practice and belief,
    54–56, 76, 103, 202; resistance, 97–98,
    101–102; Saddam Hussein and, 35, 51,
    78, 181; sectarian conflict, 35, 135–140;
    sectarian division, 73–78, 104, 126,
    132–135, 159, 204, 253, 324, 326. See
    also Da'wa; Hakim; Sadr; sectarianism;
    Sistani; United Iraq Alliance
Shock and Awe, 40–41, 139, 212
Simpson, Alan, 111
Sinar (Kurdish man), 232
Sinclair, Anthony, 154
Sistani, Grand Ayatollah, 97, 103, 120,
    160–161, 210, 214–215, 268
Sluglett, Peter, 18
Snow, Tony, 212
Solagh, Bayan Jabr, 136
Solidarity Center, 185–189
South Africa, 63, 124, 150
South Gas Company, 239
South Korea, 212, 245
South Oil Company (SOC), Iraq, xiii;
    achievements of, 257, 262–263; control
    over, 239; oil contracts and, 257, 268,
    270, 276, 283, 286, 290, 327; trade union
    in, 48–49, 51, 53, 112–113, 114–115, 187,
    189, 209, 240, 296
Soviet Union, 17, 153, 154

special inspector general for Iraq
    reconstruction (SIGIR), U.S., 141
Special Police Commandos, Iraq, 98–99, 137
Special Republican Guard, Iraq, 64
Speckhard, Dan, 155
stabilization clause, 93, 153, 156, 161, 169,
    173, 259, 261
Standard Oil, 8
Standby Arrangement, 149, 168, 198, 201
State Company for Oil Projects (SCOP), Iraq,
    xviii, 233, 262
State of Law bloc, xxii. See also Maliki
State Oil Marketing Organization (SOMO),
    Iraq, xvii, 45–46, 47, 81, 191, 271
State, U.S. Department of, 16, 35, 37, 45,
    88–89, 158, 278, 291
Statoil, 280
Status of Forces Agreement (SOFA), xvii,
    245–249, 252, 254
Steele, Jonathan
Stelzer, Irwin, 34
Steyne, Simon, 240
Stinson, Mike, 70, 93–94
Stoner, Rod, 250
Strategic Framework Agreement (SFA), 247
Straw, Jack, 78–79
Strobel, Warren, 136
Ströbl, Wolfgang, 9, 90
Sulaymaniya, 123, 183, 186, 232, 234, 307
Sullivan, John, 260
Sultan, Hazim, 17–19, 264
Sunni Muslims, xxix, 56; demography, 126,
    202–203; discrimination, 84; political
    parties, xxii–xxiii, 73–74, 96, 120, 124,
    128, 172, 180, 215, 221–222, 234, 299,
    300; resistance, 97–98, 101–104; Saddam
    Hussein and, 77–78; sectarian conflict, 35,
    135–140; sectarian division, 35, 73–78,
    99, 101–104, 122, 126, 132–135, 159, 253,
    324, 326; See also Association of Muslim
    Scholars; Iraq Islamic Party; Tawafuq
Supreme Council for the Islamic Revolution in
    Iraq (SCIRI), xvi, xxi, 54–55, 56, 80, 120,
    126, 136, 181, 204, 326. See also
    al-Hakim; Islamic Supreme Council of
    Iraq (ISCI)
Supreme Council on Oil Policy, Iraq, 107
the surge, xxvii, 180–182, 195, 196, 201, 205,
    211, 212, 238, 242–246, 254, 275
Sweeney, John, 210
Symons, Baroness, 5
Syria, 16, 140, 148, 267

Tahrir Square, Baghdad, 218, 307–308
Tahrir Square, Cairo, 313
Talabani, Jalal, 78, 122–123, 125, 183, 237,
    277, 294, 300
Talabani, Qubad, 230
Taq Taq oil field, 277
Tarhouni, Ali, 315

Tatweer project, xix, 197
Tawafuq bloc, xxiii, 213, 215, 221, 223, 237
Tawfiq, Adnan, 251
Tawke oil field, 277
technical service contracts, 3, 147, 169, 175, 233, 239, 259, 266, 270; bridging contracts, 237–238; reconstruction, 3, 32, 34, 47, 69, 322; subcontracts, 289, 291, 292. See also Halliburton; Kellogg, Brown & Root; oil contracts
Texaco, 15, 28. See also Chevron
Texas City, Texas, refinery, 12
Thabit, Adnan, 99
Thatcher, Margaret, 88
Tigris, river, 8, 42, 43, 183, 278
Tigris Petroleum, 9
al-Tikriti, Abdullah, 263
Tokarev, Nikolai, 6
Total oil, 8, 92, 238, 258, 279
Trade and Industry, U.K. Department for, 86
Trade and Investment Framework Agreement, 260, 298
trade unions, xii, xiii, 49, 115, 116–118, 156, 172, 185–189, 205, 216, 219, 228, 302–304, 308, 329. See also Federation of Workers' Councils and Unions in Iraq; General Federation of Iraqi Workers; General Federation of Workers' Councils and Unions in Iraq; Iraq Federation of Oil Unions; Law 150
Trades Union Congress, 240, 308
Transitional Administrative Law (TAL), Iraq, xvii, 119, 121–122, 124, 330
Transparency International, 93, 291
Treasury, U.S. Department of, 229, 284. See also Kimmitt
Tripoli Military Council, 317
Tripp, Charles, 43
Trump, Donald, 311–312
Truth and Reconciliation Commission, South Africa, 63
Tunisia, xxviii, xxxiii, 313, 330
Turkey, 4, 7, 74, 140, 151, 153, 267
Turkish Petroleum Company, 100, 233
Turkomans, 74, 202, 234, 329

Ullman, Harlan, 40
al-Uloum. See Bahr al-Uloum
Umara, Faleh Abood, 52, 116–117, 276, 296, 307
Umayyad Dynasty, 54
Umm al-Qura mosque, 56, 75, 96
United Arab Emirates (UAE), xvii, 27, 29, 172–173, 277. See also Dubai
United Iraq Alliance (UIA), xvii, xxii, xxv, 120, 136, 214, 215–216, 238, 269
United Kingdom (U.K.), 239, 265; Financial Services Authority, 292; history in Iraq, 6–9, 15, 58, 97, 100, 104, 164–165, 199, 248–249; international oil policy, 4, 31;

International Tax & Investment Center and, 111; Iraqi constitution and, 123, 125; Iraq War and, 4, 31; Libya, 311, 313, 314; meeting oil companies before war, 3, 4–6, 89; military, 46, 66, 69; oil law and, 170; oil plans in Iraq, xxx, 29, 34, 85, 86–87, 91, 148, 220; See also Blair; Cameron; Chaplin; Energy Department; Foreign Office; Greenstock; International Development Department; Trade & Industry Department
United Nations (UN), xvii, 44, 80, 131–132, 160, 204, 274, 313, 314–315; Human Rights Office, 137, 235; International Compact and, 168, 172, 197–198, 201; mission in Libya, 314; Security Council resolutions, 9, 31, 87, 105, 245, 312, 314; weapons inspectors, 29. See also Oil for Food program; names of UN agencies
United Nations Assistance Mission to Iraq (UNAMI), 129, 145–146. See also Dead Sea meeting
United Nations Children's Fund (UNICEF), 44
U.S. Agency for International Development (USAID), xvii, 49, 93, 151, 158, 326
U.S. Army Corps of Engineers, 69, 263
U.S. Constitution, 200
U.S. Labor Against the War (USLAW), xvii, 115, 116, 118, 240, 303
U.S.-Russia Energy Summit, 6
U.S.-U.K. Energy Dialogue, 31
USS Abraham Lincoln, 85

Vast Exploration company, 278
Venezuela, 93, 146, 148
Vieira de Mello, Sérgio, 80
Vietnam War, 35, 166, 211, 281
Visser, Reidar, 234, 299, 333
Vogler, Gary, 66
Voinovich, George, 200

Wade, James, 40
Wadi as-Salaam (Valley of Peace), 97
Waheed, Kareem, 302
Wahid, Mr., 12
Wälde, Thomas, 110
Wall, Marc, 256
War on Want, 116n, 171
"Washington clock", 195–196
Watson, John, 274
Watts, Phil, 89–90
withdrawal of U.S. troops, xxvii, 300, 309, 310, 320; American calls for 117, 135, 178, 179, 181, 195–196, 200–201, 245; Bush rejection of, 178, 182, 195, 201, 246–247; of combat troops, 251–252; Iraqis and, 121, Status of Forces Agreement and, 246, 248. See also occupation, Status of Forces Agreement

weapons of mass destruction (WMD), xvii,
    xxvii, 29, 31, 38–39, 202, 313
Wells, Peter, 288
West Qurna oil field, 18, 270, 274, 276, 280,
    282, 288
Western Desert, 202–203
WikiLeaks, 214, 231, 247, 282
Wildig, Tony, 5–6
Wilding, Jo, 96
Witt, Dan, xii, 91–92, 108–111, 155, 275. *See
    also* International Tax & Investment
    Center
Wohlstetter, Albert, 24
Wolf Brigade, 137
Wolfowitz, Paul, 23, 25, 60, 70, 196
Women for a Free Iraq, 50
Women for Peace, 330
Wood Mackenzie, 4
Woodward, Bob, 211
Woolsey, James, 6
Workers' Communist Party, 186, 218

World Bank, xxix, 111, 146–147, 174, 198, 314
World Food Programme, 44
World Health Organization (WHO), 44
World War I, 6–8
World War II, 7n, 63, 121–122

al-Yacoubi, Mustafa, 97
Yamani, Sheikh Ahmad Zaki. *See* Centre for
    Global Energy Studies
Yarmouk Hospital, 43–44
Yazid, 54
Yemen, 148
Yezidis, 227
Younge, Gary, 80

Zainy, Muhammad-Ali, xiii, 58, 60, 70, 80,
    160–161, 257
Zaki, Muhammad, 295
al-Zarqawi, Abu Musab, 135, 166
Zarubezhneft, 6
Zubair oil field, 270, 273, 282–283, 288, 291